ANCIENT GREEK CULTS

Incorporating recent archaeological discoveries and scholarly perspectives, Jennifer Larson explores the variety of cults celebrated by the Greeks, how these cults differed geographically, and how each deity was conceptualized in local cult titles and rituals. This volume will serve as a companion to the many introductions to Greek mythology, showing a side of the Greek gods to which most students are rarely exposed. For example, the worship of Zeus Meilichios in the form of a snake strongly contrasts with the Homeric image of the Olympian god. Similarly, some literary portraits of Aphrodite indicate that she was sometimes worshiped as an armed (or even a bearded) goddess.

Surveying ancient Greek religion through the cults of its gods and goddesses, heroes and heroines, *Ancient Greek Cults: A Guide* is detailed enough to be used as a quick reference tool or text, yet provides a readable account focusing on the oldest, most widespread, and most interesting religious practices of the ancient Greek world in the Archaic and Classical periods. Including an introductory chapter on sources and methods, and suggestions for further reading, this book will allow readers to gain a fresh perspective on Greek religion.

Jennifer Larson is Professor of Classics at Kent State University. Her research lies in the fields of Greek poetry, mythology, and religion, and she is the author of *Greek Heroine Cults* (1995) and *Greek Nymphs: Myth, Cult, Lore* (2001).

ANCIENT GREEK CULTS

A guide

Jennifer Larson

Routledge
Taylor & Francis Group

NEW YORK AND LONDON

First published 2007
by Routledge
270 Madison Ave, New York, NY 10016

Simultaneously published in the UK
by Routledge
2 Park Square, Milton Park, Abingdon, Oxon OX14 4RN

Routledge is an imprint of the Taylor & Francis Group, an informa business

Typeset in Sabon by
Book Now Ltd, London
Printed and bound in Great Britain by
The Cromwell Press, Trowbridge, Wiltshire

Library of Congress Cataloging in Publication Data
Larson, Jennifer (Jennifer Lynn)
Ancient Greek cults: a guide/Jennifer Larson.
p. cm.
Includes bibliographical references and index.
1. Mythology, Greek. 2. Greece–Religion. I. Title.

BL783.L37 2007
292.08–dc22   2006030370

British Library Cataloguing in Publication Data
A catalogue record for this book is available from the British Library

ISBN10: 0–415–32448–3 (hbk)
ISBN10: 0–203–98684–9 (ebk)

ISBN13: 978–0–415–32448–9 (hbk)
ISBN13: 978–0–203–98684–4 (ebk)

FOR MY MOTHER,
JANEAN LENNIE STALLMAN

CONTENTS

CONTENTS

ILLUSTRATIONS

Frontispiece maps

Figures

PREFACE AND ACKNOWLEDGMENTS

Limitations of space have made it necessary to resist the urge to document every fact; instead, I have cited primary sources only where they are directly quoted or otherwise indispensable. Secondary sources in the notes are also kept to a minimum, with emphasis on more recent scholarship, and citations of standard handbooks and reference works are generally avoided; a full list of works consulted can be found in the bibliography. I chose the further reading at the end of each chapter for its accessibility to undergraduate students, and it is therefore limited to items in English. Students who desire full coverage of a given subject will need to venture into other languages. All dates in this book are BCE unless otherwise specified. For Greek authors and the most familiar Greek names (Oedipus, Achilles) I use the conventional English spellings; other Greek words are transliterated. For the purposes of this book, I treat as singular the names of certain Greek festivals that are plural in form (Thesmophoria, Panathenaia). Abbreviations of journals are those used in *L'Année philologique*. Abbreviations of ancient authors and other primary sources conform to the usage of the *Oxford Classical Dictionary* (Third edition).

In order to write this guide, I synthesized a massive amount of existing scholarship, so I must thank the colleagues, too many to name, whose specialized work in philology, epigraphy, archaeology, and other fields has made this book possible. Most are cited in the notes and/or bibliography; for any inadvertent omissions, I apologize. Thanks are owed to Christina Clark and Daniel Ogden for reading sections and offering useful comments, and to the anonymous referees for Routledge. Art Resource, Bildarchiv Foto Marburg, and the Heraklion Museum assisted with the illustrations, and Mark Rubin helped me with foreign currencies. The work was carried out with the support of the Kent State University Research Council. As always, thanks to my dear husband Bob.

Jennifer Larson
Kent State University
June 2006

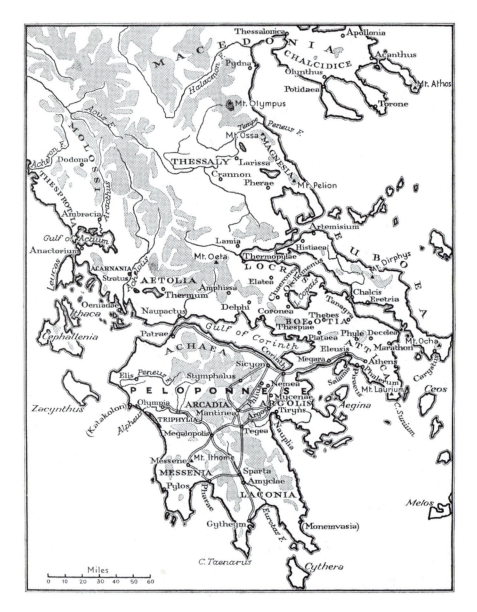

Map 1 Greece (reproduced from Cary 1949 by permission of Oxford University Press).

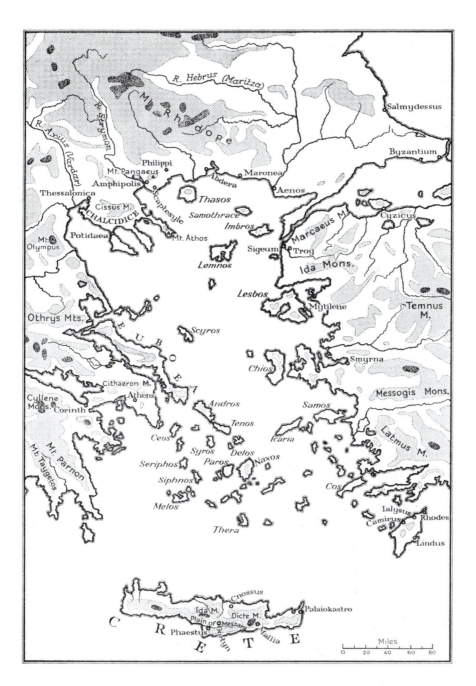

Map 2 The Aegean area (reproduced from Cary 1949 by permission of Oxford University Press).

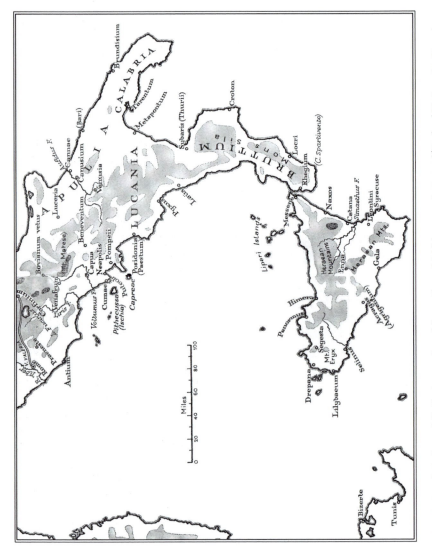

Map 3 South Italy and Sicily (reproduced from Cary 1949 by permission of Oxford University Press).

1

METHODS, SOURCES, AND CONCEPTS FOR THE STUDY OF ANCIENT GREEK CULTS

This book focuses on the ancient Greeks' relationship with the many supernatural beings of their pantheon(s). These gods, goddesses, heroes, heroines, and assorted *daimones* (a neutral word for deity that does not carry the negative connotations of English "demon") were acknowledged and honored by the Greeks in myriad ways. "Cult" comes from the same Latin root as "cultivate," which is fitting because ancient worship was predicated less on faith or belief (which was normally taken for granted) than on concrete actions such as sacrifice, votive offerings, and festivals, repeated as one might repeatedly water a garden in order to encourage its growth. Some gods were favorably disposed toward mortals; others were neutral or even hostile. All had to be cultivated according to age-old customs.

I have not provided a complete account of Greek religion, for not every activity that we think of as "religious" was primarily directed toward supernatural beings. Complex systems of traditional belief and custom addressed individual rites of passage (birth, adulthood, and death), relations with other people (family obligations, interpersonal ethics), ritual acts such as supplication and purification, and so on. These acts, beliefs, and stories were sometimes combined with worship of the gods, but recognizing a specific deity was not always their primary purpose. The *amphidromia*, a ritual by which a newborn infant was carried around the hearth in order to indicate its acceptance into the family, is an example. While Hestia was the goddess of the hearth, there is no indication that the ritual was directed to her as a personal deity. Furthermore, the communal nature of much Greek worship, and the fact that it was so often sponsored by the state, means that there is much more material in this book about civic worship than about the experience of small groups or individuals. Funerary ritual and beliefs about the afterlife, surely an important part of most religions, are for the most part unexplored here. Curses and sorcery too, which I would assign to "religion" rather than the methodologically suspect category of "magic," are only lightly touched upon.[1] Finally, cult is only one facet of a god's character. Greek cults do not always reveal a fully rounded picture of a god, just as

1

poetic descriptions leave out much that is necessary toward the full under-
standing of a deity.

Even within these limits, I make no claim to comprehensive coverage, for
the sheer number and variety of attested cults would defeat any scholar who
attempted to fully document them. Lewis Richard Farnell's magisterial *The
cults of the Greek states* (1896–), which was the inspiration for my efforts,
fell far short of this goal even though it comprised five hefty tomes on the
Greek gods, followed by a separate title on heroic cults in 1921. Therefore,
the present work is selective, and the principles of selection were as follows: I
have limited the discussion to cults attested for the Archaic and Classical
periods, or those that I believe existed before *c.* 340. Within this group, I have
selected the oldest and most widespread cults, those with special aspects of
anthropological interest (such as human sacrifice or "sacred prostitution"),
and those most familiar from canonical literary sources. I have also included
cults that illustrate specific aspects of Greek religion, such as the import and
adoption of foreign deities, and the distinctive habit of hero and heroine
worship. Throughout, I incorporate new archaeological discoveries, and I
try to present a more geographically balanced picture than Farnell did by
including as much evidence as possible from the Greek colonies. The goal is
not to replace Farnell's work, which is still widely used, but to provide a more
easily consulted and updated alternative. Although I devote a chapter to each
of the major gods, my intention is not to create the impression of a fully
integrated, consistent personality for each deity. The Greek gods were perceived in different ways depending on the time, the place, and the individual
worshiper, and it is important to let these contradictions stand. At the same
time, as a result of Panhellenism, the major gods gained some degree of con-
sistency in personality and function by the Archaic period.

The concept of the pantheon

Greek cults can be viewed from the perspective of cultural evolution: the
details of each cult are determined not only by the specific god to whom the
cult is addressed, but by a plethora of local conditions that change over time.
These include the roles of other deities and heroic figures in local and external
pantheons, manipulation of cults for the political and social benefit of
individuals and groups, and the power of historical events (such as a battle
near a sanctuary or a widely reported vision) to capture the popular imagination. In spite of the ancient Greek tendency toward religious conservatism,
cults can be said to develop, flower, reach maturity, and wither in a competitive process, for people had only limited resources to devote to worship, and
their preferences demonstrably changed over the centuries. Lack of evidence
makes it difficult to track short-term changes in most parts of the Greek
world (with the possible exception of Athens), but any account of Greek
religion should acknowledge that gods and rituals were far from static and

unchanging. As in biology, the proper application of the term "evolution" to this process implies no directional development from a "primitive" to an "advanced" state, nor a specific end goal.

Jean-Pierre Vernant, followed by many others, has argued that individual Greek gods have no identity outside the framework of the pantheon and that it is only by virtue of their associations with and oppositions to other gods that they achieve a personality and a functional range.[2] Yet there is no such thing as "the" pantheon at the level of individual religious experience as opposed to the artificial synthesis of Panhellenism: pantheons vary by place and time. Therefore, we should speak of a Theban pantheon in the Archaic period, or the Athenian pantheon of the fifth century. Even this formulation is too broad, for within the polis or other political unit, each individual was familiar with a pantheon determined by place of birth, family ancestry, neighborhood of residence, and ethnicity.

Using his recommended method to define Hermes in opposition to Hestia, Vernant achieved a fresh perspective on these deities and the way they concretize Greek habits of thought about space and movement.[3] Such structuralist approaches tend to be synchronic and to focus on the relationships to be detected in a set of facts, gathered from different centuries, about a given cult or cultic milieu. The underlying assumption is that cultic systems are predicated on the binary oppositions that are basic to human culture: life/death, male/female, hot/cold, sterile/fertile, and so on. This method can yield valuable insights, but it may neglect the historical development and local idiosyncrasies of a given cult or deity, and it does not always acknowledge that some aspects of a cult, even quite important ones, may be due more to historical contingencies than to the inner logic of a pantheon. Order and symmetry are not always apparent in systems that have grown and evolved blindly over long periods of time, though we surely have to do with complex *systems* and not random accretions.

Still, it is certain that the most methodologically sound format for the study of Greek cults is the detailed account of a particular city or region (e.g. Jost 1985, Parker 2005), which permits examination of the interrelationships between the deities and festivals, yet also allows diachronic analysis. One drawback of the organizational format I have chosen (cults grouped by deity) is that it does not place in the foreground the interconnectedness of cults in the same sanctuary, polis pantheon, or region. Mindful of the dangers of studying any god in isolation, I have tried to address this issue by pointing out the special affinities between certain members of the pantheon, for example Poseidon's regular relations with Demeter, Apollo's with Artemis, and Zeus' with Athena. Also, each chapter on the major deities includes discussion of selected minor figures whose cults are closely associated.

Throughout the book, I stress geographic and ethnic distinctiveness. The importance of ethnicity, already noted by Farnell as a crucial variable in Greek religious practice, has recently received new emphasis as scholars

3

investigate the "cultures within Greek culture." In particular, the work of Irad Malkin and Jonathan M. Hall has demonstrated how different Greek populations defined themselves against others and how the cults of various deities (Poseidon Helikonios, Apollo Karneios, etc.) contributed to this activity.[4]

Sources

Readers should be aware that the sources for Greek cults are lacunose and of widely varying date and reliability; they include the testimony of ancient poets, historians, and scholars; inscriptions; reports of excavated sanctuaries and their contents; and other bits of evidence. Scholars typically reconstruct rituals and festivals by judiciously weighing and combining information from these sources, and this practice has its pitfalls. For example, all scholars of ancient Greek religion are dependent to some degree on the testimony of the antiquary Pausanias, who lived in the second century CE and wrote a voluminous travelogue listing sights "worth seeing" in mainland Greece, with a heavy emphasis on sanctuaries. The accuracy of Pausanias' eyewitness descriptions has been repeatedly verified by archaeologists, and he is generally considered a reliable guide with respect to the places and objects he himself observed. But while Pausanias had a strong personal interest in the Archaic and Classical Greek periods, and a good eye for distinguishing their products, his reports of festivals and rituals as they were practiced and understood c. 160 CE are not necessarily accurate guides to what was done and believed centuries earlier. Therefore, the synthetic descriptions of festivals in this book must be viewed not as established facts, but as "best guesses" based on the available evidence.[5]

The remainder of this chapter is a (very) brief introduction to a few more of the terms, concepts, and methodological issues that are most critical for the study of ancient Greek cults. Specialists will already be familiar with these terms and the debates surrounding them; for those new to the discipline, one of the introductions to Greek religion cited at the end of the chapter, or Walter Burkert's classic handbook *Greek religion* (1985) will provide further context for the cults described in this book.

Ritual

The use of the term "ritual" has been criticized as imposing an artificial distinction between thought and action. Especially in scholarly traditions of religious studies influenced by Protestantism, "ritual" may carry a negative connotation of mindless repetition. "Performance," which recognizes the scripted nature of ritual behavior, yet avoids the baggage attached to "ritual," is sometimes preferred, though I choose to retain the latter term in this book. Established scholarly understandings of religious ritual point to its role in transmitting ideas, socializing the young, and creating group solidarity. In these ways, it functions much like a language and similarly has a vocabulary of acts that can be repeated in different combinations to convey different meanings. Burkert and other experts on ancient Greek ritual have stressed the way rituals create temporary disorder, fear, or uncertainty, only to decisively reaffirm order and convention. More recent approaches emphasize human agency in the construction of ritual/performance and view it as a fluid activity shaped by individuals, who use it to create culture. This perspective suggests that while some individuals may be passively indoctrinated by their participation in ritual, people are also agents who may create and modify rituals for their own ends.[6]

There is no ancient Greek word for ritual; the closest equivalents are perhaps *ta nomizomena* (customary things) and *ta patria* (ancestral customs). The basic components of Greek ritual practice include various forms of sacrifice, libation, and the offering of gifts to the gods; purifications; processions, dances, and competitions held in festival contexts; hymns and prayers; and divination. Of these rituals, which are common to the ancient cultures of the Mediterranean, animal sacrifice has attracted the most scholarly attention. Starting in the nineteenth century with Edward B. Tylor and W. Robertson Smith, animal sacrifice was explained by turns as a gift to the gods, a form of communion with them, a method of exchange between humans and gods, a conduit for human contact with the sacred, and so on. The concept of sacrifice as a gift has been the most enduring of these, for anthropological studies of reciprocity suggest that offerings to supernatural figures can be understood as an extension of "secular" gift exchange and systems of food distribution.[7]

Karl Meuli and Burkert sought the origins of sacrifice in the transition from Paleolithic hunting to the raising of domesticated animals, and in the fundamental anxiety produced in human beings by slaughter, while René Girard saw in the ritualized killing of animals an outlet for human aggression and even the substrate of all later culture. These influential theories have lost ground in recent years. Anthropologists no longer place hunting at the center of Paleolithic life, and the emotional impact of killing an animal is difficult to detect among many modern practitioners of sacrifice. The abundant evidence for sacrifice as a joyous and festive occasion in antiquity also seems to outweigh the hints of guilt and anxiety, though these are indisputably present.[8] A different approach is represented by Vernant and Marcel Detienne, who focus on the role of sacrifice in articulating the relationships between gods (who enjoy only the savor), humans (who carve and cook), and beasts (who consume raw food). Sacrifice also involves a formal distribution of food that reflects social and political structures: for example, meat may be divided into strictly equal portions among a group of political equals, or portions of honor may be allotted to certain individuals, while others are excluded from participation.[9]

5

Figure 1.1 A sacrificial bull is led to the priest at the altar, overseen by the cult statue of a goddess. Attic red-figured *pelikē*, fifth century. Kunsthistorisches Museum, Antikensammlung, Vienna. Erich Lessing/Art Resource.

The religious experience of the Greeks was organized by a lunar calendar of festivals and sacrifices unique to each place and time. Such calendars were in use as early as the Mycenaean period, for the Linear B tablets contain the names of months (including a month named after Zeus) and festivals. Festival calendars and month names correspond broadly to the ethnic background of a given city or region: Karneios and Agrianios are common Dorian months, while Anthesterion and Poseideon are found among Ionians. The month-names typically refer to gods and festivals (which allowed for arbitrary changes in order), rather than seasonal events or the rhythms of the agricultural year.[10]

A standard feature of Greek communal worship was the *pompē* or procession. While the endpoint was usually the sanctuary of the deity to be honored, the starting point varied. Starting at the city gates and moving toward the citadel emphasized that a deity on the akropolis was at the heart of the city. Starting at the *prutaneion* (city hall) emphasized the state sponsorship of the cult in question. Because most processions culminated in sacrifice, the participants led the victims and carried certain items to be used in the ritual. They might also escort the cult statue of the god on a given route.

6

While processions often included members of different social classes and categories, they were typically organized so as to draw attention to these differences and to highlight the gulf between citizens and noncitizens.[11]

Prayers were offered, above all, at the beginning of any endeavor, large or small: a season's ploughing, a meeting of citizens, the start of a journey. Greek worshipers usually prayed standing, with one or both arms raised. Prayers were spoken aloud rather than silently. Communal worship often involved the singing of hymns, and hymnic genres developed with respect to specific deities and occasions. An aspect of Greek worship far less familiar to moderns is the constant emphasis on *agōn*, competition. Many festivals, especially those that gained wide popularity and drew a Panhellenic audience, involved contests. The best drama, song and dance by a chorus, flute composition, display of horsemanship, or athletic performance would please the god or goddess, and the winners dedicated statues and other gifts in thanks for their victory.[12]

Myth, ritual, and cult

In the early twentieth century the "Cambridge ritualists," as they are known, shocked Classicists by pointing out the similarity of certain Greek religious practices to those of so-called "primitive" tribal peoples. Insisting on the priority of ritual in the study of Greek religion, they argued (in the most extreme form of the theory) that myths were nothing more than "misunderstood rituals." Although much of their work is outmoded today, the work of the ritualists (James G. Frazer, Jane Ellen Harrison, Gilbert Murray, and others) coincided with the great surge of interest in folklore and popular culture that influenced continental scholars from Wilhelm Mannhardt to Martin P. Nilsson. Their influence endures in that "Greek religion" as a discipline now has a strong anthropological/comparative strain, and focuses on rituals and material culture as much as (if not more than) myth. Countering this trend is the continuing impact of the "Chicago school" founded by Joachim Wach and Mircea Eliade. Their phenomenological method emphasizes the importance of myth, symbol, and the experience of the sacred, and sees ritual as a response to myth.

The fact that there are no broadly accepted definitions for either "myth" or "ritual" complicates the continuing discussion about their relationship. If we think of ritual as "performance," it may include a retelling of a myth or presuppose knowledge of it, so that the assumed distinction begins to dissolve. Many rituals were perceived as recapitulations of acts originally performed by a founder: Theseus and the youths he rescued from the Minotaur were the first to perform the crane dance on Delos. Often, a rite had to be performed as expiation for an ancient offense against a god (thus, the Attic Arkteia appeased Artemis' anger at the slaughter of her sacred bear). Still, many traditional narratives about gods and heroes appear to have no corresponding rituals (in the sense of acts to be performed with reference to the narrative), and vice versa. In this book, "cults" are understood to include both rituals and, where applicable, corresponding myths.

Sanctuaries

From the eighth century at the latest, most Greek gods were worshiped in a *temenos* (from *temnō*, cut), a space set aside for sacred use. These sanctuaries were typically marked by a low wall (*peribolos*) or inscribed boundary stone (*horos*). At a minimum, they included a space set aside for sacred use, and an altar (*bōmos* or *eschara*), the indispensable point of contact with the divine. Sanctuary altars were nearly always open to the sky rather than indoors. They varied from simple fire pits on the ground, to marble blocks the size of a piece of furniture, to elaborate stone monuments hundreds of feet long with sculpted relief decoration. The altar served as a platform on which to deposit and burn offerings: incense, cakes, blood and other liquids, or animal flesh. To the altar also came suppliants, outcasts seeking refuge within the inviolate boundaries of the sanctuary. Certain sanctuaries were renowned as places of asylum, and it was possible (though presumably not very comfortable) to live on their grounds for months at a time.[13]

The structures most often found in sanctuaries are the temple and the dining room or *hestiatorion*. Common meals taken in the sanctuary were central to many cults; usually the participants consumed boiled or spit-roasted pieces from sacrificial animals. The number of people who could be accommodated in such a dining room (or even a series of rooms) was quite limited, which suggests an inner circle privileged to partake of the food. Dining rooms of the Classical period typically had couches positioned against the walls, and might include kitchens and drains. Earlier examples, built before the introduction of reclining banquets, are more difficult to identify; recently, a number of early Archaic structures first classified as temples have been reinterpreted as dining rooms.[14]

Some Greek deities, such as Hermes, only rarely occupied a temple. Other gods like Apollo, Artemis, and Hera were temple deities from at least the eighth century, and cult statues played an important role in their worship. The Greeks had no regular word for "cult statue" but instead used a variety of terms such as *agalma* (delightful thing), *xoanon* (carved image), *hedos* (seated image). As substitutes for the deity, Archaic cult statues were bathed, clothed, oiled, garlanded, paraded about the city, and otherwise ritually manipulated. During the early Classical period, a new trend toward colossal cult statues emerged in tandem with the fashion for ever-larger and more elaborate temples.[15] The temple (*nāos*, Attic *neōs*) was not a house of worship, but a dwelling place for the deity and a storehouse for the god's possessions, to which access was often restricted. Many surviving inventories list the contents of temples: wooden furniture and sacrificial implements;

armor and war booty dedicated to the deity; statues and figurines of the resident deity and other gods; caches of coins and jewelry; and valuable textiles.[16]

Over time, sanctuaries grew more and more crowded with votive gifts to the gods. Strictly speaking, a votive gift was offered to the deity in fulfillment of a vow made in a time of trouble: travelers caught in storms at sea and people who became ill promised a gift if the god provided assistance. In the broader sense, votives include all the items dedicated to a god. Visitors to large sanctuaries purchased clay, wood, or bronze votive objects from artisans who worked nearby. The most common gifts were ceramic vases and figurines, but almost anything could become a votive, from personal items such as rings to captured warships. Sculpted votive monuments of various types dotted most large sanctuaries, and because the property of the gods could not be discarded, excess or damaged offerings were deposited in pits inside the sanctuary.[17]

Around 700, people in central Greece and the Peloponnese began to allocate fewer gifts to tombs and more to sanctuaries, a change that roughly coincides with the advent of monumental temples. The increased investment of resources in sanctuaries, which were emblems of the emerging poleis, implies new ideals of citizenship and state-regulated, communal worship.[18] François de Polignac's work has given a further stimulus over the past two decades to the study of the relationship between sanctuaries and civic organization. De Polignac argued that sanctuaries, particularly those located on frontiers and political boundaries, played an important role in the development of the emergent polis, and suggested a "bipolar" model of interaction between an urban nucleus with a civic sanctuary (usually of Athena or Apollo) and a major rural sanctuary. Through extraurban sanctuaries such as the Argive Heraion or Isthmia, nascent poleis were able to assert territorial claims. More recent work in this area shows that sanctuaries developed in a variety of social and political contexts, yet confirms de Polignac's insights about the important relationships between sacred and political space, and shows that early Archaic (and later) Greek religion and politics are difficult to separate.[19]

Initiation

"Initiation" is used in modern scholarship to refer to two types of personal transition mediated by ritual. The first and less controversial use describes the rites by which an individual gained access to the secret knowledge and experiences offered by such cults as the Eleusinian or Samothracian Mysteries. The second type involves rituals performed to mark the transition from childhood or adolescence to adult status, which is to be distinguished from sexual maturity. The Greeks agreed on a specialized terminology to describe the first type (*muēsis* or *teletē* and related words), but not the second. With respect to both types, initiation is conceived as a kind of death and rebirth. Many scholars have detected in ancient Greek culture parallels to the "puberty rites" and "initiation rituals" described in modern tribal cultures by social anthropologists. These rites are characterized above all by a period of physical withdrawal and marginal or liminal social status.

While Greek initiation rituals for both males and females have been posited, there is much more evidence involving the transformation of boys into men; that this transition might be the focus of greater concern and ritual elaboration is not surprising, since the status of adult male was a necessary prerequisite for citizenship and its privileges in the developing Greek polis. In fact, there is a fair amount of evidence for institutionalized age-classes of young men who were required to undergo a period of marginalization and specialized training before they were considered adults (the Spartan *agōgē* and *krupteia*, the Kretan *agelā*, the Athenian *ephēbeia*). For many scholars, an underlying assumption about this second type of initiation is that it existed as the remnant of a prehistoric initiation rite practiced by the Indo-European ancestors of the Greeks, but this hypothesis is difficult to prove. The Spartan *krupteia* in particular has the look of an institution that developed relatively late in tandem with the militaristic, totalitarian state. Another oft-noted problem with some of the female "initiations" is that while the rituals appear to follow an initiatory pattern, the participants are not an entire age-class, but only a few representatives of that class (as with the Athenian *arrhēphoroi*, girls who served Athena). In the end, coming of age remained a pivotal concept in Greek culture, a fundamental source of inspiration for both myths and rituals. Whether these were the relics of an early "age of initiation" or more recent productions must be the subject of further study.[20]

Pollution and purity

Pollution and purity are concepts shared by most cultures, yet the sources of pollution and the means of dispelling it vary widely, as does the significance of being "polluted." Mary Douglas suggested that the impure can be defined as whatever is "out of order" in a given context: an unburied corpse no longer fits in human society, but belongs with the other dead in the graveyard, which is itself maintained outside the city walls. Rules about pollution and purification are attempts to create order and deal with change, particularly as it relates to events beyond the reach of normal social rules, like birth and death. Among the Greeks, to incur pollution meant that one could not enter a sanctuary or participate in a festival. If the pollution resulted from such common sources as a death in the family or sexual intercourse, it wore off after a prescribed period of time (which varied by city or sanctuary). If it resulted from the killing of another person, its contagious nature made the killer an outcast until he or she underwent ritual purification and was re-integrated into society.

Places as well as people could be polluted and purified. Sanctuaries had to be kept free of the taint caused by sex, birth, and death; purity regulations were common components of sacred laws. Purification could be achieved in many ways. For example, people bathed after sex and sprinkled themselves with water before entering a sanctuary or participating in a sacrifice. Before meetings of the Athenian council and assembly, a young pig was killed and carried around the perimeter of the area to be purified. Its body was then discarded outside the city, taking the pollution with it.

Normally pollution was invisible, but sometimes it was thought to manifest itself in the form of madness or disease. Skin conditions and epilepsy were the ailments most often attributed to pollution. In the Archaic period, wonder-working healers and purifiers such as Epimenides and Empedokles were highly respected, but their successors in the next centuries were a lesser breed, offering a regimen of baths, drugs, abstentions, and incantations to the unfortunate, and considered predatory charlatans by the educated. Although the physicians of the nascent Hippokratic school heaped scorn on these purifiers, their own methods were heavily influenced by traditional ideas about purity and pollution.[21]

Olympian and chthonian

In the conceptual world of Greek polytheism, divinities took part of their character from the realm where they dwelt. The gods who lived in heaven were sometimes known as Olympian, while those whose abode was subterranean were considered chthonian, from *chthōn*, earth. The powers under the earth, not surprisingly, included the heroes and heroines, who exerted influence from their tombs, and the dead themselves, as well as the gods and goddesses who ruled and interacted with the dead. Overlapping with this group because of their shared relationship to the earth are the agricultural deities. Demeter and Persephone afford the best example of divinities concerned with both souls and crops. Equally, the heroes and other chthonians, such as the Athenian Semnai Theai (Reverend Goddesses) or Eumenides (Kind Ones), have the power to affect agricultural prosperity. Chthonians tend to have dual personalities and manifestations, alternately beneficent and hostile. Their "true" names are often avoided in favor of euphemisms.

Traditional scholarship made the Olympian/chthonian opposition parallel to others, such as Indo-European/Mediterranean, Greek/prehellenic, or even patriarchal/matriarchal. None of these juxtapositions can withstand critical scrutiny, especially given that the categories of Olympian and chthonian themselves cannot be used to construct a rigid classification of supernatural beings. First of all, the traditional Olympian gods have decidedly chthonian

11

personalities in certain cults. Zeus Meilichios (the Mild) is an underworld counterpart of heavenly Zeus. Even an "Olympian" deity such as Athena Polias at Athens may have chthonian features, such as her association with the snake, a creature symbolic of the earth. Second, some deities evolved a cultic personality that blended Olympian and chthonian elements (the hero-gods Asklepios and Herakles are good examples), while others (such as the river gods and nymphs) can be comfortably assigned to neither category.

The other traditional assumption about the Olympian/chthonian distinction is that it corresponds to differences in sacrificial practices and terminology: in an Olympian sacrifice (generally termed a *thusia*), for example, the victim is light in color, the ritual is conducted in daylight on a raised altar, and the participants joyfully share in the meat. In a chthonian sacrifice (denoted by *enagismos* and other terms), the victim is black or dark, the somber sacrifice is performed at night on a low altar or over a pit, and there is no meal: the animal is burned completely. Chthonians are also thought to prefer wineless libations of milk, honey, and water. These generalizations fail because many supernaturals with a strong chthonian character, especially the heroes, regularly received festive, participatory sacrifices. In the study of Greek cults, it may be preferable to abandon the concept of a strong opposition between Olympian and chthonian deities, since the character of a given deity depends upon the context. The term "chthonian" remains useful as a marker for a set of divine characteristics and ritual acts which are more often than not found together, and which connote relations with the land, the dead, or the underworld.[22]

Religious authority

It is often observed that Greek religion possessed no denominations or central organization, no dogmas, no scriptures, and no creed. The lack of these features, which in modern religious contexts provide the basis for religious authority, along with the polytheism of the Greeks, might mislead us into thinking that individuals exercised a great deal of individual choice in the matter of religion. Instead, the gods one worshiped and the manner in which one did so were for the most part predetermined by tradition and enforced by the state. Participation in the cults of one's family, tribe, village, city, and region was an important component of personal identity, while rejection of these cults was considered deviant, and exclusion from them was traumatic. Christiane Sourvinou-Inwood argued that the polis (and to a lesser extent, the ethnos or tribal state) "anchored, legitimated and mediated all religious activity."[23] Depending on how "religious activity" is defined, one might argue for numerous exceptions to this dictum, but her main point is valid: the polis not only exercised more religious authority than any group or individual, it provided the structural and conceptual foundations on which the system of worship was articulated. The construction of monumental temples, symbols of a city's sovereign power as well as its piety, was only the most obvious manifestation of this communal religion. Greek assemblies and councils considered themselves empowered to enact all manner of religious legislation, from rules about dress and conduct within sanctuaries to purity laws and sacrificial calendars. Recent research on religious authority in the ancient world emphasizes that the modern distinction between religious and secular spheres, including the concept of a separate "church" and "state," is anachronistic when applied to the Greeks.

Although the polis controlled the selection of many priesthoods, the oldest and most respected offices were inherited. Certain priestly families, such as the Eumolpidai and Kerykes at Eleusis or the Branchidai at Didyma, exercised special authority over their respective cults. A wide variety of religious specialists, from charismatic sectarian leaders to oracle-sellers and purifiers, operated more or less independently, claiming direct access to the divine and sometimes falling foul of local authorities. Other independent sources of religious authority were the oracles, particularly the Delphic oracle, which played an important role as arbiters of ritual questions felt to be beyond the expertise of citizen bodies.[24]

Figure 1.2 A priest examines a ram's entrails to determine the will of the gods. Attic red-figured *skuphos*, 490–80. National Museum, Warsaw. Erich Lessing/ Art Resource.

Further reading

For introductions to Greek religion organized by concept and theme, see Mikalson 2004, Price 1999, and Zaidman and Schmitt Pantel 1992 (the latter provides a good introduction to structuralist approaches). Bremmer 1994 is valued for its bibliographical notes. On sanctuaries see Pedley 2005. Parker 2005, Parts I and III, offers more detailed discussion of the pros and cons of structuralism in the study of Greek cults.

2

PROGENITOR AND KING

Zeus

The supreme god of every Greek pantheon, Zeus appears in Greek cults not only as a sovereign god of kings and city councils, the "father of gods and men," but in a multitude of other, humbler and less familiar guises. Zeus Pater, or "Father Zeus" is one of the few Greek gods whose name can be traced with certainty to Indo-European origins; the same name has been recognized in the Indic god *Dyaus pitar* and in Roman *Juppiter* or *Diespiter*. These are deities of the sky, perceived as divine fathers. Bronze Age Greeks knew the god Zeus, a feminine counterpart of Zeus called Diwa, and a month Diwos, which survived to historical times in Aitolia and Macedonia.[1] This proto-Zeus probably bore only a partial resemblance to the Zeus of the Classical period, who took over the functions of a number of prehellenic deities, and also borrowed certain characteristics of Near Eastern deities in both myth and iconography. Like Babylonian Marduk and Hittite Teshub, Zeus rises to become the supreme deity of the divine assembly. Like West Semitic Baal, he is a storm god who wields the thunderbolt.

Early Archaic Zeus was a rain-making, agricultural deity, sometimes paired with Ge or Demeter, and worshiped at altars constructed on mountain peaks. Disturbing myths of child sacrifice were elements in several of his cults. These can be explained as imported Near Eastern themes or as the mythic expression of initiation practices through which symbolic death led to rebirth in a new stage of life. Later, Zeus was drawn from his rural haunts into the city center, where he presided in a general way over the realm of politics, yet rarely became the patron deity of an individual city. Instead, he was acknowledged as the most powerful of the Olympians through the establishment and growth of his Panhellenic sanctuaries at Olympia, Nemea, and Dodona. His cults typically reinforce traditional sources of authority and standards of behavior, whether in the family, the kinship group, or the city.

Zeus of rain

As a deity of the sky and therefore of rain, Zeus' natural home was the mountain peak where clouds are seen to gather, presaging a storm or shower. In myth, Zeus' home was of course Mt. Olympos, a high peak in northern

15

Thessaly, but in cult too he was often worshiped on mountain summits. Eighth- and seventh-century Attica saw a vogue for the worship of Zeus on the local peaks of Hymettos and Parnes. Zeus Ombrios (Showery Zeus) had an altar on Hymettos where local farmers came to make offerings for rain. An excavated site at the summit of Hymettos revealed a cache of cups and jugs inscribed to Zeus, from the period when writing was first introduced to the area. This cult site, which dates back to the tenth century, is one of the earliest attested in Attica. Similar early sanctuaries of Zeus existed on Mt. Parnes and other Attic peaks, but all declined in popularity during the Classical period.[2]

Zeus' association with mountains was not confined to his role as a rain god, nor must all prayers for rain be conducted on mountaintops, but the practice was fairly widespread. Another example is the cult of Zeus Hellanios or Panhellenios in Aigina, where the highest peak was known as Oros, "The Mountain." There, the founding myth of the sanctuary told how the pious king Aiakos sacrificed to Zeus on the mountain and ended a drought that threatened all of Greece. On the island of Keos, a mountaintop sacrifice was conducted for Zeus Ikmaios (of Moisture) and for the Dog-star, Sirius, which heralds the greatest heat of summer. Likewise in Thessaly, Mt. Pelion was the site of a strange ritual performed for Zeus Akraios (of the Heights) at the time of Sirius' rising. The elite citizens of the district sacrificed sheep and donned their fleecy skins, then climbed to the cave of the centaur Cheiron and the associated shrine of Zeus. This poorly understood rite was perhaps an institutionalized version of the old sacrifices for rain.[3]

Zeus Laphystios and Lykaios

The Pelion sacrifice also shares certain features with other, more sinister cults and myths of Zeus. A Thessalian example concerns king Athamas, who attempted to sacrifice his son Phrixos and his daughter Helle to Zeus Laphystios (the Devourer) in order to stop a drought. Either Zeus himself or the children's mother Nephele (Cloud) arranged their escape on a flying golden ram, and this miraculous creature was the source of the famous Golden Fleece. Here again we see the juxtaposition of drought, sacrifice to Zeus, and the skin of a sheep that is thought to possess special powers or attributes. A related myth declared that Athamas himself was to be killed as a scapegoat to purify the land, but was rescued in the nick of time, just as Phrixos had been. According to Herodotus (7.197), the descendants of Athamas in Thessaly were liable to be sacrificed to Zeus Laphystios if they set foot in the town hall, which for some reason they were constrained to do (there are problems with the text in this passage). Herodotus himself seems convinced that such sacrifices took place, but it is also possible that the ritual involved an elaborate "rescue" reflecting the mythic rescues of Phrixos and Athamas, or that a ram was substituted for the human victim.[4]

16

Rain-making and human sacrifice are associated with yet another of Zeus' mountain peaks, Mt. Lykaion in Arkadia. The inhabitants of this remote area in the central Peloponnese were widely considered backward and primitive, and they preserved a number of customs and rituals that seemed strange to other Greeks. Mt. Lykaion, the birthplace of Zeus and the center of religious life in the district, was an important focus of ethnic unity for Arkadians. Fifth-century coins from Arkadia display the image of Lykaian Zeus, and the annual festival of Zeus, known as the Lykaia, included athletic competitions and attracted participants from other districts. Xenophon (*An.* 1.2.10) reports that the four thousand Arkadian mercenaries who served the general Kyros *c.* 400 stopped their march to celebrate the Lykaian

Figure 2.1 Votive bronze from Mt. Lykaion, Arkadia. Enthroned Zeus holds the thunderbolt (left hand) and an unidentified attribute (right hand). Sixth century. Ht 12 cm. National Archaeological Museum, Athens. Erich Lessing/Art Resource.

games, even though they were far from home. On the mountain, there was a sacred enclosure of Zeus where none might enter (it was said that anyone who did cast no shadow and would die within the year). During times of prolonged drought, the priest of Zeus made a sacrifice and stirred the waters of the spring Hagno (the Pure) with an oak branch in order to bring rain.[5]

But the most mysterious activity of the cult took place on the summit of the mountain. At the very top, a large mound of ashes and blackened soil contained knives, small tripods and burnt bones, while the sanctuary 20 m below included two fifth-century Doric columns topped by gilded eagles. Here, a secret nocturnal sacrifice was held during which participants ate portions of "mystery meat" from a tripod kettle reputed to contain not only entrails of animals, but also a piece taken from a human victim. According to Plato (*Resp.* 565d) "he who tastes of the human entrails minced up with those of other victims inevitably becomes a wolf (*lukos*)." Tradition said that at least one person at the sacrifice was always transformed; if during his time as a wolf he abstained from human flesh, he would become human again after ten years, but otherwise he would remain a wolf forever. What are we to make of this ancient story of lycanthropy? And could it be true that people were regularly sacrificed to Zeus Lykaios? The latter possibility is not the most likely, considering that no human remains have been found in the excavation of the site, and that human sacrifice seems to have been far more common in Greek myths and symbolic rites than in actual practice. On the other hand, the participants in the ritual may well have believed that the pot contained forbidden meat. As for the werewolves, it has been suggested that the ritual originally served as a rite of passage, through which youths entering adolescence (girls were apparently excluded) began a period of rugged training as warriors by hunting and living in the wild as "wolves." After this probationary period, the young men would be eligible to marry and enjoy other rights of full manhood.[6]

The Arkadians believed that their ancestral king Lykaon and his fifty sons once played host to the gods, who in those days dined among humans. They incurred the wrath of Zeus, however, by serving a cannibalistic feast that contained the flesh of a slaughtered boy, in some accounts the king's own grandson Arkas. Lykaon's punishment was to be turned into a wolf. Thus, the re-enactment of the meal was an annual reminder of a past epoch in which the savage ancestor of the Arkadians failed to distinguish properly between human and animal, and offended the gods with a perverted sacrifice. The descendants of Lykaon were fated to suffer his punishment, but this special burden of identity with the wolf also set them apart from other Greeks. In spite of the Arkadians' belief in the great antiquity of this custom, the oldest artifacts in the sanctuary are no earlier than the seventh century.[7]

Zeus of the city

As the sovereign and father of the gods, Zeus presided over normative civic, social, and family relationships. He endorsed the power of early chieftains and kings (in Hom. *Il.* 2.100–8, for example, Agamemnon's scepter is an heirloom from the god), but in the later age of the Greek polis, Zeus was the upholder of civic authority. Zeus Polieus (of the City) was worshiped in many Greek cities, often with Athena Polias, the citadel goddess, as his partner. The Athenians preserved an ancient and curious ritual for this god, carried out on the Akropolis at his annual festival, the Dipolieia. Already considered old-fashioned by the Classical period, the Dipolieia ritually linked Zeus' Archaic role as an agricultural deity with his civic function as a guarantor of justice. According to Pausanias (1.24.4):

> They put barley mixed with wheat on the altar of Zeus and leave no guard there. The ox that they have ready for the sacrifice goes to the altar and touches the grains. They call one of the priests the Ox-Slayer (*Bouphonos*); [after striking the ox] he drops the axe and flees, for this is the custom. And refusing to recognize the man who did the deed, they put the axe on trial.

The ritual has received attention for its special focus on the ox: many sacrifices included oxen, but only this one had a special priest known as the Ox-Slayer, and the alternative name of the festival was the Ox-Slaying or Bouphonia. This indicates that the festival was concerned with the value of the ox as a domesticated animal. The ritual expresses tension between the ox's value as a meat animal and the need to keep oxen alive as draft animals, vital for agriculture. Hence, the man who kills the ox commits a "crime," but also re-enacts the first sacrifice and the pleasurable sacrificial meal of meat.

The location of the altar on the Akropolis and the priest's use of a double-edged sacrificial axe (*pelekus*), well known from Bronze Age Aegean icon-ography, suggest that this ritual has roots in Mycenaean religion. The Swiss ethnologist Karl Meuli, followed by Burkert, would take the origins of this rite back much further, to the time before cattle were domesticated. A later but more detailed source for the Dipolieia says that after the sacrifice, the hide of the dead ox was stuffed and set up as if it were still alive. This reminded Meuli of the customs of tribal peoples who subsist by hunting; often the hunter tries to maintain the goodwill of the animal and its kind by shifting blame for the kill to others, or even to a weapon. Attempts to reconstruct the animal symbolically, so as to ensure its future abundance, are also attested.[8]

Under other titles associated with civic functions, such as Boulaios (of the Council) and Agoraios (of the City Center), Zeus preserved order and over-saw the political and legal systems of the Greek polis. He is also associated with victory in battle. After a battle, soldiers honored Zeus Tropaios (of the

Rout) by setting up an effigy in the form of a pole with armor placed on it. The first literary description of this practice occurs in Sophocles' *Antigone* 141–47, where the chorus describes how six of the Seven Against Thebes "left behind their bronze armor for Zeus Tropaios." Such images were normally temporary, but Zeus Tropaios appropriately possessed a sanctuary of his own in warlike Sparta.[9]

Cults of Zeus Eleutherios (of Freedom) were instituted on special occasions when Greeks believed they had experienced divine deliverance from tyranny. After the battle of Plataiai in 480, an altar was built for Zeus Eleutherios to commemorate the united defense of Greece against the invading Persians. The poet Simonides wrote an epigram (fr.15 Page, *FGE*) to be inscribed on the altar, including the words: "Having driven out the Persians, they set up the altar of Zeus Eleutherios, a free (*eleutheron*) ornament for Hellas." The commemorative games instituted at this time, which included a race of fully armed men around the altar, were still observed hundreds of years later. An existing altar in the Athenian agora, most likely belonging to Zeus Soter (Savior), was rebuilt *c.* 430 together with a stoa, which formed a new sanctuary of Zeus Eleutherios/Soter. The timing of the construction suggests that the power of Zeus was now being invoked against the invading Spartans. In Sicily, the cult of Zeus Eleutherios was first established when the tyrant Thrasyboulos was overthrown in 466. The city of Syracuse erected a colossal statue of Zeus and, as at Plataiai, founded games.[10]

The cult of Zeus Soter was more geographically widespread, and similarly marked occasions when disaster was averted or battles won. Zeus Soter was also invoked broadly as a god who saved individuals in times of trouble. At his temple in the Peiraieus, which was shared with Athena Soteira, sailors made offerings upon returning home from dangerous journeys, and the ephebes, or young warriors-in-training, rowed trireme races in his honor at an annual festival, the Diisoteria. Finally, Zeus Soter was an important god of the household. With other deities such as Hygieia (Health) and Agathos Daimon (the Good God), he traditionally received the third libation at symposia. The first libation was poured to Zeus and the Olympian gods, who represent the cosmos; the second to the heroes, who stand for the city; and the third to Zeus Soter, the patron of home and family. In his *Suppliants* and *Oresteia*, Aeschylus alludes several times to Zeus Soter as the deity who upholds the authority of the male head of the household, and the physical integrity of the home itself, which were felt to be interdependent.[11]

Zeus of the family

Because of his position as head of the divine family of Olympian deities, Zeus was the archetype of the patriarchal father. In myth, Zeus' many amorous alliances with mortal women produced heroes, who gave rise to aristocratic lineages. Thus he was worshiped as Zeus Patroös (Ancestor) by Dorians, who traced their lineage to his son Herakles, and more generally as a god of familial bonds. At Athens, Zeus Phratrios and Athena Phratria presided over the enrollment of boys into the phratries, or brotherhoods, that guaranteed their status as legitimate offspring of citizens. Shrines of individual phratries sometimes had altars dedicated to the pair.[12] But most widespread of all were Zeus' many domestic cults. Zeus Herkeios (of the Courtyard) received sacrifices on behalf of the household at an open-air altar. An anecdote from Herodotus (6.67–68) illustrates the role that Zeus played as the guarantor of the male line. When confronted by his enemies with claims that he was illegitimate, the Spartan king Demaratos sacrificed to Zeus and brought his mother a portion of the entrails. Placing them in her hand, he beseeched her in the name of Zeus Herkeios to tell him the truth about his parentage, and she complied. Zeus Herkeios is attested as early as Homer (*Od.* 22.333–37), who mentions that Odysseus and his father sacrifice to the god outside their ancestral home. Zeus' importance to fathers may also explain the unusual votive offerings uncovered in the hilltop sanctuary at Messapeai near Sparta. The sanctuary of Zeus Messapeus contained weapons, armor, and athletic gear, but these were far outnumbered by crude, handmade clay statuettes of males with huge, erect *phalloi*. The site was frequented mostly by men, who may have sought Zeus' aid in becoming fathers.[13]

Zeus Ktesios (of Possessions) was a humbler deity. In Athens, it was customary for the head of the household to wreathe a two-handled jar with wool tufts around its "ears" and "from its right shoulder to its forehead," and to empty into the jar a mixture of pure water, olive oil, and various fruits and grains, referred to as ambrosia. The finished jar stood in the storeroom as a "sign" of Zeus and acted as a charm to increase the household goods. That the ritual has many points of contact with funerary customs suggests a relationship to domestic ancestor cults. Though he had public altars in some cities, Zeus Ktesios was primarily an intimate, family god. The orator Isaeus (8.16) tells of an Athenian who admitted only family members to the sacrifice for this god, though his practice was not necessarily universal. Like certain other manifestations of Zeus discussed below, Ktesios could be represented as a snake.[14]

Chthonian Zeus

Rather surprisingly in view of his origins as a sky god, many cults of Zeus are chthonian or semi-chthonian in character. One of the most widespread was that of Zeus Meilichios (the Mild). Like many chthonian gods, Meilichios bore a euphemistic name. In truth he was by turns angry and kindly, a deity who required regular appeasement in order to keep the beneficial side of his personality to the fore. By calling him "mild" or "kindly," his worshipers expressed their hopes rather than their fears. Because they governed the fruitfulness of the earth, chthonian deities had the power to be givers of good things if properly propitiated. Xenophon (*An.* 7.8.3–6) describes how he once fell short of money while working as a mercenary commander in Asia Minor. A seer told him that his financial straits were due to his failure to sacrifice to Zeus Meilichios. Xenophon admitted that, although he had regularly sacrificed when living at home, he had not done so since leaving Greece. The next day, he sacrificed two pigs and burned them whole for the god, and his piety was immediately rewarded with the return of a horse he had been forced to sell.

Personal or family offerings to Zeus Meilichios were the rule in the Greek world, but in Athens there was an important public festival for this god, the Diasia.[15] In early spring, people gathered just outside the city at the banks of the river Ilissos for the rites, which involved bloodless offerings of agricultural produce and pastries shaped like animals. For the average citizen, the festival was a time to gather with family members and to enjoy a fairground atmosphere. In Aristophanes' *Clouds* (864), Strepsiades recalls how he bought a toy cart for his young son on this occasion. Yet Meilichios was also an awesome and somber deity. On votive reliefs, he usually appears not in human form, but as a huge coiling snake, rearing up to meet his worshipers. (In Greek art, the snake as companion or attribute often indicates that the deity or hero in question belongs to the underworld. Such theriomorphic epiphanies, in which the gods took animal form, were unusual among the Greeks.) Zeus Meilichios was recognized in the Pompaia (Procession), another Athenian festival that took place while the fields were being plowed and the crops sowed. At this crucial time, it was important to be sure that the land was purified and free from evil influences, such as those introduced by the shedding of a kinsman's blood. Therefore, a ram was sacrificed and its fleece, known as the *Dios kōidion* or Fleece of Zeus, was carried in procession.[16] We have already seen that the fleeces of rams sacrificed to Zeus carried special powers; their purifying function was one of the most important.

As an upholder of social norms, Zeus presided over the purification rituals conducted when a homicide took place. Persons who had killed, even accidentally, could not participate in family, religious, or political life until they were purified. They turned for help to householders in neighboring communities, or to sanctuaries, where they were protected by divine law from the vengeance of angry relatives. The role of Zeus in purifications is illustrated in one of the oldest extant sacral laws, a mid-fifth-century inscription from Selinous in Sicily dealing with procedures to be followed by a man who has killed and "wishes to be purified against the avenging spirit." The killer is to announce his intentions, provide a meal for the hostile spirit, and sacrifice a piglet to Zeus Meilichios at his own expense.[17] From other sources we know that in such rituals, the piglet's blood was allowed to flow over the killer, since the participants believed that blood could wash away blood.

A person in need of this purification was known as a *hiketēs*, "one who comes," but the angry ghost of his victim was similarly a "visitant," *hikesios*.

Figure 2.2 Zeus Meilichios as serpent, votive relief from the Peiraieus, *c*. 400. Berlin, Staatliche Museum. Bildarchiv Foto Marburg.

Zeus Hikesios, the god of "ones who come," protected suppliants and guests from violence, but could himself be a supernatural avenger. He and Zeus Meilichios are invoked in rock-cut inscriptions made by family or clan groups in Thera, Kos, and Kyrene. His importance to the extended family arises from the belief that the religious impurity of one member affected the entire group.

Other manifestations of Zeus as a chthonian deity were common in domestic and public cult. Zeus Philios (the Friendly) was similar to Meilichios but more concerned with banqueting and friendship, and his cult was of more recent origin. He is shown on a fourth-century votive relief in a pose usually reserved for heroes, reclining at a banquet and accompanied by his consort, Good Luck (Tyche Agathe). He too can be depicted as a huge snake.[18]

Righteous Zeus

In Greek literature and popular belief, Zeus is a righteous god who punishes the arrogant and the wicked. His companion or daughter is Dike (Justice), and he is closely associated with the Moirai (Fates) in myth and cult. Many cults of Zeus had a moral dimension, and focused on enforcing behavior that was expected by society. Among the most revered of traditional beliefs was the idea that one was prohibited from harming strangers, guests, beggars, and suppliants, all of whom fell under the protection of Zeus. Instead, one ought to respect guests and strangers, and give aid to beggars and suppliants.[19] According to Plato (*Leg.* 729e), "being without friends or relatives, the stranger has more claim on the pity of gods and men." Anyone who refused these obligations could expect punishment from Zeus.

Under the law instituted by Solon in the sixth century, judges at Athens had to swear an oath of office by Zeus Hikesios (of Suppliants), Katharsios (of Purification) and Exakester (of Making Amends).[20] Likewise, there was a Zeus Horkios (of Oaths). Pausanias (5.24.9) describes the solemn oaths taken by athletes and their fathers at Olympia beneath a statue of Zeus Horkios brandishing his thunderbolt in a threatening fashion: a boar was sacrificed and over its dismembered body the athletes promised "to do no wrong to the Olympic Games." A bronze inscription in front of the statue told of the divine punishment in store for oath-breakers.

Kretan Zeus

As we have seen, the Arkadians considered their land the birthplace of Zeus, but there were many claimants to this distinction. In the Peloponnese alone, the Messenians, the Arkadians, and the Achaians preserved myths and cults relating to Zeus' birth, his escape from the evil designs of his father Kronos, and his upbringing. Perhaps the most venerable traditions of the young Zeus, however, were those of the Kretans, who maintained ancient traditions of a youthful god they identified as Zeus. The Bronze Age Minoan civilization, predecessors of the Greeks in Krete, worshiped a young god as part of their pantheon. Though little is known about this god, modern scholars have suggested that he was the partner of an older goddess, and that the relationship arose from the same pattern of myth and ritual that gave rise to the Near Eastern worship of Inanna and Dumuzi, Ishtar and Tammuz, Isis and Osiris, and Kybele and Attis.[21]

Zeus Diktaios was the most important deity of eastern Krete, and a deity of this name was worshiped in Mycenaean Knossos. He appears in a number of inscribed treaty oaths between Kretan cities in the Hellenistic period, but the oath formulas themselves appear to be of Archaic date.[22] All refer to the god whose cult was localized at Mt. Dikte, where Rhea gave birth to him in a cave and he was protected by a band of youthful warriors, the Kouretes, and nourished with the milk of the goat Amaltheia. There has been much debate in both ancient and modern times about the location of Dikte: modern scholars once linked Dikte with Psychro cave near Lyktos, because Hesiod (*Theog.* 477–79) mentions this area in his description of Zeus' birth. But this

24

identification was refuted when excavation of an ancient sanctuary at Palaikastro brought to light an inscribed hymn that begins "Io, greatest Youth (*Kouros*), welcome, son of Kronos, all-powerful Brightness, here now present, leading the gods (*daimones*), come for the New Year to Dikte, and rejoice in this song." The hymn was inscribed at a late date, but its content and style show that it goes back to the Classical period or earlier.[23] It tells how, with the coming of Rhea's divine child, Justice and Peace attend the earth, and it urges the Kouros to "leap into" the herds, fields, and cities. Diktaian Zeus appears to be primarily a god of vegetative and procreative energies who is "born anew" every year.

The excavations also brought to light rich votive offerings showing that the sanctuary was most prosperous from the seventh to fifth centuries. Mt. Dikte, then, is probably the peak overlooking Palaikastro, known today as Mt. Petsophas. Significantly, the Classical site of Palaikastro overlay a Middle Minoan settlement, and on Mt. Petsophas was a Minoan peak sanctuary that yielded terracotta figures of a young deity. The most spectacular find, discovered within a hundred meters of the inscribed hymn, was a magnificent Minoan statuette of gold and ivory, depicting a youth in the same pose as the Petsophas figurines. The striking spatial juxtaposition of the Minoan and Greek cults of a youthful god suggests that memories of the Bronze Age persisted into Classical times. At the same time, there is a gap in archaeological continuity at the site from the Bronze Age to the early Archaic period, so the cult was presumably interrupted and re-established. In those intervening centuries, it must have undergone significant changes.[24]

Another famous cult site of Zeus was the cave below the summit of Mt. Ida in central Krete, which served as a sanctuary for over a thousand years. Excavated in the nineteenth century, it contained many layers of burnt sacrificial offerings, and an unusually rich hoard of votive objects, including bronze and gold items. Some of the objects from the Idaian cave, including a famous group of bronze shields with orientalizing decorations, date to the time of Homer, the eighth or seventh centuries.[25] The cult here, as at Dikte, was concerned with the youthful Zeus and his band of protective warriors, the Kouretes, who clashed their shields to conceal the infant's cries from his hostile father. Idaian Zeus was a mysterious god into whose rites young men were initiated on the model of the Kouretes, according to a fragment of Euripides' *Cretans*.[26] The chorus of this play tell how the god's worshipers led a life of purity, wearing only white clothing and abstaining from all meat except the raw flesh of the bull sacrificed to Zeus. The celebrations are described as ecstatic and involved torch-lit processions over the mountain. There is a story that the philosopher Pythagoras was initiated into this cult: after strenuous preparations, he descended into the cave for twenty-seven days and viewed the "tomb of Zeus."[27] This concept of a tomb for Zeus would have seemed reasonable to Egyptians or Syrians, who were familiar with dying gods, but it was alien to other Greeks, who never questioned that the gods were immortal. The poet Callimachus, commenting on the tomb in his *Hymn* to Zeus (1.8–9), concluded: "Kretans always lie."

Oracular Zeus

Zeus was the ultimate source of oracular wisdom, but generally did not give oracles at his own shrines, delegating this task instead to his son Apollo. There were a few exceptions to this rule, including the oracles of Zeus read from sacrificial omens at the Panhellenic sanctuary of Olympia, and the oracle of Ammon in the Libyan desert, where the Egyptian god Amun-Ra was syncretized with Zeus as early as the sixth century.[28] But the most important oracular center of Zeus, established in the eighth century, was Dodona in northwestern Greece. Zeus' cult title here was Naios (the Flowing), probably from the abundant springs in the area, and he shared the sanctuary with a consort, Dione, whose name is merely a feminine form of his own. Homer (*Il.* 16.233–35) mentions the Selloi, interpreters of Dodonaian Zeus, who have unwashed feet and sleep on the ground. These early prophets apparently obeyed an ascetic rule designed to preserve and increase their contact with the earth, often viewed as a source of oracular knowledge. But in the *Odyssey* (14.327–28), we hear that Odysseus went to Dodona to get Zeus' advice "from the god's high-leafed oak tree." In some descriptions of the oracle, an oak tree sacred to Zeus speaks with a human voice. Other accounts tell of messages from doves perched in the tree's branches, or from dove-priestesses who presumably replaced the male Selloi. Evidence from the excavations, however, shows that by the Classical period, one consulted Zeus and Dione by writing a question on a ribbon-shaped lead tablet and handing it to the priestess. Most questions dealt with personal matters, such as whether to undertake a voyage or whether to marry. Often, the oracle advised people on which gods they should sacrifice to in order to ensure health, the birth of children, or prosperity.[29]

Zeus at Olympia and Nemea

Two of the "big four" sanctuaries that hosted Panhellenic athletic festivals, Olympia and Nemea, were dedicated to Zeus. The younger of the two was Nemea, controlled by Kleonai in the sixth century (when the first temple was built) and later by Argos. The founding myth of the festival linked the cult of Zeus with that of a child-hero, Archemoros/Opheltes, for whom funeral games were established. The recently excavated hero shrine of Opheltes consisted of a long, mounded embankment containing some forty drinking vessels left as foundation deposits. On the broad end of the embankment, from which spectators could view the stadium, was a pentagonal wall enclosing at least two stone altars and a fire pit with the remains of sacrifices. The pottery from this shrine dates no earlier than the early sixth century, when the Nemean games were established, though a few scraps and sherds suggest cult activity at Nemea as early as the eighth century. The Archaic temple of Zeus was destroyed by fire during the late fifth century, probably as a result of warfare to judge from the remains of weapons in the burnt layer of soil.[30]

As early as the tenth century, Olympia was a meeting place where local chieftains displayed their wealth by dedicating valuable bronze sculptures and tripods to Zeus. The traditional date for the founding of the games themselves is 776, and during the eighth century, Olympia gradually developed into the most elaborate and important cult site of Zeus. In place of local Peloponnesian chiefs, it now became the arena for rivalries between developing city-states.[31] The center of the sanctuary was a walled precinct called the Altis (Sacred Grove), where stood the primitive altar of Zeus, a great conical pile of molded sacrificial ashes. Every four years, the high point of the festival was the sacrifice of one hundred or more cattle, whose thighs were burned on the altar by Olympic victors. Zeus' altar was also the seat of an oracle; at its summit a *mantis* (prophet) drawn from the Klytiad or Iamid families would observe and interpret the burn pattern of the offerings for those consulting the god.[32]

An early structure near Zeus' altar was the Pelopion, or tomb of Pelops, an ancestral hero who gave his name to the Peloponnese; his archetypal chariot race was immortalized in the eastern pediment of Zeus' temple. This tomb consisted of a mound on which stood a polygonal enclosure wall (probably the model for the similar hero shrine of Opheltes at Nemea). At every festival the hero received a black ram, whose blood flowed into a pit in the Pelopion, as well as preliminary offerings whenever sacrifice was made to Zeus. There has been vigorous debate over the age of Pelops' cult; though Early Helladic walls were found beneath the Pelopion, they may be unrelated to the Archaic cult, and the stratigraphy is not well enough preserved to draw conclusions about continuity. On the other hand, the mound on which the Pelopion sat was itself prehistoric, and the fact that this site was chosen shows a desire on the part of the sanctuary's founders to forge links to the heroic past.[33]

Over the centuries, hundreds of secondary and minor deities became attached to the sanctuary. Among the most important of these were Hera, whose temple dated to the seventh century, Kronos (on the Hill of Kronos), Rhea (in the Metroön), and Herakles, who was credited with founding the games. Once a month the Eleans, inhabitants of the surrounding district, made offerings at the roughly seventy lesser altars on the site. In the time of Pausanias (5.14.4–10), these included at least eight altars of Zeus in various aspects, including Zeus Katharsios (of Purification), Kataibates (of Descending Lightning), Chthonios (of the Underworld), and Hypsistos (the Highest).

As we have seen, Zeus' cults seldom required a temple or image, and the first temple on the site was that of Hera. None was supplied for Zeus until the fifth century, when the Eleans defeated the Pisatans, their rivals for control of the sanctuary, and began a building program with the spoils. Completed before 457, the Doric temple was furnished with a colossal ivory and gold statue of Zeus, which became one of the Seven Wonders of the ancient world. The god was depicted in a restful pose that departed from the standard Archaic representations of him striding forward with raised thunderbolt, and drew instead on Homer's description (*Il.* 1.497–99) of a majestic Zeus enthroned on Mt. Olympos. Seated on an elaborately ornamented, gem-encrusted throne, he held Nike (Victory) in his raised right hand, and his left hand grasped a staff, on which perched an eagle. It was said that when the sculptor Pheidias completed the statue, he prayed to Zeus to make a sign if the work pleased him, and a flash of lightning immediately appeared. Few visitors to the temple failed to be moved with religious awe at the sight of the image, which measured about 13 m in height and could be viewed from a second-floor gallery. But in spite of its huge size, viewers received the impression of a calm and peaceful deity. According to Dio Chrysostom (*Or.* 12.51), "whoever is deeply burdened with pain in his soul, having borne much misfortune and grief in his life and never being able to attain sweet sleep, even this man, I believe, standing before this image, would forget all the terrible and harsh things which one must suffer in human life."

Further reading

Cook 1964 [1914–] is still valuable for its collection of primary sources, but this massive study should be used with caution because its materials and methods are outdated. Much of Burkert 1983b focuses on cults of Zeus in relation to sacrificial practices. Jameson, Jordan, and Kotansky 1993 and Lalonde 2006 collect information about Zeus Meilichios and his role in purifications. Parke 1967 is still the best account in English of the oracles of Zeus. Sinn 2000 provides a popular account of Olympia by an excavator and scholar of religion who knows the site intimately.

3

LADY OF GRAND TEMPLES
Hera

Major cults of Hera were not evenly spread over the Greek world, but instead were characteristic of certain regions and peoples. The Dorians of the north-east Peloponnese (Argos, Korinth, Tiryns) and the Peloponnesians who colonized southern Italy honored her the most. A famous Ionian seat of her worship was the island of Samos. Her cult enjoyed its greatest prosperity during the Archaic period, when Argos and Samos were at the height of their power. Hera's origins are generally thought to lie in a powerful prehellenic goddess (or goddesses) whose cult was adopted by the Mycenaean Greeks. Her name has been connected with the word *hōra*, season, indicating fertility and ripeness for marriage, and appears on Linear B tablets from Pylos (in connection with Zeus) and Thebes. The same etymology makes Hera a feminine form of *herōs*, and this background may help to elucidate the goddess' complex ties to heroes, Herakles above all, and the genesis of the Greek concept of the mythic and cultic hero.[1]

Greek poetry and myth tell us of a goddess who vehemently opposes her husband's extramarital affairs and attempts to punish her rivals and their offspring. She is a scheming and vengeful deity, who plots against the Trojans when she loses the beauty contest judged by Paris, but she also has favorites such as the hero Jason, whom she aids in his quest for the Golden Fleece. She is not a tender mother, but Homer describes her sexual union with Zeus as a source of fecund power (*Il.* 14.347–49): "under them the divine earth grew newly-sprouted grass, dewy clover, crocuses, and hyacinths, thick and soft." In some of her cults, Hera is likewise viewed primarily as a bride or wife, and her status as Zeus' consort is central for worshipers. But in her most famous cults (Argos and Samos) Hera is a powerful city goddess who fosters economic and military success. In these cases her relationship to Zeus is not a crucial factor, and the literary portrait of a jealous, scheming wife seems far removed from the cultic experience of an awe-inspiring deity who brings success in battle, multiplies the herds of cattle, frees the enslaved, and protects the young for her chosen people.

Argive Hera

Despite Homer's Panhellenizing tendencies, he recognizes Hera's regional character as goddess of the Argive peninsula, giving her the epithet Hera Argeia (e.g. *Il.* 4.8). In historical times she became the city-goddess of Argos itself, and her Argive sanctuary was the most venerable and famed center of her worship. Her festival there, known as the Heraia or Hekatombaia (Sacrifice of one hundred Oxen), was held in the first month of the year. A grand procession escorted the priestess, who rode in an ox-drawn wagon from the city to the sanctuary several miles distant. The youth recognized as most virtuous carried a sacred shield in the procession, marking his and his age-mates' transition to adulthood and warrior status. After the procession, there were athletic competitions for which the prize was, again, a bronze shield.[2] Hera's cult at Argos shows a preoccupation with two aspects of the Argolid's prosperity: the herds of cattle on which its wealth was based, and its military might. Terracotta figurines from the Heraion indicate that Hera was also viewed as a kourotrophic deity, one who nourished and protected the young. Often she is shown holding a child in her lap. Sometimes she holds not a child but a horse, an emblem of aristocratic privilege. Hera's cult seems to have been closely bound up with the efforts of the early Archaic Argives to define their relationship with the heroic past.

The Argive Heraion was constructed over the remains of a Mycenaean settlement, but there is no clear evidence of continuity of cult from the Bronze Age to the ninth century, when activity at the Heraion becomes archaeologically visible. Around 700, a terrace was built using huge "Cyclopean" blocks in imitation of the Bronze Age architectural style, and shortly thereafter a temple of stone and wood with a colonnade was added. This Archaic structure was not superseded by a newer temple until the fifth century, when the sanctuary was transformed from a rallying center for the towns in the region to a symbol of the power of Argos, by then the dominant city. In 2000–01, excavators found (*SEG* 51 [2001] 410) a cache of inscribed bronze tablets recording, among other things, the sums borrowed from the state treasuries of Pallas and Hera to pay for the construction of this temple. It possessed sculptures depicting not myths of Hera herself, but subjects of interest to the Argives: the birth of Zeus, the battle of the gods and giants, the Trojan war, and the saga of Orestes.

In Pausanias' time, one entered the temple after walking through a series of statues of the former priestesses (styled *kleidouchoi* or Keyholders), whose tenures provided a chronological framework for the city's history. The list of priestesses was already ancient in the fifth century, when Hellanicus (*FGrH* 4 F 74–82) used it as the basis for an account of the Greeks from the Trojan war to his own day. The cult image of the Classical period was a famous one by Polykleitos, fashioned of gold and ivory over a wood core. The seated goddess held a scepter and a pomegranate, symbols of temporal power and fertility. A more ancient wooden image must have existed, but presumably was destroyed when the Archaic temple burned in 423/2. When Pausanias (2.17.3) visited the temple, he saw a venerable image of pearwood taken from nearby Tiryns, another ancient Heraian cult center, which the Argives had installed on a pillar beside Polykleitos' statue. The pillar itself may have held special significance, for a fragment of the Argive epic *Phoronis* (fr. 3 Davies, *EGF*) describes Hera's priestess adorning "the high column of the Olympian queen, Hera Argeia" with fillets and tassels. Another item of interest in the temple was the "couch of Hera," a symbol of Hera's status as the bride of Zeus.

The Asterion river near the Heraion was regarded as the father of Hera's three nurses, the nymphs Akraia, Prosymna and Euboia, who were named after features of the sanctuary's topography. Local tradition, therefore, held that Argos was Hera's birthplace. Women conducted secret rituals at the Heraion, involving purifications, sacrifices, and the offering of garlands twined from a local herb also called *asterion*. The women wove a robe for Hera, as they did at Olympia, first taking a ritual bath in the waters of the spring or well called Amymone. The hundreds of miniature water vessels (*hudriai*) from the excavations further attest the importance of water in these activities. Perhaps the ritual involved a bath for Hera's image; a legend describing how Hera took an annual bath to restore her virginity was attached to the spring Kanathos in nearby Nauplia. The "water of freedom" of the stream Eleutherion, near the Heraion, was used for the women's secret rites, and was also drunk by slaves and prisoners about to be emancipated. Hera's daughter Hebe (Youth), whose statue stood beside hers in the Heraion, similarly granted asylum to suppliants and freed prisoners at her ancient sanctuary in Phlious.[3]

Hera of Samos

Half of one column from the Heraion at Samos has been reconstructed, scarcely hinting at the former glory of this sanctuary. A succession of temples stood in the marshy site, beginning with the late eighth-century *hekatompedon* or hundred-foot temple. One of the later temples was a truly gigantic Ionic structure with a forest of columns, which Herodotus (3.60) called the largest temple of his time. Among the dedications at the Samian Heraion were over thirty house models in stone and terracotta. The Hera sanctuaries at Argos and Perachora have also produced models with Geometric decoration, causing speculation that the houses are intended to represent the earliest temples, before the construction of *hekatompeda*. Given the fact that Hera's temples are everywhere among the earliest attested, this is likely, but other explanations are possible. If the models represent chieftains' houses, they could symbolize Hera's association with political authority and social status.[4]

Figure 3.1 Terracotta house or temple model from Perachora. End of the ninth
century. Athens, National Archaeological Museum. Bildarchiv Foto
Marburg.

The center of the sanctuary, and its earliest feature, was the altar, which
existed from the tenth century. Like the temple, it was rebuilt several times,
culminating in a monumental 40 m structure.[5] All this grandeur, however,
came after the sanctuary was well established. While not of Panhellenic
stature, its fortunes rose with those of the maritime state of Samos in the
seventh and sixth centuries. Asius, a poet of this period, described the wealthy
Samians visiting the sanctuary dressed in flowing white tunics, with long hair
bound in golden bands, and adorned with gold cicadas. A stunning variety
of imported objects was uncovered in the excavations: Egyptian ivories,
Babylonian bronze figurines, and a collection of exotic animal trophies
including crocodile and antelope skulls. In spite of the cosmopolitan nature
of the sanctuary, the dedications show that it was also a local center of
worship. The excavations turned up many humble, crudely carved vessels
and figurines, as well as natural curiosities like coral and rock crystal.[6]

There were conflicting stories about the origins of the sanctuary and to
what degree it was dependent on the Heraion at Argos. One tradition said
that it was founded by the Argonauts, who brought the cult statue from
Argos, while the Samians themselves said that Hera was born here under
the *lugos*, a willow-like tree preserved in the sanctuary, and that the place
was founded by non-Greek Karians. Still, their tradition allowed that the
first Greek priestess of the sanctuary was the Argive Admete, daughter of

Eurystheus. Once, Karian pirates had attempted to steal the cult image of Hera, but found their ship immobilized when they placed the statue on board. Terrified, they left the image on the beach with a food offering and made their escape. There the searching Samians found it, and believing that it had run away, bound it to the *lugos* with the tree's flexible branches. Admete herself purified the image and restored it to its place in the temple. This myth provided the background for the annual festival called the Tonaia (Binding), during which the goddess' statue was carried to the sea, purified, and given a meal of barley-cakes. At some point during the rite, it was probably also bound with *lugos* branches. Celebrants at the feast wore wreaths made of *lugos* and reclined on beds of it. This festival has been interpreted as a drama of the deity's disappearance and return, in which the recovery of the goddess is symbolic of the yearly cycle of vegetative abundance. A related possibility is that the drama expresses the Samians' anxiety lest Hera, the protector of their city and guarantor of their good fortune, abandon them. The goddess is annually bound to her birthplace and her proper residence at Samos is reaffirmed. The myth itself asserts that even should outside forces attempt to move the goddess, she would express a preference for her home and actively resist leaving it.[7]

There are indeed indications that Hera at Samos was a goddess concerned with fertility. Among the objects dedicated to her were pinecones and pomegranates (real fruits as well as clay and ivory models), symbols of fecund reproduction. The offering of pomegranates, however, appears to cease after about 600. Joan V. O'Brien suggests that this is due to a shift in the perception of Hera, through which her role as bride of Zeus came to be emphasized over her earlier manifestation as a powerful, independent goddess. In any case, Hera's role at Samos was never limited to assuring fertility, but must have been closely connected with the Samians' successful trading ventures. Stylized wooden ship models were common votives, and in the Archaic period two full-size ships were dedicated in the sanctuary.[8]

The cult image of Samian Hera has been described by ancient witnesses as crudely carved and planklike. It was wooden, small and light enough to be carried annually to the shore for the Tonaia, but spent the rest of the year ensconced in the temple, dressed in rich garments and wearing a high crown. It also wore a pectoral ornament, resembling an extended collar or series of necklaces, which was characteristic of East Greek and Anatolian deities (the so-called "multiple breasts" of Artemis at Ephesos are another example). When the Samians built the huge Classical temple, they supplied it with a new cult image that resided in the cella, the normal location. The venerable old image was kept in the *pronaos*, or front room, of the temple. This arrangement was perhaps dictated by the need to keep the old image in its original location: its base in the *pronaos* stood on the same spot it had occupied in the cella of the old temple. As we have seen, keeping the goddess fixed in her proper place was a major cultic concern for the Samians.[9]

Hera at Korinth and Perachora

The Heraion at Perachora was among the richest minor sanctuaries in Greece. Literary sources are almost completely silent about this sanctuary, but the archaeological finds show that it was of great importance during the Archaic period. In the territory of the prosperous mercantile state of Korinth, it was founded in the eighth century and saw the construction of yet another of the very early temples to Hera we have noted. The first temple had a curved (apsidal) back wall and was only about 7.5 m in length. Nothing is known about the cult image, but the goddess here was called Hera Akraia (of the Headland), a reference to the Perachora promontory on which the sanctuary was situated near a small harbor. Sixth-century dedications to Hera Limenia (of the Harbor) have also been found; surprisingly, these appear on a terrace above the harbor itself and the main part of the sanctuary. An Archaic structure on the terrace, once thought to be a separate temple of Hera Limenia, is now considered an auxiliary building, probably a dining room. Blocks used in this building contain dedications to Hera under yet another title, Hera Leukolene (of the White Arms). These early (seventh- and sixth-century) dedications echo one of Homer's favorite epithets for Hera (e.g. *Il.* 5.711, 8.381, etc.).

The pattern of votives shows that this was an important cult site for local people, as well as for sailors traveling up and down the Gulf of Korinth. The many imported objects, including Egyptian-style scarabs and Phoenician bronzes, illustrate the wide trading contacts of the Archaic Korinthians. The earliest, eighth-century temple at the harbor was accompanied by a deposit of Geometric votive objects, including drinking vessels, wine jugs, clay models of cakes presented as offerings to the goddess (*koulouria*), and house models. This temple was replaced in the sixth century with a new Doric stone temple, and a monumental altar was added. North of the altar the excavators found a flight of steps, which probably functioned as a spectator area for viewing the sacrifices.[10]

The myth of Medeia, the young sorceress whom Jason brought back from his travels in the Black Sea, is best known from the play by Euripides. This work portrays her as a spurned wife who kills her children by Jason in order to avenge herself for his abandonment, then buries the children in the sanctuary of Hera Akraia and founds their cult (Eur. *Med.* 1378–83). There were, however, other myths about how the children of Medeia died. According to one, Medeia took each of her children in turn to the sanctuary of Hera to "hide them away" (*katakruptein*), thinking that this operation would make them immortal. (The word may mean that she buried them.) When her hopes were disappointed and Jason discovered what she had done, he abandoned her. Another version held that Medeia instructed her children to bring a poisoned robe to her rival Glauke. When Glauke perished as a result of the gift, the enraged Korinthians stoned the innocent children. The murdered children took a supernatural vengeance by causing Korinthian infants to die, until the desperate citizens consulted an oracle and were told to institute annual sacrifices to Medeia's children. They also set up a statue known as Deima, or Terror, which took the form of "a frightening woman." In antiquity, infant mortality was often attributed to female demons (Mormo, Lamia) who had a hideous appearance; the statue seems to have been designed to ward off such malign influences. Other sources tell us more about the relationship between the children's cult and that of Hera. Every year, seven boys and seven girls from noble families were dressed in black and sent to live in the sanctuary of Hera Akraia (it is unclear whether this refers to a sanctuary in Korinth itself, since no such sanctuary has been identified, or to that at Perachora). They cut their hair and dedicated it to Medeia's children, and presumably participated in the *thrēnoi*, or laments, sung for the children, and the *enagismata*, or sacrifices for the dead.[11]

All these myths and related customs have been taken as evidence of a real (in the distant past) or symbolic child sacrifice to appease hostile divine forces, or as an initiation rite by which the youths and maidens, after a period of separation from the community, reached adult status. Certainly they indicate that the Korinthians thought it was necessary to devote elite children to the service of the goddess, and that upon this service depended the health and welfare of the entire community's children. The rituals originally may have been conducted for Medeia herself, since some scholars view her as a divine figure whose cult was superseded by Hera's.[12]

Hera at Olympia

One of the paradoxes of the Panhellenic site of Olympia is that its earliest temple was erected not for Zeus, the primary deity of the sanctuary, but for Hera. During the late seventh century, a Heraion was built in the Altis, or sacred enclosure, which then contained no other major structures. Originally, only the foundations were of stone, while the walls were mud brick, and the rest of the structure, including the colonnade, was wood. The temple was refurbished in such a way that the columns were gradually replaced in stone, and each one was slightly different in style, thickness, and the type of stone used. The mismatched columns were probably the result of contributions by many donors, each of whom supplied one column and wanted it to be recognizably different from the rest.

Some scholars, disturbed by the anomaly of a Heraion as the only temple in a sanctuary of Zeus, have suggested that the temple was from the beginning dedicated jointly to Zeus and Hera, or that it was originally a temple of Zeus, and was rededicated to Hera only after Zeus' Classical temple was built in the fifth century. The question is still open, but we should keep in mind that a temple was never a requirement for a sanctuary, and was often absent from sanctuaries of Zeus in particular (as at Dodona, another Panhellenic Zeus sanctuary). The focus of Zeus' cult was not a cult statue, but the great ash altar where he received sacrifices. Furthermore, Hera was, as we have seen, one of the earliest temple deities, and one who was consistently provided with temples in the early Archaic period. Hera's cult in the Altis may have been introduced by Pheidon, the seventh-century king of Argos who established a military presence in Elis and reorganized the Olympic games. If this is the case, the Hera temple originally served as an offshoot of the Argive Heraion, and a reminder of the political and military supremacy of Argos in the early Archaic period.[13]

Pausanias (5.16.1–20.5) provides a detailed description of the temple's amazing contents. The cult image of Hera was seated, and behind it stood a statue of Zeus wearing a helmet. The positioning of Zeus' statue suggests that he was not the primary deity of this temple, but that his role as Hera's spouse was important to the cult (this is borne out by other aspects of the cult described below). Both statues are described as "simple" works, and thus probably belonged to the Archaic period. Nearby were images of many other deities in ivory and gold, some by famous sculptors and others by unknown artists: the Horai (Seasons) and Themis their mother, Athena, Demeter and Kore, Apollo and Artemis, Hermes, and so on. A richly decorated cedarwood chest was dedicated by the family of Kypselos, the seventh-century tyrant of Korinth; this famous chest was covered with labeled episodes from heroic myths. There was also a small bed, recalling the "couch of Hera" in the Heraion at Argos; a disc on which was inscribed the ritual formula for the Olympic truce forbidding men in arms to enter the sanctuary, and the ivory and gold table used to hold the wreaths for Olympic victors.

Hera's cult at Olympia was administered by a college of sixteen women chosen from the most venerable and respected matrons of the district. These women organized the Heraia, or games held to honor Hera, concurrently with the quadrennial Olympic games. While women were generally excluded from the Olympic games both as competitors and as spectators, the Heraia involved a footrace for girls of three different age categories. They ran in the same stadium as the men and boys, though the track was one-sixth shorter. The winners received a portion of the meat from the cow sacrificed to Hera and a crown of olive. The sixteen women of Elis also wove a robe for Hera, which was presumably dedicated in the temple and may have adorned the cult image. They arranged choruses for Physkoa, a Dionysiac heroine, and for Hippodameia, the heroine who figures in one of the founding myths of Olympia.[14] It was to win the hand of Hippodameia that Pelops raced against her father, the king of Elis, thus inaugurating the chariot races at Olympia. The sixteen women traced their origin to Hippodameia, who first formed the college in order to give thanks to Hera for her marriage to Pelops. An alternative story said that the women were brought together as arbiters to settle disputes between the Eleans and the Pisatans, who fought over the control of the sanctuary in the seventh and sixth centuries. If the story is accurate, this is one of the rare cases in which women's religious authority translated into a limited form of political authority.

Hera in Italy

The city of Poseidonia/Paestum in southern Italy was settled by Greeks from the Argolid. Within the walls to the south of the city, the new inhabitants built a Doric temple of Hera in the sixth century. The temple is notable for its double cella; the two halves are separated by a central row of columns. Since there was no technical need for this feature, which had been used in early temples to support the roof, scholars have speculated that there may have been two cult images. Perhaps Zeus was worshiped with Hera, as he was at Olympia. Terracottas from the sanctuary show the king and queen of the gods enthroned together. A second temple to Hera was built beside the first in the fifth century, and must have contained a newer cult image. Another theory about this temple holds that it was consecrated to Poseidon, the patron god of the city.[15]

The Hera cult in the city was linked to an extraurban sanctuary at the mouth of the river Sele, north of Paestum. The medieval lime kilns on the site show that the sanctuary's structures were long ago dismantled and the marble components burned, yet here one of the most significant caches of Greek sculpture to be uncovered in the twentieth century escaped destruction. Buried in the sand, excavators found more than thirty sculptured metopes from what was probably the earliest Hera temple at the site (c. 560). Many of these metopes illustrate the deeds of Herakles; others are scenes from the epic cycle of poems about Troy.[16] A second, larger temple of Hera, dating to about 500, was differently ornamented, with metopes depicting dancing pairs of maidens. The terracotta votives in this sanctuary are very reminiscent of those in the other Heraia we have studied: they show the enthroned goddess holding a spear, a child, a horse, or a pomegranate. Not coincidentally, the Virgin of the eighth-century CE church built near this site is known as the Madonna of the Pomegranate. Other typical gifts to the goddess, also found at both Argos and Samos, are implements of war: miniature terracotta shields and armor. Like the Heraion at Samos, this famous sanctuary was supposed to have been founded by Jason and the Argonauts to honor Argive Hera.[17]

The sanctuary of Hera Lakinia at Kroton has been described as the most important sanctuary in southern Italy during the Classical period because of its role as the seat of the Achaian and Italian Leagues. Its rich votives begin in the seventh century and include a bronze ship model and a diadem decorated with leaves and acorns that may have adorned a wooden cult image. Like the other Olympian goddesses, Hera often received gifts of clothing, among which an elaborate purple cloak, embroidered with figures in gold and silver and presented by Alkistenes of Sybaris, was renowned. The nearby sanctuary

Figure 3.2 Metope from Hera sanctuary at Foce del Sele: Centaur, 570–60. Museo
Archeologico Nazionale. Bildarchiv Foto Marburg.

of Vigna Nuova contained numerous chains and tools, which may have been
dedications to Hera by prisoners captured during Kroton's destruction of
Sybaris (510) and ultimately freed.[18]

Hera and marriage

Hera often receives the cult title Teleia (the Fulfilled) in reference to her status
as an archetypal bride and consort. In Greek culture, marriage and mother-
hood were the only acceptable goals for most women, and while Hera is not
an enthusiastic mother in myth, we have seen that she functions as a nurturing
goddess in some cults. Myths of Hera often illustrate the socially sanctioned
status of the legitimate wife. The "marriage month" Gamelion, which
appeared in many city calendars and involved sacrifices to Hera, was an
auspicious time for weddings. Her union with Zeus was celebrated in the

villages of Attica during the minor festival of Hieros Gamos (Sacred Marriage), while Zeus Teleios and Hera Teleia are invoked by Athenian poets in contexts that have to do with marriage.[19]

In Boiotian Plataiai, the site of a major Hera festival, the temple contained two statues of the goddess. One was called Hera Nympheuomene (Led as a Bride) referring to the marriage procession, and the other was Hera Teleia. The goddess' festival, the Daidala, was celebrated every four (or six) years. According to Pausanias' account (9.2.5–3.4), this involved the felling of an oak tree selected when the Plataians set out food for the crows in a sacred grove. The first tree the birds settled in was cut and fashioned into a crude statue called Daidala. At much longer intervals of sixty years, the festival called the Great Daidala took place. Unlike the annual observance, this involved the participation of cities all over Boiotia, each of whom contributed a cow and a bull. One of the wooden figures produced at the quadrennial festival was dressed as a bride and ceremoniously conducted in a cart from the river Asopos up to the peak of Mt. Kithairon. There, along with the other wooden figures and the sacrificial animals, it was burnt in a huge bonfire on the altar.[20]

The myth that explained the origin of this custom told how Zeus had quarreled with Hera, who "hid herself away" in the area of Mt. Kithairon. On the advice of a local king, Zeus devised a method to find and reconcile her: he pretended to marry a rival, the oaken statue. Hera and the outraged matrons of Plataiai disrupted the wedding procession, only to discover that the bride was a wooden image. Amused at the trick, Hera nevertheless insisted on the burning of the false rival. In the historical period, the festival was understood to commemorate the reconciliation of Zeus and Hera, and was therefore a celebration of divine and human marriage. Both the images in Hera's temple, Nympheuomene and Teleia, refer to aspects of Hera's concern with legitimate, socially sanctioned unions, and the myth likewise stresses how Hera and the women of Plataiai jealously protected their prerogatives as wives in a culture that considered extramarital sex for men normal, yet took seriously the rule that a man must have only one wife. Otherwise, issues of social status and inheritance could become muddied.

On the other hand, the festival seems to incorporate elements that predate the myth of Hera's feminine jealousy, and point to the worship of an independently powerful goddess. Zeus has no place in the ritual itself, which seems to be akin to other sacred log processions attested in Boiotia and elsewhere, such as the Daphnephoria (Carrying the Laurel). Sacrifices on mountain peaks were characteristic of Minoan religion, and a shrine known as the Daidaleion is attested from Mycenaean Knossos. Hera's cult, with its marital preoccupations, may have been superimposed upon rituals that were once carried out for a prehellenic tree or mountain goddess who disappeared and returned on a seasonal basis. At the same time, the myth of Hera's quarrel with Zeus should not be dismissed as a comical tale concocted to explain the ritual. At Stymphalos in Arkadia, there was a similar myth of Hera's quarrel with and separation from Zeus, and there too the goddess' cult titles referred to marital status. Hera, it was said, grew up in Stymphalos, and possessed three sanctuaries, one as Pais (Girl), one as Teleia, which she received upon her marriage to Zeus, and one as Chera (Widow). She received the latter because she returned to Stymphalos "while she was quarreling with Zeus" and was without a husband. Thus, in the Stymphalian cult Hera provided models for the three stages of female life as the Greeks conceptualized it, but it was her period of separation from Zeus that provided the impetus for the goddess' return to her own land. Hera's identity as a local goddess could best be manifested when she was apart from Zeus, not installed as his bride on Olympos.[21]

Further reading

Clark 1998 compares several festivals of Hera in relation to the institution of marriage. Kyrieleis 1993 is a useful account of the sanctuary of Hera at Samos by one of its excavators. O'Brien 1993 argues, speculatively at times, for continuity in Hera's cults from the Bronze Age to the Archaic period and gives detailed archaeological information. Tomlinson 1992 is a good introduction to the material record at Perachora, while Pedley 1990 (cf. Pedley 2005.167–85) provides one of the few accounts in English of the Hera sanctuaries at Poseidonia/Paestum and Foce del Sele.

4

MISTRESS OF CITADELS
Athena

Athena's name probably comes from the city of Athens and not the other way around. In a Linear B tablet from Knossos, we hear of the Potnia (Mistress) of At(h)ana, and there is a consensus that Athena was in origin a Minoan or Mycenaean deity, perhaps identical with the shield goddess who appears on a painted tablet at Mycenae itself.[1] As a warrior goddess who protected the king and citadel, this Mistress had parallels in the Near East (Ishtar, Anat) and Egypt (Neith). Still, the exact relationship between the Bronze Age goddess and the Athena of the Classical Greeks is unclear, for gaps and inconsistencies in the archaeological evidence mean that we cannot demonstrate continuity of worship. Athena's sanctuaries and temples are very often to be found at the city center, particularly on fortified heights like the Athenian Akropolis. In Greek towns of the early Iron Age, her dwelling place was often juxtaposed to that of the local chieftain or king; later she championed the polis with its varied forms of government. She presided over the arts of war, such as the taming of horses, the training of warriors, and the building of ships. As a goddess of crafts, particularly weaving and metalworking, she evokes the palace economies of the Bronze Age.

The Athenian Akropolis

Fittingly, the center of Athena's worship in her namesake city was a most impressive citadel, the Akropolis. Among the many riddles of Athenian cult topography, the question of Athena's temples on the Archaic and Classical Akropolis is perhaps the most vexing. Nobody has yet achieved a definitive reconstruction of the sequence of major Athena temples and how these match up with the structures mentioned in the inscriptions and literary sources. Archaeological remains provide evidence of several temples. First, there is the so-called Bluebeard temple, named for the triple-bodied, snake-legged creature in its pediment, which belonged to the second quarter of the sixth century. This Doric temple, the first monumental temple on the Akropolis, may have stood on the north side, directly over the old Mycenaean palace, or on the south side where the Parthenon was later built; it is sometimes called

41

the "grandfather of the Parthenon." Second, well-preserved foundations on the north side, excavated in the nineteenth century by Wilhelm Dörpfeld, belong to a splendid late sixth-century temple, also Doric, which possessed two porches and a cella divided into four chambers. Sculpture from this temple, including a striding Athena attacking a giant, has been identified. A number of sculptures from unidentified buildings, such as the "Olive tree pediment," are also known. Finally, immediately following the victories of 490, the Athenians began to build a splendid, large temple as a thank offering to the goddess. Located on the south side of the Akropolis, this was the Older Parthenon, the direct predecessor of the great Periklean temple. When the Persians sacked the Akropolis in 480, they burned the existing temples, including the unfinished Older Parthenon, and the remains of these were incorporated into the north Akropolis defensive wall.[2]

It is safe to say that Athena possessed a temple from the eighth or seventh century, since this is the most likely date of the ancient olivewood cult image around which the central rituals for the goddess were organized.[3] Two Homeric passages are relevant; in the *Iliad* (2.549) she establishes the cult of Erechtheus "in her own rich temple" while in the *Odyssey* (7.78–81) she travels across the sea and enters "the strong-built house of Erechtheus." The Ionic building we call the Erechtheion was known to the Classical Athenians as "the temple with the image" or the *archaios neōs* (Old Temple), even though it was quite new at the time. It took over this name from its predecessor, either the Dörpfeld temple or a "pre-Erechtheion." Active controversy attends the question of whether the Ionic building, in addition to housing Athena's olivewood statue, is also the shrine of Erechtheus; some say the latter, described by Pausanias (1.26.5–27.4), is to be found elsewhere on the Akropolis. Though the question must remain open, the Homeric passages above suggest that Athena's holiest shrine always housed Erechtheus' cult as well. The same sacerdotal family, known as the Eteoboutadai, supplied the priests for both Poseidon-Erechtheus and Athena Polias. If the cults were housed together, we also have an explanation for the four-chambered cellas of both the Dörpfeld temple and the Ionic temple.[4]

An early fifth-century decree (*IG* I[3] 4) was carved on a metope from the Bluebeard temple and therefore postdates the dismantling of that structure. It refers to a *neōs* (Temple) and a *hekatompedon* (Hundred-Footer) as separate sacred areas, but there is no consensus on which labels fit which places. This inscription does however illustrate the pattern, probably dating to the early sixth century, of maintaining two Akropolis temples dedicated to Athena. One, situated on the north side, held the olivewood statue (and perhaps the associated cult of Erechtheus) and was the focus of the most ancient rituals. The other, on the south, came about as a result of the competitive vogue for elaborate "Hundred-Footers" that swept the Greek world in the seventh and sixth centuries, and the final representative of this tradition was the Parthenon, with its colossal gold and ivory cult statue sculpted by Pheidias.[5] The

Figure 4.1 Athena Parthenos. Roman marble copy of the cult statue in the Parthenon at Athens, 447–39. Ht 1.045 m. National Archaeological Museum, Athens. Alinari/Art Resource.

southern temples, whose primary function was to store and display the increasing number of rich objects dedicated to Athena, were themselves a form of offering from the citizens to their goddess.

Some two hundred marble fragments preserve the inventories of the *tamiai* (treasurers) of Athena, officials who were responsible for keeping track of the valuable ritual objects and dedications stored in the Parthenon and the Erechtheion in the Classical period. These inventories show that the interior walls of the temples were fitted with shelves or cupboards. For smaller items, baskets (often gilded) and bronze boxes were used. The earliest inventory of objects in the Parthenon (434/3) includes gold and silver ritual vessels, armor, at least fifty-seven items of furniture, several lyres, and six Persian daggers inlaid with gold. Many of these objects were used in Athena's festivals and returned to the temple, while others were simply valuable or decorative items owned by the goddess. The inventories for the Ionic temple describe the contents of the room where Athena's olivewood cult statue stood, including a gold incense burner fitted into the floor and a lustral basin held by a male statue. The cult image itself is said to possess a gold circlet, earrings, a neck-band, five necklaces, a gold owl (probably on the statue's shoulder), a gold aegis with a gorgon's head, and a gold libation bowl.[6]

The bastion flanking the south entrance to the Akropolis was the site of a cult of Athena Nike (Victory) dating to the early sixth century. During the modern restoration of the gemlike Classical temple perched on the bastion, workers found remains of the Archaic sanctuary, which had been incorpor-ated into the newer structure. Beneath the new altar, a block from the old was preserved with its sixth-century inscription: "Altar of Athena Nike. Patrokles erected it." The theme of victory relates to the reorganization of the Pana-thenaia in 566 and that festival's association with Athena's victory over the giants. The Archaic sanctuary was presumably destroyed by the Persians, though the cult statue, a wooden Athena holding a pomegranate in the right hand and a helmet in the left, survived to be reinstalled in its new home.[7] The mid-fifth-century Nike Temple Decree (*IG* I³ 35) commissioned Kallikrates to design the temple that still stands and established the office of priestess of Athena Nike, which was awarded based on the drawing of lots from all Athenian citizen women.

Figure 4.2 Bronze votive statue of Athena in battle from the Athenian Akropolis, *c.* 480. Athens, National Archaeological Museum. Bildarchiv Foto Mar-burg.

Athena's festival year

Athena's great festival, the Panathenaia, fell in midsummer during the first month of the Athenian calendar, Hekatombaion (named for the customary hecatombs or sacrifices of multiple cattle to the goddess). The preparations for the Panathenaia began nine months earlier, with the fall celebration of the Chalkeia (Festival of Bronze-workers) in honor of Athena Ergane (of Labors) and Hephaistos as deities of handicrafts. Weavers too honored Athena Ergane, and as part of the Chalkeia the *ergastinai* (women workers) set up a loom on which to weave the *peplos* destined to be presented to Athena during the Panathenaia.[8] They were assisted by little girls clad in white, about seven years old, and chosen from elite families to serve Athena. These girls, known as the *arrhēphoroi*, lived on the Akropolis "with the goddess" for the rest of the year, just as the daughters of king Kekrops once did.

As early summer drew near, the ritual and logistical preparations for the Panathenaia began in earnest. The purificatory month of Thargelion brought two holy days involving the cult statue of Athena, both associated with Aglauros, the daughter of Kekrops and priestess of Athena who leapt to her death from the Akropolis. The first day, called the Kallynteria (Beautification), is often described as the sweeping out of the temple (the verb *kallunein* can mean both "adorn" and "sweep, scour"). Alternatively, the ritual may have involved the *kosmēsis* or adornment of the image with jewelry and other items, for it was said in connection with this festival that Aglauros was the first to adorn the gods' images.[9] Next, women of the Praxiergidai, an Athenian sacerdotal family, performed the Plynteria (Washing festival). They removed the garments of the statue and cleaned them. They may also have bathed the image itself, but our sources do not specifically say this. The naked image was veiled for one day, on which it was considered unlucky to conduct either private or public business; Athenian sanctuaries were closed during the Plynteria as well, and some Attic towns (also known as demes), such as Erchia and Thorikos, held their own observances. At this time the Praxiergidai conducted secret rites, and a cake made of figs, the first domesticated fruit, was carried at the head of a procession as a reminder of Athens' primitive origins. The somberness of the day was attributed to the mourning for Aglauros, but it was clearly part of a cycle of purification and a necessary preliminary to the celebration of the New Year and Panathenaia. A month called Plynterion, attested in the Ionian islands of Paros, Thasos, and Chios, suggests that this observance predates the Ionian migration, though it is not certain that "Washing month" refers specifically to the same ritual.[10]

During Skirophorion, the *arrhēphoroi* were called on to perform a secret nocturnal rite. According to Pausanias (1.27.3), Athena's priestess gave them sacred objects in baskets, which they carried on their heads to an enclosure in the city not far from the sanctuary of Aphrodite in the Gardens, accessible by a "natural underground descent." Neither the priestess nor the girls knew what the objects were, but when they reached their destination, they exchanged what they were carrying for other hidden objects, and returned to the Akropolis. This curious ritual has been interpreted as a fertility rite and/or a rite of passage, especially given the mention of Aphrodite and the comment of one scholiast that the secret objects were dough models of male genitalia and snakes. Although Pausanias does not identify Aphrodite's sanctuary as the actual destination of the *arrhephoroi*, it has been suggested that the girls climbed down a passageway on the north slope of the Akropolis toward an area that served in Classical times as a shrine of Aphrodite and Eros.[11] Their journey reflects the myth that Athena gave the daughters of Kekrops something secret to carry in a basket, which turned out to be the snake-legged, earthborn infant Erichthonios. When the girls disobeyed the goddess' command and peeked into the basket, they were terrified and leapt from the Akropolis. Pandrosos (All-Dew), the one daughter who obeyed Athena, had a shrine beside the Ionic temple of Athena, and the families of former *arrhephoroi* sometimes made dedications to Athena and Pandrosos.[12] The term *arrhephoros* (also spelled *errhephoros*) refers to a "bearer" of something; ancient commentators suggested that the unknown first element in the word came from *arrheta* (unspoken things) or *herse* (dew).

The New Year brought the Panathenaia, held on 28 Hekatombaion, the anniversary of Athena's triumph in the battle of the gods and giants. The battle of the gods and giants was the scene intricately woven into Athena's *peplos*; Elizabeth Barber has shown that such story cloths were an inheritance from the early Archaic period, if not the Bronze Age, and required months to create.[13] Every four years the weeklong annual festival became the Great Panathenaia, when games were celebrated on a lavish, Panhellenic scale. The wide variety of events included musical competitions and recitations of Homer, chariot racing, men's and boys' athletics, a dance in armor (*purrhike*), a regatta in the harbor, and a torch race. Winners received commemorative jars filled with olive oil, many of which have survived for modern study.

The highlight of the festival was the Panathenaic parade, which followed the Sacred Way from the Dipylon gate through the potters' quarter and agora to the Akropolis, a distance of about 1 km. Unlike the games, the procession was an inclusive event with representatives from many segments of the Athenian population, who were given different ritual duties: non-citizens, freed slaves, women, and old men. Still, members of aristocratic families played the most important roles. On the Parthenon frieze, the procession is shown entering the company of the gods (i.e. the Akropolis?) and presenting the newly woven robe to the goddess. Perhaps the olivewood statue was now fully dressed and adorned for the first time since the removal of its *kosmos* during the Plynteria. Meanwhile, a massive sacrifice took place and the meat was distributed to the gleeful residents of the city. The management of this elaborate festival was the responsibility of a number of officers, some of whom administered the games while others, the *hieropoioi* (doers of sacred things), organized the sacrifices. While the Panathenaic festival was "founded" in 566, this date probably represents a reorganization and elaboration of existing rituals, such as the weaving of the *peplos*, that reach back to the eighth century or earlier. In later centuries many changes were introduced, such as the inclusion in the parade of a ship on wheels with a giant "*peplos*" displayed as its sail. This elaborate cloth was produced by professional male weavers, but it did not take the place of the women's *peplos*, which was approximately 1.8 by 2 m, the size of an actual garment.[14]

Other Athenian cults

To judge from the evidence of the surviving deme calendars, many of the Attic demes held local celebrations of Athena's great city festivals. At Thorikos there was a sacrifice for the Plynteria, and at Erchia a sacrifice to Kourotrophos (Nurturer of Youths), Athena Polias, Aglauros, Zeus Polieus, Poseidon, and Pandrosos fell on 3 Skirophorion, the same day the *arrhēphoroi* carried their secret objects for the goddess.[15] In the coastal deme of Phaleron, the Salaminioi, an extended family with strong ties to the nearby island of Salamis and its cult of Athena Skiras, maintained a sanctuary of the goddess. This Attic sanctuary of Athena Skiras played a role in the vintage festival of the Oschophoria and Athena herself, in association with the hero Skiros, received the clan's offering of a pregnant sheep in the winter month of Maimakterion.[16]

The little-known cult of Athena Pallenis (of Pallene) is important for the light it sheds on the process by which the cults of Attica were absorbed into the larger system of the Athenian polis during the eighth and seventh centuries, and their continuing relations. Athenaeus (6.234f–235a) preserves the rather mangled texts of a dedication and a sacred law pertaining to this Athena Pallenis. From them we learn that several of the inland demes, including Pallene, were gathered into a league centered on the worship of Athena. No later than the seventh century, this cult was brought under the supervision of the state in the person of the *archōn basileus* (the King Archon, who had inherited the original king's religious authority). He selected a group of officials known as *archontes* (rulers), who in turn designated *parasitoi* (fellow diners) from each member deme. The parasites and archons, the social elite of their communities, enjoyed a yearly banquet funded by the goddess in a building maintained for this purpose. Like several gods whose sanctuaries were located outside the urban area of Athens, Athena Pallenis possessed considerable wealth and her sanctuary easily financed the annual feast. A fine fifth-century temple in the agora, moved from its original site in the Roman period and previously assigned to Ares, is now thought to be the shrine of Athena Pallenis.[17]

Goddess and Palladion

Pallas was a common literary title of Athena, and the name appears on Archaic dedications from the Athenian Akropolis. There are two possible etymologies, one from the verb *pallein*, to brandish, and one that makes Pallas a synonym for girl or maiden.

The epic cycle told of a covert mission by Odysseus and Diomedes to enter Troy and carry off a small statue of Athena known as the Palladion (statue of Pallas). Sent down from heaven by Zeus, the talismanic image ensured the security of Troy as long as the Trojans possessed it. Many late sources speak of this tradition, and vase paintings illustrate the theft of the diminutive statue. Athens, Argos, Sparta, Rome, and other cities had protective images of this type, and each boasted that its Athena was none other than the original Palladion of Troy. The Argive claim was the oldest, for the Athenians and Spartans said that their Palladia were confiscated from the Argive hero Diomedes.[18] The Palladion of Argos was most likely the image housed in the akropolis temple on Larisa, which existed from the sixth century or earlier. (The cult itself, in which Athena and Zeus were closely associated as poliad deities, dated to Geometric times.) Callimachus recorded the annual ritual of the statue's purification in his fifth *Hymn* (5.1–2, 33–34), which indicates that female members of the clan or phratry of Arestor served as "bath pourers" (*lotrochōoi*) for Pallas. A procession accompanied the Palladion, carried on the shield of Diomedes, to the river Inachos about 4 km from the city, where it was bathed in the river. The only other attested Greek ritual in which a statue is carried out of its temple in order to be bathed belongs to another Palladion, this one at Athens.

Trials for accidental homicide and the murder of non-citizens were conducted at a court in the place called Palladion, located on the southeast side of Athens on the Ilissos river. The origins of this court were tied in legend to the sanctuary of Athena "at Palladion," which contained an image thought to be the celebrated Trojan Palladion, confiscated by King Demophon from Diomedes and his men at the port of Phaleron. During the scuffle, Demophon either killed the Argives themselves, or accidentally caused the death of an Athenian. He was brought to trial in the court at Palladion, which ever after served the same function. Two old priestly families, the Gephyraioi and Bouzygai, oversaw the sanctuary, and during an annual festival the statue was carried in a procession to Phaleron, where it was washed in the sea. The washing ritual for the Palladion has often been conflated with the ceremonies of the Plynteria, but there is no basis for this idea. The bath in the sea (or in sea water) was clearly connected with the need to "cleanse" the image from the miasma brought about by repeated exposure to the killers who were tried in the court, and the original bathing of the statue was ascribed to King Demophon himself. Because it was made of wood and small enough to carry about, the Palladion was probably of Archaic date.[19]

Ionian Athena

Though a less dominating presence than at Athens, Athena was a prominent civic goddess in virtually every Ionian city by the eighth century. At Miletos, where Apollo was the patron deity, the seventh-century Athena temple was constructed in a commercial district on the site of a former Minoan and Mycenaean colony. It was repeatedly damaged and rebuilt over the succeeding centuries.[20] An unbroken series of votive offerings, including metal items such as a fragmentary bronze griffin cauldron, stretches from the eighth century on and hints at the wealth of the sanctuary. Likewise, the earliest activity at Athena's sanctuary in Erythrai is dated to the eighth century; among the oldest structures found there were a temple (rebuilt in the sixth century) and a ruler's dwelling. Pausanias (7.5.9) describes the cult statue of Athena Polias at Erythrai as a large enthroned Athena made of wood, holding a distaff and crowned with a *polos*, a cylindrical headdress often worn by goddesses. He attributes it to the Archaic sculptor Endoios. Such representations of Athena with spinning tools are virtually absent from the Greek mainland, although facilities for sacred weaving in her sanctuaries were not unusual.[21]

At Old Smyrna, the Athena cult seems to have been introduced by Ionian refugees from Kolophon who seized the city from its Aiolian founders in the late eighth century. The first temple to Athena, a modest apsidal structure, appeared shortly thereafter (*c.* 690), and its successors grew ever more elaborate. Excavation has revealed a wealth of faience, ivory, terracotta, and stone objects traceable to Rhodes, Krete, Cyprus, and Syria, evidence of the cosmopolitan city's flourishing trade in the Orientalizing period. Around 600, the Lydian ruler Alyattes sacked the city and looted the temple, but the people quickly rebuilt it. Several mushroom-shaped capitals from the early sixth-century temple, influenced by Phoenician and Hittite models, have survived. Alyattes also burned the temple of Athena at Assessos, in the territory of Miletos. As a result of this sacrilege he fell ill, and the Delphic oracle ordered him rebuild the temple as penance for the offense to the goddess. Investigation of the ancient site, where excavators found the remains of an Archaic city and at least one temple destroyed and rebuilt in the seventh century, supports the general outline of Herodotus' account (1.16, 19–22).[22]

At the citadel of Emporio on Chios, the eighth-century sanctuary of Athena shared the space inside the circuit wall with a ruler's *megaron*, while the townspeople lived on the slopes below. Around 600, the hillside town was abandoned for a settlement in the harbor below, yet the Athena sanctuary was kept in use and a temple was added in the mid-sixth century. The temple design carefully preserved an earlier structure, an irregular stone box less than a meter high, touching the bedrock and filled with earth. This crude altar or basis for offerings, once the center of the open-air sanctuary, shared the focal area of the cella with the cult image. Nine small griffin protomes of lead, found in the cella, may have been attached to the helmet of this statue.[23] Priene, Phokaia, Ephesos, Teos, Kolophon, and Klazomenai too had their cults of Athena Polias or Poliouchos (Protector of the City), demonstrating the great popularity of Athena among the Ionians. Herodotus (1.147–49) relates that all these cities except for Ephesos and Kolophon celebrated the Apatouria, a coming-of-age festival celebrated by the phratries. Athena and Zeus presided over the Apatouria at Athens, so the same may have been true in the Ionian cities.

Boiotian Athena

Homer (*Il.* 4.8, 5.908) gives Athena the epithet Alalkomeneïs, which literally means "she who protects" and evokes the warlike goddess of the Palladion. Several cults of Athena under this name existed, but its oldest home was perhaps her ancient sanctuary in the Boiotian town of Alalkomenai. Excavated but never published, it lay in a plain between the towns of Haliartos and Koroneia. According to Strabo (9.2.36), the venerable sanctuary was held in such respect that the city was never ravaged by a hostile army. His account is contradicted by Pausanias (9.33.5–6), who reports that Sulla impiously looted the temple's celebrated ivory statue. With the loss of the sacred image, the sanctuary at last fell into decline, and was overgrown with vegetation by the second century CE. Local legend held that Athena was born or grew to adulthood here; her poetic epithet Tritogeneia (Triton-born) was associated with the river Triton.[24]

Oddly enough, nearby Koroneia boasted another Athena sanctuary of equal antiquity and renown, which served as the site of the Pamboiotia, or festival of all the Boiotians. This gathering, already old in Pindar's time, involved contests in chariot racing, music, and athletics. A series of sixth-century Boiotian vases showing a festival in progress and an armed Athena standing before an altar and temple have been attributed to this cult. The worship of Athena Itonia originated in the Thessalian town of Iton, but was brought to Boiotia when the Boiotoi moved south in the early Iron Age. In the seventh century Alcaeus (fr. 3, 325 *LP*) sang of this Athena, whom he addresses as Queen Athena *polemadokos* (Sustainer of War). The goddess' companion was a chthonian deity represented as a snake and understood to be either Zeus or Hades. In the fifth century, Agorakritos, the pupil of Pheidias, created bronzes of Athena and Zeus for the Itoneion. Athena was served by a priestess, successor of the legendary priestess Iodama, who ventured at night into the sacred area and saw a vision of the goddess wearing the aegis with its gorgon head. Iodama was turned to stone (perhaps she was identified with a life-size statue) and a fire was lit daily on her altar in the sanctuary.[25]

The Lokrian Maidens

Ajax the Lesser, a native of Lokris, attacked the Trojan maiden Kassandra who had sought refuge beside the statue of Athena, and as he dragged her away he toppled the sacred image. The goddess' wrath was directed at all the Greeks for this sacrilege but especially at Ajax, who in the Homeric account was shipwrecked and drowned before reaching home (Od. 4.499–511). In the third year, a plague fell upon Lokris, and the people consulted Apollo's oracle at Delphi. They were told that their penance for Ajax's crime would last a thousand years. They must choose two of their girls by lot and deliver them to the shores of Troy as temple servants of Athena. These girls must be led to the goddess secretly by night, while the Trojan men hunted them down. Maidens killed attempting to reach the safety of the temple were to be burned with wood that bore no fruit, and their ashes cast in the sea; those who arrived unharmed had to remain in the sanctuary for life, barefoot and wearing only a simple shift, sweeping out the temple and performing other menial duties like slaves. They grew old as virgins, and when one died, another must be brought to take her place.

This tribute of maidens, reported most fully by Lycophron (Alex. 1141–73 with schol.) and mentioned by a number of late authors, has no exact parallels in Greek practice.[26] Maiden sacrifices are common enough in myth, but rarely if ever did they occur in the ritual of historical times. The Lokrians of Italy, according to some dubious sources, devoted their daughters as sacred prostitutes to the service of Aphrodite, but in these accounts the girls' lives were not threatened, nor were they forced to leave their homes forever. A ritual requirement of lifelong virginity is extremely unusual: the Greeks had no Vestal Virgins. Therefore, the amazing account of the Lokrian Maidens would likely be dismissed today as a fantasy, but for a third-century inscription (IG IX 1² 3.706), which establishes the journey of the maidens as historical fact. It declares that the Aianteioi, or descendants of Ajax, and their city of Naryx in Opuntian Lokris, shall receive significant privileges (such as tax relief and priority access to courts) in return for sending the two maidens to Ilion. The girls are to have their expenses paid, including the cost of their wardrobes (kosmos). The inscription makes it clear, however, that the girls served for a limited period, not for life; that they wore new garments, not rags; and that they were chosen from elite families, not by lot. It is reasonable to assume that the "hunting" of the maidens, though an important part of the ritual, was innocuous. The custom probably began in response to a civic crisis, not after the Trojan War when the site of Troy was abandoned, but in the sixth century and with the cooperation of the Greek colonists at New Ilion, who were eager to play the role of "Trojans." There is evidence that it lapsed in the fourth century and was revived with due ceremony, perhaps about the time of our inscription.

The journey of the Lokrian Maidens has been interpreted as a ritual counterpart of the many myths in which adolescent girls give up their lives to save their cities; it has also been called an "exemplary initiation," by which a few members of an age cohort stand in for the whole group in performing acts symbolic of that group's passage to adulthood. Finally, the putative humiliation of the maidens and the casting of their ashes in the sea are characteristic of the scapegoat or *pharmakos* rite, in which a city wards off harm from itself by expelling individuals who are treated as carriers of pollution.[27]

Athena Alea

The sanctuary of Athena Alea at Tegea in Arkadia is the richest site so far excavated in that district, and the only one to produce significant Mycenaean finds. The earliest material dates to the Late Bronze Age, and though cult activity is archaeologically visible only from about 900, the worship of a goddess on this spot may have far deeper roots. Excavations have focused on the site of the successive temples and an associated sacred spring to the north, both of which yielded a rich variety of Archaic and Classical votives including a wealth of bronzes, lead and iron objects, jewelry, and ivories. During the eighth century, the first temple was constructed of wattle and daub on an apsidal plan, and had a neighboring metal workshop. It was replaced in the late seventh century by a monumental stone temple, which continued in use for some three hundred years until it was destroyed in a fire in 392. It was the sculptor and architect Skopas who designed the third temple, one of the finest and largest in the Peloponnese. Its east pediment illustrated the Arkadian myth of the Kalydonian boar hunt, and the trophies from the great beast, including its hide and tusks, were proudly displayed within. Its other treasures, appropriate to Athena, included trophies of war: chains brought by Spartan invaders who hoped to enslave the Tegeans, but themselves suffered this fate; and a bronze vessel used to feed the horses of the Persian general Mardonios, taken as a prize by the Tegeans who captured his camp. The cult statue was a small ivory Athena attributed to the Archaic sculptor Endoios, which was looted by Augustus along with the boar's tusks and set up in his new Forum at Rome.[28]

The earliest deity worshiped on this spot was probably not Athena, but an indigenous goddess called Alea, whose name seems to mean "place of refuge." Indeed, asylum was an important function of the sanctuary in historical times, and we are told (Paus. 3.5.6) that the entire Peloponnese respected the sanctity of Athena's suppliants. The cult was so renowned that daughter sanctuaries were founded in Lakonia and on the border with Argolis. The Geometric finds from the sanctuary suggest concerns with fertility (pomegranate pendants) and women's issues (loom weights, beads and other jewelry in great numbers), but also include items more often associated with Athena's cult, such as miniature votive shields. In any case, if

Athena and Alea were distinct goddesses, they had merged by the sixth century, when a very Panhellenic bronze Athena with helmet, spear, shield, and aegis was deposited.[29]

Spartan Athena

Sparta was dotted with minor cult places of Athena; these included three separate shrines of Athena Keleutheia (of the Road), which were associated with a race run by the suitors of Penelope. In the area of the Dromos were sanctuaries of Herakles and Athena Axiopoinos (of Deserved Vengeance). The latter was connected with Herakles' punishment of Hippokoön for killing his nephew Oionos. Still another shrine of Athena was founded by Theras, the great-grandson of Orestes and colonizer of Thera. The variety of her cults illustrates Athena's regular function as a "goddess of nearness," the guardian and helper of heroes. It also reflects Sparta's background as a group of independent villages loosely gathered into a polis, but never fully urbanized or consolidated.[30]

On the Spartan akropolis, a hill of no great height, the most important structure was the sanctuary of Athena Poliouchos (City Protector) or Chalkioikos (of the Bronze House). Its origins were attributed to the mythic king Tyndareos, though excavation shows that the earliest remains are Geometric. The temple itself and its bronze cult statue by Gitiadas belonged to the sixth century. (Gitiadas was a multitalented Spartan who also composed "Dorian songs," including a hymn to Athena, and made bronze tripods for the Amyklaion.) The temple was apparently sheathed in bronze plates, some of which were found by excavators at the turn of the last century. None of the relief-decorated plates have survived, but these included scenes of Athena's birth and the feats of Peloponnesian heroes including Herakles, Kastor and Polydeukes, and Perseus.[31]

The sanctuary was well known as a place of asylum for criminals, even those under a death sentence. The ancient sources tend to draw attention to this function only when it is violated, as in the gruesome death of the Spartan general Pausanias, the victor at Plataiai in 479. Suspected of intrigue with Xerxes and of fomenting a helot rebellion, Pausanias was recalled to Sparta about 470 and, when he realized that he was to be arrested, ran into a back room of the Bronze House. The Spartan ephors sealed him in the chamber until he was dying of starvation, then carried him outdoors so as not to pollute the sanctuary with his death. Later, in the belief that they were being punished by Zeus Hikesios for violating the rights of a suppliant, they consulted Delphi about these events. The oracle commanded them to move Pausanias' tomb into the sanctuary and to "give back two bodies instead of one to the goddess of the Bronze House." Therefore they installed two bronze statues of Pausanias beside Athena's altar.[32]

Little is known of the cult at the Bronze House, but Polybius (4.35.2–4) describes a traditional observance that involved a parade of all the Spartan warriors in full armor to the altar, where the ephors waited to conduct a sacrifice. Among the finds in the sanctuary were bronze figurines of Athena and a trumpeter, and, nearby on the akropolis, a fifth-century marble statue of a helmeted hoplite, known today as "Leonidas." Unexplained is the large number of bells, forty of bronze and eighty of terracotta; they may have been dedicated by night watchmen who carried them on their patrols or warriors who used them as horse trappings.[33]

Athena Lindia

Pindar's seventh Olympian *Ode*, written for the boxer Diagoras of Rhodes in 464, celebrates the prominent cult of Athena in the city of Lindos, one of the three original Greek cities on the island. Like the people of Alalkomenai in Boiotia or Alipheira in Arkadia, the Rhodians believed that their island witnessed the birth of Athena from Zeus' head. Helios, the patron deity of Rhodes, urged his children to be the first to honor the goddess with an altar and the smoke of sacrifice. But climbing to the peak of the Lindian akropolis, they forgot to bring live embers, establishing instead the custom of fireless sacrifice. Zeus confirmed these events by sending snow of gold on the city, while Athena herself taught the Heliadai the skills to create wondrous works of art that moved like living creatures.[34] An alternative legend attributed the founding of the sanctuary to Danaos and his daughters as they fled from Egypt, while the Archaic temple was built by the sixth-century tyrant Kleoboulos, one of Greece's Seven Sages and an associate of Pharaoh Amasis of Egypt. Amasis dedicated to Athena Lindia two stone statues and a linen corselet embroidered with figures in gold thread.[35] These connections between Rhodes and Egypt are borne out by actual fragments of Egyptian sculpture discovered near the temple of Athena Polias at Kameiros.

Around 392, the temple on the akropolis and its contents were completely destroyed, perhaps in the violent struggles between the supporters of Sparta and Athens, and a lengthy period of recovery followed. Roughly a century after its destruction, the Rhodians began to rebuild the sanctuary on a lavish scale. Conscious of Athena Lindia's distinguished past, but lacking the rich variety of heirloom dedications to be seen in other sanctuaries, they eventually decided to create a list of all the famous gifts that had been lost, and to display it in the sanctuary. This inscription, known as the Lindian Chronicle, dates to 99 and contains a catalogue of fabulous gifts from ancient heroes (e.g. Herakles, Helen, Tlepolemos) and historical figures (Alexander the Great and Pyrrhos) as well as descriptions of three epiphanies of the goddess. The votive catalogue, complete with "footnotes" which cite written sources for each entry, is an interesting mixture of legend and history. In spite of its late date, it is an invaluable resource for Athena's cult. It shows, for example, how colonists from Rhodes maintained a relationship with Athena Lindia by sending gifts to her shrine. The votive catalogue lists gifts of Archaic and Classical date from Lindian colonists at Kyrene, Phaselis, Gela, Akragas, and Soloi, all of which are probably authentic dedications.[36]

Athena's cult partners

Because her functions overlap with those of Zeus and Poseidon, Athena was often worshiped in tandem with these deities. Poseidon and Athena shared space in the Ionic temple on the Akropolis and at Cape Sounion because of their common interest in the Athenian polis, though the myth of their contest for the land shows that the relationship was one of opposition as well as affinity. At Kolonos in Attica, Poseidon Hippios and Athena Hippia (of horses) had a shared altar in Pausanias' time (1.30.4). Athena's interest in horses stemmed not only from her identity as a war goddess, but also from her role as a teacher of crafts and skills. Pindar (*Ol.* 13.63–86) is the earliest written source for the story that Athena gave a golden bridle to Bellerophon, which he used to tame Pegasos. In return, he dedicated an altar to Athena Hippia in Korinth, where her worship was focused primarily on the taming and training of horses. Poseidon, on the other hand, was the creator of the horse and the source of its fierce energy and speed.[37]

Athena's mythic intimacy with her father Zeus is reflected in many dual cults, particularly those that deal with civic administration, law and justice. In Sparta they shared the titles of Agoraios (of the Marketplace), Xenios (of Strangers), and Amboulios (of Counsel), among others. In Athens, as we learn from the orator Antiphon (6.45), the Council-chamber or *bouleutērion* contained a shrine of Zeus Boulaios and Athena Boulaia (of Counsel), at which members prayed as they entered. Polieus, Zeus' title as the protector of the city, is the masculine form of Athena's common epithet Polias, while Zeus Phratrios and Athena Phratria shared altars throughout Attica as the patrons of the Athenian kinship groups known as phratries. Athena frequently accompanies Zeus when he appears in his chthonic guise as a serpent. In the fifth century, for example, a sanctuary of Zeus Meilichios and Athena existed at Athens. The same configuration of goddess and serpent companion is to be found in the cult of Athena Itonia (above) and of course in the presence of Athena's serpent familiar, sometimes identified with Erichthonios, on the Athenian Akropolis.[38]

Further reading

Deacy and Villing 2001 collects papers on Athena and includes an important study of the Athena sanctuary at Stymphalos by H. Williams and G. Schaus. Chapter 4 of Detienne and Vernant 1991 [1978], originally published in French in 1974, explores the interlocking "domains" of Athena and her relations with Poseidon. Hurwit 1999 includes full coverage of the topography of Athena's cult places on the Athenian Akropolis. Two volumes edited by J. Neils (1992 and 1996) contain papers on the Panathenaic festival, including an important article on Athena's *peplos* by E. J. W. Barber (103–17 in *Goddess and polis*). On Athena Alea, the work of M. E. Voyatzis (1990, 1998) is indispensable.

5

RULER OF ELEMENTAL POWERS

Poseidon

Homer (*Il.* 15.184–93) recounts that when the cosmos was divided among the gods, Poseidon received the sea as his lot. Yet his first worshipers probably did not live within sight of the sea. Poseidon was a powerful god among the Mycenaean Greeks, and his cult is strongest among populations established in the Greek world before the so-called Dorian invasion. His status was gradually eroded in the Archaic period, as the process of Panhellenization required that all the gods of the canon be subordinated to Zeus. Little concerned with the spheres of justice, invention, or the arts, Poseidon is in origin a god of elemental, geological forces: life-giving springs, disastrous floods, chasms through which water flows or recedes, and tremors in the earth. Ultimately he ruled the vast and unpredictable sea, causing storms and tidal waves.

He is often found partnered with Demeter, a clue to his probable origin as a deity of fresh water. The most commonly cited etymology of his name recognizes it as a compound: Greek *posis* or *potis*, "lord, spouse" is combined with an element of unknown meaning, possibly "earth."[1] Poseidon's name, then, contains the masculine version of the word *potnia*, or mistress, which is familiar from the Linear B tablets, while he himself appears in the tablets from Knossos and especially Pylos. One of his most widespread cult epithets, Asphaleios (Steadfast), was apparently a euphemism, emphasizing his power to still earthquakes rather than induce them. In both poetry and cult he is Ennosigaios (Earth-Shaker) and Gaieochos (Embracer of Earth). This control over the forces in the earth only occasionally spilled over into agricultural or chthonic, underworld functions, as at Tainaron, where Poseidon hosted an oracle of the dead.

Poseidon was also a god around whom many Greeks shaped their ethnic identities. For the Thessalians, the Boiotians, the people of Trozen, and many others, he was an ancestor, comparable to Zeus in the large number of heroes he sired with mortal maidens. Poseidon was an important amphictyonic deity, which means that his cult was the focus for many federations and leagues, whose shared interests were based sometimes on tribal affinity and sometimes on geographical proximity. According to the Homeric *Hymn* in his honor (22.5), Poseidon is "a tamer of horses and a savior of ships." Myth made him the father of the horses Areion and Pegasos, while he was honored in many places as Hippios and was a master of chariot races from earliest times. He was the central deity at the Panhellenic sanctuary of Isthmia, worshiped with his consort Amphitrite.

Poseidon Helikonios

The member cities of the Ionian League met annually at the sanctuary of Poseidon Helikonios at the Panionion on the promontory of Mt. Mykale. Very little is left of the sanctuary now, though the foundation of a huge, 18 m Archaic altar has been detected. Also found at the site were a council chamber and a large cave, which must have played a role in the cult. The sanctuary probably never included a temple, yet it was an important symbol of political and cultural identity in the Archaic period. The priests were supplied by the city of Priene. Later the meeting place was moved for safety to a spot near Ephesos. Though this cult was almost certainly brought to Asia Minor when the Ionians migrated to their new homes around the tenth century, there is debate over its source, closely tied to the question of Ionian origins. One school of thought derives Poseidon Helikonios from the city of Helike in Achaia, often cited by ancient authors as a homeland of the Ionians. The Ionians of the Classical period seem to have believed this version, for in response to an oracle, they sent representatives to Helike to ask for sacred objects (*aphidrumata*) from the ancestral altars. The Achaians' refusal to permit this privilege is said to have caused the famous earthquake and tidal wave that destroyed and engulfed Helike in 373.[2] It is certain that an ancient cult of Poseidon was present at Helike, for Homer (*Il.* 8.203–4) mentions offerings to the god from the people of Helike and Aigai. From a linguistic point of view, however, the word Helikonios is better derived from Helikon, the mountain in Boiotia. Though no Poseidon cult on Helikon is attested in historical times, the god had deep roots in Boiotia and such a cult may have largely faded from memory. In any case, Homer is also aware of the worship of Poseidon Helikonios, for he speaks (*Il.* 20.403–5) of the bellowing bulls sacrificed to "the Helikonian lord." According to Strabo (8.7.2), some in antiquity took this as a reference to the sacrifices at the Panionia, where the participants read omens if the bull bellowed as it was struck down.[3]

On Delos, another Ionian religious center, a large sacrificial feast was held during the month Posideion, which fell during the stormy period of mid-winter. Poseideia, or festivals of Poseidon, seem to have been a regular feature of this month in many Ionian cities, both in the islands and on the coast of Asia Minor. Poseidon's epithets in these places vary, from Helikonios at Sinope to Asphalios (Steadfast) or Themeliouchos (of Foundations) on Delos and Phykios (of Seaweed) on Mykonos. Noel Robertson connects the winter festival to Poseidon's function as a partner of Demeter in fructifying the fields; alternatively, the timing suggests a propitiation of the god who causes storms at the season when his anger is most evident.[4]

Isthmia and Korinth

Poseidon's sanctuary at Isthmia is one of the earliest post-Mycenaean cult places yet identified in the Greek world, having been established at the beginning of the Protogeometric period around 1050. It therefore ranks in age with Olympia and Kalapodi/Hyampolis. Yet for centuries the worship of Poseidon required no temple; the main structures were a platform for dining created in the eighth century, and temporary shelters of which only the post-holes remain. The dominant activity seems to have been sacrifice followed by extensive feasting and drinking.[5] Easily accessible by land and sea, the sanctuary was an important meeting place for the people living in the scattered communities that would evolve into the maritime polis of Korinth. In contrast to Olympia or Delphi, it attracted few dedications of precious metals, such as tripods, and there was less of an emphasis on aristocratic display in the votive practice. In spite of the focus on drinking, dedications of jewelry show that women were active in the worship. Terracotta bulls, animals symbolic of Poseidon, are present from the earliest years, though most of the bones found on the site belonged to sheep, goats, and pigs. The sacrificial area was covered with egg-sized stones that were used in the ritual. Most likely, the participants cast stones at the hapless victim in the moments before its throat was cut. In this way, all present joined in the act of slaughter, just as all would share in the feast.[6]

Constructed in the seventh century, the first temple was destroyed in a conflagration around 470. No sign of a statue base was found in the cella, and the temple may have been used mainly as a strongroom for valuable dedications and supplies. Excavation has brought to light the charred remains of storage vessels for oil, chariots, and horse trappings from the cella, while many small valuables came from the area of the east porch, including a tiny golden bull. The exterior wall was coated with stucco and brightly painted with animals and geometric designs, while within the peristyle stood a lovely marble *perirrhantērion*, a water basin used for purification before entering the temple.[7] Its Orientalizing design features a base with four women standing on lions. Outside the temple was a monumental altar over 30 m long. In 582 the Isthmian games were opened to Panhellenic participation, a stadium was added, and the sanctuary continued to grow with the patronage of Korinth and the advantage of placement on a major road. When the Archaic temple burned, it was speedily replaced with a larger Doric temple, which stood until late antiquity. A major category of dedication in this period, second only to the offerings at Olympia in abundance, is armor and weapons, which were displayed so as to be visible from the road.

A number of other gods were worshiped at the sanctuary, including

Amphitrite, Poseidon's consort, and the child-hero Melikertes-Palaimon. The games, with their prize of a pine crown (later changed to wild celery), were said to have originated as funeral games instituted in his honor by Sisyphos. According to the legend, Palaimon and his mother Ino-Leukothea were drowned in the sea, but Ino was transformed into a Nereid, while Palaimon's body was carried to shore by a dolphin. Both mother and son granted mariners' prayers for safety. An interesting and unusual feature of the sanctuary in the Classical period was the pair of underground, man-made caves, designed to serve as dining rooms. One is located near the theater, while the other sits roughly between the theater and the temple of Poseidon and is associated with a nearby altar. Each cave contained couches carved from the earth, and the theater cave also had two kitchen areas. These small rooms, each able to accommodate only five to six people, may have been used in the worship of Melikertes-Palaimon or some other chthonian power.[8]

Yet another early Poseidon cult, the source of our earliest images of the god, has been detected in the environs of Korinth. At Penteskouphia a large number of painted terracotta *pinakes* (tablets) dating to the seventh and sixth centuries were recovered from a votive dump. The location of the sanctuary itself has not been pinpointed, but much can be learned from the tablets. They record dedications to Lord (*Anax*) Poseidon and often to Amphitrite as well, demonstrating that this cult pairing, so prominent at Isthmia and the Hellenistic sanctuary of Poseidon at Tenos, was already well established in the Archaic period. Amphitrite sometimes receives dedications of her own, and is shown on one *pinax* with a small worshiper. The divine pair stand facing one another, or ride together in a chariot driven by Poseidon. Other *pinakes* from this deposit demonstrate Poseidon's patronage not only of seagoing merchants, but also of the potters and painters who helped supply the cargo. Several *pinakes* show ships, one loaded with pots, while at least twenty-eight illustrate workers using kilns, and the tablets themselves may have been used as proofing pieces in the firing process. Most of the tablets seem to be dedications by men working in the ceramics industry; often the donors made and/or painted the tablets themselves. As a deity of subterranean processes and energies, Poseidon was considered the right god to watch over kilns; as a marine deity and ruler of the Isthmos, he guarded a ceramic industry dependent on sea trade.[9]

Marine Poseidon

Several of Poseidon's cult epithets are related to his marine function. On Samos he was Epaktaios (on the Coast), at Athens and Rhodes Pelagios (Seagoing), and at Tainaron Pontios (of the Sea). Poseidon's sanctuaries are regularly found at harbors, on promontories, and on islands, while coastal cities too are frequently called Potidaia (Chalkidike) or Poseidonia (Lucania

Figure 5.1 Potter and kiln. Votive *pinax* from Poseidon sanctuary at Penteskouphia, early sixth century. Louvre Museum. Erich Lessing/Art Resource.

in Italy). Storms at sea are attributed to Poseidon, and Herodotus says (7.192) that he was credited with aiding the Greeks by scattering the Persian fleet in a storm off Artemision. At Geraistos, the only safe harbor along the coast of Euboia and a major port for ships traveling to or from the eastern Aegean, the origin of the festival called Geraistia was traced to a particularly destructive storm, probably the one in which Poseidon drowned the impious Lokrian Ajax. In the *Odyssey* (3.176–79), Geraistos was the first safe port of call for ships returning home from the Trojan War; Nestor, Diomedes, and Menelaos sacrificed bulls there to Poseidon for their safe journey. Recent discovery of the remains of the sanctuary at Porto Kastri included a Hellenistic inscription mentioning an *asulon* or safe area. Rob Schumacher has pointed out the relationship between Geraistos, Kalaureia, and Tainaron, three coastal yet remote sanctuaries that functioned as retreats for suppliants and fugitives. Various cultic and personal names related to Geraistos, a pre-Greek word of uncertain etymology, are scattered about the Aegean.[10]

Poseidon's marine character was apparent in the iconographic tradition, which invariably showed him holding a trident, a fish, or a dolphin. While the trident has usually been explained as a fishing harpoon, the tridents on the early *pinakes* from Penteskouphia display great variety in shape and size. Scholars have speculated about the possible origin of the trident as a thunder-weapon (given Poseidon's connection with storms at sea) or an Indo-European symbol of kingship.[11]

Messenian Poseidon

The Linear B tablets indicate that Poseidon was a highly regarded deity among the Mycenaeans of Pylos. A series of Pylian tablets lists contributions (*dosmoi*) to various gods among whom Poseidon is the most prominent. Pylos 171 = Un 718 breaks down the community into functional groups listed in order of descending status and offering amounts. The king's contribution consists of wheat, wine, a bull, cheeses, a sheepskin, and honey. Similar but smaller gifts are presented by the *dāmos* or village, the military leader, and the estate of the *worgiones* or cult association. Another famous tablet, Pylos 172 = Kn 02, describes ritual actions performed in the shrines of local deities. A shrine of Poseidon is mentioned, to which women bring golden cups. Later in the same tablet, a goddess Posidaeia (apparently a female version of the name Poseidon) receives a golden bowl carried by a woman.[12] The prominence of Poseidon at Pylos is reflected in the Homeric account (*Od.* 3.4–11) of Telemachos' visit. When he arrives, the people are offering black bulls to Poseidon on the shore, divided into nine companies of five hundred men each; each company offers nine bulls to the god. Nestor and his sons sit feasting in the midst of their men; Nestor's father Neleus of Iolkos was a son of Poseidon and the founder of Pylos.

In spite of his early importance, Poseidon rapidly lost ground in Archaic Messenia with the rise of the Dorian Spartans. Whereas worship of the god known as Pohoidan (a Lakonian form of the Arkadian Posoidan) continued at Helos and Thouria (Akovitika), in historical times virtually nothing remained of the Pylian cult, while the important sanctuary at Tainaron was controlled by the Spartans.[13] Located at the southern tip of the Mani peninsula, Tainaron was sacred to the helots, the occupants of Messenia enslaved by Sparta in the eighth and seventh centuries, and dates to before the time of the Messenian wars. Escaped slaves and fugitive helots fled to the sanctuary, where by religious custom they were safe from pursuers. Various late sources speak of the festival known as the Tainaria, which included a three-day feast held on the seashore, and most likely the crowning of Poseidon's cult statue by the helots. Always a wrathful god, he was particularly angry when the ritual laws protecting suppliants were violated. One example long cited as an instance of his wrath was the earthquake that hit Sparta in 464, nearly reducing the city to a pile of rubble. The god was said to be enraged at the Spartans, who had dared to remove fugitive helots from Tainaron and execute them. Though Tainaron has not been excavated, finds of votive bulls and horses in bronze as well as Classical *stēlai* (stone markers) commemorating the release of slaves have been reported. Areas set aside for the display of such *stēlai* and for the housing of fugitives are apparent at the site. Overlooking Sternis Bay is a Hellenistic temple, which may have been preceded by earlier structures, to judge from votives found in the area. The most famous feature of the site is the cave oracle of the dead, which the sources describe as an underground "house" of the gods, into which souls were gathered. This type of oracle was useful in cases where the dead needed to be placated; legend had it that the man who killed Archilochus was sent here by the Pythia in order to propriate the soul of the poet with libations. The actual age of the cave oracle, located at the head of Sternis Bay and fitted with a wall and doorway at the entrance, is unknown. When he visited, Pausanias (3.25.5) noted that the cave did not contain a great chasm or other identifiable entrance to the underworld.[14]

Poseidon at Trozen

Poseidon's sanctuary on Kalaureia, a small island off Trozen with one of the best harbors in Greece, lies high above sea level, recalling a scene in the *Iliad* (13.10–16) in which Poseidon sits on the highest peak of Samothrace, observing the far away battles at Troy. This place was another well-known refuge, famous for having hosted the orator Demosthenes when he fled from Alexander's successor Antipater in 322. Rather than pollute the sacred ground with the taint of death, Demosthenes took poison inside the temple, then staggered out as it began to take effect. The sanctuary's function as an asylum resulted from its role as the center of an early amphictyony, a league of seven communities in the area. The island's former name Eirene (Peace) probably had to do with the amphictyony as well. Scholars disagree on the purpose and date of the league, but the archaeological remains indicate that the sanctuary was founded by the seventh century at the latest, and acquired a Doric temple in the sixth.[15] Little is known of the ritual there, but Pausanias (2.33.2–3) says that Poseidon had a virgin priestess, an unusual arrangement for a male deity.

Trozen itself was unusual in honoring Poseidon as the protector of the city, Poliouchos, and as King, Basileus. He was an important ancestor, having fathered several of the city's heroes including Theseus. The people made the trident an emblem on their coins, while the city itself once bore the name Poseidonia.[16] Trozen's Poseidon cult, like that of Athens, was tied to its Ionic origins. The city fell under the sway of Argos at an early date and became increasingly Dorianized, yet it exported the worship of Poseidon to its colony of Halikarnassos in Karia.

Outside the walls of Trozen was a sanctuary of Poseidon Phytalmios (of Growth). The legend said that the angry god once inundated the crops with seawater until he yielded to prayers and sacrifices. Overlooking this shrine was a sanctuary of Demeter Thesmophoros, established by Poseidon's son Althepos. In recognition of his connection with agriculture, the god was offered *aparchai*, first fruits from the crops. This facet of Poseidon's personality is unexpected, yet the cult pairing of Poseidon and Demeter is widespread (present in Attica, Argos, Mykonos, and of course, Arkadia).[17] It is likely that Poseidon's flood was originally a freshwater inundation, for as a

63

god of subterranean forces, he controlled springs and rivers. Having caused a drought at Argos by drying up the springs, he relented and revealed the sources at Lerna to the Danaid Amymone. Aeschylus (*Sept.* 304–11) names Earth-supporting Poseidon and the rivers, offspring of Tethys, as the deities who pour forth the waters that fructify the earth. Poseidon's waters nourish the plants, yet too much water just as surely destroys them. Thus Poseidon's relationship with Demeter was both intimate and adversarial. Argos had a flood legend according to which Poseidon, angry when the land was awarded to Hera, caused an inundation, and the Argive sanctuary of Poseidon Prosklystios (of Surging Water) was located beside that of Pelasgian Demeter. The Athenians too said that Poseidon had flooded the fruitful Thriasian plain where Demeter had her sanctuary at Eleusis.[18]

A recently discovered Mycenaean sanctuary on the peninsula of Methana, facing Kalaureia, was unusual in that the finds included rare terracotta chariot groups, helmeted riders, and groups of oxen being driven or ridden. The absence of the female Psi and Phi figurines typically found in Mycenaean shrines, together with this evidence, point to a male deity connected with horses, chariots, and bulls. Thus, Poseidon may already have been the foremost deity in Trozenia during the Bronze Age.[19]

Poseidon Hippios

Onchestos in Boiotia was the site of a renowned Poseidon sanctuary often mentioned by early Greek poets (e.g. Hom. *Il.* 2.506). Pindar (*Isthm.* 1.52–54) calls this Poseidon *seisichthōn*, earthshaker, and *hippodromios*, the patron of horse races (the latter epithet is also the name of a Boiotian month probably connected with the god). Like many sanctuaries of Poseidon, this one did not possess a temple at first, though one was added in the sixth century. The early sources speak of a sacred grove, and there must have been facilities for the races Pindar mentions. The Homeric *Hymn* to Apollo (3.230–38) describes a curious custom of the shrine:

> There the new-broken colt burdened with drawing the lovely chariot gets its breath; and the driver, though skillful, jumps to the earth from the car and walks. For a while the horses, lacking a driver, rattle the empty car along. If they break (or, if he brings) the chariot in the wooded grove, they care for the horses, but tilting the chariot they leave it. For such from the first was the holy rule (*hosiē*). They pray to the Lord, and the chariot is kept as the god's share.

There is no agreement on the meaning and context of the actions described; the ritual may have involved a driver leaping from the moving car and allowing the horses to career into the grove. If the chariot was wrecked, it was left in the grove as a dedication to the god. On the other hand, if the amended reading is correct, the poet may be referring to a ritual law requiring that any chariot driven into the grove be forfeit to the god. The only certain point is that Poseidon is here celebrated in his guise as the master of horses and chariot racing.[20] This role as horse god looms as large in the cult of Poseidon as his marine aspect, and supports the idea that Poseidon originally had more to do with fresh water and horses (often connected in Indo-European and Greek thought) than with the sea.[21]

Another Boiotian tradition about Poseidon was preserved in the lost epic poem *Thebais*. In the territory of Haliartos was the spring Telphousa, where Poseidon, in the form of a horse, mated with the goddess Erinys. She in turn produced the wondrously swift horse Areion, whose name refers to his superiority, and Poseidon presented the horse as a gift to Kopreus, king of Haliartos.[22] This story finds a doublet in Arkadia, and given that both Erinys and Poseidon are Mycenaean deities, it may well have originated in the Bronze Age.

The Boiotian worship of Poseidon is tied to that of Thessaly, the ancient home of the Boiotoi. Thessaly and Boiotia were the strongholds of the Minyans, a legendary clan whose patron deity was Poseidon. Among their heroes were his twin sons, Neleus (founder of Pylos) and Pelias, the king of Iolkos. The descendants of Neleus also had ties to the cult of Poseidon in

Figure 5.2 Bronze Poseidon from Livadhostro Bay (Boiotia), *c.* 470. Inscribed to the god. Ht 1.18 m. Athens, National Archaeological Museum. Bildarchiv Foto Marburg.

Athens and the Ionian migration. Little information is available about the Thessalian cult, but as in Boiotia, it seems to have focused on Poseidon's rule over horses. A Thessalian legend told how the god created the first horse, Skyphios, by smiting the rock with his trident; Poseidon's widespread cult title Hippios (of the Horse) is connected with this story, as are the equestrian contests conducted for the god and the Thessalian sanctuary of Poseidon Petraios (he of the Rock). This sanctuary is still undiscovered, but it lay somewhere in the vale of Tempe, once a lake drained by the god when he smote the mountains with his trident and made an outlet for the river Peneios.[23] In a seminal paper, Marcel Detienne compared Poseidon's mastery of all things equestrian with the rival powers of Athena. Though both are concerned with horses and their training, he concluded, Athena's sphere tends more toward the driver's skill and strategy, while Poseidon governs the uncanny energy of the animal itself.[24]

Arkadian Poseidon

An important center of Poseidon's cult was landlocked Arkadia, where he, not Zeus, was considered the father of Demeter's daughter, the mistress of the underworld. His sanctuaries were concentrated in the central plains and valleys around Orchomenos, Kaphyai, Methydrion, and Mantineia, poorly drained areas subject to flooding.[25] At Mantineia, Poseidon was a civic god and his trident adorned the shields of the citizens, while late inscriptions show that calendar years were reckoned by the names of his priests. Like Zeus Lykaios, Poseidon Hippios had an inviolate area in his sanctuary outside Mantineia where no human being was permitted to tread; according to legend, a mere woolen thread marked the boundary of the sacred area. When the hero Aipytos cut this thread, he was blinded by a miraculous wave of seawater. Arkadia was a great repository of traditions about the births of the gods; one such legend, tied to a spring in the territory of Mantineia, said that Rhea fooled the murderous Kronos by telling him she had given birth to a horse, and gave him a foal to eat instead of the infant Poseidon, who was sheltered in a lambs' pen.[26]

In most regions of Greece, we encounter a belief in Poseidon as the creator of the first horse or as the sire of miraculous steeds such as the winged Pegasos, who was the offspring of Poseidon and Medousa. In Arkadia, the god himself becomes a horse, as in the Mantinean birth legend and the myths attached to the city of Thelpousa. Here, Demeter Erinys sought to escape the lustful Poseidon by transforming herself into a mare, but he became a stallion and mated with her. The offspring of this union were a goddess whose name was kept secret (presumably the Arkadian equivalent of Kore) and the divine horse Areion. Pausanias, our source for most of this information, speaks of the sanctuary of Demeter outside Thelpousa, but does not elaborate on the cult of Poseidon here, except to say that he had the title of Hippios. Similarly at a cave sanctuary outside Phigaleia in the Neda river gorge, the cult myth recounted the coupling of Demeter and Poseidon in the shape of horses, specifying that their daughter was the goddess known as Despoina (Mistress). Poseidon Hippios also had an altar at the important sanctuary of the Mistress at Lykosoura.[27] Here Poseidon is hardly a god of the sea, and his cults are presumably least changed from their Mycenaean antecedents (just as Arkadian Posoidan is the dialect form closest to Linear B). The few references to his marine nature are due to Panhellenizing influences during the Classical period and later.

Athenian Poseidon

Athens and Trozen shared a myth according to which Athena and Poseidon disputed ownership of the land.[28] In the lore of cities bordering the Saronic Gulf, Poseidon figures in a number of these contests; tellingly, he is never the winner. At Trozen, the contest ended in a truce under which the territory was shared, while at Athens, the story went that the victorious Athena produced an olive tree on the Akropolis as a token of her claim, while Poseidon struck the rock with his trident, creating a "sea." The nature of this sea is unclear, though Pausanias (1.26.5) describes it as a well with salt water, enclosed within the walls of the Classical Erechtheion. He also notes an altar on which sacrifices to both Poseidon and Erechtheus were made. The story of the conflict between Poseidon and Athena seems to be closely related to that of the early war between Athens and Eleusis, in which the earth-born Athenian king Erechtheus, protégé of Athena, battled Eumolpos, the Eleusinian leader and son of Poseidon. Athens was victorious when Erechtheus sacrificed his daughters to save the city, but he himself was struck by Poseidon's trident and hidden under the earth.[29] By the fifth century, Poseidon had taken the name of his antagonist as a cult epithet, an arrangement comparable to that between Apollo and Hyakinthos at Amyklai. In both cases the cults of Olympian gods were superimposed on those of earlier indigenous deities, and the earlier figures were transformed into heroes killed by the gods and worshiped side by side with them.[30]

Poseidon was an important deity in Archaic Eleusis, consistent with his usual close cult relations to Demeter. Eleusis possessed a cult of Poseidon Pater (Father), and a priest of the Kerykes served Poseidon Prosbaterios (of the Approaches) and Themeliouchos (Upholding the Foundations). It is likely that all these epithets have to do with Poseidon's role vis-à-vis Demeter as a fructifying deity of water and flooding. That Poseidon's role in Athenian cult has much to do with the relations between Athens and Eleusis is likewise demonstrated in the festival known as the Skira, when the Athenian priests of Poseidon, Athena, and Helios walked to a sanctuary near the boundary with Eleusis.[31]

Poseidon had other cults in Attica, but the most important was at the promontory of Sounion, where a temple was added *c.* 490 and rebuilt under Perikles. The Athenians held a quadrennial festival with boat races, and the vigor of the Archaic cult is attested by at least twelve *kouroi* (statues of idealized young men) found buried in a pit east of the temple.[32] The earliest cult at Sounion, however, probably belonged to the hero Phrontis, the steersman of Menelaos buried there according to Homer (*Od.* 3.276–85). In spite of the apparent antiquity of his cult, Poseidon was not a significant presence in Attica compared with Zeus, Demeter, Apollo, Dionysos, and of course Athena.

Further reading

Gebhard 1993 and Morgan 1994 summarize the development of sacred space at Isthmia from the eleventh century. Robertson 1984 demonstrates Poseidon's role as a god of fructifying waters and partner of Demeter. Schumacher 1993 discusses the function of Poseidon's sanctuaries as places of asylum. Chapter 6 of Pache 2004 is devoted to Melikertes-Palaimon.

6

MISTRESSES OF GRAIN
AND SOULS
Demeter and Kore/Persephone

Demeter's origins as a grain goddess must lie in the Neolithic period with the advent of agriculture. Her name contains the Greek word for "mother," but whether the initial syllable means "earth," "grain," or something else has long been debated. Homer had little interest in Demeter and none in her relationship with Kore (the Maiden), though Persephone appears in epic poetry as the bride of Hades. The queen of the dead (Attic Pherephatta) has a non-Greek name and must have been in origin a deity separate from Demeter's daughter. Even after the two were firmly and inextricably identified, they were often paradoxically represented in cult as two distinct personages. Eleusinian iconography and terminology, for example, juxtaposed Thea, the underworld goddess, with Kore, the daughter. The Greeks avoided pronouncing or inscribing the ominous name Persephone in cult contexts, replacing it with Kore or other euphemisms, though such caution was less often exercised by the poets. Demeter and Kore were frequently worshiped together under such names as the Two Goddesses, the Thesmophoroi, or the Great Goddesses.

Demeter sanctuaries tended to be scattered in neighborhoods rather than centralized, probably because they were used for local celebrations of the Thesmophoria, Demeter's main festival. In spite of their crucial role in the prosperity of the city, Demeter and Kore rarely functioned as civic gods. Exceptional were Thebes, where Demeter's sanctuary occupied prime civic space on the Kadmeia, and certain cities of Sicily and Magna Graecia, where the two goddesses were dominant presences in the pantheon. In the Greek West, Kore/Persephone herself was sometimes the more prominent partner of the two, and played an important role in the social construction of marriage and the rites leading to adulthood for women and men. In keeping with Kore's significance as the archetypal bride, the western colonies saw the core of the myth as the theogamy of Persephone/Kore and Hades, rather than the reunion of Demeter and Kore after the latter's abduction, which was the focus of the famous Eleusinian Mysteries.

Thesmophoria

The most widespread festival of Demeter and Kore, and one of the most popular of all Greek rites, was the women's festival known as the Thesmophoria. The term *thesmos* means "that which is laid down," hence laws, rites, or revered customs. As the presiding deities, the two goddesses were called Thesmophoroi (Bringers of the Divine Law) because the introduction of grain cultivation was considered the origin of civilized life. Some scholars believe that the "things laid down" are to be understood in a much more literal sense, as the dead piglets deposited during the central rite of the festival. Still, the epithet unquestionably conveys the respect in which the goddesses were held, as do other cult titles such as Megalai Theai (Great Goddesses) and Hagnai Theai (Pure Goddesses). Each year, normally in late summer or early fall, married Greek women gathered in the local Demeter sanctuary, often called the Thesmophorion. Although celebration of the festival was generally not centralized, one sanctuary might be more heavily frequented than the rest. Most had a few modest cult buildings or a simple shrine called a *megaron* rather than an elaborate temple, but they are relatively easy to identify as sanctuaries of Demeter and Kore by the objects left behind: ceramic tableware; water jars; terracottas of the goddesses or their votaries, often carrying a piglet; pig bones; numerous lamps for the nocturnal parts of the rites; and the remains of ritual meals.

Literary evidence for the exclusion of males is plentiful. Herodotus (6.134) tells how the Athenian general Miltiades attempted to enter a restricted building (*megaron*) in the sanctuary on Paros – perhaps to meddle with the "untouchable" things there – and as a result of divine anger was stricken with a fatal case of gangrene. Xenophon says (*Hell.* 5.2.29) that the men of Thebes kept clear of the Kadmeia while the women were performing the rites there, going so far as to hold the *boulē* (council) in the agora rather than its usual place on the akropolis. Men's dedications are often found at these sites, so we know that their exclusion was not complete. Demeter sanctuaries were apparently used for a number of different observances throughout the year, only some of which involved ritual gender segregation.[1]

The sacred objects used and acts performed during the Thesmophoria were kept secret. We hear of ritual dances, processions, and special foods, particularly bread. The Delian celebration, held in the late summer month of Metageitnion, involved an event called the Megalartia (Large Loaves), and bread seems to have played an important role in the celebrations at Korinth (below).[2] Only one source, a scholiast on Lucian (*Dial. meret.* 2.1), describes the ritual in detail, and his version refers to Attic custom. He writes that piglets are cast into the "chasms of Demeter and Kore" in honor of Eubouleus, a herdsman whose swine were swallowed in the abyss when Hades abducted Kore (Eubouleus reappears as a deity in Eleusis). After an unspecified period, the rotted remains of the piglets are brought up from the chasms (also called *aduta*, innermost chambers, and *megara*, chambers) by ritually pure women, laid on the altars, and mixed with the seed grain to ensure a good harvest. The scholiast says that pine branches and phallic shapes made of wheat dough are used the same way, all given as thank offerings for the generation of crops and the procreation of people.

The ritual deposition of piglets was probably widespread; piglets were cast into *megara* at Potniai in Boiotia, and excavations of Demeter and Kore sanctuaries at Knidos and Priene have uncovered such pits. At Eleusis, several deep shafts, which probably served this function, were found around the porch of the so-called Telesterion.[3] Apparently, the story of Kore's rape was the mythic foundation for the ritual; the piglet is also symbolic of the female genitals, and the piglets falling into the earth to be resurrected with the grain repeat the descent and ascent of Kore. Thus the Thesmophoria and the Eleusinian Mysteries shared the same myth, interpreted in different ways. Kevin Clinton has suggested that the Homeric *Hymn* to Demeter, usually thought to recount the origin of the Mysteries, is primarily an aetiological account of the Thesmophoria.[4]

The Attic Thesmophoria was a three-day festival held a few weeks before the ploughing and sowing of the fields; we also hear of such festivals celebrated as early as midsummer (Thebes) and lasting as long as ten days (Sicily). Women gathered in the sanctuaries, bringing supplies of food and setting up tents as temporary accommodations. As part of the proceedings, the women engaged in sex-talk (*aischrologia*) and ritual mockery. This seems to have been a mainstay of the goddesses' segregated worship; its mythic explanation is that when Demeter was grieving for Kore, scurrilous jokes and gestures caused her to smile.[5] The sex-talk was the verbal equivalent of the piglets, pine branches and phallic shapes handled by the participants; the women's heightened awareness of their own sexuality and reproductive ability was powerful (therefore it could be deployed to aid the growth of crops) yet dangerous to male prerogatives (therefore its unfettered expression was limited to the festival context).[6]

The first day of the Athenian festival was called Anodos (Ascent), perhaps with reference to the women's retrieval of material from the chasms. The second day was the Nesteia (Fasting), a day when no public business or sacrifice was conducted in the city. The last day was called Kalligeneia (Beautiful Offspring), making clear the connection between agricultural bounty and women's fertility. This was probably a feast day, presided over by leaders (*archousai*) elected from each deme. It is clear from Isaeus' speeches (3.80, 6.49–50, 8.19) that citizen matrons organized and attended the festival, but the sources conflict on the question of whether slaves and prostitutes could be present and in what capacities. Aristophanes' *Women at the Thesmophoria* draws a vivid tableau of male suspicion and female revelry during the Thesmophoric ritual, which he sets on the Pnyx, in the same meeting place used by the Athenian assembly. Excavation in this area uncovered a few terracottas and lamps consistent with a sanctuary of Demeter and Kore, but not enough material to confirm the existence of a Thesmophorion.[7]

Demeter, Kore, and the agricultural year

As one might expect, many festivals of Demeter and Kore were tied to the annual cycle of grain cultivation. Barley and wheat were the staple crops, sown during the fall in most Mediterranean lands. Great anxiety surrounded the fateful question of when to plough and sow, for the farmer must plant late enough to coincide with the fall rains, yet early enough to allow the shoots to become established before the onset of winter cold.[8] Therefore the most important festivals and rituals connected with grain cultivation are clustered around sowing time.

As usual, we are best informed about the Attic year. Early in Pyanopsion (October/November), the Proerosia or pre-ploughing sacrifices took place in the demes, including Eleusis. In conjunction with the Proerosia there were at least three sacred ploughings, one at Skiron, one in the Rharian plain of Eleusis, and one in Athens. The Thesmophoria, with its ritual preparation of the seed, followed soon after. During the next month, Poseideion (December/January), the grain sprouted and began to grow. By the time of the Haloa at the winter solstice, it became evident whether the farmers had chosen their sowing dates wisely. Epigraphic evidence from the fourth century (*IG* II² 1672.124, 144) shows that huge amounts of firewood were used, probably for the bonfires typical of solstice ritual. At this point in the year, the grain was quiescent because of the cold; only the returning heat of the sun could bring it to fruition. Ancient accounts of the Haloa are late and confused, but it is clear that like the Thesmophoria, the festival involved a link between human and vegetable fertility.[9] Temporarily flouting the rules of behavior for respectable females, women gathered at Eleusis drank wine, engaged in sexual banter, and handled pastries shaped like male and female genitals.

In Anthesterion (February/March) the Lesser Mysteries took place just as the grain stalks entered their prime phase of growth, celebrated in the Chloaia (Greening festival). This was probably the main festival of Demeter Chloë, though she also received a sacrifice at the harvest. Perhaps surprisingly, the main harvest observance, known in Attica and some Ionian cities as the Thargelia and in other Greek lands as the Thalysia, had early ties to Apollo and Artemis rather than Demeter. Homer (*Il.* 9.533–35) thinks of *thalusia* as first fruit offerings to Artemis, and Apollo was the patron of the Thargelia, but by the Hellenistic period Theocritus (*Id.* 7.31–38) describes the Thalysia on Kos as a Demeter festival. On the other hand, we know that Demeter was an important figure in the harvest folklore of Greek peasants, who sang songs to her as they reaped. The Kalamaia (Straw festival), probably held in the mid-summer month of Skirophorion, was an Attic/Ionian celebration of the threshing and winnowing. This was also the month of the Skira, a poorly understood festival celebrated by married women who temporarily abstained from sex. Like the Thesmophoria, it was celebrated at a number of sites in Attica.[10] Finally, the Eleusinian Mysteries were held in Boedromion (September/October), about a month before the ploughing and sowing began once more, renewing the agricultural cycle.

The Eleusinian Mysteries

For a thousand years, people traveled to the small town of Eleusis in Attica in order to experience something profound, something that soothed their fears of death and enhanced their lives immeasurably. This most prestigious of mystery cults must have begun as a local rite open only to the people living nearby, but gradually it accommodated ever-larger numbers, including slaves and foreigners. Many secrets still surround the cult, for its hundreds of thousands of initiates kept their promise not to reveal what took place within the sanctuary. Still, a surprising amount is known from archaeological investigation of the once-inviolate precinct, the assertions of hostile Christian Fathers (which must be read with caution), and other scattered bits of information. The Eleusinian Mysteries had an important public component, and contemporary sources addressing this aspect of the rites, including inscriptions and vase paintings, are numerous.

In spite of the plentiful data (or perhaps because of it), many scholarly controversies surround the Mysteries. Debate centers on the date at which the Eleusinian cult was incorporated into Athenian religion (from the beginning, or not until the sixth century?), the relationship between the cult and the Homeric *Hymn* to Demeter (to what extent does the latter reflect an "Eleusinian" perspective?) and the significance of the Mycenaean remains found in the sanctuary (do they point to continuity of the cult from the Bronze Age?). The early Mycenaean Megaron B, located beneath the later Demeter temple or Telesterion, was distinguished from nearby houses by its stepped porch and the remains of frescoes within; Mycenaean figurines were found in the vicinity. Yet its function is not clearly established; it may have served as an elite residence, a cult building, or both. A curved Geometric wall outside Megaron B could be either the remains of a Geometric Demeter temple or a retaining wall added to the still-standing Bronze Age structure. In any case, the earliest unequivocal evidence of the cult are the massive eighth-century terrace and a wall enclosing the whole area, with a sacrificial pyre full of broken figurines, pottery, and ashes at the entrance.[11]

Eleusis lies at the edge of the Thriasian plain, the "bread basket" of Attica; it was bound to be of interest to the emerging polis.[12] Legend tells of a war between the two towns when Erechtheus was king at Athens and Eumolpos, the first celebrant of the Mysteries, at Eleusis. The resulting settlement left financial control of the cult entirely in Athenian hands, while ritual responsibilities were shared between two aristocratic families, the Eumolpidai of

Eleusis and the Kerykes of Athens. The chief priest of the Mysteries, the Hierophant (Revealer of Sacred Things) was always a Eumolpid, while the Keryx (Herald) and Dadouchos (Torchbearer), other important officials, were both Kerykes. Second only to the Hierophant was the Priestess of Demeter and Kore, who might come from a number of different families. Hers was probably the oldest office associated with the cult, for her duties extended to several of the local, deme-level festivals of Demeter at Eleusis. Inscriptions reveal an ongoing struggle for ritual authority between the Hierophant and the Priestess of Demeter in the fourth century, when a Hierophant was convicted of impiety for usurping the Priestess' right to preside at the Haloa. Many of the sacred personnel connected with the Mysteries seem to have held their offices for life, a fact that sets the Eleusinian priesthoods apart from most others among the Greeks.[13]

Initiation to the Mysteries required time, effort, and a cost that, while substantial, was not out of reach even for the poor. Those who wished to participate were expected to undergo a long period of preparation, beginning with the Lesser Mysteries in Anthesterion, seven months before the Eleusinian festival. Little is known of the Lesser Mysteries, but they took place in the suburb of Agrai at Athens in the sanctuary of Meter/Rhea, and they involved purification of candidates by bathing in the Ilissos river or through the use of the *Dios kōidion*, a sacred fleece obtained by sacrificing a ram to Zeus Meilichios. Together with the Sacred Way that connected Athens to Eleusis, and the city Eleusinion between the agora and the northwest corner of the Akropolis, the Lesser Mysteries helped to cement the relationship between Athens and Eleusis and shaped the "Athenian" identity of the festival as a whole.

Candidates for initiation, or *mustai* (those whose eyes are closed), had to seek a sponsor from the Eumolpidai or Kerykes to guide their spiritual preparation, known as *muēsis*. On 13 and 14 Boedromion (September/October), the *hiera* (sacred objects) were brought in procession from Eleusis to the Athenian Eleusinion, and their safe arrival was announced to the priestess of Athena on the Akropolis. Priestesses from Eleusis carried these objects in boxes on their heads, so they cannot have been large or heavy, but we know nothing else about them except that they played a central role in the climactic rite. The next day was the first day of the Mysteries proper, the Agyrmos (Gathering). All assembled in the agora for a formal proclamation by the Hierophant and Dadouchos. Anyone unable to speak Greek, ritually impure, or conscious of having committed a crime was asked to abstain from the rite. At this time the *mustai* probably paid their fees, which have been calculated as the equivalent of several days' wages. The sixteenth of Boedromion was a day of purification. Directed by the heralds, the *mustai* brought piglets to Phaleron or Peiraieus, where they bathed in the sea and washed the animals. Each then sacrificed the piglet "on his/her own behalf." The next day was allotted to major state sacrifices, and the eighteenth was the Epidauria, a subsidiary festival of Asklepios that began in 420 when the cult of Asklepios and Hygieia was introduced at Athens on this day.[14]

The nineteenth brought the great *pompē* (procession) and escort of the *hiera* back to Eleusis. Wearing garlands of myrtle and carrying bunches of myrtle twigs or bundles of provisions attached to the end of sticks, the *mustai* set out in a merry mood to walk about 22 km to the sanctuary. They were led by Iakchos, the god who personified the ritual cry "Iakche!" Because of the boisterous tone of the parade and similarity between the names Iakchos and Bakchos, the former began at an early date to be associated with Dionysos, yet he is a distinct Eleusinian deity.[15] After arriving at the outer court of the sanctuary, where there was a temple of Artemis Propylaia (Before the Gateway) and the Eleusinian patron deity Poseidon, the *mustai* spent the rest of the evening celebrating the "reception of Iakchos" and singing and dancing at the well called Kallichoron (Place of Beautiful Dances). Perhaps this was also the day when *kernoi*, special offering trays equipped with cups of various seeds and grains, were presented to the goddess. The next day saw the offering of the *pelanos*, a massive cake of barley and wheat harvested from the sacred Rharian plain, and other sacrifices financed from the "first fruit" offerings (*aparchai*) tithed to Demeter and Kore. The *mustai* meanwhile fasted, and finally broke their fast with the *kukeōn*, a posset of barley water and an aromatic herb, pennyroyal. These actions, and others to follow, imitated the activities of Demeter when her daughter had disappeared; Demeter's fast and request for the *kukōn* is recorded in the Homeric *Hymn* to Demeter (2.208–10).

With evening began the secret part of the ritual, when the *mustai* were admitted into the confines of the sanctuary proper. This was situated on the southwest slope of the Eleusinian akropolis, and had two main components. First was the rocky cliff containing a cave that served as a cult place for Theos (God) and Thea (Goddess), the Eleusinian titles for Plouton and Persephone in their roles as king and queen of the dead. With them was worshiped a deity or hero named Eubouleus, whose role was similar to that of Hermes in the Homeric *Hymn* to Demeter: he is shown on vase paintings holding torches in the presence of Theos and Thea, ready to guide the goddess back to the upper world for a reunion with her grieving mother. The *agelastos petros* (Mirthless Rock), where Demeter is supposed to have sat mourning the loss of her daughter, was probably also in this rocky area. Passing by the cave with its small shrine, the *mustai* would have followed a path up to the principal structure, the initiation hall known to scholars as the Telesterion, but in Classical times called the *neōs* (temple) or *anaktoron* (lord's hall). Starting in the late seventh or early sixth century, a succession of ever-larger temples was built over the old Mycenaean Megaron B, each one containing an inner room whose position was kept constant. The design of this "temple" differs dramatically from those of other gods, for unlike most Greek temples, it was designed to hold a large number of people and includes seating around the walls.[16]

The sources give us only a glimpse of what took place in this room amid the forest of columns, the actual *teletē* (mystery rite). Certainly the initiates were guided on an emotional path from confusion and grief to confidence and joy, and this progression seems to have corresponded to the events in a ritual drama depicting Kore's return from the underworld and her reunion with Demeter. At a critical moment, the Hierophant appeared from the inner room in a blaze of torchlight to display the *hiera* to the onlookers. Those who had experienced the Mysteries in a previous year were permitted to remain in the Telesterion for a further revelation; such individuals were called *epoptai* (those who have seen). Following the climactic rites, bulls and pigs were sacrificed to the goddesses and other Eleusinian deities, while initiates used special vessels called *plēmochoai* to pour libations of water toward the east and west.

On the day after the Mysteries concluded, the Athenian Council met in the city Eleusinion to review the conduct of the festival and deal with any infractions of sacred law; this custom was attributed to a law of Solon. The earliest votive deposits in the Eleusinion date to the seventh century, and it received architectural elaboration in the sixth. It contained a temple of Demeter and Kore, altars, and many inscribed decrees relating to the conduct of the Mysteries, as well as a temple of Triptolemos, the Eleusinian hero who is said to have introduced the knowledge of grain cultivation to the world, flying about in his winged chariot.[17]

Particularly in the period of empire, Athens promoted the Mysteries, along with the knowledge imparted by Triptolemos, as its unique gifts to the world. Heralds were sent to other cities to declare a sacred truce of fifty-five days, which allowed time for pilgrims to travel to Athens, be initiated, and return home. The first fruits decree (*IG* I³ 78), issued *c.* 435, details the collection of an annual tithe of grain from every deme in Attica and the Athenian allies, and urges that every Greek city likewise join in the offering.[18] We don't know how many Greek cities heeded this rather high-handed request, but Athens clearly succeeded in securing for Eleusis a Panhellenic reputation and status, which it maintained until the end of antiquity. Even as the cult gained renown across the Greek world, however, the "Eleusinian version" of the Demeter/Kore myth remained surprisingly localized. Other cities often had their own versions of the myth that failed to be displaced because they, like the traditions at Eleusis, were venerable tales tied to local landmarks (wells, caves, or rocky outcroppings). Even the Homeric *Hymn* to Demeter reflects a generic, Panhellenized version of the Attic cult: Eubouleus, the titles Theos and Thea, and the Mirthless Rock are omitted from the story, while Triptolemos is barely mentioned.

Demeter at Korinth

On a steep slope of the Akrokorinthos, some fifteen minutes' walk from the city center, Demeter's principal sanctuary at Korinth was constructed in a

Figure 6.1 Demeter and Kore or Hekate. Relief sculpture, fifth century. Archaeological Museum, Eleusis. Erich Lessing/Art Resource.

series of three terraces. Though there was continuous activity on the site from the Late Bronze Age, no evidence for a cult appears until a series of pins and rings deposited in the mid-eighth century. Even at this early date the offerings give the impression of a strong female presence at the site. In the seventh century a wider variety of offerings appears in the middle terrace, including bronze jewelry, miniature vases, and terracotta figurines. A small but substantial building, probably a temple, was already present in this period. The middle terrace, with its temple, sacrificial area, bone debris (primarily from pigs), and votive collections, served as the nucleus of the cult for its first hundred and fifty years, while the upper terrace contained a theatral area that was probably used for a mystery rite.

In the sixth century came a major architectural development: numerous dining rooms were constructed on the lower terrace. Ritual dining in this area was probably not new, but the Korinthians now expended considerable resources on dining facilities. Each room held from six to eight diners, who reclined on stone couches. By mid-century, the sanctuary could accommodate about one hundred diners at once. The ritual menu seems to have focused not on sacrificial meat, but on grain-based foods. One of the characteristic votive offerings at this site was the terracotta *liknon* (winnowing fan) filled with a variety of model breads and cakes. The cooking vessels are the types used for boiling and stewing, so gruels or porridge may also have been an important menu item. Finally, numerous wine cups (*kantharoi* and *skuphoi*), mixing bowls and amphoras show that wine was consumed with the meal.

Who partook of these meals is a mystery. On the one hand, elaborate dining facilities, reclining posture, and wine consumption are associated with men's symposia. Yet the abundance of women's votive offerings, the emphasis on grain-based foods, and the fact that this was a Demeter sanctuary point toward a women's festival such as the Thesmophoria. In any case, the expansion of the dining facilities at Korinth continued through the fifth and fourth centuries. Eventually, more than two hundred diners at once could use the rooms, which were provided with extra spaces for food preparation and washing. To judge from the scarcity of imported offerings here (relative to a sanctuary like that of Hera at Perachora), the cult seems to have attracted few outsiders.[19]

The Two Goddesses are said to have played a role in the success of Timoleon, the Korinthian who was credited with the liberation of Syracuse from rule by Greek tyrants and Carthaginians. On the eve of Timoleon's expedition in 345/4, the priestesses of Demeter and Persephone reported a dream in which the goddesses appeared to them in traveling garb to announce that they would accompany Timoleon to Sicily. Much encouraged, the Korinthians dedicated a "sacred trireme" to the goddesses and set sail. On their journey, a great flame appeared in the night sky, and forming itself into a torch "like those used in the Mysteries," guided them to their destination.[20]

Demeter Chthonia at Hermione

Pausanias (2.35.4–11) is our most detailed source for the famous cult of Demeter Chthonia (of the Underworld) at the remote town of Hermione in the Argolid. Hermione was not a Dorian town, but was settled by the aboriginal Dryopes when the Dorians expelled them from Thessaly. This cult is unusual in its emphasis on the role of Hades (who is given the euphemistic name of Klymenos, the Renowned One). Examination of the site has revealed a lengthy section of wall, which probably marked off the Classical sanctuary, a series of inscribed bronze cows (which relate to the ritual described below), and numerous late inscriptions. It is difficult to know from Pausanias' second-century CE account which elements of the ritual date back to the Classical period. He reports that the Chthonia festival took place in the summer and began with a procession of all the priests, magistrates, and townspeople, even the children. Dressed in white and crowned with wreaths made from a local summer wildflower, they led a heifer to the sanctuary, where it was allowed to roam about until it entered the open doors of the temple. Inside, four old women rose from their ceremonial thrones and pursued the heifer until one of them cut its throat with a sickle. Three more cows were slaughtered for the goddess in the same way.

The indoor sacrifice is very unusual, but can be explained as the result of the strict gender segregation practiced in the cult. The cult statue of Chthonia was so sacred that only the old women were permitted to view it, and the exclusion of men seems to have extended to the sacrificial slaughter, usually a male prerogative. Although the whole city participated in the festival, its climactic ritual acts had to take place in seclusion, away from male eyes. Chthonia seems to have been an important Dryopian goddess, for the Dryopes of Asine, a neighboring town, sent a sacrificial cow and a delegation to walk in the procession even after they were forced to emigrate to Messenia (*IG* IV 679.1–2). Opposite Chthonia's sanctuary was that of Klymenos, and the area was famed for its entrance to the underworld, an opening in the earth from which Herakles once emerged, it was said, leading Kerberos. Although Kore plays no role in Pausanias' description of the cult, she appears with Demeter Chthonia and Klymenos in numerous dedicatory inscriptions from Hermione. A fragmentary hymn composed by the sixth-century poet Lasos of Hermione confirms that worship of the triad Demeter, Klymenos, and Kore was the norm in the late Archaic period as well.[21]

Demeter and Despoina in Arkadia

According to Herodotus (2.171), the *teletē* (secret rite) of Demeter which the Greeks call the Thesmophoria was mostly abandoned in the Peloponnese with the arrival of the Dorians, but was preserved among the Arkadians, whose lands were not penetrated by the invaders. Certainly the worship of Demeter was far more prominent in Arkadia than elsewhere in the Peloponnese. The Arkadia of the poets is a mountainous, wild land sparsely inhabited by goatherds and hunters, but the district also encompassed fertile lowlands where cereal crops were grown. Like so many other Arkadian cults, with their pronounced tendency toward theriomorphic (animal-shaped) gods, the worship of the Two Goddesses in this isolated district seems strange and primeval, the remnant of a very early syncretism of Greek and indigenous traditions.

The Arkadians worshiped an equine Demeter, consort of the horse-god Poseidon Hippios. They held in common with the other Greeks the belief that Demeter angrily withdrew to an earthly abode and caused a crisis in the natural world because of her rage at the abduction of her daughter. Demeter's anger was further attributed to her unwilling union with Poseidon. In order to escape his lustful pursuit, she transformed herself into a mare, but he saw through the trick and forced himself on her in the form of a stallion. Their offspring were the miraculous horse Areion and a daughter, the Arkadian equivalent of Kore, whose true name was revealed only to initiates. In public, their daughter was called Despoina (the Mistress). This story was attached to

Thelpousa, where Demeter had the title Erinys (the Wrathful One), and a similar myth about Erinys is attested for Telphousa/Tilphossa in Boiotia.[22] Demeter also had the title of Lousia (of Washing) at Thelpousa, because she purified herself in the river Ladon after intercourse with Poseidon and let go of her anger. Demeter Erinys and Demeter Lousia thus form a complementary pair representing angry and appeased manifestations of the goddess.

The Thelpousan cult is closely related to that at Phigaleia, where Demeter's Archaic statue had the head of a horse and was housed in a cave on the rocky gorge of the river Neda, well outside the city. To this cave Demeter had withdrawn, causing a famine until her anger abated. She was known as Melaina (the Black) because she dressed all in black to express her mood; scholars generally interpret her blackness, which is a feature shared by the Erinyes, as a sign of her underworld nature. The statue was seated on a rock with serpents and other creatures emerging from its mane, and it held a dolphin in one hand and in the other a dove. This Demeter is a Mistress of Animals and has close affinities with the gorgon Medousa, who similarly sported snaky hair, mated with Poseidon, and gave birth to a miraculous horse (Pegasos). Kore/Despoina has little involvement in this cult, nor is Demeter primarily a grain goddess. Every year the people set upon an altar outside the cave samples of all the raw materials produced in their land, including grapes, honeycombs, and wool, and poured olive oil over these in an attempt to appease the disgruntled goddess. According to Pausanias (8.42.5–7), this was a revival of an Archaic cult that had fallen into disuse. The original theriomorphic statue was lost to a fire in the distant past. On the occasion of a blight, the people consulted Delphi and were told to replace the statue of "stallion-mated Deo," whose anger had been renewed by the people's neglect. Onatas of Aigina, a sculptor active in the fifth century, was given the commission, and inspired by a dream and perhaps an old copy of the image, he re-created it.[23]

The Arkadian cults of Demeter resulted from a complex process combining the old Mycenaean goddess Erinys, who was early on linked to Poseidon Hippios and whose offspring was a horse, with the Panhellenic and Eleusinian Demeter who bore a daughter. The persona of the daughter seems to have been superimposed on an older Arkadian goddess, Despoina. The sanctuary of Despoina at Lykosoura was dramatically rebuilt in the Hellenistic period with sculptures by Damophon (c. 175–150), and most of the excavated remains are late. Only a few Archaic and Classical terracottas attest to the earlier life of the sanctuary, which the Arkadians considered very ancient. Pausanias' account (8.37.1–10) of Lykosoura mentions the worship of Despoina with her mother Demeter; certain mysteries (most likely derivative of the Eleusinian rites); and a platform called the *megaron* where an unusual form of sacrifice took place. Each participant sacrificed an animal, not only cutting its throat, but also chopping off a random limb for the goddess. Despoina clearly had a strong affinity with Artemis, who not coincidentally maintained a cultic presence in the sanctuary. Another clue to the nature of the cult are the theriomorphic figures found in the *megaron* area and sculpted on the robe of Damophon's statue of Despoina, fragments of which were recovered in the excavations of Lykosoura. The border of the robe shows a line of dancing male and female figures with ram and horse heads. These belong to the Hellenistic period, yet likely reveal a very old custom of masked dances for the goddess.[24]

The Two Goddesses in Sicily

The religious life of the colonists in the west developed differently from that of people in the mother cities for several reasons. First, the entire pantheon of major and minor deities could not be reproduced in a colony; the settlers were forced to focus on a limited number of cults selected from those they knew at home. As it happened, Demeter's cult was particularly well suited to the fertile soils of Sicily. Second, Greek religious assumptions required that the local gods be recognized (preferably as Greek deities in a new guise), and their cult places respected. The native Sikans and Sikels worshiped a number of goddesses, among them Hyblaia, Anna, and local water spirits, whose functions and personalities were easily assimilated to those of Demeter and Kore/Persephone. In particular, the dominance of Persephone, who was often worshiped quite independently of her mother in this part of the world, may be due to syncretism with local underworld goddesses.

During the Archaic period, much of Sicily was ruled by tyrants of the Deinomenid family including Gelon and Hieron. The Deinomenids played an important role in the dissemination of the cults of the Two Goddesses, for their ancestor Telines held a family priesthood of the *chthoniai theai* (earth goddesses, i.e., Demeter and Kore). When a group of Geloans seceded, Telines was able to win them back by displaying the sacred objects of the goddesses. In return for this service, he demanded a civic priesthood, which he passed to his descendants. The Deinomenids seem to have exported cults of Demeter and Kore/Persephone to Gela's daughter city Akragas and to several other sites in the hinterland.[25] Already in the sixth century, Pindar (*Pyth.* 12.1–2) described Akragas as the "seat of Persephone," and by the first century, Cicero (*Verr.* 2.4.106) could remark that all Sicily was sacred to Demeter and Persephone. The names of Sicilian festivals such as Anakalypteria (Unveiling of the Bride), Theogamia (Divine Marriage), and Koreia (Festival of the Maiden) suggest the importance of Kore/Persephone's cult and show that its principal focus was her marriage to Hades.[26]

Founded on the south coast of Sicily by seventh-century colonists from Rhodes and Krete, Gela lies on a hill beside the mouth of the Gela river. While Athena and Hera were worshiped in the city proper, Demeter and Kore seem to have possessed at least three sanctuaries outside the walls, all quite modest in terms of architecture, yet rich in votive gifts. A pot graffito indicates that the sanctuary across the river at Bitalemi was a Thesmophorion, and to judge from the votive deposits, the other two sites served a similar function. Excavation of Bitalemi revealed some mud-brick structures, the remains of ritual meals cooked on the spot, terracotta figurines, and interesting deposits of vessels buried upside down in orderly rows. The early settlers signaled the importance of this site by burying a hoard of ingots and other objects in bronze, a custom borrowed from the natives. They also laid down a ploughshare and other agricultural tools as offerings to Demeter and Kore.[27]

The sanctuaries of Predio Sola, on the seaward side of the Geloan akropolis, and Via Fiume to the north, similarly possessed small buildings and a wealth of votive objects including a large number of lamps and the "masks" or busts so characteristic of the worship of Demeter and Kore in Sicily and Italy. Other terracottas considered diagnostic of the cult include standing women with torches and piglets and certain types of enthroned goddesses with pectoral decoration; many of these types were locally made but derive from Rhodian models. These sites are notable for the care with which votives were buried. In many Greek sanctuaries, old votives were unceremoniously dumped in pits to make room for newer offerings, but in the chthonic sanctuaries of Sicily, burial was a form of communication with the deities, so vessels and terracottas were carefully positioned face down, and every available space was used. In some cases, rings of stones were arranged around pits in which sacrificial remains, vessels, and figurines were deposited. Sanctuaries closely resembling Bitalemi have been uncovered at Akragas and the Syracusan colony of Heloros.[28]

Founded from Gela in the sixth century, Akragas was a major center of Persephone's worship. Its tyrant Theron is portrayed in Pindar's second Olympian ode (56–83) as a believer in afterlife judgments, reincarnation, and final salvation in the Isles of the Blessed. It is very likely that Theron's convictions about the afterlife were intertwined with the cult of Persephone, who played an important role in the Bakchic/Orphic mysteries so popular in the Greek west. Several cult places at Akragas date to Theron's day or before. On the north side of the city, just outside the wall, the rupestral sanctuary of S. Biagio consists of a series of artificial caves or tunnels in the rocky hillside. These were filled with votive deposits, including many large busts. The excavation of the tunnels seems to have been a method of conveying the offerings to divine power(s) conceived of as present within the earth. Opposite the rupestral sanctuary and within the walls, the present church of S. Biagio was constructed over an early fifth-century temple, beside which are two circular altars with hollow depressions in the center. These were used to direct libations and perhaps other offerings into the earth. At the south end of the city, the area known as the "Chthonic sanctuary" of Akragas was probably devoted to Persephone and/or Demeter.[29]

Selinous, westernmost of the Sicilian Greek colonies, is famous for a group of well-preserved Doric temples, none of which can be assigned with certainty to a specific deity. West of the akropolis was a more modest, extraurban sanctuary of Demeter Malophoros (Bearer of Fruit), a goddess imported from the mother city of Megara in mainland Greece. The Malophoros sanctuary, founded in the seventh century, is actually a compound containing smaller shrines of Hekate (who appropriately guards the entrance) and Zeus Meilichios. Demeter's temple stood within a second inner boundary wall, emphasizing its inviolate nature. The rear of the temple was hidden under a large mound, giving the appearance that the entrance led into the earth. A water channel bisected this area, carrying water to the long platform altar facing the temple. Wherever visitors walked within the sanctuary, they were standing on carefully buried ritual deposits. Among these were numerous clay pomegranates, ideal gifts for the fruit-bearing goddess, and terracottas of standing women holding torches and piglets. The Malophoros sanctuary is also famous for its many early curse tablets, inscribed on lead. As the Queen of the Underworld, Persephone (or Pasikrateia, the All-ruling, to use her local name) was a particularly appropriate recipient of these missives to the underworld powers.[30]

Persephone at Lokroi Epizephyrioi

The Dorian Greek colonists of Lokroi Epizephyrioi, on the "toe" of Italy, developed a distinctive pantheon with Persephone and Aphrodite as the key deities. Demeter too was worshiped here in a typical Thesmophorion, but Persephone's role and personality overshadowed those of her mother. At the seaward end of the city was the ancient U-shaped stoa, the oldest cult place in Lokroi and the center of Aphrodite's worship. At the other end on the Mannella hillside lay the sanctuary of Persephone, which also dated to the seventh century and the founding of the city. Here excavators uncovered an amazing trove of terracotta plaques or *pinakes* decorated in relief with ritual and mythic scenes. Difficult as they are to interpret, these give us a glimpse into the religious life of the Lokrians in the fifth century, particularly that of the Lokrian women, whose votive gifts (mirrors, perfume jars, dolls) predominate in the excavated deposits.[31] Their Persephone served many of the functions in relation to female maturation, marriage, and childbirth that Artemis and Hera fulfilled for the mainland Greeks. Her union with Hades was a divine exemplar of marriage and it was she who received the pre-wedding sacrifices known as *proteleia*. She was also the protector of young children. But in the background was always the knowledge of Persephone's identity as the Queen of the Dead, and her role in the ultimate fate of the soul as set forth in "Orphic" eschatology. Thus the widespread Greek analogy between marriage and death finds at Lokroi its most complex and highly developed manifestation. The ideology of marriage had its own peculiarities at Lokroi, where social status and ritual privilege seem, uniquely in the Greek world, to have been transferred in matrilineal fashion. The wife, particularly

Figure 6.2 Persephone opens a box containing an infant. Terracotta *pinax* from Lokroi Epizephyrioi, 470–50. Museo Archeologico Nazionale, Reggio Calabria. Scala/Art Resource.

in the role of bride, seems to have held a higher status than in many other Greek cities. Furthermore, the idealized institution of marriage had an eschatological significance: just as marriage was a symbolic death, death was a symbolic marriage and the blessed afterlife state was assimilated to that of marital bliss.[32]

The *pinakes* are the primary source for this picture of marriage as a Lokrian cultural ideal. About the size of a standard sheet of paper, they are pierced for suspension and originally hung in the sanctuary, probably on trees. The main types include scenes of Persephone's abduction by Hades; the abduction of a maiden by a youthful male which is thought to be a generic representation of the bride's "capture" by her groom; wedding libations and processions; women packing and unpacking wedding gifts; Persephone enthroned alone or with Hades, receiving divine visitors and mortal suppliants including children; and various scenes with Aphrodite and Hermes, who governed the sexual aspects of marriage. Fragments of similar *pinakes* have been found at

Medma and Hipponion, towns in the Lokrian orbit, as well as Francavilla in Sicily, though the Lokrian products do not appear to have been widely exported.[33]

Further reading

Cole 1994 provides an excellent, brief review of Demeter's cults, with good use of archaeological evidence. For the Eleusinian Mysteries, Clinton's work is indispensable; Clinton 1992 develops his controversial theories about the relationship between the Thesmophoria and the Homeric *Hymn* to Demeter, and draws together visual as well as literary evidence for the Mysteries. For more on the *Hymn* and the Mysteries, see Foley 1994. Detienne 1989, to be read with Osborne 1993, argues that women's limited role in sacrificial ritual, even in the Thesmophoria, corresponds to their limited political rights. On the Athenian rites of Demeter and Persephone, see Parker 2005, Chapters 13 and 15.

7

GUARDING AND GUIDING
THE CITY

Apollo

One of the most widely worshiped deities in the Greek world, Apollo is nevertheless a relative latecomer to the pantheon. The Mycenaeans probably did not know him, though their healing god Paian, who appears in a Linear B tablet from Knossos, survived as one facet of Apollo's complex character.[1] Early dedications in Apollo's sanctuaries include bronzes of Near Eastern "smiting gods" such as the Semitic Reshep, who shared Apollo's function as a sender of plague, while Apollo's bow may be a borrowing from the Hittite archer-god Irra.[2] In keeping with his Near Eastern associations, and like his sister Artemis, Apollo is a temple deity. While temples and images were not indispensable to his cults, they were characteristic of his worship. Among the sanctuaries described in this chapter, those at Eretria, Dreros, and Thermon are noted for the wealth of information they provide about the origins of the Greek temple and the range of cult practices during the eighth and seventh centuries.

Several etymologies have been proposed for Apollo's name, but it probably derives from the Dorian Greek word for an annual tribal gathering, *apella*. At such gatherings, young men were admitted to membership and received political status as adults; thus the presiding god is almost always depicted as a beardless youth.[3] Patronage of youths approaching manhood was one of Apollo's key functions, but he is best known as the oracular god who interpreted the will of Zeus and gave advice on everything from war and colonization to private dilemmas about marriage and family. Apollo's role as the god of prophetic inspiration was closely tied to other aspects of his character, including his interests in purification, poetry, and music. The only Olympian to possess a musical instrument, the lyre, as an attribute, he regularly appears in poetry with the Muses and other divine choruses. Comparatively few cults focused specifically on Apollo's patronage of poets and musicians, but hymns and music are everywhere essential to his worship.

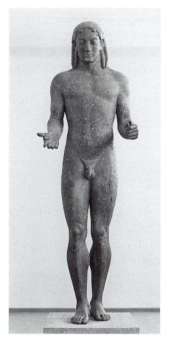

Figure 7.1 Youthful Apollo in bronze. Possibly produced as a cult statue, originally with a bow in the left hand and an offering bowl in the right, *c.* 520. Ht 1.91 m. Peiraieus Museum. Scala/Art Resource.

Widespread cults of Apollo

One of the most widely diffused types of Apolline cult is perhaps the least familiar to readers of Greek poetry: the worship of Apollo as a guardian and an averter of evil. For this role, Apollo was often depicted in aniconic form as a stone pillar on a stepped base. He was known as Apollo Agyieus (of the Street), Thyraios (of the Door), Propylaios (Before the Gate), and Prostaterios (Protector).[4] In Athens, the pillars stood in front of houses, where they were decorated with branches of laurel or myrtle, and received offerings of incense or oil. Belief in the protective powers of sacred stones was widespread throughout the Mediterranean, including the Levant, where Reshep's pillar functioned in similar fashion during the Bronze Age.[5] Apollo Agyieus was also expected to protect travelers, as Aeschylus reveals in the *Agamemnon* (1081, 1086) when he makes Kassandra bitterly reproach this god for leading her into danger. Sometimes the worship of Apollo focused on protection from very specific ills, as in the cult of Apollo Smintheus (of Mice), which thrived as early as Homer's time near Troy and in the neighboring parts of Asia Minor settled by Aiolian Greeks. Smintheus protected the harvest against incursions of mice, but he also appears as the bringer of plague in the *Iliad* (1.37–42) and like his Near Eastern counterparts, he could avert plague. Similarly, a sacred law from Kyrene in North Africa directs that if disease should come against the city, the inhabitants are to "sacrifice in front of the gates before the shrine of aversion a red he-goat to Apollo Apotropaios [the Averter]."[6]

Semitic Reshep and Hittite Irra were weapon-bearing gods whose anger could be channeled against enemies, just as Chryses called down Apollo's plague on the Greek invaders in the *Iliad*. Apollo Lykeios (of Wolves) was similarly invoked against enemies, particularly in military contexts. One of his ancient cults was that at Argos, where he was the most important god next to Hera, and his temple held the sacred fire of the city. In both Argos and Athens, he presided over the mustering of hoplite warriors who would defend the city with the ferocity of the wolf. Athenian hoplites in the fifth century paid a tax for the upkeep of the sanctuary of Apollo Lykeios, which also served as their training ground. In its earliest stages, the cult probably had to do with the need to ward off marauding wolves from the flocks.[7]

Another widespread and early cult, common to many Dorian and Ionian cities, is that of Apollo Delphinios. The Greeks believed that his name came from their word for dolphin (*delphis*), but the real etymology is unknown, and is most likely non-Greek. Both ancients and moderns have understood this god as a protector of seafarers, and have speculated that his cult is related to that at Delphi (the pun-loving author of the Homeric *Hymn* to Apollo has the god appear in dolphin form and demand that the first priests of Delphi erect an altar to him under this name). More recent scholarship has noted the important role of Apollo Delphinios in civic life, particularly with regard to inter-city relations. Official documents including treaties were stored in his temples, and he was associated with the ephebes, or youths who would soon become citizens. At Miletos, where Apollo Delphinios was the patron of the city, the annual procession to the oracular shrine at Didyma started from the Delphinion. When excavated, this sanctuary was found to contain hundreds of inscriptions recording citizenship decrees, treaties, a cult calendar, and other matters of interest to the state.[8]

Two early temples of Apollo

In the 1930s, men digging a field in eastern Krete made a stunning discovery: the undisturbed remains of a very early temple. Along the back wall, the excavators found a stone box filled with bones and goats' horns, which reminded them of the Keraton or horn altar at Delos (below). Upon this boxlike altar stood three figures made of bronze sheets hammered over a wood core. The largest, just under a meter tall, is a nude figure of Apollo, while the two clothed female figures, about half the size of the Apollo, must be Artemis and Leto. (Apollo's sister and mother are regularly worshiped with him, and this group is known as the Apolline triad.) These Late Geometric figures, contemporary with the temple, are unique examples of early Greek cult images. The back wall also supported a bench that held pots, a lamp, and terracotta figurines. A bronze gorgon mask hung on the wall or was propped on the bench. The temple continued in use for centuries, safeguarding its heirloom contents, before it was abruptly abandoned in the Hellenistic period. Epigraphic evidence shows that the city of Dreros had an important cult of Apollo Delphinios, probably to be assigned to this sanctuary.[9]

The tribes of Aitolia in northwest Greece worshiped Artemis and Apollo above all the other gods. They met at the rural sanctuary of Thermon, another truly venerable cult site where excavators have uncovered what may be the earliest Apollo temple on the Greek mainland. It did not appear, as we might expect, on the future site of a large and prosperous polis. Instead, Aitolia lacked a centralized government and was considered a cultural backwater during the Classical period. Yet in the late Bronze Age, it had been part of the Mycenaean civilization, and it escaped the violent upheavals of the centuries after the Mycenaean collapse. A mysterious building called Megaron B, dating to well before 800, served as a center for ritual feasts and perhaps as a temple. Among the earliest votive objects is a Syro-Hittite "smiting god" statuette of the eighth century. The seventh-century Thermon temple, constructed atop Megaron B, had walls of mudbrick, while its columns and

Figure 7.2 Bronze cult statues from Dreros, Krete: Apollo, Artemis, and Leto, eighth century. Ht of Apollo 0.8 m. Heraklion Museum. Photo used by permission.

entablature were wood. The roof was decorated with gorgon masks. The surviving terracotta metopes, rare examples of early Greek painting, show that the temple was Doric in style. They depict the myth of the Nightingale and Swallow (Prokne and Philomela) and the Apolline triad of Apollo, Leto, and Artemis (who had her own temple here), as well as more gorgons, whose traditional function as architectural ornaments was to repel enemies.[10]

Dorian Apollo

For the Dorian Greeks of the Peloponnese and their overseas cousins, the late summer festival of Apollo Karneios (of the Ram) was the most important of the year. They took seriously the prohibition on combat during the Karneia, which was the reason why the Spartans missed the battle of Marathon and sent only a token force to Thermopylai. The festivities involved dances by the young men and women of the community; at Sparta the Karneia grew into a major musical competition. A group of unmarried men known as the Karneatai were chosen by lot to organize and bear the expenses of the festival. They also entered a footrace as *staphulodromoi,* "grape runners," and carried fruited vine branches while pursuing a runner decked with wool fillets like a sacrificial victim. If they caught him, it meant good luck for the city in

Figure 7.3 Painted metopes and roof ornaments from the temple of Apollo at Thermon, Aitolia, *c.* 625. Athens, National Archaeological Museum. Bildarchiv Foto Marburg.

the coming year. In spite of the injunction against warfare during the festival, it celebrated the warlike nature of the Dorians, and their legendary conquest of the Peloponnese, as well as historical colonization efforts. At Sparta, the warriors set up tents and banqueted in honor of the god as if on campaign, and at Kyrene they conducted a dance in armor. The myths surrounding the Spartan festival attributed its origins to the pre-Greek inhabitants. Sometime in the Geometric period, scholars have suggested, Apollo supplanted a pastoral, ram-headed god Karnos, whether of Dorian or indigenous origin, who presided over the seasonal movements of the flocks and led them to new pastures. The journey of the flocks was eventually identified with the mythic Dorian migration and the festival took on a more military character in keeping with the theme of conquest.[11]

A more clear-cut case of a prehellenic deity whose cult was absorbed by Apollo is Hyakinthos. The -nthos termination of his name is also found in the Luwian language of Anatolia, and reveals a non-Greek origin. He is sometimes thought to be Minoan. The month and festival named after Hyakinthos are common in Dorian cities, but most of our evidence comes from the cult at Amyklai outside Sparta. Here, Hyakinthos was remembered as a hero beloved of Apollo, whom the god accidentally killed with a discus throw. His tomb was located within the base of Apollo's ancient cult statue, a colossal bronze figure that stood in the open air. It drew on Near Eastern iconography, showing Apollo as a helmeted warrior with a bow in one hand and a spear in the other. This image, created in the late seventh or early sixth century, was unusual for several reasons. It did not possess a fully human shape, but took the form of a huge bronze pillar with sculpted face, feet, and hands. Colossal statues like the Athena Parthenos made by Pheidias were celebrated in the Classical period, but most Archaic cult images were considerably smaller than life-size. The size of the Apollo, estimated by Pausanias at 30 cubits (15 m), explains why there was no temple to house it, for buildings of such height were beyond the technology of the day. Instead of a temple, the image was displayed in an elaborately decorated enclosure known as the "throne," which was added about a century after the statue was erected.[12]

The festival itself combined the worship of Apollo Amyklaios and Hyakinthos. The first day was a day of mourning and solemnity, when the blood of sacrificial animals was poured into Hyakinthos' tomb through a bronze door in the side of the statue base, which also functioned as an altar. The rest of the festival, in contrast, was a joyous celebration. The whole city joined the procession from Sparta to Amyklai, where there were spectacles of music, dance, and horse racing in which both boys and girls took part. Even the slaves joined in the celebrations. Every year, the women of Sparta presented Apollo with a newly woven tunic or *chitōn* (probably not one large enough for the statue to wear). The high point of the festival was the singing of the *paian*, the special hymn for Apollo.

Apollo Amyklaios has drawn attention from scholars because his name appears on a bilingual inscription from Idalion in Cyprus, where he was equated with Reshep Mukal. The epithet Mukal, transformed to (A)myklos, was carried at an early date to Gortyn in Krete, and thence to Sparta, supplying a name for both the cult and the town. It illustrates how Cyprus and Krete were conduits for cultural influences from the Near East during the formative period of Greek religion. Excavation of Amyklai revealed evidence for nearly continuous activity from the late Bronze Age, another unusual feature of the site. After serving as a sub-Mycenaean cult place, the sanctuary began to receive dedications again in the ninth century, perhaps the date of Apollo's introduction.[13]

Ionian Apollo

The small Cycladic island of Delos was a religious center for the Ionians, including the Athenians and many Greeks who emigrated during the Dark Age to the coast of Asia Minor. Delos was celebrated as the birthplace of Apollo and Artemis, and while Artemis was probably the original mistress of the sanctuary there, Apollo came to dominate it in the Archaic period. The Homeric *Hymn* to Apollo (3.145–61) tells how the festival was celebrated with "boxing, dancing and song" and describes the Delian maidens who were famed for their choral songs in honor of the god. The Athenians, who controlled the sanctuary for much of its life, twice purified the tiny island by removing burials (except for those of the heroes) and decreeing that all inhabitants must leave if they were soon to give birth or die. An elaborate web of myth and ritual connected Delos with Athens and its hero Theseus. The Athenians believed that Theseus visited Delos after slaying the Kretan Minotaur, and with his companions performed a winding dance called the Crane, which imitated the tortuous paths of the Labyrinth. They danced around the famous Keraton, an altar constructed from the horns of goats, Apollo's favored sacrificial animal.[14]

Apollo, Artemis, and Leto all possessed temples on the island. In Apollo's Archaic temple stood a famous cult image, the work of the sixth-century sculptors Tektaios and Angelion. About twice life-size and covered with hammered sheets of gold, the god appeared in the frontal pose of a *kouros*, holding a bow in his left hand and small images of the three Charites in his right.[15] Another feature of the Delian cult was the legend that the Hyperboreans, a mythical northern people whom Apollo visited every year, sent annual offerings of "sacred things" wrapped in wheat sheaves to his shrine. The mysterious offerings themselves seem to have some historical basis; in the Classical period they were conveyed by a long trade route until they reached Athens, where they were ceremoniously escorted to Delos. A Mycenaean tomb on the island was venerated as the gravesite of two Hyperborean maidens.[16]

The Athenians boasted of their descent from Ion, the son of Apollo and ancestor of the Ionian peoples; therefore they worshiped Apollo Patroös (Ancestor). The possession of domestic cults of Apollo Patroös and Zeus Herkeios became one of the criteria for holding office in Athens.[17] Because of their ancient kinship, the Athenians and the Ionians of Asia Minor had similar ritual calendars, and many of their common cults and festivals can be dated to the time before the Ionian migration. One of the shared Ionian–Attic festivals was the Thargelia, held at the onset of harvest time in May. The festival took place on the sixth and seventh of the month Thargelion, the birthdates of Artemis and Apollo respectively. At this time the Athenians sent sacred ambassadors (*theōroi*) to Delos with sacrificial victims and choruses for the musical competitions. Athens had to be kept pure, so executions of criminals were postponed until the return of the ship from Delos (such a delay occurred when Sokrates was to be executed). They also purified the land of Attica through a ritual involving human scapegoats known as *pharmakoi*. Two men, chosen for their ugliness and poverty, were feasted at public expense, then beaten with fig branches and driven out of the city. They symbolically carried away all the ills and impurities that might result in harm to the city or its ripening crops. On the second day of the Athenian Thargelia, the city celebrated with a cereal offering to Apollo, a mixture of produce cooked and carried in procession to the suburban shrine of Apollo Pythios. The festival was also noted for extensive dithyrambic (choral) competitions, and victors dedicated tripods at the Pythion.[18]

Pythian Apollo

Perched on a rocky slope of Mt. Parnassos, Delphi has a stunning view and a "numinous quality" noted by every visitor.[19] A thriving Mycenaean village and cult area were abandoned at the end of the Bronze Age, but in the mid-ninth century, people returned to this lovely spot and resettled it. Fifty years later, Delphi had already become a regional gathering place for the worship of Apollo. Fueled by the popularity of the oracle, its fame grew until it became the premier sanctuary of Apollo in the Greek world, exerting a unique influence on Greek colonization and interstate relations. Its only rival in this respect was the Panhellenic sanctuary of Zeus at Olympia.[20] During the Archaic period, a mythic pedigree for Apollo's sanctuary was established in order to cement its claim to be the most important Greek oracle. Before Apollo's arrival, it was said, the oracle belonged to Gaia (e.g. Aesch. *Eum.* 1–8). Although Gaia did have old oracles like the one at Olympia, the lack of archaeological or literary evidence for Gaia's presence at Delphi before the fifth century makes it difficult to accept the historicity of this tradition.[21]

What drew so many visitors to Delphi was the chance to consult Apollo, god of divination and prophecy. In myth, Apollo often predicted future events, such as Oedipus' murder of his father. In reality, he more often advised petitioners on the best course of action for addressing their problems, specializing in ritual solutions that invoked the aid of the gods. If a town suffered from a plague or crop failure, perhaps the citizens had neglected to make the proper sacrifices or purifications. If land shortages resulted in civic discord, or if new trade connections were required, Apollo might recommend that colonists settle in likely areas overseas. The oracle could be consulted on virtually any major enterprise contemplated by a city, from legal reform to military conquest. The congregation of delegates from many cities also ensured that Delphi remained a valuable resource for intelligence-gathering and diplomatic exchange. The political importance of Delphi meant that it must not be under the control of any one state. After a series of wars, the sanctuary was overseen by a federation of states known as the Delphic Amphictyony. By the Classical period, however, the oracle was consulted primarily on matters involving religious practice and procedure. Purification was an important Apolline specialty, although there is surprisingly little evidence for purification rituals (for example, the cleansing of blood-guilt) performed at Delphi itself.[22]

At the center of all this activity was the Pythia, the priestess who acted as the medium for the voice of Apollo. Consultation with the Pythia was limited to one day per month during the nine-month season when Apollo was believed to be "in residence," and this helps to explain why consultations in the early centuries of the oracle were dominated by important matters of state, rather than by individual concerns as at Dodona. Before an oracular session, the Pythia purified herself, probably with water from the Kastalian spring. She entered the inner room of the temple and sat on a covered tripod cauldron, clutching a branch of laurel. There she received the questions of the petitioners and answered them. Many reconstructions of the oracle have described the process as one of violent possession, in which the Pythia raved incoherently while priests translated her answers into verse oracles. None of the early sources presents the Pythia as frenzied or hysterical, and she is always described as responding directly to the petitioners in intelligible speech, though sometimes her answers were ambiguous and riddling.[23]

Certainly the Pythia experienced a form of religious ecstasy, and its cause has been the subject of much speculation through the centuries. According to various theories, she owed her inspiration to a drink from the spring Kassotis, to laurel leaves she chewed while seated on the tripod, to a mediumistic trance that required no artificial stimulant, or to intoxicating vapors rising from a chasm in the earth. This last possibility, taken seriously by Plutarch (Mor. 432d–438d) but scoffed at by modern scholars, was revived when geologists newly evaluated the site of Delphi in the 1990s. They concluded that ethylene, a sweet-smelling, mildly intoxicating gas present in the limestone beneath the temple, could have contributed to the Pythia's trance.[24]

The Homeric Hymn to Apollo (3.300–76) gives the foundation legend for the sanctuary, telling how the god battled a huge serpent (later known as the Python) for possession of the site and supervised the building of the first temple, which archaeologists date to the late seventh century. At the Pythian festival, held every four years, one of the most important contests was the Pythian nome, in which musicians presented their interpretations of Apollo's combat with the serpent.[25] The Pythian games originally focused upon artistic contests of lyre-playing and singing to the flute, though athletic events soon began to gain in popularity as the festival was modeled more closely on the Olympic games. The serpent combat was also considered the basis for another important Delphic festival, the Septerion. Every eight years, the Delphians enacted a ritual drama that incorporated elements of the combat myth and linked Delphi with the valley of Tempe in Thessaly. According to the Delphic myth, Apollo was purified in Tempe after killing the serpent, and returned in triumph with the laurel for his sanctuary. In ritual, a boy played Apollo's role and traveled to and from Tempe in a sacred procession, bringing laurel boughs to make crowns for the Pythian victors.[26]

Because of Apollo's sponsorship of colonization efforts and his importance for civic decision-making, the cult of Apollo Pythios/Pythaeus became widespread throughout the Greek world; he often bears the titles Archegetes (Leader/Founder) and Ktistes (Establisher), which were also given to colony founders. The Spartans believed that Apollo played an instrumental role in creating their constitution. In their marketplace they had statues of Pythian Apollo, Artemis, and Leto, and the kings appointed a board of Pythioi who were responsible for state consultations of the oracle. In Athens, the Pythion was the oldest cult center of the god. At Argos, where an important sanctuary of Apollo Pythaeus was located on the Deiras ridge between the two citadels, the cult seems to have been appropriated from Asine, which the Argives destroyed at the end of the eighth century.[27]

Other Apolline oracles

Apollo had other oracles on the Greek mainland, yet the majority of Apollo shrines there were not oracular, or their oracles faded because they could not sustain competition with Delphi. One district with a strong independent oracular tradition was Boiotia, where the sanctuary of Apollo Ptoios thrived in spite of its relative proximity to Delphi. The hero Ptoios, named for the triple-peaked Mt. Ptoion, may have preceded Apollo as the resident deity of the sanctuary. Its most prosperous period began in the late seventh century, when *kouroi* became fashionable dedications. Typical Archaic gifts to the gods, these stiffly frontal, sculpted nude youths made especially appropriate votives for Apollo, himself a divine *kouros* (youth). About a hundred *kouroi* were dedicated during the seventh and sixth centuries and discovered in the excavation of the site, providing a treasure trove for the study of Archaic sculpture.[28] The sanctuary attracted attention outside Boiotia, particularly from the neighboring Athenians. Visitors included Hipparchos, son of the Athenian tyrant Peisistratos, who left an inscribed dedication. Herodotus

(8.135) gives our only account of the oracular procedure in his story of a barbarian named Mys who consulted the oracle during the Persian wars. As soon as Mys entered the shrine, the male prophet shocked the Greeks present by uttering words they could not understand. But Mys declared that the oracle was responding in his own language, Karian, and left satisfied.

Other mainland Apollo oracles included the Ismenion of Thebes and the sanctuary at Abai in Phokis, while at the Argive shrine of Apollo Pythaeus, a female prophet gave oracles after tasting the blood of a sacrificed ewe.[29] Yet these sanctuaries were exceptional. In the Greek colonies of Asia Minor, the situation was reversed. The entire Aegean coast was dotted with oracular Apollo shrines. The East Greeks had rich Apolline traditions influenced by their non-Greek neighbors, and were distant enough from Delphi to require their own oracle centers. The most famous was Didyma, but it never achieved the prominence of Delphi in Greek affairs because its interests were too closely aligned with nearby Miletos, a powerful Ionian city. In the Archaic period, Didyma was run by a family of prophets, the Branchidai, who traced their ancestry to the beautiful herdsman Branchos. Once, Apollo spotted Branchos with his flocks and immediately fell in love with him. The god kissed Branchos and bestowed on him a crown, a laurel rod, and the power of prophecy, which he passed down to his descendants. The story explains one of Apollo's cult titles at Didyma, Philesios (Loving). When Apollo became angry with the Milesians and sent a plague, Branchos saved the people by striking or sprinkling them with the purifying laurel branch.[30]

Didyma and Miletos remained close partners throughout the history of the sanctuary. The patron god of Miletos was Apollo Delphinios, and his priests, the Molpoi (Singers), began every year with a grand procession, which traveled from the Delphinion along the Sacred Way to Didyma. The sanctuary itself can be traced archaeologically to the eighth century, when the sacred spring used to induce the prophetic trance was enclosed. Around 600 a portico was added to shelter visitors and display the increasing number of offerings. These included the Pharaoh Necho's gift of a royal garment, worn at his victory over Josiah, King of Judah, in the battle of Megiddo (609). Didyma also received treasures from the rich Lydian king Kroisos, who sent gifts to a number of Greek oracles. In the sixth century, a huge temple was constructed in the tradition of the colossal Ionic temples of Hera at Samos and Artemis at Ephesos. Differing from temples in mainland Greece, it was designed as an unroofed courtyard enclosing a grove of laurels and the sacred spring. At one end a small roofed shrine (*naiskos*) was provided to house the cult statue of Apollo Didymeus, commissioned from the sculptor Kanachos. He created a roughly life-sized, cast bronze figure of the nude god in a standing, frontal pose with one leg forward. In the left hand was a bow; in the outstretched right palm, the god held a stag. With respect to ritual practice, osteological analysis of the finds from Didyma has revealed that the sacrificial procedure was nonstandard: thigh bones of cattle were not burned on the altar, but were deposited unburned and whole in special places. The accumulation of these bones, like the "horn altars" of other sanctuaries, must have formed an impressive visual record of the gifts allotted to the gods in the sanctuary.[31]

The Milesians and their neighbors consulted the oracle for much the same reasons as other Greeks consulted Delphi. Didyma, or Branchidai as it is often called, played an important role in Miletos' vigorous colonization program. A few sixth-century consultations are recorded in inscriptions: one petitioner asked for advice on whether to engage in piracy and was told to follow the practices of his ancestors, while another query dealt with whether women should be permitted in the sanctuary of Herakles. A recently discovered Archaic inscription from Olbia, found on a bone tablet, preserves an enigmatic text linking the colony's fate with multiples of Apollo's sacred number, seven, and different aspects of the god:

> 7: Wolf without strength. 77: Terrible lion. 777: Bowbearer, friendly with his gift, with the power of a healer. 7777: Wise dolphin. Peace to the Blessed City (Olbia). I pronounce her to be happy. I bear remembrance to Leto.

A second inscription on the same tablet mentions Apollo of Didyma, and the tablet has therefore been interpreted as a record of an oracular response. It is also possible that the tablet represents a hitherto unattested Apolline cult with Orphic or Pythagorean connections.[32]

The highly prosperous operations of Didyma came to an abrupt end in 494, when Darius captured Miletos. The sanctuary was pillaged and burned, and the Branchidai were deported according to the usual Persian policy of resettling war captives far from home. After about a hundred and fifty years of silence, the oracle was revived under state-appointed priests to welcome Alexander the Great when he took the city. Alexander is said to have discovered the descendants of the Branchidai when he arrived in Bactria, but instead of restoring them to their ancient role, he cruelly slaughtered them.[33]

Apollo Daphnephoros and Ismenios

Many gods possessed sacred groves, but they are especially characteristic of Apollo, whose major shrines were often located outside the cities. At Kourion, his most important sanctuary in Cyprus, he was known as Hylates (He of the Grove).[34] Apollo's special tree was the laurel or bay (*daphnē*), and he was worshiped particularly in central Greece as Apollo Daphnephoros (the Laurel-Carrier). The laurel had a purifying effect because of its sweet aromatic leaves, and in Euripides' *Ion* (102–6) we hear how the title character, an orphan raised at Delphi, sweeps the temple entrance with laurels and hangs up garlands every morning. Processions of laurel-carriers may have served a similar purpose of purification long before the advent of Apollo in Greece. We are best informed about the celebration of the Daphnephoria at Thebes, the leading city of Boiotia. In his discussion of ancient hymns, Proclus says that it involved a procession led by a boy with both parents living. His nearest male relative carried an olive log adorned with laurel branches, small bronze globes, and purple fillets. A man or boy designated as the *daphnēphoros* and a chorus of girls carrying branches followed this group. Such festivals of "bringing in the tree" to symbolize prosperity are found in connection with other deities including Hera and Dionysos; the ritual, not the god, is primary.[35]

A sanctuary of Apollo Daphnephoros has been discovered in Eretria, where a very early, apsidal *hekatompedon* was constructed about 740. (The cultic function of an even older building, which may have been a chieftain's house, is disputed.) In addition to its early date, the Eretria temple is noted for the find of a bronze horse's blinker, inscribed in Aramaic to a ninth-century Syrian ruler. This was part of an heirloom set of horse trappings, dedicated piecemeal by some ancient traveler, and it is the earliest example of a West Semitic script to appear in Greece so far. Even more amazing, a forehead piece from this set, with the same inscription, has been found in the Heraion on Samos. Other finds at the sanctuary, including gold ornaments, bronzes, faience amulets, scarabs, and amber beads, further illustrate the wide trading contacts of the Geometric Eretrians and the prominence of Apollo Daphnephoros in their city.[36]

One of the most important gods of Thebes was Apollo Ismenios, named for the Ismenos river running through the city. Visitors to his temple were impressed by the numerous dedications of tripods, including one of gold dedicated by Kroisos of Lydia. Others were reputed to date to the heroic age. Writing in the fifth century, Herodotus (5.59–61) attributed some of the tripods he saw to the time of King Oedipus. He says they were inscribed with "Kadmean letters," a reference to the Phoenician immigrant Kadmos who settled in Thebes, bringing with him the alphabet. The tripods were probably early gifts to the sanctuary, which was founded at the end of the eighth century. Other tripods were dedicated by youths after they served as *daphnēphoroi*. Apollo's oracles here were delivered through omens, as priests observed sacrificial animals burning in the flames on the altar. A number of subsidiary heroes and heroines were venerated at the Ismenion, including Teneros, the first seer at the shrine.[37]

Apollo Maleatas

The site of Apollo Maleatas' sanctuary on Mt. Kynortion (Dog's Climb) at Epidauros is noted for its Bronze Age remains, which include an altar, auxiliary buildings, and a terrace where ritual meals were consumed. Though continuity with the Bronze Age cannot be demonstrated, medical instruments contained in the altar here show that the subsequent Geometric cult was addressed to Apollo (at least in part) as a healer.[38] Apollo's healing function is a legacy from the deity Paian, who is attested in Mycenaean Greek and in Homer (e.g. *Il.* 5.401, 899–900). In later Greek, *paian* was a song, and Archaic medicine frequently made use of healing charms sung over the sick person. Apollo's power to control plagues and his status as an authority on purification also contributed to his healing abilities. Yet in the Classical period, Apollo ceded the role of healer to his son Asklepios, whose cult rapidly grew in popularity. At Epidauros, Apollo's sanctuary spread to the plain, where it was eventually taken over by Asklepios. Pilgrims to the shrine, hoping to be healed, still sacrificed first to Apollo before entering. The votive inscriptions they set up to describe their miraculous cures are addressed to both Apollo and Asklepios as saviors. In the fourth century, a *paian* composed by Isyllos was inscribed on a block near Asklepios' temple. It describes how a sacred procession of Epidauros' "best men" carry garlands of laurel to Apollo's temple, and shoots of olive to Asklepios.[39] Neither the Asklepios precinct nor Apollo's shrine on Mt. Kynortion possessed a monumental temple until the fourth century. Scholars disagree on whether Maleatas was initially the name of a separate deity, but inscriptions show that the cult was fairly widespread in the Archaic Peloponnese.

Apollo Epikourios at Bassai

During his journey around Greece, Pausanias (8.41.8) was struck by the beauty of the temple of Apollo at Bassai, a remote site in the highlands of Arkadia. Here, Apollo and his sister Artemis were provided with twin temples in the seventh century. An Archaic temple of Aphrodite stood on the summit of Mt. Kotilion in the same precinct. Pan was worshiped here too, and like the more famous Arkadian peak of Lykaion, all of Mt. Kotilion seems to have been considered sacred space.[40] Many Arkadians who served as professional mercenaries (*epikouroi*) made offerings of miniature armor and weapons for Apollo, who had the dual titles of Bassitas and Epikourios (of Allies): helmets, shields, corselets, and spear-heads. In the fifth century, they raised the money for a magnificent new temple to be built by Iktinos, the architect of the Parthenon. Iktinos' temple, still standing today, is Doric on the outside with an interior Ionic colonnade and a sculpted frieze depicting Centaurs fighting Lapiths and Greeks fighting Amazons. It conservatively retained some of the features of its predecessor, such as its extra length and north–south orientation. A single column with a very early Korinthian capital was placed at the focal point of the cella where one would expect the cult statue to stand. This column may have had cultic significance, since we know that Apollo was sometimes worshiped in the form of a pillar. But the temple also possessed an *aduton*, or inner room, which was separated from the cella only by this column. An entrance created in the east side of the structure allowed the morning sun to enter the *aduton* (most temples are oriented east–west, and receive the sun through the main entrance). The *aduton* may have held the larger than life-size bronze statue of Apollo Epikourios that was created for the temple, but later moved to Megalopolis.[41]

Further reading

Dietrich 1996, a chapter in a longer work about Kourion on Cyprus, contains an important general discussion of Apolline cults. Malkin 1994 includes an illuminating chapter on Apollo Karneios. On Apollo's oracles, Parke and Wormell 1956 (Delphi) and Fontenrose 1988b (Didyma) are essential works. Solomon 1994 gathers several useful articles, including Burkert's paper on the Archaic "oracle" inscription from Olbia (to be read with Onyshkevych 2002).

8

THE TENDER AND
THE SAVAGE

Artemis

Artemis' cults are numerous and more widespread than those of any other
Greek goddess, extending from Massilia (modern Marseilles) to the Greek
colonies of Sicily, to mainland Greece, north Africa, and Ephesos on the coast
of Asia Minor. She is a paradoxical goddess: a virgin who aids women in
childbirth, a fierce huntress who fosters wild beasts, and a bloodthirsty deity
who both nurtures the young and demands their sacrifice. Standing at the
borders, both conceptual and physical, between savage and civilized life,
Artemis oversees the transition of girls to adult status, but is also a patron of
warriors. The young, regarded as untamed and akin to the unruly natural
world, are her special concern. Archaic and Classical Artemis is a composite
figure with close ties to the Near East, like her brother Apollo, whose cults
are regularly juxtaposed with hers. Among her antecedents we recognize the
powerful mother goddesses of Asia Minor, a number of local Greek goddesses
who presided over rites of passage, and the ancient figure known to students
of iconography as the Mistress of Animals. Of unknown etymology, her
name was sometimes associated with the Greek verb *artameō*, which means
"to butcher, cut to pieces." She is perhaps included among the deities of
Mycenaean Pylos, but there is disagreement on this point.[1]

The Mistress of Animals

The Artemis of cult bears only a partial resemblance to the Homeric goddess,
an adolescent girl who delights in the hunt and is celebrated as the divine
prototype of the virginal maiden, ripe for marriage. Still, hints of Artemis'
cruelty and power appear in the Homeric portrait. Hera (*Il.* 21.483) calls her
"a lion to women," pointing out that she brings death to any woman she
wishes, though her power is dependent on the will of Zeus. Homer (*Il.*
21.470–71) also gives Artemis the titles Agrotera (of the Wilds) and Potnia
Theron (Mistress of Animals). Because Artemis is a goddess of game animals
and takes special delight in "the suckling young of every wild creature"
(Aesch. *Ag.* 140–43), she has been compared to certain deities of hunter-
gatherer cultures around the world, whose function is to protect and regulate

101

the supply of game. Wild animals, particularly deer, were considered sacred to Artemis, and her sanctuaries sometimes possessed sacred and inviolate herds, as at Lousoi in Arkadia.[2]

A Mistress of Animals is familiar in the shared iconography of Bronze Age cultures in the Aegean; she stands flanked by paired animals or birds, which she grasps firmly by their necks or tails. This motif occasionally appears in representations of other Greek goddesses, but is found most often among Archaic votive gifts to Artemis. In societies where hunting is reduced in the main to an aristocratic pastime, the powerful deities of the hunt are not forgotten but modified; Artemis' interest in the death-dealing potential of the hunter is transferred to the warrior.[3] The widespread cult of Artemis Agrotera, found all over mainland Greece and beyond, focused often on victory in battle. According to Xenophon (*Hell.* 4.2.20), at the crucial point when the enemy was within sight, the Spartans slaughtered a goat for Artemis Agrotera, "as was their custom," and charged. Athenian sacrifices to Artemis Agrotera were conducted by the *polemarchos*, a military official, and made in conjunction with those to the war god Enyalios. In thanks for their victory at Marathon in 490, the Athenians annually organized a large procession to Agrai outside the city, a pleasant spot where the young Artemis was supposed to have hunted for the first time. Dressed in their armor, the ephebes escorted five hundred female goats to be sacrificed at Artemis' small Classical temple on the Ilissos river. The battles of Artemision and Salamis were also commemorated with festivals for Artemis, whose saving power was felt in times of dire peril.[4]

Artemis' identity as mistress of wild nature is expressed through the placement of sanctuaries (often in rural areas, especially near rivers or wetlands) and through epithets and unusual sacrificial practices. In Samos, she was known as Kaprophagos (Boar Eater), presumably because wild boars were offered to her. The wild boar also appears as a sacred animal in the legends of Kalydon in Aitolia, where the angry goddess once sent a huge boar to ravage the countryside. The Laphrion or sanctuary of Artemis Laphria in Kalydon was the most important in the district, next to Apollo's sanctuary at Thermon. It was established in the Geometric period, while the first temple of Artemis appeared at the end of the seventh century and was rebuilt several times. In the fifth century (*c.* 460) the Kalydonians added a gold and ivory statue of Artemis in huntress garb with one breast exposed, sculpted by Menichmos and Soidas of Naupaktos. A second temple at the site was devoted to Apollo Laphrios, just as the Thermon sanctuary of Apollo in Aitolia included a temple of Artemis. The remains at the site show that the sacrificial animals here included boars, deer, and horses. Pausanias' description (7.18.8–13) of the later cult at nearby Patrai, where Augustus transferred it after destroying Kalydon, may give us some idea of earlier practices, though we cannot be certain that there was continuity. Each spring the people of Patrai held a grand procession to the altar, and last of all came the priestess of Artemis in a

Figure 8.1 Artemis from the east frieze of the Parthenon. Erich Lessing/Art Resource.

chariot drawn by yoked deer. Creatures of all sorts, including deer, game birds, bear cubs, and domesticated animals, were driven into a large enclosure around the altar. A bonfire of logs within was kindled and the fire consumed the animals alive. The offerings also included fruit from the local orchards, which suggests that the animals too were considered "first fruits" for the goddess. This ritual has been compared to the spring fire festivals of other Indo-European cultures, including the Celtic practice of burning live animals and people in wicker enclosures.[5]

The themes of salvation in wartime and mastery over the animal world are again united with a fire festival in the Phokian cult of Artemis Elaphebolos (Shooter of Stags). The people of Phokis in central Greece long remembered a sixth-century conflict with their neighbors to the north, the Thessalians. They told how on the eve of the most desperate battle, the men of Phokis constructed a huge pyre and placed on it all their valuable possessions and the images of the gods. If the battle was lost, the men guarding the pyre were to kill the Phokian women and children, place them on the pyre, light it, and then commit suicide. When the Phokians instead won the battle, they commemorated the victory during the important festival called the Elaphebolia at the sanctuary of Artemis and Apollo near Hyampolis. This site (modern Kalapodi) held symbolic and strategic importance because it guarded the entrance into Phokis. In all likelihood the festival, and certainly the sanctuary, were far older than the war with the Thessalians. Recent excavations have revealed that Kalapodi is one of the extremely rare cases in which continuity of worship can (arguably) be demonstrated from late Mycenaean times to the Geometric period. While this does not prove that Artemis was a goddess of the sanctuary in the Bronze Age, the remains of sacrificial deer from the Mycenaean levels are consistent with her title of Elaphebolos.

In the ninth century the sanctuary was reorganized and two small temples (presumably for Artemis and Apollo) were constructed, one over the previous Mycenaean installation. These were followed by a succession of later temples, in the early phases characterized by interior hearths for cooking sacrificial animals (now the more conventional goats and sheep). About 560, major renovations were undertaken and the character of the offerings changed, with a new preponderance of weapons and armor. These developments are consistent with local memories of the war with Thessaly and the development of the sanctuary as a regional place of worship and a key factor in Phokian self-definition.[6]

The bloodthirsty goddess: Artemis Tauropolos and Ortheia

Like Dionysos, Artemis embodies much that stands in opposition to Greek cultural ideals: she is an untamed, powerful female, a deity of the wilds more than of the city, and her personality includes a savage element which must be suppressed in the making of a civilized society. Both deities are so challenging to cultural norms that they are sometimes presented as "foreigners," gods who have arrived from strange and savage lands. This was the case in a number of cities, including Athens and Sparta, which attributed the founding of their Artemis cults to Orestes and his sister Iphigeneia.[7]

Attic myths about Artemis tell of an angry goddess who must be appeased. At Aulis in nearby Boiotia, Agamemnon is said to have outraged Artemis by killing a sacred stag, causing her to demand the sacrifice of his daughter Iphigeneia. In some versions of the story, Iphigeneia perished at the altar, but in others she was saved by Artemis and made immortal, or spirited away to a distant land. Herodotus (4.103) tells of the barbarian Tauroi on the shores of the Black Sea, who sacrifice strangers to a goddess they call Iphigeneia or Parthenos (the Maiden). His account may have inspired Euripides' *Iphigeneia in Tauris*, in which Orestes discovers his sister serving as priestess of Artemis in the land of the Tauroi. Obeying an oracle, they escape the barbarians and bring the barbarian statue of Artemis Tauropolos (Bull Tender) to Attica, where it is installed in a temple at Halai Araphenides. There a strange rite of bloodletting takes place: a sword is held to a man's throat in order to draw a small amount of blood, "so that the goddess may have her proper honors" (Eur. *IT* 1459–61). This practice may have been an attenuated form of human sacrifice, though there is no additional evidence for this. What it does demonstrate is the uncanny and savage aspect of the goddess and the *belief* that she desired such sacrifices. While it is unclear whether the Greeks ever actually practiced human sacrifice, the concept was deeply embedded in their culture. Instead of recognizing their own fascination with the topic, they disavowed it by giving the practice, and even the goddess herself, a barbarian origin.[8]

At Sparta, a bloody ritual was again linked to the putative origin of the goddess' image in the land of the Tauroi. Spartan boys underwent a series of trials designed to toughen them and to produce ideal warriors worthy of inclusion among the ranks of citizens; one of these tests took place at the altar of Artemis Ortheia. According to our earliest source, Xenophon (*Lac.* 2.9), it was a sort of war game between two teams. One team attempted to steal cheeses piled on the altar, while the other wielded whips against them. Later sources speak of a simple test of endurance in which boys were whipped so that blood fell on the altar, while the priestess of Artemis stood by holding the ancient statue. If the men wielding the whips were too lenient, the statue became heavier in her hands. The boys who withstood the most punishment, called "victors at the altar" (*bōmonikai*), were greatly honored. In Roman times this ritual became a popular spectacle, and an amphitheater was built around the altar to accommodate tourists.[9]

Ortheia seems to mean the Upright Goddess, and folk etymology derives the name from the discovery of the statue tangled in the boughs of the *agnus castus* bush, which held it upright.[10] In the cult legend related by Pausanias (3.16.9), the strange character of the goddess was immediately manifested when the men who found her went mad. The early inscriptions speak of Ortheia, who was probably an independent goddess, only later syncretized with Artemis. Known as the Limnaion (the Marsh), the sanctuary was founded in the late eighth century, and originally consisted of a pavement and altar located in a hollow beside the river Eurotas. An Archaic temple was added and restored after a flood destroyed the original installation. The excavators found an unbroken series of votive objects from the late Geometric period to Roman times; among these the sanctuary is famous for its ivory and bone plaques inspired by Phoenician models, more than one hundred thousand lead figurines, and an array of unusual terracotta masks.

Found immediately north and south of the temple, the masks are votive copies of wood or cloth masks worn during ritual dances in the Archaic period, and depict a variety of stock characters: grotesque demons, youths, warriors, satyrs, and gorgons. The most numerous are the masks covered with wrinkled ridges, featuring gaping toothy mouths. The iconography of these rather fearsome-looking masks, based on Phoenician models, can be traced back to the male Babylonian monster Humbaba. Most modern scholars, however, think the masks represent grotesque females, for an ancient authority speaks of Spartan dances performed by males wearing female masks and clothing. Such dances, described as "funny and obscene," were a regular part of the Dorian and Peloponnesian worship of Artemis, and were probably related to rites of passage.[11]

The ivories and the far cheaper molded terracotta and lead figurines include numerous images of a winged goddess, holding animals in the heraldic Mistress of Animals pose or grasping a wreath in each hand. Initially, Artemis' favorite animal, the deer, is absent from the animals depicted, but becomes increasingly popular after 600, suggesting that the syncretizing of Ortheia and Artemis took place in the sixth century. The lead figurines, including many hoplite warriors, are characteristic of Peloponnesian sanctuaries but little known elsewhere. Among the early votive gifts, limestone sculptures of heraldic lions and bronze double axes show that artistic motifs from the Mycenaean period were still remembered here.[12]

Artemis and the vulnerable maiden

In many if not most Greek cities, adolescent girls danced for Artemis. These dances had social as well as religious functions, as they signaled a girl's readiness for marriage and made her visible to potential suitors. Also, transitions in the female life cycle governed by Artemis were linked to the prosperity and safety of the community as a whole. Many of Artemis' sanctuaries were located on the borders of a given polis, in lands that formed territorial boundaries. Rituals conducted safely by girls at these vulnerable sites demonstrated the strength of the polis, just as the very placement of such border sanctuaries asserted territorial claims. Likewise, a number of myths and legends draw a clear analogy between the rape of young women celebrating Artemis' festivals and the penetration of polis territory by enemies. The Spartans traced the origins of their hostility toward the Messenians to such an incident. During a festival, they said, Spartan girls were raped in the sanctuary of Artemis Limnatis (of the Marsh), which stood on the borderlands between Lakonia and Messenia and was disputed territory.[13]

Artemis' concern for the nurture of human young overlaps with her control over the fertility of the natural world. Particularly in the Peloponnese, where her cults are extremely numerous, Artemis has the characteristics of a nature goddess who promotes the growth of vegetation and is to be found in green, moist places. The cult of Artemis Karyatis (of the Nut Tree) was famed throughout Greece for its dancing maidens, often said to be the inspiration for the columns in maiden form (caryatids) that support the porch of the Athenian Erechtheion and other ancient buildings. Located on the border between Lakonia and Arkadia, Karyai was sacred to Artemis and the nymphs who served as her companions. The girls of Lakonia made an annual pilgrimage there to dance "a traditional local dance" before the goddess' statue, which in Pausanias' day stood in the open air. Here too, the maidens were vulnerable: it was said that the Messenian general Aristomenes and his men kidnapped the daughters of their Lakonian enemies from this sanctuary.[14]

As a virgin goddess, Artemis is not asexual but fosters a constant awareness of the maturing sexuality of the community's adolescent girls. From a patriarchal perspective, the asset of female fertility is always complicated by fears of poaching by rival males (or the desire to engage in such poaching), which helps to explain the regular appearance of the rape motif in Artemis' myths and cults. Still another Peloponnesian cult, that of Artemis Alpheiaia (of the river Alpheios) at Letrinoi, incorporated a legend about the attempted rape of Artemis by the local river god. Artemis escaped recognition by daubing her own face and those of her nymph companions with river mud, an act that probably reflects a lost ritual practice. Artemis and Alpheios shared an altar at Olympia, and the cult spread to the Dorian colony of Syracuse in Sicily, where Artemis Potamia (of the River) was worshiped at a spring said to be the local manifestation of the river Alpheios.[15]

Artemis Brauronia

All over the Greek world, women prayed to Artemis for help with gynecological problems, childbirth, and the nurture of young children. Artemis' cult at Brauron, one of the oldest and most important in Attica, was concerned with these functions. The sanctuary, which included a temple and a dining facility, was arranged around a sacred spring and a cave-like cleft in the rocky hillside nearby. This "cave" area was appropriate for a goddess of childbirth, both from a symbolic standpoint and because the Kretan childbirth deity Eileithyia, who is sometimes syncretized with Artemis, was also worshiped in a cave. It is possible that Iphigeneia, whose name means something like "strong in birth," was originally the goddess of Brauron, and that she was demoted to the status of a heroine upon the arrival of Artemis. In Euripides' day (Eur. *IT* 1462–67), Iphigeneia was remembered as the first priestess at Brauron, and garments of women who died in childbirth were dedicated at her tomb. Excavation has failed to pinpoint the location of this tomb, but it may have been associated with the complex of structures found in the cave area.

Here and in the spring, archaeologists discovered costly gifts to Artemis from the women of Attica: gold jewelry, stone seals and scarab gems, glass beads and vases, and bronze mirrors.[16] But the most frequently dedicated items were articles of women's clothing: belts, tunics, long robes, shawls, and headgear. After using the garments for a time, women gave them to the goddess, often embroidered with their own names or the words "sacred to Artemis." The items were displayed in the temple in boxes and on racks, and the officials in charge of the sanctuary kept careful records of them. No trace of them exists today, but the temple inventories were carved in stone in the fourth century and set up both at Brauron and at a sister sanctuary on the Athenian Akropolis. These lists make it clear that women gave the best they had to the goddess:

Pheidylla, a white woman's *himation* in a display box. Mneso, a frog-green garment. Nausis, a lady's *himation* with a broad purple border in wave pattern around the edge. Kleo, a delicate shawl. Phile, a bordered textile. Teisikrateia, a multi-colored Persian style shirt with sleeves.[17]

Some of the garments were draped over the cult images of Artemis in the temple, which was first constructed in the sixth century and rebuilt after the Persian invasion in the fifth. There were at least two statues and possibly three, referred to in the inventories as "the old image," "the stone image," and "the standing statue." As many as five garments at a time were worn by these images, a practice that allowed worshipers to feel they had achieved the closest possible contact with the goddess.[18]

Old Attic stories, dating to the founding of Brauron and beyond, tell how Artemis became enraged when local inhabitants killed a sacred bear. The ensuing plague could be stopped only by a maiden sacrifice or by the institution of a ritual in which young girls "played the bear" (arkteuein).[19] The bear was noted in Greek lore for both its fierceness and its maternal devotion; though presumably not commonly encountered in Classical Attica, it had a long history as a sacred yet prized game animal in the prehistoric hunting cultures of Europe. At Brauron, girls between the ages of five and ten danced and ran races beside the altar of Artemis. They wore special yellow robes, which they shed at some point in the rite, for the small painted jars dedicated at the end of their service depict both clothed and naked girls.[20]

When the Attic towns were united under Athens, the state took over the Brauronia and entrusted the quadrennial festival to the hieropoioi (doers of the sacred things), the same officials who ran the Panathenaic festival for Athena. Not every girl in Attica could serve as a bear at Brauron, though the painted cups have turned up in several other sites, suggesting that some of the Attic villages held their own Brauronian festivals. "Playing the bear" is often described as a puberty or initiation ritual that prepared the girls for the next stage of life, but clearly they were pre-adolescent, too young to be married even by Greek standards. Rather, the ritual has to do with Artemis' role as a goddess who alternately nurtures and destroys the young of both humans and wild animals. By serving the goddess, the young "bears" appeased her and placed themselves under her protection. Many statues of young children, both boys and girls, were dedicated at Brauron. These were apparently given in thanks for the children's survival, because mortality rates were highest in the first few years of life.[21]

Artemis Ephesia

Almost nothing remains of the Artemision at Ephesos, one of the Seven Wonders of the ancient world. This monumental temple was an expression of the awesome power attributed to the goddess, the patroness of the city. The plan consisted of an unroofed central court surrounded by an outer phalanx of over a hundred columns, each nearly sixty feet tall. Thirty-six of the columns in the front had bases carved with relief sculptures, a feature inherited from Hittite palace architecture, so that entering the temple was like walking through a gallery of gods and heroes. At the heart of the temple was the famous cult image, mysteriously un-Hellenic in appearance. When Paul of Tarsos (*Acts* 18:19–20:1) visited Ephesos as a missionary in the first century, he found a thriving city that owed much of its prosperity to the popular cult of Artemis.

The Greek settlers who reached the Anatolian coast about 1000 encountered the deities of the indigenous peoples. Most prominent among these was a mother goddess who held a dominant position in the pantheons of this region. She was worshiped under many local names and in many variations, but is best known as Kybele or the Great Goddess. The Greeks chose to recognize their own Artemis in this foreign deity, in spite of the fact that Artemis was emphatically a virgin, not a mother. Yet like her Anatolian counterpart, Artemis was a mountain-roving goddess and a Mistress of Animals.

It is likely that the Greeks found a pre-existing cult at the site of the later Artemision, for legends attributed the founding of the cult to the native Amazons. According to Callimachus (*Hymn* 3.237–42), the women warriors set up the goddess' statue beneath an oak tree and danced around it in their armor. Both Artemis' early epithet Oupis/Opis and the name Ephesos itself seem to be etymological descendants of the Hittite town Apasa, which occupied the site in the Bronze Age. While there are Mycenaean and Proto-Geometric potsherds at the site, the earliest archaeological remains securely attributed to the cult are those of a hundred-foot eighth-century temple (*hekatompedon*) with a surrounding colonnade. Following the local practice, the entrance faced west rather than east. By the next century, there was a large altar opposite the entrance with a special base for the cult image; presumably it was brought out of the temple to witness sacrifices at close quarters. Beside the altar was a sacred spring, perhaps the focus of the earliest cult, and the entire site was marshy and wet.

The evidence suggests that a statue of the goddess was an important element of the worship from at least the seventh century onward. We know little about the earliest cult image, but a new statue seems to have been commissioned with the construction of the massive Archaic temple in the sixth century. Literary sources tell us that the sculptor Endoios, who made several other famous cult statues, created the Artemis. It was similar in appearance to the Archaic Hera of Samos: a rigidly frontal standing figure with legs together, swathed in a tight garment. The arms were bent at the elbows and held forward, and the goddess wore a high crown called a *polos*. This basic wooden image, probably smaller than life-size, was adorned with a variety of objects: from her hands hung long knotted ribbons, she was draped with cloth garments including a veil, and she wore fine necklaces. Eventually, she was given an elaborate chest ornament, a feature characteristic of Anatolian cult images. Covered with globe-like objects, this pectoral was later misunderstood by both ancients and moderns, who thought that the goddess was many-breasted. Votive reliefs depicting the Zeus of Labraunda with a similar pectoral falsify the breast theory, though it was a favorite of early Christian authors, and a few ancient copies of the Ephesian statue actually have nipples, suggesting that the globes seemed breastlike to some pagan worshipers.[22] A recent hypothesis holds that the globe-like objects were scrotal sacs from sacrificed bulls, symbols of fertility. More likely suggestions are that they represent the large, globular dates harvested from the date palm under which Artemis was born in Ephesian Ortygia, according to local legend, or that they can be traced back to a leather bag considered a divine attribute in Hittite religion. It is unclear whether the pectoral was added in the Hellenistic period or had Archaic origins. The panels of Artemis' skirt were covered with a profusion of small relief images. These were a development of early modes of ornamentation for cult statues, in both the Near East and Greece, which involved fixing hammered plates of gold to the statues.[23]

Figure 8.2 Artemis Ephesia. Roman alabaster and bronze copy of cult statue, original *c.* 500. Ht 2.03 m. Naples, Museo Nazionale. Alinari/Art Resource.

Beneath the Archaic temple, the original excavators found a collection of valuable objects including ninety-three Lydian coins (the earliest known coinage) and intricately crafted items of gold, ivory, terracotta, and bronze. More recent investigations revealed a cache of jewelry contemporary with the Geometric temple, including many amber beads that may have been used to adorn the cult statue. The Archaic stone temple was constructed with help from the Lydian monarch Kroisos, who had his name inscribed on one of the column drums. It endured until the fourth century, when it was consumed in a fire set by a madman. The Ephesians, men and women, gave their own jewelry toward its restoration, which took more than a century.[24]

The archaeological remains from the sanctuary include large numbers of animal bones, primarily those of sheep and goats, but cattle, pigs, and a wide variety of wild animals are also attested. Slightly fewer than one hundred deer bones were found around the *hekatompedon* in the same areas as the ovicaprid bones; this suggests that they were sacrificed. Other bones of wild animals, such as bear teeth, may have been brought to the sanctuary as offerings. A "horn altar" composed of goat horns within a stone casing recalls similar Apolline altars on Delos and at Dreros in Krete.[25]

We know surprisingly little about the rituals conducted for Artemis at Ephesos in the Archaic and Classical periods; we can only make guesses based on later evidence. A first-century inscription describes a sacred procession including a singer and several individuals specially chosen to carry salt, wild celery, a garment or cloth, and the *kosmos*, or accessories, of the goddess. A late lexicographer provides context for this inscription, telling of a ritual in which the cult image is brought down to the sea, laid on a bed of wild celery, and given a meal of salt.[26] According to the temple legend, Klymene, the daughter of the king, once treated the goddess to this meal as a game, and she responded by demanding an annual reenactment of the ritual. Such rites focused on the dressing and feeding of cult images are not unknown in Greece, but are more often attested in Near Eastern and Egyptian sources.

A typically Anatolian feature of the Artemision, perhaps borrowed from the cult of the Great Mother, was the eunuch priest called the Megabyzos, a word of Persian origin. The Athenian mercenary Xenophon (*An.* 5.3.6) speaks of his dealings with one of these priests, with whom he deposited money for safekeeping. The Megabyzoi were held in great honor among the Ephesians, though they faded away during the Hellenistic period.[27] Like many other ancient sanctuaries, the Artemision was a place of asylum for fugitives and suppliants of all kinds. The inviolate aura of the sanctuary was so strong that according to legend, when the Ephesians came under attack by Kroisos, they stretched ropes about a mile from the gates of their city to the columns of the temple. By remaining in physical contact with the sanctuary, they attempted to extend its protection to the city itself.[28]

Ephesian Artemis, unlike her mainland counterparts, was a city goddess concerned primarily with the prosperity and safety of the Ephesians, yet her great fame encouraged the spread of her cult. When sending a colony to Massilia (Marseilles) around 600, the people of Ionian Phokaia were instructed by an oracle to bring with them a guide from Ephesos and a copy of the cult image. Meanwhile, an Ephesian woman named Aristarche dreamed that the goddess stood beside her and commanded her to go with the Phokaians. Strabo (4.1.4) tells how she became the first priestess of the goddess at Massilia, where a temple was constructed and the rituals performed at Ephesos were preserved unchanged. Another example shows how the cult could be spread through private devotion. After visiting the Artemision, Xenophon (*An.* 5.3.4–13) decided to build a miniature copy of the temple for the goddess on his land in Skillous near Olympia. Within it he placed a cypresswood copy of the cult image, and every year he held a banquet in honor of Ephesian Artemis for the people living in the district.

Artemis on Delos

Ephesos and Delos put forward competing claims to be the birthplace of Artemis, but the Delian claim became more widely accepted. Here the triad of Apollo, Artemis, and Leto was worshiped from the eighth century onward, and these cults, particularly that of Artemis, may have had Mycenaean antecedents. One of the enduring riddles of Delian archaeology is the nature of the cache of precious objects found beneath the Archaic (*c.* 700) temple of Artemis. This was a foundation deposit like the one discovered beneath the temple at Ephesos, but it consisted of true antiques: Mycenaean gold ornaments, a cache of ivory pieces including plaques carved in relief, bronze arrowheads, and potsherds spanning the gap to the Geometric period. The excavator suggested that these were the collected votives from a Mycenaean temple of "pre-Artemis" that preceded the Archaic one and stood on the spot until it was replaced. Others have questioned this reconstruction of a continuous cult because there is little evidence that the island was inhabited from the eleventh to ninth centuries.[29] Still, the deposit suggests that the Archaic temple builders wished to emphasize links to the past. Perhaps they chanced upon a long-buried hoard and piously placed the ancient treasures beneath the new temple.

The richest concentrations of Mycenaean and Geometric votives on Delos were found around Artemis' sanctuary, not that of Apollo, the dominant deity in later centuries. Even in the Classical period, the Artemision remained the spot where the most important votive offerings and heirlooms were preserved. Among these was the famous seventh-century *kore* (maiden) dedicated by Nikandre to "the Far-Shooter," the oldest Greek example of a larger than life-size marble statue. Because the hands are pierced to hold attributes, the statue probably represents Artemis rather than a worshiper. Its size and proportions were inspired by Egyptian art. In the temple itself was a seated image of the goddess. Hellenistic inventories of the temple's treasures record that this statue possessed an extensive wardrobe including crowns, robes, and a necklace.[30]

Artemis' sanctuary was associated with two tombs said to be those of maidens from the land of the Hyperboreans, the legendary northern people who sent offerings to Apollo. According to Herodotus (4.35), Arge and Opis came to the island "at the same time as the gods themselves." Upon their tomb, located behind the Artemision, the Delians scattered ashes from the thighbones burned at the altar. The maidens were the subject of ancient songs, and the Delian women had a custom of taking collections on their behalf. When excavated, their shrine turned out to be a real tomb of Mycenaean date. Another pair of maidens, Hyperoche and Laodike, had a monument in the Artemision itself. Legend said that they came to bring thank offerings for the birth of Apollo and Artemis, but they died without returning home.[31] The tale of these girls who died young formed the basis for a Delian rite of passage to adulthood: both girls and boys cut their hair at adolescence and laid it on the tomb as a sign of mourning. For the girls, this was a prelude to marriage. The reason for the location of the monument in the Artemision is clear, for Artemis herself often presided over such rites. Plutarch (*Vit. Arist.* 20.6) tells us that Artemis Eukleia (of Glory) had an altar and image in the marketplace of every Boiotian and Lokrian town, where she received offerings from couples about to be married.

Further reading

Vernant 1991 gathers some essential writings (Chapters 11–14) on the "otherness" of Artemis, a quality she shares with Dionysos. Cole 2004 (Chapters 6–7) deals with the goddess of the wilderness in relation to the civilized spaces of polis and sanctuary. The web of connections between Artemis, Gorgo, and the prehistoric Mistress of Animals, and the goddess' patronage of warriors are explored in Marinatos 2000. Faraone 2003 rejects the consensus view that the rites at Brauron pertain to female initiation and focuses instead on the way the ritual functions to placate the anger of Artemis. On Iphigeneia, see Bremmer 2002.

9

THE PERSUASIVE GODDESS
Aphrodite

Aphrodite was universally recognized as the Lady of Cyprus, the cosmopolitan island where Greek colonists and mariners were exposed at an early date to the cultures of the Near East. Because of the many similarities between Aphrodite and Semitic Ishtar/Astarte, and the lack of clear evidence for a Mycenaean Aphrodite, many scholars view the goddess of sexual desire as a relatively late addition to the Greek pantheon, borrowed from the Phoenicians. A persistent minority, however, argue that her roots were Indo-European, and that she was a cousin to Ushas, the Vedic dawn goddess, brought to Cyprus by the Mycenaeans. A third view holds that her ancestor was a Bronze Age Cypriot goddess who incorporated both indigenous and Phoenician elements by the time the Greeks adopted her.[1]

In poetry as in cult, she was associated with blooming gardens and all the paraphernalia of female beauty: perfumed textiles, jewels, and mirrors. Incense, dove sacrifices, and myrtle crowns were distinctive features of her worship. Aphrodite was typically honored at several smaller shrines in a given city rather than one major sanctuary, which indicates an important popular element in the development of her cult. Her sanctuaries often included a cult statue, which required housing, but only rarely were grandiose temples built for her. Similarly, few state festivals in her honor are attested except in the case of Aphrodite Pandemos, though private activities such as vows and banquets were common, particularly in connection with the securing of husbands or sea journeys safely completed. Though a mother, she is not a "mother goddess." Above all, as in myth and poetry, she rules sexual unions of every variety, and is therefore incidentally associated with marriage and the conception of children.

Kypris: The Lady of Cyprus

Around 1200, longstanding trade between the Mycenaean Greeks and the Cypriots culminated in Greek colonization at several sites on Cyprus, including Paphos. At about the same time, a monumental sanctuary was constructed in the local style, with an open court and a covered colonnade.

This sanctuary was destined to endure more than a thousand years, and to become the best-known cult site of Aphrodite. Here, according to Homer (*Od.* 8.361–66) and Hesiod (*Theog.* 199), was the goddess' home, the spot where she was born from the sea, and where the smoke of fragrant incense rose from her altar. Not surprisingly, given the multicultural nature of the site, the ancient sources do not agree on whether the origins of the sanctuary were Greek, Cypriot, or Phoenician. One of the legends says that its founder was Agapenor, a king of Arkadia returning from the Trojan war. Archaeological and linguistic evidence of close contacts between Arkadian and Cypriot Greeks in this period suggests that this story contains a grain of truth, but a competing version holds that the sanctuary was founded by Kinyras, an indigenous king whose descendants became the historical kings of Paphos and priests of Aphrodite. For his part, Herodotus (1.105) says that the Cypriots borrowed the cult of Aphrodite Ourania (that is, Astarte) from Ashkelon in the Levant.[2]

In spite of the fame of Paphos, few details of its early cult are known. Inscriptions show that Aphrodite had the Mycenaean title Wanassa (The Lady) until the end of the Classical period, and it is clear that her cult was closely associated with kingship on the Near Eastern model. The older structures in the sanctuary were mostly obliterated by the later Roman temple, and our only sources for the ritual life there are of Roman date. According to Tacitus (*Hist.* 2.3–4), the Paphians practiced divination from the entrails of sacrificed animals, but the blood was not allowed to touch the altar, which had to remain pure. This is consistent with the early accounts of incense as a key offering. Tacitus also describes the strange image of the goddess: a large conical stone. A dark grey-green stone of matching shape, slightly over a meter high, was recovered in the excavations.[3] Other sources emphasize the importance of flowers and fragrant botanicals in the cult. The use of perfumed oil, mentioned as part of Aphrodite's toilet in her Paphian shrine in the Homeric *Hymn* to Aphrodite (5.61–63), has Mycenaean precedents. Nearby was the Hierokepia (Sacred Garden), perhaps the source for the rose garlands that filled the sanctuary. An important feature of the early cult, not mentioned in the literary sources, is the relationship between the sanctuary and the industry of bronze metallurgy. Copper slag was found in the sanctuary itself and close by, a pattern that is repeated at other Cypriot cult sites from the Late Bronze Age, where the goddess was worshiped in conjunction with a male deity. This patronage of the island's main export product by a divine pair throws new light on the mythic (but not cultic) association of Aphrodite with the smith god Hephaistos.[4]

Among the numerous Cypriot sanctuaries of the goddess, that at Amathous, where the population was of indigenous and Phoenician stock, was noted for its unusual, bi-gendered deity. Here the image of the goddess wore female garb, but was bearded and held a scepter. The locals called this deity Aphroditos, a name that was also known in fifth-century Athens. The androgyny of Aphrodite at Amathous again points to the Near East, for Phoenician Astarte is likewise known to have had a male aspect, but it is also compatible with Greek ideas of Aphrodite as the goddess born of Ouranos' genitals, who governed male sexuality.[5]

The export of Aphrodite

The Greeks thought that the oldest cult place of Aphrodite in their lands was the island of Kythera, where an ancient sanctuary of Aphrodite Ourania was attributed to Phoenician founders by Herodotus (1.105) and others. Archaeology provides no support for the hypothesis of Phoenician influence on the island, though the sanctuary itself remains unexcavated, and the murex shells exploited by the Phoenicians for purple dye were locally abundant. Certainly this cult was well established by the time of Hesiod (*Theog.* 191–99), who mentions Aphrodite's brief sojourn there before her emergence from the sea at Cyprus. The remains of a fifth-century Doric temple survive on the island, and the cult statue was an armed Aphrodite who recalled the warlike goddesses Ishtar and Astarte.[6] The goddess probably made her way into mainland Greece during the tenth and ninth centuries from three locations: Cyprus, Kythera, and Krete. Excavations have revealed that the Kretan sanctuaries are among the oldest after those of Cyprus. At Kato Symi, the Archaic sanctuary devoted to Hermes and Aphrodite had a history of continuous use stretching back to Middle Minoan times, though the Minoan predecessors of the pair must have had different names. Again, at Olous there was a Geometric temple of Aphrodite and Ares. (Ares is not attested at the site until the double temple of the Roman period, but in other parts of Krete the pair was worshiped from an early date.) All over the Greek world, Aphrodite is regularly found with a cult partner, either Hermes or Ares, and this appears to be an archaic feature of her worship rather than a later development.[7]

Aphrodite Ourania and Pandemos

At Paphos, Kythera, Korinth, Athens, and many other places, Aphrodite was known as Ourania (Heavenly). For the Greeks, this most widely disseminated of her titles evoked the Hesiodic story of the goddess' birth from the severed genitals of Ouranos, Father Sky. They also associated the title with Aphrodite's putative Eastern origins, perhaps because Ishtar/Astarte was known as the "Queen of Heaven" and was likewise a daughter of the sky god. Aphrodite's abode was the heavens, and artists visualized the goddess transported through the night sky, or descending from heaven on a ladder, an Egyptian and Near Eastern symbol of travel between heaven and earth.[8] Much evidence for the cult of Ourania comes from Athens, and its observance there was attributed to the mythical King Aigeus. The goddess had a sanctuary in the city center near the Stoa Poikile with a statue attributed to Pheidias, and an altar excavated in the area was constructed around 500. In the vicinity of this altar lay a fragmentary, fifth-century votive relief of Aphrodite descending a ladder and later reliefs of the goddess riding on a goat, her favorite sacrificial animal. The iconography of Aphrodite on a goat must have been popular with Greek women, for it was often used to decorate bronze mirrors and jewelry. We find the goat and ladder motifs combined on votive reliefs from outside Attica, as well as on a silver medallion from a brothel in the Kerameikos that shows the goddess riding through a starry sky accompanied by Hermes and Eros.[9]

The sanctuary of Aphrodite by the Ilissos river, situated in a suburban area known as the Gardens, has not been located and is known only from Pausanias' description (1.19.2). Here was an image of Aphrodite Ourania in the shape of a herm, a squared-off pillar topped by a head. This shape was not unusual in the cult of Aphrodite, though it is primarily associated with Hermes or Dionysos. It may have been a sign of Aphrodite's bisexual nature, for the gods portrayed in this way were highly phallic; or it may have been a reminder of the goddess' aniconic image at Paphos. While the herm stood in the courtyard, the temple itself contained the best-known work of Pheidias' pupil Alkamenes, "Aphrodite in the Gardens." Pausanias called this much-admired statue "one of the most noteworthy sights in Athens," but unfortunately failed to describe its appearance, leaving modern scholars to speculate based on minimal clues. A prevailing theory holds that two other Aphrodite sanctuaries in the Athens area are duplicates of the one on the Ilissos. Certainly the small sanctuaries at Daphni and on the north slope of the Akropolis are similar to one another, for both were bounded by stony hillsides with niches cut into the rock, both linked the worship of Eros with that of Aphrodite, and both received offerings of anatomical votives in the shape of male and female genitalia. These charming spots, surely filled with greenery in antiquity, correspond to the vase paintings of the Meidian school that show Aphrodite seated on a rock in a garden setting. Aphrodite's connection with vegetation at these shrines recalls the sacred gardens of Near Eastern Astarte and Cypriot Aphrodite Ourania.[10]

Pheidias sculpted an Aphrodite Ourania for the Eleans, sponsors of the Olympic games. This work of ivory and gold showed Aphrodite standing with one foot resting on a tortoise, an animal associated with women in Greek folklore because it was always confined to its home.[11] In the sanctuary at Elis, Pheidias' Ourania was juxtaposed with a bronze statue of the goddess riding on a ram, by the fourth-century sculptor Skopas. This image was called Aphrodite Pandemos (of All the People), another widespread cult title of the goddess. Plato (*Symp.* 180d–181c) attempted to differentiate Ourania and Pandemos as two distinct goddesses, one the celestial deity of "Platonic love" and the other concerned with fleshly pleasures. There is no evidence, however, to suggest that this distinction reflects cult practices or assumptions. Ourania, as we will see, is by no means aloof from fleshly pleasures, while

Pandemos shares the iconography of the "celestial" goddess who travels through the sky.

The epithet Pandemos had to do with Aphrodite's political function as a goddess who unites the citizens in harmony. An Athenian legend about Pandemos says that Theseus founded her worship with that of Peitho (Persuasion) after he united all the people of Attica into one city.[12] Equally indispensable in matters of *erōs* and politics, Peitho was an important concept for the emergent Athenian democracy. It is probable that the cult was established around 500, and helped to promote *sunousia*, the fellowship of citizens. We hear of Athenian *tetradistai*, or men who gathered to feast in honor of Aphrodite Pandemos on the fourth of every month, a day sacred to both Aphrodite and Hermes.[13] Remnants of the sanctuary have been excavated on the southwest slope of the Akropolis, including a small fourth-century temple with sculpted doves. A later Hellenistic inscription from the site shows that preparations for the state-sponsored festival (known as the Aphrodisia) involved the purification of the sanctuary with a dove sacrifice and the washing of the statues. The cult of Pandemos was an exception to the rule that Aphrodite's worship tended to be less centralized and state-supervised than that of most other Olympian deities. At Erythrai in Ionia, an oracle solicited by the state toward the end of the fifth century advised that the citizens build a temple of Aphrodite Pandemos and supply it with a statue "for the preservation of the people."[14]

Figure 9.1 Aphrodite with dove, votive bronze from Dodona (?), *c.* 450. Athens, National Archaeological Museum. Bildarchiv Foto Marburg.

An analogue to the legend of Theseus' establishment of the cult of Aphrodite Pandemos and Peitho is found at Thebes, where the city's Phoenician founder, Kadmos, is said to have married Harmonia, the daughter of Aphrodite and Ares. Thebans believed that Harmonia, whose name connotes the unity of the citizens, dedicated three ancient wooden statues of Aphrodite on the akropolis. These were named Ourania, Pandemos, and Apostrophia (Averter of Evils). According to Xenophon (*Hell.* 5.4.4), the three Theban civil and military officials known as *polemarchoi* always celebrated a festival of Aphrodite when their term of office was completed. Similar customs are attested for city officials in Megara, Ionia, and the Aegean islands through dedicatory inscriptions, the earliest of which belongs to fifth-century Keos.[15] While the emphasis at Thebes is on Aphrodite's partnership with the war god Ares, many of these dedications pair her with Hermes. In either case, the union of polar opposites (masculine and feminine or war and love) expresses metaphorically the concepts of civic concord and harmonious order.

Spartan Aphrodite

On the Spartan akropolis, we find an arrangement similar to that at Thebes, with a temple of Aphrodite Areia (of Ares) containing at least two Archaic cult statues. Based on inscribed potsherds from the area, one of these was probably Aphrodite Basilis (Queen). In the seventh century, Spartan colonists of Taras and Satyrion in Italy chose to carry this cult to their new home. Taras built an akropolis temple for the goddess, and at neighboring Satyrion worshipers deposited huge numbers of terracotta figurines and pots from the seventh to the third centuries, including one inscribed with the cult title Basilis. The choice of Aphrodite as a patroness may be connected with the legend that the settlers were illegitimate sons of Spartan women.[16] A second Spartan temple was unusual in that it had two stories, each containing its own cult statue. The lower level housed Aphrodite Enoplios (Armed), an Archaic type that may have been copied from Kythera. The upper room contained an unusual cedar statue called Morpho (the Beautiful One). Here the goddess, presumably Aphrodite, was shown enthroned, veiled, and wearing fetters on her feet. She belongs to a category of cult statues deemed to be so powerful and dangerous that they required binding and restraint. The veil too fits this interpretation, for such images were often hidden from view.[17]

Aphrodite and "sacred prostitution" at Korinth

On Akrokorinthos, the high rocky citadel of Korinth, Aphrodite was installed as a goddess of the city, probably under the rule of the Bakchiad aristocrats in the eighth century. As in other early cults of Aphrodite, she was depicted with weapons and had the title Ourania, signs of her Near Eastern affinities.[18] The

Korinthian cult, however, differed from most other Greek cults of Aphrodite because the goddess owned slaves who worked as prostitutes. According to the traditional scholarly view, the practice of "sacred prostitution" originated as a fertility rite, and is attested in relation to Ishtar and Asherah. For example, a class of women known as *ishtaritum* is described in a Babylonian text alongside courtesans "whose favors are many" and prostitutes "whose husbands are legion."[19] On the other hand, this interpretation of certain Mesopotamian cultic functionaries has been vigorously criticized as a scholarly construct, overly reliant on nineteenth-century assumptions about "fertility cult" in the ancient Near East. While the vast textual evidence from cuneiform tablets reveals a bewilderingly large variety of female cultic personnel, some of whom are regularly mentioned alongside prostitutes or in contexts that hint of sexuality, they offer no clear-cut example of a "cultic prostitute," and it is likely that this conceptual category simply does not correspond to the more nuanced and complex roles of Mesopotamian women in relation to their goddesses.[20]

Not surprisingly, the practice of "sacred prostitution" at Korinth has also been called into question, since it was assumed to derive directly from the cult of Ishtar. In the Greek instance, however, the evidence is much more convincing, and it is important to keep in mind that prostitution for Aphrodite need not be an exact imitation of any Near Eastern model. It could have been based on Greek (mis)understandings of the roles of female cultic personnel in the Near East, or it could even be an independent development. Athenaeus remarks (13.573d) that it was the practice of individuals to "render" *hetairai* (courtesans) to Korinthian Aphrodite in payment of vows when their prayers were fulfilled. An example was Xenophon, a citizen who vowed one hundred girls to the goddess in return for victory at the Olympic games. He commissioned Pindar to write a song (fr. 122 Snell-Maehler) for the thanksgiving sacrifice, attended by the girls:

> Young women, hospitable to many, handmaidens of Peitho in rich Korinth, you who burn the golden tears of pale incense; often you fly in your thoughts to Aphrodite Ourania, the mother of Loves. She gave to you, girls, without blame, to pick the fruit of soft youth on beds of desire. With necessity, all is good ...

Strabo (8.6.20) reports that both men and women dedicated sacred slaves, or hierodules, to the goddess, and that the sanctuary at one time owned more than a thousand of these courtesans, who were a major source of income.[21]

As a thriving port and trade depot, Korinth was famous for its prostitutes. Sanctuaries were often expected to be self-supporting, and their income usually derived from estates belonging to the resident deity. In this case, the goddess profited from one of the main industries of Korinth, the sex trade, through her ownership of slaves who worked as prostitutes. Most, if not all of these slaves must have worked near the harbors, rather than on the Akrokorinthos itself. To modern ears, this arrangement sounds incompatible with "the sacred," yet there is further evidence that the prostitutes of Korinth had a special relationship with Aphrodite. It was an ancient custom that whenever the city had great need, it recruited as many prostitutes as possible to participate in the supplication of the goddess. The most famous instance occurred in 480 when, with the Persian invasion at hand, the *hetairai* of Korinth prayed to Aphrodite on behalf of the Greeks and the Korinthian soldiery.[22] Still, there is no evidence that Aphrodite's prostitutes acted as priestesses of the goddess, or that consorting with them was in itself a religious act, so "sacred prostitution" is probably a misnomer for their role.

Aphrodite in Lokroi Epizephyrioi

A different form of "sacred prostitution" involving temporary service to Aphrodite is attributed to the people of Cyprus, Lydia, and Lokroi Epizephyrioi by late authors including Clearchus of Cyprus, who says that parents prostituted their freeborn daughters.[23] The case for prostitution in connection with Aphrodite at Lokroi is considerably less credible than that at Korinth, for the sources are not considered reliable and the practice described by Clearchus would have been shocking to standard Greek sensibilities. He may have in mind the story that when the Lokrians were under attack from the rival city of Rhegion in the fifth century, they vowed to prostitute their virgins during the festival of Aphrodite if they were victorious. Hieron of Syracuse intervened on their behalf, and the city was saved; it is unclear whether the promised offering of virgins actually took place.[24]

The gift of female sexual services in fulfillment of a vow evokes the customs of Korinth, and it is at least possible that the vow was made in a similar context, where prostitutes were a standard offering to Aphrodite. On this hypothesis, the exigencies of war drove the Lokrians to vow not merely slaves but their own daughters to the goddess, just as the Lokrians of mainland Greece devoted citizen maidens to the temple service of Athena. The famous Ludovisi throne, a ritual object of unknown function which originally stood in a Lokrian temple of Aphrodite, is carved with reliefs showing a nude courtesan playing the double flute on one side and a matron burning incense on the other: a reference to the vow, or perhaps to the different modes by which married women and (non-sacred) prostitutes served the goddess.[25]

There is no question that Aphrodite's worship at Lokroi was anomalous in some ways. The oldest known structure at Lokroi is a dining complex near the seashore dating to the seventh century, not long after the initial founding of the colony (later, in the sixth century, a three-room temple was added). The U-Shaped Stoa, as it is known, enclosed three hundred and seventy-one separate pits, each with the buried remains of one or more ritual banquets, including pottery inscribed with Aphrodite's name. The contents of the pits were laid down from the mid-sixth to the fourth century. While dining facilities are not unusual in sanctuaries, this example is particularly early and the careful deposition of the debris – with each pot and figurine deliberately broken – is unparalleled. Whatever the function of the ritual, the early date of the stoa shows that Aphrodite's cult was of crucial importance to the colonists.[26]

At Lokroi, Aphrodite's cult was closely intertwined with that of the most important goddess of Magna Graecia, Persephone. The large collection of fifth-century terracotta *pinakes* from the Persephone sanctuary at Mannella contain a significant number illustrating mythic and cultic scenes involving Aphrodite, including her birth from the sea. Three *pinax* types show Aphrodite with her cult partner Hermes, while Eros too seems to have played a role in her worship here. In one type, she stands in a chariot drawn by a winged boy and girl as Hermes steps up beside her; in another she presents Hermes with a flower as Eros sits on her arm. A third shows cult statues of the pair standing in a temple while a young couple pours libations upon an altar decorated with a copulating satyr and deer. The general impression is that while Persephone's cult focused on pre-nuptial rites and the protection of young children, Aphrodite's cult had to do with women's sexual experience, including that of brides.[27]

Figure 9.2 The birth of Aphrodite on the Ludovisi "Throne," probably from the sanctuary of Aphrodite at Lokroi Epizephyrioi, 460–50. Museo Nazionale Romano. Art Resource.

Maritime Aphrodite

Aphrodite's sanctuaries were regularly located at port cities along the major trade routes used by Greek and Phoenician merchants, important disseminators of her cult. An anecdote quoted by Athenaeus (15.675f–76a) illustrates this point. Herostratos, a merchant plying the waters between Cyprus and the Greek trading emporium of Naukratis in Egypt, purchased a small statue of Aphrodite at Paphos and continued south. Buffeted by a terrible storm, all aboard his ship prayed to the goddess to save them. Fresh myrtle sprouted around the statue, permeating the air with its sweet scent and soothing the seasick men as the skies cleared. The crew arrived safely at Naukratis, and Herostratos was moved to dedicate the image at the sanctuary of Aphrodite, and to distribute crowns of the miraculous myrtle to her worshipers. Herostratos is supposed to have lived in early Archaic times, and excavation has shown that the temple in the sanctuary of Aphrodite was one of the oldest structures at Naukratis, founded *c.* 600 by East Greek traders. Several vases were dedicated here to Aphrodite Pandemos, an appropriate choice for a colony composed of immigrant citizens from varied backgrounds. As a goddess of sea and sky who aided in navigation, Aphrodite was called Euploia (of Good Sailing), Epilimenia (She at the Harbor), and Pontia (She of the Sea). The sanctuary of Aphrodite Euploia at Knidos was famous for its cult statue by Praxiteles, the first Classical sculptor to show the goddess nude. Surrounded by fine gardens, the temple was constructed on a circular plan so that visitors could enjoy the delights of the statue in the round.[28]

Aphrodite and Hippolytos

At both Athens and Trozen, which faced each other across the Saronic gulf, Aphrodite's cult was closely linked with that of Hippolytos. Euripides' play *Hippolytos* tells how the hero incurred the goddess' wrath because of his devotion to chastity, and how Phaidra, the young wife of Theseus and stepmother of Hippolytos, became the tool of Aphrodite's vengeance. The Athenian cult of Hippolytos was an offshoot of that at Trozen, the result of the popularization of Theseus as an Athenian hero. On the south slope of the Akropolis, in the same area as the sanctuary of Aphrodite Pandemos (and perhaps identical to it) was a shrine of Aphrodite "at Hippolytos," also known as the Hippolyteion. Here the hero received regular sacrifices at his tomb.[29] At Trozen, on the other hand, Hippolytos was a local god whose sanctuary contained a shrine of the goddess, so that their relative status was inverted. The meaning of his name is not transparent, but it contains the root *hipp-* (horse), suggesting a relationship with the city god Poseidon (both Poseidon and Aphrodite were responsible for his death according to the myths). He was the principal deity in a large, important extramural sanctuary that included a number of interrelated cults. Here, the debris from the site of his small temple indicates activity as far back as the Geometric period.[30] Pausanias (2.32.1) saw the temple with its ancient statue and reported that a priest was dedicated for life to Hippolytos' service. Before marriage, maidens offered a lock of hair at his sanctuary. The complex also included a stadium, overlooked by a temple of Aphrodite Kataskopia, (She Who Observes). Near this temple was a myrtle tree, sacred to the goddess, and the supposed tombs of Hippolytos and Phaidra.

Aphrodite and Adonis

The cult of Aphrodite's paramour Adonis held a special appeal for Greek women, combining the erotic adoration of a beautiful youth with the emotional catharsis of lamentation for his death. The Adonis cult was an early import from the Levant, probably via Cyprus, but while many of the outward forms remained the same, its cultural context and significance changed. Adonis was modeled upon Tammuz, the consort of Ishtar whose death was annually lamented by women, and his name is a direct borrowing of the West Semitic *adon*, Lord. At Phoenician Byblos there was a sanctuary of "Aphrodite and Adonis," that is, the city goddess Astarte and a consort who corresponded to Tammuz. Whereas the cult of Tammuz (Sumerian Dumuzi) enjoyed near-universal recognition in Mesopotamia and his festival was so important that a Babylonian month was named after him, the worship of Adonis was tolerated by many Greek city-states but rarely gained the status of a state-sponsored cult. Adonis was viewed with some ambivalence, probably because his main adherents were women, and in spite of his popularity in certain areas, he retained a fundamentally "foreign" aura. At the core of the cult lay a ritual with no connection to acknowledged sacred space; in Greek contexts before the Hellenistic period, Adonis only rarely possessed a sanctuary, temple or even an altar, making his rites anomalous.

To perform the Adonia, which took place in late summer, women ascended to the roof, where they sang dirges, cried out in grief, and beat their breasts. Sappho (fr. 140a *LP*) mentions that the women tore their garments, a standard sign of mourning. Other features of Adonis' ritual belong to the cult in Classical Athens. A few days before the Adonia, garden herbs and cereals were sown in broken pots. These tender young plants were brought to the rooftops during the festival, to be withered in the hot sun as emblems of the youthful Adonis' death. Another custom involved the laying out of Adonis dolls as for burial. While the traditional Frazerian concept of Adonis and similar figures as dying "fertility gods" has been increasingly criticized, Detienne's analysis of Adonis as the paradigm of illicit sexuality and sterility, to be set against the fruitful union of husband and wife, has not achieved full acceptance, perhaps because it neglects the Adonis cult's Near Eastern background.[31]

Aphrodite and marriage

Aphrodite is sometimes associated with weddings, as we saw at Lokroi, but her involvement has to do specifically with the sexual component of marriage, not its social aspects. On the road from Trozen to Hermione, Pausanias (2.32.7) noted a sanctuary of Aphrodite Nymphia (Bridal Aphrodite), which was connected with Theseus' abduction of the young Helen. In Hermione itself, both virgins and widows who wished to "go with a man" had to sacrifice to the goddess before marriage. The inclusion of widows shows that this was not a rite of passage, but an acknowledgment of Aphrodite's role in successful marriages. Similarly, widows at Naupaktos went to Aphrodite's cave to pray for husbands. The participation of women at varying stages of life is also evident in the venerable cult of Aphrodite at Sikyon, where the temple was served by a female warden (neōkoros) "for whom it was no longer permitted to go with a man" and by a maiden priestess, consecrated for one year. Whereas the warden had once been married, the priestess soon would be. The cult statue was a gold and ivory image by Kanachos, the Sikyonian sculptor who created other masterworks for the Thebans and Milesians around 500. The goddess was shown seated, wearing a *polos* and holding a poppy in one hand and a fruit in the other. Access to the temple was restricted, so visitors gazed upon the statue and offered their prayers from the doorway. This cult is similar in nature to those of the old Achaean goddesses such as Hera or Athena and shows few signs of the Near Eastern influences we saw in other cities. Still, it is typically Aphrodisian in its emphasis on fragrance: the sacrifices were burned on juniper wood with a local aromatic herb that had erotic associations.[32]

Further reading

Budin 2003 provides a detailed examination of the goddess' journey to the west from Cyprus and her prehistoric roots, with emphasis on the material evidence. MacLachlan 1992 defends the historicity of sacred prostitution against the growing number of skeptics; it should be read with Westenholz 1989, Assante 2003 and the papers collected in Part I of Faraone and McClure 2006. Williams 1986 summarizes the material evidence for Aphrodite's cult on the Korinthian citadel. Rosenzweig 2004 has full coverage of cults in Athens, primarily from an art-historical perspective, while Redfield 2003 offers many insights about Aphrodite's important role in Lokrian culture.

10

EPIPHANY AND TRANSFORMATION

Dionysos

The traditional view of Dionysos' worship as an import from Thrace or Phrygia was called into question with the discovery of the name Dionysos on Linear B tablets from Pylos, which show that the name, and probably the god, was known to Bronze Age Greeks.[1] While Dionysiac myths present this most exotic of the Olympians as a literal stranger, an emigrant from foreign lands, they also maintain that he was born in Greece. At the same time, his worship shares features with the cults of Phrygian Kybele, who was likewise celebrated with ecstatic dancing to percussive music, and Egyptian Osiris, a chthonian vegetation god who experienced dismemberment and resurrection. The ecstatic nature of some Dionysiac rites, together with their special appeal to women, set the worship of Dionysos apart from that of any other Olympian deity. Though clearly a god of the vine and its product, Dionysos' identity cannot be so easily delimited. He is also a deity of intoxication and madness, whose followers experience both profound surrender and glad liberation; this element of *enthousiasmos*, having the god within, is anomalous in Olympian worship. From the Archaic period, he offers hope for afterlife salvation through private initiatory rites. He is not a major civic or federal god, though his festivals can become essential to civic identity (as they do in Athens). The archaeological remains of his sanctuaries and temples are not impressive, but their modesty belies his great popularity. With respect to ritual, the most commonly recurring concept is the epiphany or advent of Dionysos and his reception. The *dithurambos*, often on the theme of Dionysos' birth, was his characteristic hymn. Though the details of the process are unknown, it is clear that Greek tragedy and comedy arose in a ritual context from choral songs performed for Dionysos.

Dionysos has attracted a great deal of critical attention because a profound theology, analogous to certain Christian doctrines, can be extracted from his myths and cults in a way that is not true of the other Olympian gods. A suffering god, an ecstatic religious experience in which worshipers are united with the deity, the consumption of wine as part of the ritual, and the belief in the god's ability to offer salvation from death: all these elements have contributed to theories that Dionysiac religion was co-opted by Christianity, on

126

the one hand, and attempts to recast the pagan Greeks as Christian precursors, on the other. More recently, the psychosocial dimensions of Dionysiac religion have been extensively studied to reveal how the god offered temporary escape from normal modes of being into alternate states such as trance, masquerade, madness, and of course, intoxication, and how he subverted gender roles and other societal norms. These analyses are largely based on the portraits of Dionysiac worship in Greek poetry and myth, above all the *Bacchae* of Euripides. While they provide a valuable description of the god's symbolic significance and cultural meaning, a study of Dionysos' cults and the historically attested behaviors associated with them yields a picture rather different from what myth and poetry lead us to expect.[2] In practice, the worship of Dionysos was not truly subversive; instead, it offered outlets for physical and emotional self-expression within socially acceptable contexts. Furthermore, Dionysiac cult was smoothly integrated into Greek civic systems of worship, with ecstatic and private components balanced by state-sponsored festivals and conventional sacrifices.

Dionysiac festivals and the calendar

While drama was a Panhellenic development, the major Dionysiac festivals can be assigned to the Ionian and Athenian Greeks (Anthesteria, Lenaia) or to the Dorians and the Aiolic speakers of Thessaly and Boiotia (Agriania and its variants, Theodaisia). This division also corresponds to two early centers of Dionysiac activity, the Aegean islands and Boiotian Thebes. The islands, particularly Chios and Naxos, were leading producers of wine and proponents of Dionysos as the god of viticulture whose sacred marriage with Ariadne ensured prosperity. The rituals and myths that involve Dionysos' arrival from the sea, as in the ship processions of East Greece and Athens, seem to reflect the influence of the islands. The silens or satyrs, who are featured in the vase iconography of several myths set in Naxos (e.g. the return of Hephaistos and the meeting of Dionysos and Ariadne), are also a part of this Aegean Dionysiac tradition.[3] They are conspicuously absent from the myths of Boiotian origin that involve resistance to Dionysos by royal women (the daughters of Kadmos, Minyas, Eleutheros, and Proitos). The Boiotian/ Theban strand of Dionysiac cult, exported to the rest of the mainland and beyond, focused on the god's birth, themes of death and resurrection, and various benefits and purifications obtained through initiation into Dionysiac *thiasoi* (groups organized for worship). Mainadic activity seems to have been present in both traditions, though emphasized far more heavily on the mainland. The geographical position of Attica ensured that both the Aegean and Boiotian strands played an important role in the Athenian worship of Dionysos.

Dionysos, rather surprisingly, is a winter god. His festivals everywhere take place in the months we call December, January, February, and March:

127

the seasons of winter and early spring. The biennial nature of many of these festivals, generally the winter ones with mainadic elements, has never been satisfactorily explained. One theory relates the phenomenon to the need for intercalary periods to reconcile the lunar and solar calendars and keep the months synchronized with the seasons.[4] The Dionysiac festivals of winter have been described as rites by which the quiescent grape vines and other vegetation were recalled to life. While Dionysos is certainly a god who dies or vanishes and reappears periodically, it is difficult to plausibly match his comings and goings with the growth cycles of plants. On the other hand, he unquestionably has affinities with certain trees (pine, fig, plane) and vines (grape, ivy). The ivy, ubiquitous in art, actually eclipses the grapevine as the emblem of the god, perhaps because it retained foliage through the winter and was thus available for ritual use.[5] The spring festivals are more easily explained because they correspond to the tasting of the new wine, but it is notable that no major Dionysiac festival addresses the vintage.

Cycladic Dionysos

On the island of Keos some 40 km from the Attic coast, archaeologists have uncovered the earliest known Dionysos sanctuary. The Cycladic people who occupied the site of Ayia Irini in the Bronze Age built a temple and filled it with large-scale terracotta sculptures of women wearing typical Minoan dress. The statues, produced in large numbers, do not represent the resident deity. Instead, they were placed in the sanctuary for some unknown reason, perhaps as perpetual witnesses of the god's epiphany or as pleasing gifts from worshipers. Eventually the temple collapsed and the town was deserted in the twelfth century. Around 750, votives began to accumulate in the innermost room of the same sacred building the Bronze Age inhabitants had used. The focus of this cult was a terracotta head that originally belonged to one of the Minoan-type statues in the sanctuary, many of which were buried at the site. The new occupants dug up this object or received it as an heirloom, and set it up on the floor of the temple in a specially made ring base, where the excavators found it *in situ*. With the head were found Geometric *kantharoi*, the characteristic wine cups of Dionysos; that he was the god of the sanctuary by the end of the sixth century is confirmed by a vase graffito. It has been suggested that the shrine originally belonged to a Minoan goddess, but it is also possible that a Bronze Age Dionysos was the occupant, surrounded by groups of dancing women just as he was in historical times. On the other hand, despite the unusual degree of continuity in the use of the temple at Ayia Irini, the cultic focus on the terracotta head shows that its original function was not well understood. Dionysos was apparently worshiped at Ayia Irini in the Geometric period, but how much earlier remains an open question.[6]

The Cyclades were famous for their wines, and Naxos in particular was considered sacred to Dionysos from at least the seventh century. The first coins minted there, *c.* 600, displayed the *kantharos*, and other emblems of the god followed. The island was the source of a cycle of Dionysiac myths, including tales of the god's birth and nurture by nymphs, and his meeting with Ariadne.[7] Unfortunately, we know little of the cults there. According to Plutarch (*Vit. Thes.* 20), there were two festivals of two Ariadnes, one a joyful occasion celebrating the bride of Dionysos, and the other a time of sorrow with sacrifices for the dead heroine (Ariadne was also honored as a heroine in Argos and Amathous). The Naxians possessed a pair of sacred masks, objects that signaled the god's presence and served as cult images. One, made of grapevine wood, was known as Bakcheus, and the other, of wood from the fig, was Meilichios, the mild or sweet. The combination of an important god and a secondary female cult figure (Dionysos and Ariadne) is consistent with the finds from the recently excavated sanctuary at Hyria on Naxos, where a temple stood from Geometric times over the remains of a Mycenaean cult site. Later structures at the site included an Archaic dining room and a successor temple. The rich and varied votive gifts included some types, like terracotta female busts, that were typically offered to female deities.[8]

Phallic processions and images

Processions including wooden *phalloi* on poles or large painted *phalloi* in carts were a common mode of celebration for Dionysos throughout Greece; according to Herodotus (2.48–49), it was the Argive hero Melampous who first introduced this custom. Processional *phalloi* were a familiar sight in the rural and city celebrations of the Athenians, while epigraphic evidence starting in 301 shows that every year, the Delians created a winged, brightly colored *phallos*-bird and drew it through the streets in a wagon. This fanciful object was considered the image of the god himself, and while the direct evidence is Hellenistic in date, it is likely that the phallic parade was practiced from the Archaic period. Excavators found no temple of Dionysos on the island, but there was a deposit of items dedicated to the god including an Archaic stone *phallos*.[9] The Delian *phallos* image of Dionysos, like the masked columns seen on Attic vase paintings, was intended to serve as a temporary simulacrum of the god, just as the *phalloi* used in the Athenian City Dionysia had to be replaced every year. The use of such ephemeral images is typical of Dionysiac cult but rare in other Greek worship.

The representation of the *phallos* in art and poetry is linked in sacred narratives with the proper reception of Dionysos. In Athens, for example, the men who failed to receive Dionysos Eleuthereus with honor made model *phalloi* in order to regain the god's favor, while an inscription from Paros tells a similar, presumably apocryphal story about the poet Archilochus. When his attempt to introduce obscene Dionysiac poetry was rebuffed, the men of Paros were rendered impotent until they accepted the new mode of worship. Paradoxically, though the *phallos* has an important role in many Dionysiac cults, the god himself is rarely portrayed nude or in a state of sexual excitement; in fact he remains detached from sexuality except in the context of the sacred marriage. The Dionysiac *phallos* does not signify male sexuality or masculinity per se but the exuberant, animating force that makes arousal and procreation possible.[10]

The Anthesteria

Thucydides (2.15.4) notes that the "older Dionysia," which takes place at Athens in the month of Anthesterion, is a festival also celebrated by the Ionian cities. Post-Classical inscriptions confirm that this was the case in Ephesos, Priene, Miletos, and Smyrna, and scholars have therefore included this festival among those that predate the Ionian migration of *c.* 1000. The month name Anthesterion is even more widely attested, from Eretria in Euboia to the Ionian colonies of Massilia and Kyzikos. Sometimes the celebration is called the Anthesteria (Festival of Blooming); otherwise it is the Dionysia or the Katagogia (Bringing Home) of Dionysos. The latter most likely refers to the advent of the god in a ship on wheels similar to a parade float and ultimately derived from Egypt; Attic vases illustrating this ritual scene suggest that it was an element of the Archaic and Classical Athenian festival, probably one of the initial events of the ritual sequence.

Whereas the vintage took place in the fall, the true advent of Dionysos as the wine god came in the early spring, when the casks of new wine were broached for the first time. This first day of the festival, 11 Anthesterion, was known at Athens as the Pithoigia (Cask-Opening). The second day, called Choes (Jugs), was a day of revelry and feasting even for slaves. It also included what has been described as a rite of passage for little boys who had reached the age of three, the usual age of weaning. They were crowned with spring flowers and given presents, including miniature versions of the wine jugs called *choes*, a shape produced for about fifty years during and after the Peloponnesian war. Infants who died before they could participate were sometimes buried with these jugs, which are gaily painted with scenes of chubby boys, naked but for their amulet strings, playing with small dogs, riding in carts, or making offerings of libations and cakes.[11] As we learn from Aristophanes' *Acharnians* (959–1234), adult males too looked forward to the Choes, when serious drinking was the order of the day. Each man was supplied with his own *chous*, a container which held about three liters of wine. (This custom was explained by reference to the hospitality shown Orestes when he came to Athens to be tried for matricide: to avoid sharing his pollution, all drank from separate jugs.) If we can take Aristophanes' comic description as an accurate reflection of ritual, the *archōn basileus* (King Archon) conducted a drinking competition with a skin of wine as the prize for the first man to empty his *chous*. In any case, numerous private contests and festive dinners were held around the city. At the end of the day, the revelers wrapped their *choes* in the garlands they had won and headed to the Limnaion, or sanctuary of Dionysos at Limnai (the Marshes), where they poured libations from whatever was left of the wine in the presence of a priestess.[12]

The Choes was the only day of the year when the Limnaion was open, and the sanctuary now witnessed an ancient and venerable rite: the sacred marriage of the King Archon's wife (the *basilinna* or Queen) and Dionysos himself. A law stating that the *basilinna* was required to be of Athenian birth and a virgin at the time of her wedding to the King Archon was inscribed on a stone set up in the Limnaion. In a speech preserved in the Demosthenic corpus (*Against Neaira* 59.73–78), Apollodorus is indignant that an alien woman of questionable virtue was permitted to assume the title of *basilinna* and perform the sacred acts on the city's behalf; he stresses the great antiquity and solemnity of the rite. This part of the festival was carried out in secret, and little is known of what actually constituted the "marriage." Perhaps there was a wedding procession from the Limnaion to the old city center east of the Akropolis, where the sacred union is said to have taken place in the so-called *boukoleion* (cattle shed), the headquarters of the King Archon. Modern scholars have speculated that the King Archon himself played the role of Dionysos in order to consummate the marriage. He further chose fourteen women attendants known as the *gerarai* (Reverend Ones), who assisted with offerings at fourteen altars, witnessed the secret things, and were apparently present at other Dionysiac rituals during the year. According to Apollodorus, they took the following oath: "I lead a holy life and I am pure and chaste from intercourse with men and other polluting things, and I will hallow the Theoinia (Wine God's Feast) and the Iobakcheia for Dionysos according to ancestral custom and at the appointed times."[13]

The third day of the Athenian celebration was also named after a type of vessel: Chytroi (Pots). Unfortunately, there are no detailed contemporary sources for the events of this day, nor do the sources make a clear distinction between Choes and Chytroi. It is logical that the pots, like the casks and jugs of the first two days, should have something to do with wine, and they have been connected to Phanodemus' account (*FGrH* 325 F 12) of Athenians mixing sweet wine with water for Dionysos Limnaios. The mixing of wine and water is attested for other Dionysiac festivals (below), and while mixing vessels came in a wide variety of specialized shapes, they were all essentially wide-mouthed pots. The scholiasts on Aristophanes and various lexicographers, however, give a different account, characterizing the Choes (or the month Anthesterion) as a time when ghosts rose from the underworld. They derive the name Chytroi from the cooking pots in which the Athenians prepared a mixture of grains as an offering to Hermes Chthonios (of the Underworld), with special reference to those who perished in the Flood. The sources portraying the Choes/Chytroi as a Halloween-like festival of the dead are late and somewhat confused accounts. On the other hand, Aristophanes' *Frogs* places Dionysos' visit to the underworld in the context of the Limnaion and the Anthesteria, lending plausibility to the connection between this festival and the dead.[14] It should be noted that while the celebration of Dionysos' advent in the month of Anthesterion seems to have been widespread among the Ionian peoples, the details of the Choes and Chytroi are apparently unique to Athens.[15]

The City Dionysia

While all the Athenian festivals of Dionysos included dramas or dithyrambs, the City Dionysia was transformed during the sixth century into the premier dramatic festival of the Athenian year, and, with the Panathenaia, played a crucial role in the construction of Athenian civic identity. Originally the urban version of the winter festivities held in the demes, the City celebration was moved to the spring month of Elaphebolion for the convenience of spectators and visitors traveling to Athens. Unlike the ancestral rites of the Lenaia and Anthesteria, which were the responsibility of the King Archon, the City Dionysia was treated like a newer festival and placed under the jurisdiction of the eponymous Archon. A preliminary to the festival was the "bringing in (*eisagōgē*) of Dionysos from the altar," the ceremonial torch-lit escort of the god's image from a temple near the Academy to its permanent home in the theater precinct. Dionysos Eleuthereus was the god of this festival, and tradition held that a man named Pegasos had first brought the image to Athens from the town of Eleutherai on the border with Boiotia. When the Athenians failed to receive the god with honor, they found themselves stricken with a disease of the male genitals. An oracle advised the Athenians to make model *phalloi* and honor the god with them. Scholars view the *eisagōgē* ritual either as a re-enactment of Dionysos' original advent in Athens, or more specifically as a commemoration of the Athenian annexation of Eleutherai and adoption of its Dionysiac cult. Our main sources for the *eisagōgē* are Hellenistic inscriptions, but it is likely that this complex of myth and ritual dates to the sixth century, when the modest temple of Dionysos Eleuthereus was built beside the theater at the foot of the south slope of the Akropolis.[16]

The main ritual of the Athenian festival was a relatively inclusive *pompē* or procession which, like the Panathenaic parade, featured women and scarlet-robed metics as well as male citizens. A *kanēphoros* (basket-bearer), a maiden of noble birth, led the procession with a golden basket, followed by people carrying loaves and libations of water and wine, or guiding sacrificial animals. (The goat was probably the preferred victim, given that tragedy seems to have the root meaning of "goat song.")[17] The colonies of Athens were required to send *phalloi* for the festival and presumably had their own representatives in the parade. The most colorful participants were the *chorēgoi* or sponsors of the plays, who wore elaborate robes embroidered with gold and golden crowns. The procession traveled through the agora, pausing at various altars to allow choruses to perform. Perhaps that evening was the time for the *kōmos*, a male-oriented, wine-soaked revel. The competitions included ten dithyrambic choruses made up of boys and ten of men, as well as comedies, tragedies, and satyr-plays. Before they began, the theater was purified with piglets' blood and libations were poured for the god, whose statue was present during performances. The crowds in the theater also witnessed the proclamation of crowns for honored citizens, the display of tribute from Athens' subject states, and the introduction of citizen youths reared at public expense because their fathers had fallen in battle.[18]

Dionysos in Attic Ikarion

The Country Dionysia of Attica, as its name implies, was a decentralized celebration that focused on Dionysos as an agricultural deity. Throughout the winter month of Posideion, villagers in the various demes of Attica organized processions such as the one described in Aristophanes' *Acharnians* (237–79), which includes a basketbearer with a sacred cake, slaves holding a large *phallos* on a pole, and the protagonist Dikaiopolis as a reveler, singing a ribald hymn to Phales, personification of the *phallos*. According to Aristotle (*Poet.* 1449a), comedy developed from these phallic songs. Many of the demes had their own theaters and presented comic and tragic performances. Ikarion, a wine-producing village at the northern foot of Mt. Pentelikon, had a unique status among the Attic demes as the first to receive Dionysos. According to legend, Ikarios welcomed the god and received the gift of wine, which he offered to his unsuspecting fellows. When they passed out from overindulgence, their relatives thought Ikarios was a poisoner and killed him. His daughter Erigone discovered the body with the help of Ikarios' faithful dog, and in her grief, she hanged herself from a tree. As a result of their impiety toward Dionysos, the villagers were struck with a plague, and the Delphic oracle directed them to hang up a female effigy to swing in the trees as an appeasement of Erigone. This story was connected with a purification ritual called the Aiora (Swinging), during which girls sat in swings suspended from trees. It has sometimes been assigned to the Anthesteria, though similar rituals involving boys and girls may have taken place at other times in the year.[19]

Its material remains show that Ikarion was indeed the home of a venerable Dionysiac cult. Beneath a Byzantine church were found the fragments of a massive cult statue once housed in the Dionysion. This marble image is dated to about 520, making it one of the earliest known cult statues in stone (most early examples were sculpted in wood or ivory). The seated, draped god held a *kantharos* and originally measured 2 m from head to foot. His history can be tentatively reconstructed with help from several inscriptions detailing the

Figure 10.1 Head of Dionysos cult statue from Ikarion, Attica, *c. 520*. Athens, National Archaeological Museum. Bildarchiv Foto Marburg.

cult and the system of liturgies for the presentation of dramatic performances in Ikarion. A fifth-century inscription (*IG* I³ 254) mentions that the *chorēgoi*, the demesmen organizing the dramas for the Country Dionysia, were sworn in with one hand on a statue – presumably that of Dionysos. Ancient repairs to the statue are suggested by the present state of the head (which has sometimes been mistaken for a mask) and confirmed by a fourth-century inscription (*IG* II² 2851). When first sculpted, this statue would have been one of the most impressive in Attica. It was certainly housed in a temple, though the extant architectural remains are not complete enough to tell us more.[20]

The Lenaia

Like the Anthesteria, the Lenaia was a widespread festival among the Ionians, to judge from the appearances of the winter month name Lenaion in inscriptions. At Athens, the festival was celebrated in the corresponding month Gamelion, and was overseen by the King Archon and officials connected with the Eleusinian mysteries, who organized a procession and musical contest, later expanded to include dramas. These competitions, at which several of Aristophanes' comedies debuted, were held in the Lenaion, a sanctuary that has left no trace but was probably located in the agora. Little is known about the ritual activities of the Lenaia, except that Dionysos was invoked as "Iakchos, son of Semele, giver of wealth." In a custom common to the Lenaia and Anthesteria, scurrilous gibes were cast at the spectators by young men in the processional wagons.[21]

The name Lenaia is usually derived from the Ionic term *lēnai* (wild women or mainads), though an alternative theory links it to *lēnos* (a vat for treading grapes). If the former etymology is accurate, it points to an early mainadic element in the festival. Mainads (also known as *bakchai*) worshiped Dionysos in a "maddened" state of ecstasy, which was expressed primarily through physical movement: energetic dancing performed out of doors, particularly on the mountainsides. They wore distinctive animal skins over their dresses, left their hair unbound, and carried ivy-tipped staffs called *thursoi*. Their activities simulated those of the female half of Dionysos' entourage, the band of nymphs who reared him in Nysa. Archaic and Classical sources have much to say of these madwomen who leave the confines of their homes for the wild mountains, but rather surprisingly, there is no unambiguous evidence of real-life mainads as opposed to mythic ones before the Hellenistic period. Still, the wealth of literary evidence strongly suggests that mainadism was practiced in at least some areas (Boiotia, the Peloponnese, and Delphi) from an early date. Again, the literary accounts often focus on mainadic transgressions (those who reject the god are driven to crimes such as the dismemberment of their own children) or tell of superhuman invulnerability and strength (e.g. the rending of a bull in Euripides' *Bacchae*). It is difficult to separate the mythic elaborations from the authentic ritual core in these accounts.

A different type of evidence for Classical mainads are the so-called Lenaia vases, which depict women moving about a temporary, outdoor cult image of Dionysos, a draped column or pole topped with a bearded mask. This masked column appears first on black figured vases, mostly *lekuthoi*, where the presence of satyrs suggests that the female figures in attendance are to be understood as nymphs. Red figured examples (mostly *stamnoi* produced for export) include vases showing ecstatic, mainad-like females dancing around the column and altar of the god. On one side, we typically see stately women ladling wine from twin *stamnoi* set up on a table before the masked column; the other side shows women walking or dancing and holding drinking cups. Whether any of these scenes can be assigned to a specific Attic festival has been the subject of debate since the early twentieth century, with one camp opting for the Lenaia as the "festival of madwomen," another for the Anthesteria, and a third suggesting that the scenes are generic or mythical. It is probable that the use of the masked column was not limited to a specific festival, for the vases do not form a coherent group. The scenes of dancing women are consistent with the hypothesis of cultic mainadism in Classical Attica, but they cannot confirm it in the absence of other evidence.[22]

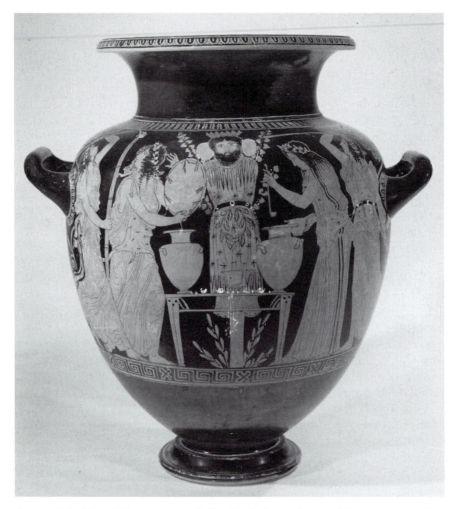

Figure 10.2 "Lenaia" vase: women ladle wine before an image of Dionysos (a masked and draped pole). Attic *stamnos* exported to Italy, fifth century. Naples, Museo Archeologico Nazionale. Scala/Art Resource.

Mainadism: myth and history

Epigraphic evidence of cultic mainadism from the third century and later can be used to construct a model of Classical mainadic ritual, but there are nagging questions about the origins of Hellenistic mainads: were they the direct recipients of authentic ancient traditions, or were they creatively drawing from poetic descriptions, such as the *Bacchae*, to "revive" cultic traditions that had long since lapsed? The possibility that the *Bacchae* may have played

136

an instrumental role in such mainadic revivals is especially relevant to the famous Magnesian mainad inscription. In the reign of Hadrian, a time of keen antiquarian interest, a Hellenistic inscription recording an oracle of Apollo was copied onto a new stone (*IMagn.* 215). The inscription told how the inhabitants of Magnesia on the Maiandros river consulted Delphi after finding an image of Dionysos in a plane tree. The Pythia told them, "Go to the holy plan of Thebes to get mainads who are from the race of Kadmeian Ino. They will give you *orgia* (ecstatic rites, or perhaps sacred objects) and noble customs and will establish *thiasoi* (worship groups) of Bakchos in your city." The inscription continues with the story of how three Theban mainads were indeed brought to Magnesia and ultimately buried in places of honor. The organization of the Magnesian *thiasoi* closely follows the scheme laid out in the *Bacchae*: Kadmos' daughters Ino, Autonoë, and Agave lead three mainadic groups who rove over Mt. Kithairon. Whether this arrangement reflected Classical Theban ritual practice, we simply do not know. In any case, this inscription, taken together with others, shows that post-Classical mainads were highly respected members of the community, performing state-sponsored and presumably decorous rituals.[23]

When conducted under state auspices, sacrifices for Dionysos usually followed the same conventions as those for other gods, but non-standard sacrifices are prominent in Dionysiac myth, particularly in mainadic contexts.[24] Many Attic vases depict the mainads or Dionysos himself holding the torn remains of an animal, a fawn or goat. This motif refers to a specialized form of sacrifice: the mainads violently tore animals limb from limb (*sparagmos*). Scholars and late antique sources, particularly the Christian fathers, often assume that mainads ate the raw flesh of animals so sacrificed (*ōmophagia*), but this is less clear. The chorus in the *Bacchae* (138) speaks of "the joyful act (*charis*) of eating raw meat," but they are describing Dionysos' behavior, not necessarily their own. Later, the raving mainads tear apart a herd of cattle (734–47), but there is no mention of omophagy. The consumption of raw flesh, however, may have played a role in certain Dionysiac mysteries. A fragment of Euripides' *Cretans* (472 *TrGF*) alludes to a sacred meal of raw meat, which formed a stark contrast to the pure vegetarian diet of the initiates. Dionysos Omestes (Raw-Eater) is mentioned already by Alcaeus, a native of Lesbos, and the related epithet Omadios is attested for Chios and Tenedos, where there are rumors of human sacrifice.[25] Greek myth is full of accounts of men or infants torn to pieces by the mainads, who fail to distinguish between human and animal quarry, yet there is no credible evidence that such forms of "sacrifice" were regularly practiced in any Greek city.

Delphi and Dionysos

The Panhellenic sanctuary of Delphi, primarily dedicated to Apollo, welcomed Dionysos during the months of winter and early spring, when Apollo was

137

said to be visiting the Hyperboreans. Delphic theology emphasized an intimate fraternal relationship between the two deities. Excavation of the Sacred Way brought to light a stele inscribed in 340/339 with a *paian* in which Dionysos is urged to appear "in the holy season of spring" for the Theoxenia (Hospitality to the Gods), a festival at which deities were provided with food, drink, and entertainment.[26] It also describes major additions to Dionysos' Delphic cult: the establishment of a sacrifice and dithyrambic competition, the erection of a statue of Bakchos "in a chariot drawn by golden lions" and the building of a grotto "suitable for the holy god."

Already in the fifth century, tragedians speak of the ecstatic worship of Dionysos high on the slopes of Mt. Parnassos. Here the entourage of Dionysos, whether mortal women or nymphs, were called Thyiads (Raving Ones), and they are described as scaling the twin peaks above the Korykian cave, roving over the mountain with torches to light their way and wetting the rocks with sacrificial blood.[27] No special altar or cult place is mentioned either on the mountain or in the sanctuary itself, though by the fourth century Dionysos and some rather sedate Thyiads, whose fragmentary remains have been recovered, were sculpted in the west pediment of Apollo's new temple. Like other mainadic festivals, this one took place every other winter; the Thyiads must have experienced great dangers and discomforts on the cold, dark slopes of Parnassos. It would be difficult to believe that Greek women actually danced on the mountain at night, were it not for the testimony of Plutarch (*Mor.* 249e–f, 953d), who served as a priest at Delphi during the turn of the first century CE. In his day, the Thyiads once had to be rescued when they were caught in a snowstorm on Parnassos. Pausanias (10.4.3) reports that he spoke with Thyiads from Attica, who joined with their Delphic counterparts every other year to perform mysterious rites for Dionysos.

Agriania/Agrionia

An early spring month Agrionios and a corresponding festival called Agr(i)ania/Agr(i)onia are well attested among the Dorian Greeks and in Boiotia. The name seems to be related to the adjective *agrios* "wild, savage," and the myths and rituals associated with this festival involve women who run wild under the influence of Dionysos. What distinguishes the Agriania from other mainadic traditions is the role played by men, who oppose and check the women's ravings, yet are themselves led by the priest of Dionysos or his surrogate. At Boiotian Orchomenos, the three daughters of Minyas were driven mad when they refused to participate in Dionysiac dances. Tearing apart an infant in their care, they dashed outdoors, only to be chased away as murderers. During the Agrionia, women said to be descended from the Minyads were pursued by a sword-wielding priest of Dionysos who was empowered to kill any woman he caught. Yet if this power was ever more than symbolic, it had lapsed by Plutarch's day (*Quaest. Graec.* 299c–300a), when the priest Zoilos actually killed a woman and his family was deprived of the priesthood as a result.

At Argos, we are told, the Agriania was held to honor Iphinoë, another victim of the Dionysiac pursuit. According to Hesiod (fr. 131 M–W), the three daughters of Proitos refused to join Dionysos' worship and fell into a murderous frenzy, soon joined by the other women and girls of the city. With the strongest youths of the city, the Dionysiac prophet Melampous pursued the women to Sikyon, where Iphinoë met her fate (a fourth-century inscription marking her tomb in the agora has been excavated). Other versions tell how Melampous cured the women of their madness and purified them, marrying one of the surviving daughters and succeeding to the kingship.[28] Thus the Agriania, performed on a biennial basis like other mainadic rituals, enacted a dissolution of social order and gender norms followed by a return to stability. The ritual segregation of men and women, not unusual in itself, was escalated into an overt opposition between raving women and pursuing men. The earliest attested version is the Homeric story (*Il.* 6.130–40) of Thracian Lykourgos, who drove the nurses of raving Dionysos over the sacred plain of Nysa, striking them with an ox-goad while the god himself leapt fearfully into the sea and was received in the bosom of Thetis. King Perseus of Argos carried out a similar pursuit, killing the mainadic Haliai (Sea Women), but ultimately honoring their tombs and founding a temple of Dionysos. These myths probably arose from pursuit rituals like those attested for the Agrionia.[29]

Wine miracles and the Elean hymn

More than the other Olympian gods, Dionysos is credited with supernatural wonders: springs of wine gush from the ground, *thursoi* drip with honey, vines spring up in minutes and bear fruit. These miracles are strongly associated with Dionysiac ecstasy (e.g. Eur. *Bacch.* 699–707) and with the epiphany of the god, particularly in his bull form. Such wonders, including magic "ephemeral" vines that grow and bear fruit in one winter day, are mentioned in Greek tragedies, but it is unclear what role they played in cult during the Archaic and Classical periods.[30] Later sources speak of sanctuaries in which miraculous springs of wine were to be found, sometimes in connection with a lesser-known Dionysiac festival, the Theodaisia (God's Feast). Haliartos in Boiotia celebrated the Theodaisia by the spring Kissousa, where local tradition held that the infant Dionysos was bathed. The water of Kissousa was delicious and "had the color and sparkle of wine," the result of the holy bath.[31] The month name Theodaisios and/or the festival were observed in Kyrene, Rhodes, and Krete, where *arrhēta* (unspoken things) were performed in connection with the Theodaisia of the city Olous. Springs of wine are also found in Ionian contexts. Pliny (*HN* 2.106, 31.13) says that wine flowed in the sanctuary of Dionysos on the island of Andros for the seven days of the Theodaisia in the winter. Similar wonders are attested for Teos and Naxos, where the miracle was inaugurated when Dionysos and Ariadne met. Based on the little evidence we have, the Theodaisia seems to have been a biennial winter festival, hence mainadic in origin, concerned with the mysteries of the god's birth and characterized by supernatural signs of his presence.

We see a similar combination of wine miracle, epiphany, and women's ritual in Elis at the celebration of the Dionysia or Thyia (Raving). According to Pausanias (6.26.1–2), the Eleans believed that Dionysos attended the festival, manifesting himself in the wine. At his sanctuary outside the city, the priests placed three empty pots in a room and sealed the doors in the presence of witnesses. The next day, when the seals were broken, the pots were found filled with wine. Plutarch (*Quaest. Graec.* 299a–b) reports that the Elean women sang a song of invocation to the god: "Come, hero Dionysos, with the Charites to the holy Elean temple, raving (*thuōn*) to the temple on bovine foot, worthy bull, worthy bull." This hymn, which scholars consider one of the most ancient attested cult songs, was most likely sung as part of the Thyia. It illustrates the visualization of Dionysos as a bull, a recurrent feature of his worship.[32] In the *Bacchae*, for example, the ecstatic chorus praises Dionysos as the bull-horned god (100) and he appears to the demented Pentheus in the form of a bull (922). The designation of Dionysos as "hero" has not been satisfactorily explained.

Thebes and Semele

The tradition of Dionysos' birth at Thebes was very ancient, attested by both Homer (*Il.* 14.323–25) and Hesiod (*Theog.* 940–42). There the god was called Dionysos Kadmeios because his sanctuary was located on the akropolis (Kadmeia) near that of Demeter. It included the part of the old palace where Kadmos' daughter Semele, the lover of Zeus, was destroyed by a thunderbolt. In keeping with Greek custom regarding places hit by lightning, the shrine/tomb (*sēkos*) was delimited by a wall and declared off limits for human feet. Euripides (*Bacch.* 7–8) describes it as "smoldering with the still-living flame of Zeus," perhaps an eternal flame of some sort, yet overgrown with lush vines. Centuries later, Pausanias (9.12.3) viewed the same spot, now called the bridechamber (*thalamos*) of Semele, and was told that the ancient image of Dionysos Kadmeios consisted of a log that fell from heaven with the thunderbolt.

Considering the importance of Thebes in the history of Dionysiac cult, we know surprisingly few specifics about the rituals performed there. The existence of a mainadic ritual conducted on Mt. Kithairon, probably the Agrionia, can be deduced from the myth of Pentheus' pursuit of the mainads as told in Euripides' *Bacchae*. As we have seen, the authority of Thebes in Dionysiac matters was supported by the Delphic oracle, and certain Theban cults were imitated by other cities. For example, the Pythia instructed the Korinthians to obtain the tree from which Pentheus was dragged and to "worship it just like the god." Two images made of pinewood from Thebes were called Dionysos Lysios (Liberator) and Bakcheios. Sikyon too had a statue of Dionysos Lysios, brought from Thebes at the behest of the oracle, and paired with a Bakcheios. The sanctuary in Sikyon was located beside the theater, and one night each year the citizens escorted the god's two images to this Dionysion while carrying torches and singing hymns.[33] The Athenians practiced a similar ritual with respect to Dionysos Eleuthereus, originally a Boiotian god, who was installed beside the theater. The cult pattern can be traced ultimately to the sanctuary of Dionysos Lysios near the theater at Thebes.

Semele's cult was observed at both the major Theban sanctuaries of Dionysos, on the Kadmeia and at the theater. Euripides (*Phoen.* 1755–56) mentions Theban women's dances in the mountains for Semele. The cult spread to Attica, for Pindar (fr. 75.19 Snell-Maehler) speaks of Athenian "choruses for Semele with her circlet wreath" in a dithyramb composed for the City Dionysia, and the deme Erchia sponsored sacrifices for Dionysos and Semele during the same festival. Scholars often call Semele a "faded" earth goddess because she is shown on Greek vases, like Persephone/Kore and Ge, rising from the earth. The Greeks, however, always thought of her as a heroine who both suffered and transcended mortality. Hesiod notes her special character as a mortal who birthed a god, and narratives about her focus almost exclusively on her death and Dionysos' descent to the underworld to retrieve her. Every eight years the Delphic Thyiads conducted the Heroïs, a festival of Semele that included both public rites and secrets kept hidden from men. From what he was able to observe, Plutarch (*Mor.* 293b–c) concluded that the Heroïs celebrated the *anagōgē* (bringing up) of Semele from the underworld.[34]

Dionysiac mysteries

According to the Ionian philosopher Heraclitus (fr. 15 *DK*), Hades and Dionysos were the same. The concept of a chthonian, underworld Dionysos who had a role to play in the fate of the soul was widespread, though not fully manifested in state religion. Instead, it was disseminated through private Bakchic mysteries, which seem to have arisen in the late Archaic period. An inscription from a chamber tomb at Cumae in Southern Italy restricts use of the tomb to Bakchic initiates (*c.* 500). At the other end of the Greek world, Dionysiac mysteries were celebrated in the Black Sea colony of Olbia. Herodotus' story (4.78–79) of the Skythian king who had himself initiated at Olbia finds support in the excavations there, which yielded a sixth-century mirror inscribed with the names of a couple and the Bakchic ritual cry *euai*. Here too were collected a scattering of bone tablets from the fifth century, one with the message "life, death, life, truth … Dio(nysoi), Orphik(oi)."[35] Discoveries like these have made it clear that the movement scholars call Orphism, which consisted of teachings and rituals concerned with the secret knowledge and purifications necessary to achieve a blessed afterlife, overlapped with Dionysiac religion. An esoteric Orphic tradition held that Persephone was the mother of Zagreus, who as a child was torn apart and consumed by the Titans, yet came to life again as Dionysos in the womb of Semele.[36] This unique experience meant that Dionysos, in conjunction with Persephone, was able to grant release from the miserable lot of the dead; thus his epithet Lysios (Releaser) had one meaning for the general public and another for the initiate. In the late Classical and Hellenistic periods, many initiates went to their graves with tiny folded leaves of gold, inscribed with the special instructions and passwords they would require. A small trapezoid of beaten gold from a grave at the south Italian city of Hipponion (c. 400) advises its owner to avoid the spring on the right when entering the house of Hades. Instead, she must look for the cold water flowing from the Lake of Memory, and speak the right words to the guardians. If she succeeds, she will "travel a road, a sacred road, which other famous initiates and *bakchoi* also tread." Roughly a century later, a Thessalian woman was buried with two gold tablets shaped like ivy leaves positioned over her breasts, tablets which also provided the password to life after death: "Tell Persephone that the Bakchic one himself has set you free!" More than forty of these gold leaves have been uncovered in Thessaly, Krete, Italy, and other sites, witnesses to a form of religious experience that is rarely described in literary sources.[37]

Plato and other authors speak scornfully of the itinerant prophets who offered initiations and purifications to the ignorant, and it is clear that Orphic/Bakchic initiation did not have the same cultural prestige as the Eleusinian or other state-sponsored mysteries. Instead of journeying as pilgrims to a sanctuary and becoming a member of a public cohort of initiates, Bakchic devotees received initiation privately or as part of a small group from prophets who traveled about plying the family trade with their heirloom sacred books and spoken formulas. (Although written texts seem to have played an important role in the Orphic traditions, recent scholarship on certain hexameter texts from the gold leaves suggests that they can be traced to an oral archetype.)[38] The Dionysiac prophets, who induced "telestic madness" as a remedy for physical and spiritual ills, had a long history reaching back to mythic figures like Melampous and Polyeidos. What is less clear is how such rites were related to those of Bakchic *thiasoi*, particularly those that engaged in mainadism. Euripides' *Bacchae* (e.g. 22, 73, 238) is sprinkled with allusions to Dionysos' *teletai*, initiatory rites, which were an integral part of the "Theban strand" of his worship.[39] The Delphic Thyiads, for example, had a limited membership, generally restricted to females who had experienced *teletai* preparing them for the mystical aspects of the cult.

Further reading

Henrichs 1983a provides an excellent, brief survey of Dionysiac religion, and Gould 2001 usefully examines recent scholarly perspectives. Otto 1965 (originally published in 1933) is still essential reading, a sensitive and seminal discussion of "the god who comes." Carpenter and Faraone eds 1993 collects several excellent essays. Chapter 4, "Orpheus and Egypt," in Burkert 2004 provides an account of recently discovered texts pertaining to Dionysiac mysteries, with current bibliography. Parker 2005, Chapter 14, provides detailed discussion of the festivals in Athens.

11

DEAR TO THE PEOPLE
Hermes, Pan, and nature deities

Relative to the other Olympian deities, Hermes had few sanctuaries, festivals, and temples. Instead, he was pre-eminent in private, neighborhood, and domestic contexts, often in connection with other deities worshiped in the countryside. Hermes' name is derived from an object: *herma* refers to a pillar-like prop or support, as well as to the cairn or stone-pile that marks a path or border. Essentially a god of travel and boundaries, Hermes came to preside over a host of related domains, such as thievery, lucky finds, and transitions between the lands of the living and the dead. Like Apollo and Pan, Hermes has an important pastoral function, especially in the oldest center of his worship, Arkadia. His cults are most prominent on the Greek mainland, particularly Attica, Boiotia, and the Peloponnese. His mythic function as the herald and messenger of the gods, probably borrowed from Near Eastern epic, is not emphasized in worship, though he is a patron of heralds and ambassadors.

Hermes in Arkadia

If, as seems likely from the Linear B tablets, Hermes had a Mycenaean predecessor, it is not surprising to find his cult vigorously maintained in mountainous Arkadia, one of the regions least affected by the upheavals at the close of the Bronze Age.[1] For people who support themselves by herding sheep and goats, as most Arkadians did, maintaining boundaries and pre-venting the theft of one's flocks (or thieving a neighbor's flocks undetected) are of paramount importance. Panhellenic myth recognized Arkadia as the god's birthplace, and his worship was unusually prominent in this land, where myth and cult tie him to mountain peaks, especially Kyllene. In a late stratum of Homer (*Od.* 24.1) and other Archaic poetry, he receives the epithet Kyllenios. No cave on Kyllene has been confirmed as a cultic counterpart of the one described in the Homeric *Hymn* to Hermes, but Pausanias (8.17.1–2) speaks of a ruined temple on the mountain with a cult statue made of wood from a conifer. The people of neighboring Pheneos dedicated at Olympia a statue by the Aiginetan master Onatas (*c.* 500), which showed Hermes carrying a ram under his arm. Small Archaic bronzes of the same subject have been found in Arkadia, so it is probable that the Arkadians visualized him as a fellow herdsman. He was also an ancestor, having fathered the local heroes Evander, Myrtilos, and Aipytos, whose name means "of the heights." Homer (*Il.* 2.604) mentions the latter's tomb near Kyllene, while a temple of Hermes Aipytos stood at Tegea. The relationship between god and the hero whose name he adopts parallels that between Poseidon and Erechtheus at Athens. Another Archaic cult of Hermes was centered on the hill and town Akakesion, which were etymologically related to the god's Homeric epithet *akakēta*, "doing no wrong" or "benevolent." With the synoecism of Megalopolis *c.* 365, the most venerable Parrhasian cults, including that of Hermes Akakesios, were moved to the new city.[2]

Lucky Hermes

To a large extent, the cult of Hermes was conducted at the popular level, meaning that people used modes of worship other than standard city-sponsored sanctuaries and festivals. The fourth day of the month, mentioned as Hermes' birthday in the Homeric *Hymn* to Hermes (4.19), was the day to present offerings of food, often figs or small cakes, at neighborhood herms. Hermes was a "hungry" god, parodied in comedy as a food gobbler.[3] His fondness for tasty food and drink is probably a reflection of his role as a provider of good things. Lucky finds and other unexpected goods were called *hermaia*, and Hermes sometimes had the epithet Tychon (Lucky). Prayers, inscriptions, and votive reliefs, many from the area around Athens, demonstrate that Hermes was grouped in worship with other gods believed to inhabit the surface of the earth and to exert an influence over the prosperity of herdsmen; "Hermes, Pan and the nymphs" was a common triad in prayers and dedications at rural shrines. Early poets agree that Hermes could aid in the multiplication of flocks. According to Homer (*Il.* 14.489–91, 16.180–86), Hermes favored Phorbas, a Trojan rich in flocks (*polumēlos*), and made him wealthy. On the Greek side, his affair with the aptly named Polymele resulted in a son Eudoros (Generous).

In popular belief, Hermes oversaw the operation of what we might call "poor man's oracles," those that could be consulted by people who lacked the wherewithal to travel to a major oracle and offer sacrifices there. Instead, they divined by casting knucklebones or other small objects and searching the resulting patterns for messages from the gods. The Homeric *Hymn* to Hermes (4.550–68) says that the youthful god desired to share the prestige that his brother Apollo derived from Delphi, but had to be satisfied with a lesser form of divination involving the observation of bees. Hermes did possess at least one proper oracle, at Phares in Achaia, but even this was an informal affair compared to the pomp of Delphi. In the market square at Phares stood a Hermes Agoraios (of the Marketplace) facing a hearth surrounded with lamps. In the time of Pausanias (7.22.2–3), whoever wished to consult the oracle entered the agora at dusk, burned incense on the hearth, lit the lamps, and placed a coin on the altar. Then, having whispered a question in the god's ear, the petitioner covered his own ears so as to block out all sounds. Once out of the agora, he unstopped his ears and received as the oracle the first phrases he heard.

Hermes as guide and protector

Of all the Olympian gods, Hermes is the most "down to earth" (*epichthonios*), a deity who eschews the heavenly, watery, and underworld abodes in favor of the places inhabited by mortals. His patronage of travelers grows not only from his territorial concerns but also from his role as a herdsman, for Hermes accompanies and protects the traveler just as the shepherd guides and watches over his flocks. In the last book of the *Iliad* (24.334–38), Zeus asks him to protect Priam on his mission into the Greek camp because Hermes loves "to be a man's companion." Roadside cairns and guideposts marking the path belonged to Hermes, and multi-headed images of him, like those of Hekate, were placed at crossroads. The Classical herm, a stone image of Hermes consisting of a squared pillar with a bearded head of Hermes on top, a cross-bar where the "shoulders" should be, and erect male genitals halfway down, probably developed from wooden versions used as markers. Around 520, Hipparchos, brother of the Athenian tyrant Hippias, set up stone herms marking the halfway points on the roads from each Attic village to the agora, where the Altar of the Twelve Gods had been designated the city center. Edifying verses supplied by Hipparchos himself, such as "walk with just intent" and "deceive not a friend" were carved upon the herms. These were enthusiastically received, and soon so many herms were clustered at the principal entrance to the agora that the spot became known as "the Herms." Magistrates and victorious generals like Kimon dedicated them, and one in particular, known as Hermes Agoraios, had its own altar.[4]

From the late sixth century on, herms served the Athenians and other Greeks not only as milestones and boundary markers, but also as guardians, warding off any evil spirits (or thieves) who might try to enter a home. They became an important focus of popular piety, and were regularly saluted, anointed with oil, and garlanded. Scenes of private sacrifice before herms are very common on Attic figured vases. Thus it was a terrible shock for the Athenians when they awoke one morning to find that someone had gone about the city knocking the noses and genitals from their beloved herms. This sacrilege took place on the eve of the Sicilian expedition in 415, and augured ill for the Athenian war effort.[5]

Phallic Hermes

Burkert has linked the function of the herm as a territorial marker to its phallicism, for in the primate world phallic display is used to warn potential trespassers to keep their distance.[6] It is unclear, however, whether Hermes' phallicism is an ancient part of his cult. According to Herodotus (2.51), the Athenians learned to use ithyphallic images (those with erect members) from the Pelasgians, the pre-Greek inhabitants of the Aegean. He connects the herms with the ithyphallic statues used as guardians in the cult of the Samothracian gods, which was "Pelasgian" in origin. Yet phallic herms are not attested in the early Archaic period, and Athenian contact with Samothrace was minimal before the Classical period. Another theory holds that the *phallos* is borrowed from the cult of Dionysos, whose phallic aspects are attested much earlier. Dionysos is sometimes worshiped in the form of a draped post and crosspiece topped with a mask, the same arrangement that most likely developed into the stone herm. Ancient authors commented on the unusual statue of Hermes Phales at Kyllene in Elis, which was simply an erect *phallos* set on a base. Similar statues are attested in Dionysiac cult.[7] Less widely accepted, though still plausible, is the view that Hermes' phallicism is tied to his pastoral and generative function.[8] Like his equally phallic compatriot Pan, Hermes multiplies the flocks. Since gods typically become practitioners of the activities they rule, it is not surprising to find that Hermes has a lusty side. The Homeric *Hymn* to Aphrodite (5.256–63) tells how he and the silens mate with the nymphs in the recesses of caves, and Hermes is the constant companion of the nymphs on votive reliefs and in the private observances of herdsmen, such as the swineherd Eumaios who sets aside portions for Hermes and the nymphs at his meal (Hom. *Od.* 14.434–36). On this reading, the *phallos* is "lucky" because it is symbolic of animal fecundity, hence prosperity. Hermes' regular cultic connections with Aphrodite are also relevant to his phallicism; where they appear as a pair, the focus of the cult is usually on human sexuality.

Ephebic Hermes

In the fifth century, Hermes was increasingly recognized as "Lord of Contests" (Agonios or Enagonios) and, with Herakles, became a patron of the gymnasium and *palaistra* (wrestling ground). From this time he was usually portrayed as a beardless, athletic youth with great homoerotic appeal, though stone herms continued to be sculpted with archaizing bearded heads. The games for Hermes (Hermaia) at Achaian Pellene, where warm cloaks were awarded as prizes, were recognized at a Panhellenic level by the fifth century, and Hermaian games were celebrated at many other sites, including Pheneos beneath Kyllene. Pindar's victory odes often mention Hermes as the giver of victory, a god who "has charge of contests and the awarding of prizes." In this guise of a youthful god associated with the physical education of boys, Hermes became an archetype of the ephebe, or young male citizen on the cusp of manhood.[9] While the ephebic god is typical of the late Classical and Hellenistic periods, a few Archaic cults, particularly in the Peloponnese and Krete, also featured a youthful Hermes.

Recent excavations at Kato Symi in east-central Krete near Mt. Dikte show that cult activity in the Middle Minoan period continued unbroken through Archaic times, when the deities of the shrine were known as Hermes and Aphrodite. This sanctuary is noted for its fascinating series of bronze cut-out plaques from the seventh and sixth centuries. The subjects include hunters with bow and arrow, youths lifting or wrestling animals, scenes of homosexual courtship, and Hermes himself, who seems to have been the dominant partner at the sanctuary, to judge from the surviving dedications. The votives suggest a mostly male clientele engaged in typical Dorian aristocratic maturation and socialization rituals. At Kato Symi, Hermes appears as both beardless youth and mature adult, as if to illustrate his patronage of youths approaching manhood. Hermes' title here was Kedrites (of the Cedar), and a seventh-century bronze plaque illustrates his epiphany as a beardless god sitting in a tree, gazing at the viewer. This concept is probably a Minoan survival, since he is only rarely connected with trees in other parts of the Greek world, and on the coins of Phaistos Zeus Welchanos similarly appears as a youthful god sitting in a tree.[10]

Hermes of Tanagra

The Boiotians contested the Arkadian claim that Hermes was born on Kyllene, asserting instead their own local traditions that Mt. Kerykeion (Herald's Mountain), or perhaps Thebes, witnessed the god's nativity. Tanagra, home of the poet Corinna, was particularly devoted to Hermes. As in Arkadia, he was regarded as an ancestor, the partner of the eponymous nymph Tanagra. One of Hermes' titles at Tanagra was Kriophoros (Ram-Bearer). The cult statue, sculpted by Kalamis in the early Classical period, is reproduced on Tanagran coins, which show a youthful, nude Hermes with a ram draped over his shoulders. It replaced an older, bearded and cloaked type. During the festival of Hermes, the town chose its most beautiful youth to walk the length of the walls carrying a lamb on his shoulders, just as Hermes once warded off a plague by carrying a ram. The ritual can be interpreted as a purification by which the unfortunate animal, like the scapegoat, absorbs into itself all the noxious influences threatening the town, or again as a means by which the god, in his guise as "the good shepherd," wards off evil.[11] As the city god and protector of Tanagra, Hermes turned away military threats as well. Another of his sanctuaries was dedicated to Hermes Promachos (Battle-Ready), who led the Tanagran youth in battle against invading men from Euboia, wielding a strigil as his weapon. The emphasis upon Hermes' youthful beauty and his association with ephebes and athletics suggests an origin in the fifth century or later for these Tanagran legends, but the cult of Hermes there is doubtless much older.

Hermes of Ainos

The Greek colonies of Thrace seem to have shown a special interest in Hermes as evinced in the devices on their coins. Many of these are Hellenistic or later, but Herodotus (5.7) says that the Thracian royal families worshiped "Hermes" the most and considered him their ancestor. This syncretism of a Thracian deity with a Greek one probably had its effect on both sides of the cultural divide. At Ainos the cult of Hermes was certainly well established by the mid-fifth century, when coins depict an unusual, pillar-like statue standing on a high-backed throne.[12] The body has no arms or legs, nor is it equipped with a *phallos* like standard herms. The head is anthropomorphic and bearded; in some examples the god wears a hat or is draped. The throne, an elaborate piece of furniture sometimes decorated with a goat attribute or the god's wand, conveys the message that the image is sacred. According to a legend related by Callimachus (fr. 197 Pf.), some fishermen of Ainos netted a block of wood and recognized in it a god, which Apollo's oracle instructed them to set up in the city. Epeios, maker of the Trojan horse, had sculpted the image, and it was washed to the sea from the Skamandros river. The statue was known as Hermes Perpheraios, probably a reference to a ritual of *periphora* in which the god was ceremoniously conducted about the city to spread his benefactions.

Hermes Chthonios

In the last book of the *Odyssey* (24.1–10), Hermes shepherds the souls of the dead suitors to the underworld with a lovely golden wand, which he also uses to lull mortals to sleep and to awaken them. Hermes' mythic role as the *psuchopompos* or guide of souls is reflected in religious practice through prayers and offerings to Hermes Chthonios (of the Underworld) at the grave-site, attested in Thessaly and Argos.[13] As the god of ways and boundaries, closely associated with the standing stones and cairns that marked graves, Hermes was an ideal guide for journeys between the worlds of the living and the dead. In Aeschylus' *Libation Bearers* (1–5, 124–25), Orestes and Electra pray at their father's grave to Hermes Chthonios, the deity who can summon spirits from under the earth. Usually invoked in private contexts, including curses and binding spells, Hermes Chthonios occasionally plays a role in public festivals honoring the dead. After the Persian wars, the heroic dead of Plataiai were summoned to an annual banquet in their honor by means of prayers to Zeus and Hermes Chthonios, and the Attic Anthesteria supposedly included a meal offered to Hermes Chthonios for the dead.[14] The ghoulish, necromantic aspect of Hermes is balanced by his beneficent protection of souls in the vulnerable state between sleeping and waking. Homer (*Od.* 7.136–38) mentions that the Phaiakians offered libations to Hermes before retiring, while Apollodorus of Athens (*FGrH* 244 F 129) calls Hermes the *oneiropompos* or conductor of dreams, and says that he is a guardian of sleepers; people orient their beds so that the foot of the bed faces Hermes' image, and pray to him before sleep.

Pan

Pan is distinctive among the Greek gods because of his hybrid human-animal form (theriomorphism). The earliest images of Pan, in bronze sculpture and in a Boiotian vase painting of the early fifth century, show a goat-headed god with a human torso atop a goat's hind legs.[15] Originally a guardian of the goats whose character he shares, he achieved Panhellenic status only in the

Figure 11.1 Skuphos with an early depiction of Pan, from the Theban Kabirion, fifth century. Athens, National Archaeological Museum. Bildarchiv Foto Marburg.

150

fifth century, when his cult was introduced from Arkadia to Athens and rapidly diffused to the rest of the Greek world. Many etymologies have been put forward for his name, which is also known in the compound form Aigipan (Goat-Pan). The most convincing makes it a cognate of Latin *pastor*, so that Pan is "one who grazes the flocks."

In Arkadia itself, Pan's myth and cult were not standardized. There were conflicting views of his genealogy, the most common being that he was the son of Zeus and twin of the national hero Arkas, or that he was the son of Hermes and Penelope. His connection with Zeus sprang from their association on Mt. Lykaion, the sacred mountain of the Arkadians. Pan possessed a sanctuary on the south slopes of Lykaion, where in keeping with his identity as both goat and goatherd, he offered asylum to any animal being pursued by a wolf (*lukos*). A votive dump excavated here revealed many late Archaic and early Classical bronze figures, cut-out plaques, and terracottas with subjects reminiscent of those at Kato Symi: hunters, men carrying animals for sacrifice, and Hermes. Both youthful and mature males are depicted, and the bronzes include dead foxes, a standard courtship gift presented by adult males to their favorite youths. Inscribed pots show that the sanctuary was sacred to Pan, whose role as a god of the hunt and Master of Animals made him well suited, like Hermes, to sponsor maturation rituals.[16]

The Athenians believed that Pan sent them a message on the eve of Marathon (490) via Philippides, who ran 233 km to ask for aid from the Spartans. Passing through Arkadia, he saw an apparition of the god, who asked why the Athenians did not honor him in spite of the good deeds that he had done and would yet do for them. When they learned of Pan's epiphany, the Athenians concluded that he had contributed to the victory at Marathon and instituted his worship with an annual festival including a torch race. Pan's official sanctuary was a grotto on the northwest slope of the Akropolis, but he quickly became a resident of the Attic countryside, where he was worshiped together with the nymphs and other rustic gods in numerous cave shrines.[17] Contrary to the practice in Arkadia, where Pan possessed temples and sanctuaries like those of other deities, the rest of the Greek world viewed the cave as the proper dwelling for this god of the wild places. After 490, the cults at these caves, including one near Marathon, gained a wider and more affluent clientele who dedicated pots, small metal items, and marble votive reliefs. Menander's comedy *Dyscolus* is set at one such shrine, the cave at Phyle in Attica. In the play, Pan rewards a pious maiden by causing a wealthy youth to fall in love with her, and punishes her neglectful father Knemon, whose sour misanthropy offends against the god's rule of laughter and good cheer.[18]

Folk traditions illustrate the less benevolent side of Pan, connecting him with mysterious noises, particularly the echoes heard in mountainous terrain; with "panic," the phenomenon of sudden terror, seemingly without cause, that comes over armies in the night; and with certain types of illness involving apparent possession by the god (seizures). Pan's theriomorphism and association with madness also brought him into connection with ecstatic forms of worship such as the cults of Dionysos and Meter/Kybele, though always as a subordinate figure. Pindar refers to the Boiotian Pan as "the dog of Meter."[19]

The nature deities: rivers and nymphs

Most of the Greek gods were connected in one way or another with natural phenomena: Zeus was a god of rain, Poseidon of earthquakes, Artemis of wild beasts. A number of minor deities, however, were truly nature gods in the sense that they personified specific features in the landscape or phenomena in the environment. Pre-eminent among these were the river gods and the spring nymphs, whose cults appeared everywhere the Greeks lived. Closely tied to human fertility, the care of children and love of one's homeland, these minor gods made up for their strictly local influence by their great numbers: "it is difficult for a mortal to tell the names of all, but those who dwell near them know their own" (Hes. *Theog.* 69–70). Babies were often given names evocative of local rivers: Asopodoros, Ismenodoros, Acheloios. In fifth-century Athens, a man named Kephisodotos (Gift of Kephisos) co-founded a shrine to the river Kephisos and other gods, including Hermes and the nymphs. The other founder, Xenokrateia, made offerings for the welfare of her son. She established an altar for a number of gods concerned with children, including the rivers Kephisos and Acheloös; the trio Apollo, Artemis, and Leto; Eileithyia; and the local nymphs. In the *Iliad* (23.140–51), Peleus similarly directs his prayers for his son's safety to the local river: upon Achilles' safe return to his dear homeland, Peleus vows that a hundred cattle and fifty rams will be sacrificed into the waters of the Spercheios, while Achilles himself will cut his hair, grown long for the purpose, and offer it to the god. The offering of a lock of hair to the local river was a widespread custom; in Aeschylus' *Libation Bearers* (6), Orestes calls this offering to Inachos a *threptērion*, a recompense for his upbringing.[20]

Popular taboos and cult regulations protected the purity of rivers and springs against the taint of human dirt, excrement, and other wastes, and rituals such as hand-washing or sacrifice before crossing a river are attested.[21] In the *Iliad* (5.77–78, 23.140–51), the cults of river deities are well developed: Skamandros has his own priest and Spercheios has an altar and sanctuary. Animal sacrifice was performed either on an altar in a sanctuary or at the river bank itself so that the blood flowed into the water. Immersion sacrifices are also attested; Homer speaks of live horses cast into the Skamandros (*Il.* 21.124–32).

In the early twentieth century, a Swedish team investigated the sanctuary of the river Pamisos, the major waterway of Messenia. Located at a group of warm and cold-water springs feeding the stream, it was founded in the

Archaic period and had a reputation as a place for healing. It included a small Doric temple with an unusual feature, a votive pit incorporated in the temple wall, which connected with one of the springs feeding the river. Into this pit were deposited gifts of all sorts, including a number of small bronzes, which can be divided into animal figures (primarily horses, bulls, and goats) and human figures (mainly naked youths of Classical date). There are signs that the god's sanctuary was used in rites of maturation: a number of small lead stars were found, originally attached with wire in wreaths. These are paralleled at Lakonian sanctuaries and were apparently dedicated by ephebes. According to tradition, the kings of Messenia brought annual sacrifices to the river. If accurate, this would place the origins of the cult as early as the eighth or seventh century.[22]

The only river god to achieve Panhellenic status in cult is Acheloös, god of the longest river in Greece, who shared many sanctuaries with the nymphs by the fifth century. His popularity was fostered by Zeus' oracle at Dodona, which often recommended sacrifice to Acheloös. A boundary stone marking a shrine of the nymphs and Acheloös was unearthed in Oichalia in Euboia, accompanied by a bronze of the god (c. 460), shown as a bearded, draped figure holding a cornucopia. The full anthropomorphism of this bronze seems to be characteristic of fifth-century sculpture. River gods are likewise shown in human form on pediments of the temple of Zeus at Olympia and the Parthenon in Athens, but in other media they are shown as theriomorphic, man-bull hybrids, the bull symbolizing both the terrifying force of a flooding river and the fertilizing potency of its waters. Acheloös was also worshiped in the form of a mask, (a marble example dating to about 470 was found near Marathon) and his bearded, horned face was used as an amulet in jewelry.[23]

The nymphs, spirits of lakes, mountains, trees, and above all springs, were ubiquitous in the ancient Greek world, and their cult was probably an Indo-European inheritance. Much as described in Homer (Od. 13.102–12, 349–51; 17.205–11), they were worshiped at simple open-air spring sanctuaries and in caves formed by the action of water. Often considered the first inhabitants of the land and cited as divine ancestors, they helped define local identity in the same way as rivers, and were similarly concerned with the welfare of the young. In myth, the nymphs often appear as companions of Olympian gods including Artemis, Dionysos, and Aphrodite, but in cult they are most often linked with pastoral deities including Apollo, Hermes, Acheloös, and Pan. They were worshiped as individuals or as pluralities, usually shown in Greek art as triads. Nymph sanctuaries securely dated to the Archaic period include Saftulis cave near Sikyon, where unique examples of Archaic painting on wood were discovered in 1934. Visitors in the sixth century hung painted wooden *pinakes* in the cave to commemorate their gifts to the nymphs. One well-preserved *pinax* shows a family preparing to sacrifice a sheep at a low altar; another features a triad of women, probably the nymphs. The terracottas of pregnant women found at this cave, while not

Figure 11.2 Cave shrine of the nymphs with three nymphs led by Hermes. Pan is present in the upper right. Hellenistic. Kunsthistorisches Museum, Antikensammlung, Vienna. Erich Lessing/Art Resource.

standard offerings to the nymphs, are consistent with the general Greek belief that nymphs aided in childbirth, the nurture of the young, and girls' transition to adulthood at the time of their weddings. Many girls brought dolls and other toys to the nymphs when they entered adulthood, and the nymphs were among the goddesses who might receive formal prenuptial offerings. The word *numphē* means "bride," so it is fitting that the nymphs were always pictured as beautiful women, divine models for mortal brides.

In contrast to the a strictly local cult at Saftulis cave, the Korykian cave of the nymphs and Pan at Delphi was famous because of its location in a Panhellenic sanctuary and contained an unusual volume of cult-related deposits. Pilgrims to Delphi brought hundreds of seashells from the Korinthian gulf as gifts for the nymphs. The cave was also a center of divination with *astragaloi* or "knucklebones" from sheep and goats, which were cast like dice. This form of fortune-telling was associated with Hermes, whose relationship with the Korykian nymphs is mentioned in the Homeric *Hymn* to Hermes (4.552–68).[24] In the Archaic and Classical periods, the nymphs were credited with the ability to "seize" individuals and inspire them; some of these nympholepts claimed oracular powers. Others withdrew to cave shrines and devoted themselves entirely to the worship of the nymphs, tending their gardens and

154

adorning their caves with sculptures. During the Classical period, nympholepts lived at caves in Attica (Vari) and Thessaly (Pharsalos).[25]

Further reading

The discussion of Hermes in Athanassakis 1989 is most useful for students who have completed an introductory course in ancient Greek. Marinatos 2003 describes the finds from the sanctuary at Kato Symi and includes good illustrations. Osborne 1985 is the first full treatment in English of the origin of herms, the herms of Hipparchos, and the mutilation of the herms in 415. Borgeaud 1988 sensitively explores the cultural impact of Pan's cult through the themes of the Arkadian landscape, the human/animal divide, and the god's reception in Athens. Connor 1988 is the seminal article on nympholepsy, and Larson 2001 is a comprehensive study of the nymphs in myth and cult.

12

DIVINE SPECIALISTS
Other Panhellenic deities

All the gods discussed in this section appear in the Panhellenic poetry of Homer, Hesiod, or both. All were presumably known to Greeks of the Archaic and Classical periods, whether or not they were part of an individual's local pantheon. Popularity in art and poetry did not always translate into widespread worship; Hephaistos is an obvious example. Conversely, a deity such as Hestia, whose cult was indispensable to the polis, seldom found her way into art and played a role in very few myths. Most of the gods described in this chapter have well-delineated functions and spheres that simultaneously ensured their survival, but retarded the development of the complex personalities and multiple roles characteristic of major deities like Athena, Zeus, and Artemis. Hekate, as so often, is exceptional.

Ares and Enyalios

In Homer, Ares is both an abstract noun denoting "war" and the deity, blood-stained and bellowing, who personifies the grim and horrific aspects of war (e.g. *Il.* 2.381, 5.859–63). Not surprisingly, Ares enjoyed only a limited worship, concentrated in the Peloponnese and central Greece. Yet he was father to numerous ancestral heroes, and played an important role in the legendary origins of Thebes. As god of war, Ares was early paired in myth and cult with Aphrodite, goddess of sexual desire, and their relations were a favorite subject of artists and poets from Homer on. Their daughter was Harmonia, bride of Thebes' founder Kadmos, and Ares was the patron (or father) of the great serpent that guarded the spring on the site where Thebes was founded. The pair had a double temple in Argive territory, with ancient statues said to be gifts of Polyneikes before his march on Thebes.[1] Cults of Ares were often connected to battle lore, and as the ancestor of the Amazons, Ares was associated with stories of women warriors. In Argos and Tegea, legends told how the women of the city took up arms to battle invading Spartans, and having achieved victory, established cults of Ares from which men were excluded. The Tegeans, who often served as mercenaries, also worshiped Ares Aphneios (of Abundance), in hopes that he would increase the spoils of war.[2]

Both Ares and Enyalios appear in lists of deities on Linear B tablets from Knossos, and in later centuries the two were syncretized. Enyalios, a war deity, and his female counterpart Enyo also survived as independent cult figures in many parts of the Greek world. Again, the strongest evidence comes from the Peloponnese, particularly Arkadia and Lakonia. The Arkadian city of Mantineia possessed a sanctuary of Enyalios, which ultimately gave its name to one of the civic tribes designated during the political unification of Mantineia in the fifth century. The Spartans had a thriving cult of Enyalios, whose statue was kept in chains, probably to hold its dire influence in check. The same deity presided over a ritual fight between adolescent boys, who made a preliminary sacrifice of puppies. Finally, an Argive bronze plaque inscribed to Enyalios shows a rider on one side and a spearman on the other; it belongs to the seventh century.[3]

Because of their shared functions as deities of war, Ares and Athena (often with the title Areia) could be worshiped together. A decree from the Attic deme of Acharnai (*SEG* 21 [1965] 519) shows that the demesmen, having consulted the oracle of Delphi, constructed new altars for the local sanctuary of Ares and Athena Areia. The sculpted scene on the inscription depicts Athena crowning a youthful Ares in hoplite armor. Several clues suggest that the worship of Ares and Enyalios was an ancient, if minor, institution among the Athenians. Solon is said to have founded a sanctuary of Enyalios, and the Athenian *polemarchos*, a magistrate who was responsible, among other things, for the funerals of the Athenian war dead, offered sacrifices to Artemis Agrotera and Enyalios. The Athenian ephebes swore an oath to protect their homeland with Enyalios, Enyo, Ares, Athena Areia, and other ancestral deities as witnesses. Though the oath is first explicitly attested in the fourth century, it probably dates back to the fifth or earlier; the preservation of the distinction between Enyalios and Ares is an archaic feature.[4]

Ge and Helios

Hesiod (*Theog.* 117) describes Earth as "the ever-sure foundation of all," a divine progenitor who also plays an instrumental role in bringing about the lasting rule of Zeus. At first portrayed as the enemy of the status quo, she eventually comes to support the hegemony of the Olympians. In the mythic imagination, Earth's primordial status and uncontrolled powers were necessarily superseded by a male-dominated regime representing order and stability. The same idea is expressed in the myth of Gaia's prominence at Delphi as the "first prophet" of the oracle, which was taken over by Apollo (e.g. Aesch. *Eum.* 1–2).[5]

While the Earth is often named Gaia in poetry, in cult she is usually given the more prosaic name of Ge. Her cults were widespread yet rarely prominent at the civic level. She is frequently paired with Zeus, a combination that reflects the age-old partnership of sky god and earth goddess. Sacrificial calendars from the Attic towns of Erchia and the Marathonian Tetrapolis, inscribed in the fourth century, provide us a glimpse of the rural contexts in which Ge was typically worshiped, presumably in connection with agriculture. The Erchian calendar specifies that on a certain day the nymphs, Acheloös, Alochos (a birth goddess), and Hermes will each receive a sheep, while Ge will receive a pregnant sheep. In the Tetrapolis calendar, Ge is given a pregnant cow "in the fields" and a black ram "at the oracle (*manteion*)." The offering of a pregnant animal has obvious symbolism, while a black animal is standard for deities who are associated with the underworld.[6]

Ge was depicted anthropomorphically, but never fit comfortably into the cadre of Olympians or exhibited as distinct a personality as they did. Her dual ontological status as "Earth" and "Earth goddess" hindered such development. Reflecting this uncertainty, vase painters show her as a woman whose head and torso are rising from the ground.[7] In her cosmic aspect as one of the three great domains (heaven, earth, and underworld), she appears in oaths. In the *Iliad* (3.103–4, 276–80) she is invoked with Zeus, Helios, the rivers, and the underworld deities to witness the oath attending the single combat of Paris and Menelaos. Two lambs, a white male and a black female, are sacrificed for the Sun and Earth. The group of Zeus, Ge, and Helios as witnesses to oaths and other official business is also widely attested in Greek inscriptions.

Although Helios, whose name is clearly of Indo-European origin, was an oath deity, occasionally cited as an ancestor (particularly in myths connected with Korinth) and recognized everywhere as divine, worship of the Sun was limited among the Classical Greeks, who tended to associate purely astral cults with the barbarians. Helios began to be syncretized with Apollo as early as the fifth century in philosophical speculation, but widespread identification of Apollo with the Sun god was a later phenomenon.[8] Just as Ge at Delphi was considered a primordial deity who yielded to Apollo, Helios was the original possessor of the Akrokorinthos, the citadel of Korinth, but gave the land to Aphrodite. The scattering of minor cults in the Peloponnese (Sikyon, Argos, Hermione, Epidauros, Mt. Taleton in Lakonia) and the holy flocks of Helios at Tainaron mentioned in the Homeric *Hymn* to Apollo (3.410–13) suggest that this worship was deeply rooted in Greece. Thus it may be that Helios' cult was carried to Rhodes by Dorian settlers in the seventh century, although Farnell holds that the Sun worship there was prehellenic in origin. Against these theories of early Rhodian cult stands the lack of evidence for worship of Helios on the island before the late fifth century. In spite of this gap, Helios clearly held a privileged place in the pantheon during the Archaic period. Pindar's seventh Olympian ode (54–75) conveys the unique relationship between the Rhodians and their patron god, who chose the island as his portion and fathered the seven Heliadai to whom the Rhodian elite traced their ancestry.[9] With the founding of Rhodes city in 408, the annual festival of the Heliaia drew athletes and musicians from around the Greek world, and the cult gained even more fame when the bronze statue of Helios known as the Colossus of Rhodes, some 33 m in height, was erected in 282.

Hephaistos

Hephaistos was a beloved member of the Olympian pantheon by the eighth century, but his popularity was expressed primarily though poetry and the visual arts, not cult. He is unique among the Olympians in his physical imperfection, which to the Greek mind made him by turns comic and pathetic. A favorite of Homer, who describes both his awesome skills as a craftsman and his role as a peacemaker among the gods, Hephaistos' origins lie in the Bronze Age sacralization of metalworking. His name is certainly not Greek, and most likely his worship was brought to mainland Greece from Anatolia via Lemnos, an ancient seat of his cult where the capital city was called Hephaistia. The pre-Greek Lemnians, known to Homer as Sinties, were credited with the invention of fire and the technique of forging weapons. Hephaistos is similar to craft-related *daimones* like the Telchines of Rhodes, the Idaian Daktyloi, and the Kyklopes who forged Zeus' thunderbolts, though his individual personality is more fully developed. In certain myths he is a craftsman-magician, creator of fabulous animated statues with talismanic and apotropaic powers. Corresponding rituals intended to imbue real statues with such powers are unattested for our period in Greece, but were well known in Assyria, Anatolia, and Egypt.[10]

Yet Hephaistos is also an elemental deity whose name functions (e.g. Hom. *Il.* 2.426) as a synonym for fire. He is perhaps the god of the famous yearly fire festival at Lemnos, which involved the extinguishing of all fire on the island for nine days, until a ship brought new fire from which all the domestic hearths and forges could be kindled anew and purified. In the time of Philostratus of Lemnos (*c.* 215 CE), our source for this festival, the fire was brought from Delos, but if the festival existed in the Classical period, the new fire may have been the gift of the island's patron deity. In Sophocles' *Philoctetes* (986), the title character stranded on Lemnos cries out to "Lemnian earth and the all-powerful flame wrought by Hephaistos."[11]

The major locus of Hephaistos' cult outside Lemnos was Athens, where the god was integrated very early into the local pantheon and had a special affinity with Athena. The two were honored in the Chalkeia (Bronzework) festival as patrons of craft workers. As a fire deity, Hephaistos was particularly important to those who worked with forges and kilns. People set up clay statues and plaques of the god beside hearths and kilns as an "overseer" of the fire. Local legend also held that the birth of the primordial king Erechtheus from the Earth came about as a result of a comically unsuccessful rape attempt by Hephaistos, who had conceived a passion for Athena. Hephaistos therefore was ancestral to the people and had an altar in the Erechtheion.

Figure 12.1 Temple of Hephaistos in the Athenian agora. Erich Lessing: Art Resource.

During the Apatouria, the festival at which a man's sons were presented for enrollment as citizens, certain Athenians dressed in magnificent clothing and lit torches "from the hearth" while singing hymns for Hephaistos.[12] A fragmentary decree of 421/20 (*IG* I³ 82) shows that the Hephaisteia was reorganized in that year as a large-scale celebration including a torch race, sponsored by the tribes, and an interesting contest of "ox-lifting" to be performed by two hundred chosen youths, with the oxen subsequently sacrificed to the god.[13] In the same year, Alkamenes began work on the cult statues for the new temple of Hephaistos, which overlooked the busy commercial center of the city and, uniquely, was destined to survive into modern times almost fully preserved. Sadly, the same cannot be said for the bronze cult statues, one of Athena and one of Hephaistos, though later copies give us clues to their appearance. Ancient visitors praised this statue of the god because it minimized his deformity.[14]

Hestia

The perpetual virginity of Hestia, whose name simply means "hearth," reflects the Greek belief that fire and the fireplace must be kept pure and inviolate. The hearth was the center of domestic cult; it symbolized the integrity of the individual household, and by extension, the chastity of the resident women. Hesiod (*Op.* 733–34) advises men not to expose their genitals before the hearth after sex, and hearth fires polluted by proximity to corpses or violated by enemies needed to be extinguished and lit anew from a pure source. In spite of her great antiquity and her status as an Olympian god, Hestia remained one of the least anthropomorphic of Greek deities, without a fully developed mythology. The newborn child was carried around the hearth and laid upon the ground to indicate its acceptance into the family, while the outcast suppliant crouched at an alien hearth to indicate his homeless state. Hestia as a divine personality appears to have no role in these rituals, yet the hearth, *hestia*, is no less revered. Homer does not mention a personal goddess Hestia, but in the Homeric *Hymn* to Aphrodite (5.30–32), she "sit[s] in the center of the house, taking a rich portion" of daily offerings and is honored in all temples. Hestia's priority is the distinguishing feature of her cult. According to a widely observed ritual protocol, Hestia was mentioned first of the gods when oaths were sworn, and received an offering first when sacrifices were performed. This was the custom followed at Olympia, where Hestia was honored before Olympian Zeus himself.[15]

During the Bronze and early Iron Ages, the sacral power of the domestic hearth was extended to the king's or chieftain's hearth as the symbol of civic continuity and integrity. With the development of the polis, this function was transferred to a communal civic hearth, usually located in the city hall or *prutaneion*. With a few exceptions, state cults of Hestia were conducted in these halls, which often functioned as dining rooms, rather than in separate sanctuaries. The civic hearth was in many ways analogous to the home hearth, for it was here that important guests were brought to receive the city's hospitality. Inscriptions from around the Greek world show that civic officials honored Hestia when they began their service. One such man was Aristagoras, who served on the governing council of the island Tenedos in the fifth century. Pindar's eleventh Nemean ode (11.1–7), commissioned for his installation, asks Hestia to welcome Aristagoras to the *prutaneion*, where "they often worship you first among the gods with libations, and often with savory smoke." Finally, when a city was founded, the colonists brought cinders from the *prutaneion* in their hometown to light the fires on their new hearths and altars.[16]

Hestia's special relationship with Hermes is recognized in the Homeric *Hymn* to Hestia (29.7–12), where the two are invoked as dear friends who dwell in and protect the house together. Both are the objects of domestic cult and both are concerned, more than the other gods, with the doings of *epichthonioi*, those "who live on the surface of the earth." Also present in this pairing is an implicit recognition of the way the two deities govern gendered space and movement in relation to the home. Hestia, the most immobile of goddesses, marks and anchors the center of the home, just as the women of the house ideally remain indoors and aloof from contact with strangers. Conversely, Hermes guards the door and governs movement in and out, just as the masculine role is to work under the sun and deal with strangers. Iconographic convention also linked these two gods. They appeared as a pair, for example, on the altar of Amphiaraos at Oropos and on the statue base of Pheidias' Olympian Zeus.[17]

Charites

The Charites (Graces) are familiar in Greek poetry as companions of the Olympian gods. They are beauty experts who bathe, anoint, and dress Aphrodite in her shrine on Paphos, and they ensure the success of every entertainment on Olympos, enthroned beside Apollo or dancing around him while he plays the lyre. Greek *charis* denotes, among other things, joy in the giving and receiving of gifts, divine favor that results in athletic or military glory, and anything that is beautiful to the senses, as well as the response it engenders.[18] "All things sweet and pleasant for mortals" come about through the Charites according to Pindar (*Ol.* 14.4–6, 13–15), whose ode for a victor from Boiotian Orchomenos celebrates the "much-sung queens of the city," naming them Aglaia (Shining), Euphrosyne (Joy), and Thaleia (Blooming). Rather unexpectedly, these paragons of pleasure and beauty were worshiped in Orchomenos as a triad of stones. The city was a Mycenaean stronghold, occupied in the prehistoric period by a Greek tribe known as the Minyai and long remembered for its fabled riches. Later accounts firmly link the worship of the Charites to these early inhabitants, while the founder of the cult was said to be a primordial king, Eteokles. The stones representing the goddesses fell from heaven, and Eteokles was the first to sacrifice to them.[19] The Greeks occasionally used unworked stones as cult objects, a practice that was common in the Near East and is paralleled in the Boiotian cults of Eros at Thespiai and Herakles at Hyettos.

Strabo (9.2.40) links the riches of Orchomenos with the cult of the Charites and the strong reciprocal element in the Greek concept of *charis*: the wealth of the city allowed it to give and receive abundantly. Usually the Charites are considered goddesses of water and vegetation, essentially nymphs in origin, and indeed they were closely associated with both the local river Kephisos and a spring Akidalia (or Argaphia). Orchomenos owed its prosperity to the fertility of the marshy Kopaic plain, and the grateful citizens allotted the Charites a share of its produce.[20] Yet the habit of personifying abstracts was an old one, and the concept of *charis*, so fundamental to Greek culture, surely shaped the worship from its earliest days. Certainly it was instrumental in the spread of the cult. According to Aristotle (*Eth. Nic.* 1133a), shrines of the Charites were set up to serve as reminders of the special quality of *charis*: one ought not only to repay favors, but also initiate them. The Classical sanctuary of the Charites at Orchomenos, including their temple, has been identified but not fully excavated. Little else is known about their Archaic and Classical cult, though the dramatic and musical contests of the Hellenistic Charitesia may have begun in the late Classical period when the theater was built.[21]

The Charites were worshiped at an early date on Paros, where legend had it that Minos was sacrificing to them when he received word of his son's death in Athens. Because he ripped the garland from his head and stopped the music, ritual law decreed that the sacrifices ever after be conducted with neither garland nor flute. This story has been taken as evidence of the antiquity of the cult (because the islanders associated it with the reign of Minos) and its chthonian orientation (because it was associated with mourning and the ritual was austere). A relief sculpture of the three goddesses from Paros, now in Munich, confirms the Archaic date of the cult and features heavily draped Charites, for the familiar iconography of three entwined nudes is a late development. Callimachus (fr. 7.11–12 Pf.), pictures these Parian goddesses garbed in resplendent gowns with unguents dripping from their hair. Colonists carried the cult to Thasos, where Apollo with the nymphs and Hermes with the Charites, sculpted in the fifth century, adorned the entrance to the old city.[22]

In Athens, the Charites were worshiped, again with Hermes, on a much-copied relief at the entrance to the Akropolis. Popular belief held that the sculptor was the philosopher Sokrates, whose father was a stonecutter, though scholars are skeptical. While the Akropolis sculpture was produced in the Classical period and showed a canonical triad of Charites, Pausanias remarks (9.35.1–7) that in the oldest Athenian cult the Charites were two, Auxo (Increase) and Hegemone (Leader). He mentions a third goddess, Thallo (Blossoming), whom he says is properly one of the Horai (Seasons), another divine plurality often associated with the Charites. Auxo, Hegemone, and Thallo were among the witnesses to the oath of the ephebes, and they represented agricultural abundance, the powers that invigorated the land and ripened the crops. The fact that a secret *teletē* (initiation) was conducted at the Akropolis shrine is consistent with this function.[23]

Eileithyia

While a Panhellenic tradition made Eileithyia one of the younger goddesses, child of Hera and Zeus, she is one of the few Greek deities who demonstrably existed in the Bronze Age. A Linear B tablet from Knossos mentions a jar of honey sent to Eleuthia at Amnisos, and others record offerings of wool. A large cave faces the sea at the harbor of Amnisos, probably the same one the *Odyssey* (19.188) calls "the cave of Eileithyia." It contained Neolithic, Bronze Age, Archaic, and Roman pottery clustered around a stalagmite used as a focus of worship, but no other identifiable votive objects. Near the cave, however, is a sanctuary constructed over an old Minoan site, which yielded votive objects from the eighth and seventh centuries: bronze bovines and men, Orientalizing nude females, and Egyptian figurines including the fertility god Bes. Perhaps both sites were sacred to the goddess of birth pangs. The use of cave sanctuaries was, of course, a well-established feature of Minoan religion. Another Kretan cave at Inatos is assigned to the goddess because of its votives: from the late Minoan through the early Archaic period, people left figurines of pregnant and nursing women, erotic groups, jewelry, and other items. As at Amnisos, Bes figurines imported from Egypt were present; these may have been used as amulets during childbirth. The idea that Eileithyia should be worshiped in a cave seems to have been exported to Paros, where a cave sanctuary functioned from late Geometric through Roman times.[24]

Eileithyia's name is not Greek in origin and probably derives from the little-understood Minoan language. Its early diffusion and initial unfamiliarity to Greek ears led to a plethora of dialect forms; the Peloponnesian Eleuthia or Eleusia is closest to the Mycenaean spelling. During the Archaic period, Eileithyia's cult was most prolific in Krete, the Peloponnese (particularly Lakonia, which had close relations with Krete), and the Cyclades. From an early date, she was associated with the Apolline triad. On Delos, birthplace of Apollo and Artemis, she was especially honored. Olen of Lykia, a legendary hymnist and prophet, was credited with the suite of ancient hymns, including one to Eileithyia, that celebrated Delian sacred history. None survive, but we know that they told how the goddess came to the island from the land of the Hyperboreans in preparation for Leto's travail. In her hymn, Eileithyia was lauded as the "good spinner" (*eulinon*), "older than Kronos," and "mother of Eros." The Homeric *Hymn* to Apollo (3.95–116) gives her a less exalted but still indispensable role, and recounts Hera's spiteful scheme to delay her visit to Delos. Summoned at last by Iris, Eileithyia's arrival allowed Apollo to spring forth from the womb. She possessed a temple on Delos, perhaps within the boundaries of Apollo's sanctuary. Hellenistic inscriptions give us information about repairs to the temple, sacrifices and banquets during the Eileithyiaia in the month of Posideion, and an inventory of offerings to the goddess (vases, jewelry, votive plaques of gold and silver), which were given exclusively by women.[25]

In Sparta we find the oldest record of Eileithyia's cult on the Greek mainland. Pausanias' description (3.17.1) of a sanctuary of Eileithyia near that of Artemis Ortheia was confirmed by the discovery of part of a bronze dress pin and a bronze die, both inscribed with the birth-goddess' name and both from the seventh or sixth century. Other scattered artifacts of Archaic and Classical date, together with Pausanias' description of seven sanctuaries and three temples, complete the picture of a cult well established in all areas of the Peloponnese. At Olympia, Eileithyia seems to be cast as a divine *kourotrophos* or nurturer of the young. There she was worshiped near the hill of Kronos in an Archaic temple shared with the mysterious infant *daimōn* Sosipolis (City-Savior). According to local legend, a woman guided by a dream brought the suckling child to the Elean army when the city was under attack by Arkadians. Placed at the head of the army, the child turned into a serpent as the enemy charged, throwing them into confusion. Eileithyia's kourotrophic function is a natural outgrowth of her concern for pregnant and parturient women, and many of her sanctuaries featured thank offerings made for the survival of children.[26]

Whereas in Boiotia and Thessaly the functions and name of this ancient goddess were absorbed by Artemis, worship of an independent Eileithyia continued in Attica, which followed the Delian/Kretan cult traditions. Describing the shrine of Eileithyia near the Athenian Olympieion, Pausanias' informants (1.18.5) said that "the women" attributed two of the three ancient wooden statues to Krete and one to Delos. The fact that women were the authorities in this matter is consistent with the sacerdotal arrangements at the sanctuaries of Hermione and Olympia: only women served Eileithyia and access to her inner sanctum, with its sacred images, was sometimes restricted.[27] The orator Isaeus (5.39) provides an interesting footnote on the significance of this cult for women. In a speech against Dikaiogenes, the narrator tells how the malefactor's mother seated herself as a suppliant in the shrine of Eileithyia and publicly reproached her son for crimes "too shameful to repeat." Presumably the goddess could be relied upon to punish an ungrateful child.

Hekate

According to the current scholarly consensus, Hekate originated as a goddess in the pantheon of Karia on the west coast of Asia Minor. In Lagina, the home of her largest known sanctuary, she was the preeminent deity, ensuring the security and prosperity of the inhabitants and maintaining close relations with the Karian equivalent of Zeus. So far, none of the archaeological evidence for her cult at Lagina predates the Hellenistic period. Yet a number of Karian personal names contain the *Hekat-* root, suggesting that it is not Greek in origin, and that her worship was native to this area. In the Archaic period, her cult was apparently adopted by the Karians' Greek neighbors, and was particularly prominent at Miletos, where she had an altar before the *prutaneion* as early as the sixth century and a shrine at the city gates by the fifth. A single terracotta figure inscribed with her name reveals her presence in Athens by the late sixth century.[28]

Her absence from Homer and the paucity of myths about her suggest a relatively late entry into the Panhellenic pantheon, and while her role in Hesiod's *Theogony* (411–52) is substantial, it is also anomalous. For Hesiod, Hekate is a mighty goddess who has a surprisingly wide range of special prerogatives from Zeus: she assists kings and speakers in the assembly, gives victory in battle and athletics, helps mariners, fishermen, and herdsmen, and acts as a *kourotrophos*.[29] While this portrait of the goddess conflicts with most of what we know about her Classical Greek cults, it closely resembles the Karian conception of her, right down to the special relationship with Zeus.

One of our few other Archaic sources is the Homeric *Hymn* to Demeter, in which Hekate, together with the sun god Helios, witnesses the rape of Persephone (implicit in these lines is the later concept of Hekate as a moon goddess). At the end of the poem, Hekate becomes the companion of Persephone, who "goes before and follows after" her as she travels between the upper and lower worlds. This is our first evidence of what was to become Hekate's most important role, as a deity who provided protection during transitions of all kinds, which were by nature perilous. It was in the interstices between safely defined territories (home, sanctuary, city) and times (new and old month) that dangerous spirits were emboldened to attack the unwary. Her very power to protect, of course, derived from her intimacy with and control over these spirits, the untimely and restless dead. By the Classical period, protective statues of Hekate (*hekataia*) were ubiquitous in Athens, functioning as complements to the older herms, and monthly garlanding of the family statues was a sign of conventional piety. The triple-formed Hekate sculpted by Alkamenes (*c.* 430) for the entrance to the Athenian Akropolis is the most famous example. A Hekate who simultaneously faced in different directions was presumably a more efficacious guardian; the form also expresses visually the goddess' role as mistress of the crossroads, dangerous transitional spots where one was likely to encounter prostitutes and other dispossessed persons as well as angry ghosts. In Sophocles' *Rhizotomoi* (Root-cutters), Hekate has a place on Olympos but also dwells at the crossroads; she is a terrifying figure crowned with oak leaves and serpents.[30] Aristophanes (*Plut.* 594–97) and others tell how those who could afford it sent *deipna* (dinners) to Hekate at the crossroads when the new moon arrived. A related practice was the use of sacrificial dogs for the purification of private houses; the remains were set out at the crossroads for the goddess. Because the Greeks did not normally consume the meat of dogs, these sacrifices were doubly marked as outside the norm. Only extreme poverty or impiety would move someone to eat such food.[31]

Just as Kybele was assimilated to Greek Rhea, Hekate was sometimes accommodated in the Greek pantheon as an aspect of Artemis (both were thought to have an interest in weddings, childbirth, and the care of the young). Aeschylus (*Supp.* 676–77), for example, described Artemis-Hekate as a guardian of women in labor. An important Archaic version of Iphigeneia's myth (recounted by Stesichorus among others) held that when Artemis demanded her sacrifice, the heroine was transformed into Hekate or Artemis-Hekate.[32] Sometime before the fifth century, Hekate was also fully syncretized with the Thessalian goddess Enodia (She in the Road) and began to use her name as an epithet. Lacking evidence for the early nature of Enodia, we cannot say which of the two goddesses contributed the many characteristics they share, but given the longstanding association of Thessaly with drugs and witchcraft, it is logical to assume that Hekate's role as a patron of magical practitioners originated here. Hekate's interest in sorcery is attested first in

Sophocles' *Rhizotomoi* (fr. 534 *TrGF*), where she is invoked by Thessalian women as they gather powerful herbs. Enodia also functioned, like Hekate, as a guardian of private houses and a protector of children. Fifth-century Thessalians set up small statues of the goddess in front of or inside houses, asking her aid "for a child's sake."[33]

Another relatively early center of Hekate's Greek cult was Aigina, where Myron's wooden statue stood in the goddess' sanctuary. We do not know whether the mysteries of Hekate mentioned by Pausanias (2.30.2) were already celebrated in the Classical period, but the Aiginetan cult is unusual in any case because the goddess rarely achieved such full integration into any civic pantheon. Sanctuaries devoted primarily to Hekate were unusual, and the development of civic cult was probably hampered by the continuing growth of the goddess' reputation as a deity invoked for private and nefarious purposes. As early as the mid-fourth century, Hekate Chthonia (of the Underworld) and Chthonic Hermes are the deities named in an Attic curse tablet incised on lead, which was intended to bind and neutralize the author's opponent in a lawsuit.[34]

Erinyes

Erinys is named in offering lists on at least two Linear B tablets from Knossos. We do not know how much, if any, of the Mycenaean goddess' personality persisted in the Erinys and plural Erinyes of later centuries, but an Arkadian word *erinuō*, "to be angry," seems to be derived from her name. Anger is also an important component in the personality of Arkadian Demeter Erinys, a descendant of the Mycenaean goddess.[35] The Homeric Erinyes (or Erinys), who inhabit the underworld (*Il.* 9.571–72, 19.259, etc.), are concerned with the punishment of deviant behavior, especially transgressions of filial duty and respect. Outraging a parent, committing a murder of a blood relative, or breaking an oath were all actions that aroused the anger and merciless pursuit of the goddesses. Both dead and living relatives, especially mothers, were thought to have the power to awake the Erinyes through curses. Although by nature inimical to the processes by which the claims of the family and blood ties give way to the demands of larger social groups, they were successfully integrated into polis religion. This process is memorialized in Aeschylus' *Eumenides*, which shows how the goddesses' enduring powers could be harnessed for the benefit of the state through a program of propitiation.

In local cult contexts, the Panhellenic name "Erinyes" was assiduously avoided in favor of euphemistic titles.[36] The Athenians consistently used the name Semnai Theai (Revered Goddesses) in their principal cult, an ancient observance that was closely related to the Council of the Areopagos. A relic of Athens' earliest constitution, the Council lost most of its political clout by Solon's day but remained highly respected as the court before which homicides were tried. The abode of the Semnai Theai was a chasm beside the *Areios pagos* (Hill of Ares), where according to legend the goddesses were persuaded to descend after their unsuccessful prosecution of the matricide Orestes. We learn from the Attic orators and their scholiasts that legal proceedings were limited to the last three days of the month, which were sacred to the three Semnai Theai (and inauspicious days for any other business to be carried out). Each party at the start of a trial took a solemn oath over the cut pieces of a boar, a ram, and a bull, calling down ruin on himself and his descendants if he lied. When a man was acquitted of murder, sacrifice to the Semnai Theai was required to satisfy their anger. The Athenians also conducted an annual torchlight procession for the goddesses, in which the family of the Hesychidai (the "silent ones," referring to the solemn silence kept during the proceedings) played a leading role. The women of the Hesychidai formed a college of priestesses attending the goddesses. Other citizens, of whom the orator Demosthenes was one, were also selected to serve as *hieropoioi* (doers of sacred things). Wine was excluded from the worship (a feature typical of old chthonian cults), and offerings consisted of cakes and libations of milk or honey. The grove of the Eumenides (Kindly Ones) in the Athenian town of Kolonos, associated with the hero Oedipus, hosted an independent cult of the goddesses (who were also locally known as Semnai Theai) with its own unique rituals. Both sanctuaries were known as places where suppliants could find refuge.[37]

Worship of the Eumenides and similar goddesses was widespread in the Peloponnese, where it was associated with Orestes, or less often, Oedipus. Near Megalopolis in Arkadia was a sanctuary of the Maniai (Crazes), who maddened Orestes until he bit off his own finger. This is an extreme form of expiation, the sacrifice of an expendable body part. The satisfied goddesses, who had previously appeared black, now turned white and Orestes, recovered from his madness, established the custom of sacrifice to each group, *enagismos* to the black and *thusia* to the white. That the sanctuary was located in a place called Ake (cure) suggests that people sought healing there, perhaps for mental illnesses.[38] Material evidence of an Argive cult exists in the form of several votive reliefs dedicated to the Eumenides. One, inscribed as a thank offering, shows three benevolent-looking goddesses, each holding a flower in the left hand and a snake in the right. They are greeted by a couple approaching from the right side of the relief. These dedications from the fourth century illustrate a more personal, family-oriented cult practice, and show how the actual worship of these goddesses invariably focused not on their dark and threatening aspects, but on the benefits they could provide if properly appeased.[39]

Further reading

Harrison 1977a, b reconstructs the interior sculptures of the splendidly preserved temple to Hephaistos in the Athenian agora, while Faraone 1987 shows how the myths of Hephaistos as a maker of talismanic statues reflect ritual practices in the Near East. Vernant 1983a, a classic article, uses structuralist analysis to define Hestia in relation to Hermes. Marinatos 1996 reexamines the traditional identification of the Kretan cave at Amnisos as the shrine of Eileithyia. Johnston 1999 (203–87) includes the fullest recent discussions of Hekate and the Erinyes.

13

STRANGERS AND INDIGENES

Latecomer and regional deities

The "latecomers" of this chapter were adopted by Greeks only after the polis system, which implied regulation of the civic pantheon, was established in the eighth century. Therefore these deities faced a more challenging path to local, regional, and (in some cases) Panhellenic acceptance. Native to Phrygia, Thrace, Lydia, and elsewhere in the Aegean, they illustrate the fluidity of culture in the ancient world, and show that Greek pantheons were open to change well before the revolutionary developments of the Hellenistic period. On the other hand, the cults of "regional" deities such as Themis, Diktynna, Damia, and Auxesia were ancient but remained geographically restricted. They exemplify the resistance of local pantheons to the homogenizing pressures of Panhellenism, and – in the case of Aphaia/Athena – show how anomalous deities might eventually succumb.

Kybele

The most important goddess in the Phrygian pantheon was Matar Kubileya, the Mother of the Mountains. From the sixth century on, Greek religion knew her as Meter (the Mother), and poets called her Kybele, a personal name derived from her Phrygian title. In her homeland, her places of worship were door-shaped niches carved into rocky cliffs and hillsides. These were filled with high relief or freestanding images of the goddess, often holding a bird of prey or flanked by lions. A mistress of wild nature, Matar Kubileya was a close relative of the Bronze Age goddess who is depicted in Minoan gems standing on a mountain peak, flanked by twin lions; many variations of this goddess were worshiped throughout Anatolia. Some of the Ionians who first adopted her cult, like the Chians and Phokaians, continued the tradition of rural, rock-cut sanctuaries, but more often the motif of the goddess in the niche was transferred to the portable medium of stone votive reliefs. The popular appeal of Meter's cult is attested both by its rapid spread through the Greek world in the sixth century and by the abundance of votive reliefs and figurines depicting the goddess, found not only in sanctuaries, but also in domestic contexts and tombs. On the other hand, "Meter" iconography was used to depict a wide range of goddesses, so without an inscription, secure identification of artifacts can be difficult.[1]

Meter was quickly syncretized with Ge/Gaia, with Demeter, and especially with the Titaness Rhea, mother of Zeus and the other elder Olympians. Rhea's Kretan cult, perhaps a Bronze Age survival, was focused on the birth of Zeus and was celebrated in an ecstatic dance during which the participants imitated the mythical Kouretes, youths who clashed their shields to cover the infant's cries. One of the centers of this cult, Mt. Ida in Krete, was closely associated with the Phrygian Mt. Ida, the haunt of Meter. Like Idaian Zeus and Rhea, Meter was worshiped with percussive music and ecstatic dancing, and she was accompanied by the Korybantes, youths who were analogous to the Kouretes. The characteristic instruments in her music were the *tumpanon*, a tambourine-like drum, and the flute. Herodotus (4.76) tells how the Greeks of Kyzikos celebrated Meter's festival at night, striking *tumpana* and decking themselves with small images of the goddess. Most ancient and modern observers have traced the ecstatic elements of the cult, as well as the use of the *tumpanon*, to Phrygia. These features, negatively stereotyped as "Eastern" in the wake of the Persian wars, are most likely Greek developments originating in Krete. Less is known about the origins of the mendicant priests of Meter known as *mētragurtai* (Gatherers for the Mother); they too are considered somewhat disreputable in surviving sources.[2]

During the Meter cult's period of explosive growth in the late Archaic period, she was quickly incorporated into civic worship. In Athens, the emerging democracy seems to have welcomed this popular goddess by the end of the sixth century. Meter's cult was established in or near the *bouleutērion* (council chamber) in the agora and Athenian council members began to sacrifice to the Mother of the Gods along with the other major civic deities. In the late fifth century, with the construction of a new *bouleutērion*, the old one became known as the Metroön, or temple of Meter. Like the temple of the Mother in Kolophon, the Metroön was used as a state archive.[3] Private sponsorship of Meter was also widespread and was prompted by dreams and visions. Pindar is said to have founded a Theban shrine of Meter after he had a vision of the goddess' statue walking, and Themistokles brought the cult to Magnesia after the goddess warned him in a dream of an assassination attempt.[4] In the succeeding generation, however, the cult of Meter was viewed less favorably, at least by the elite men of Athens, and was associated with women, the poor, and excessive emotional displays. Attis, who later became known as the consort of Kybele, does not become a prominent figure in the cult until the fourth century. While the Phrygian priests of Matar bore the title Attes, the myth of Attis seems to be a Greek invention.[5]

The Kabeiroi and the Megaloi Theoi

Scattered about the Aegean, particularly in its northern half, were a number of sanctuaries devoted to groups of deities who were the guardians of mysteries. These deities are sometimes known as the Megaloi Theoi (Great Gods) and sometimes as the Kabeiroi, a name related to the Semitic *kabir*, "mighty." Like the Kouretes and Korybantes who surround Meter, the Kabeiroi are sometimes portrayed as subordinate to a goddess or a divine pair, ministers or servants of more powerful deities whose names are only for the ears of initiates. Yet they are potent cult figures in their own right, and they seem to function as intermediaries between the human and the divine. In origin, these deities were non-Greek, but they were rapidly accepted by Greek worshipers, and their mysteries were developed and administered using Greek models.

Though its material remains are venerable, dating to the late seventh century, the Kabeiric cult in the territory of Thebes was surely imported from the northeastern Aegean. Located about 6 km west of Thebes, the sanctuary site was apparently selected because of its natural features: a small stream bisected the area, a hillside served as a natural amphitheater, and a rock formation on the hill seems to have provided a focus for the cult. The resident deities included a mother goddess, her consort, and two attendant Kabiroi (to use the local spelling), an elder and a younger. We know little about the identity and nature of the first pair, who must have been the subject of the secret mysteries. Within a circular cult building (*tholos*) dating to the fifth century, excavators found a clay tub buried with its rim slightly protruding from the ground, and inscribed "of the Husband." A hole pierced in the bottom shows that it was intended for liquid offerings, which drained into the earth, and the sequestering of this basin inside the *tholos* suggests that these offerings were secret. Far more accessible were the Kabiroi themselves, who were the recipients of many of the inscribed gifts left in the sanctuary. Prominent among these were bull figurines, first of bronze and later of terracotta. The site also yielded an unusually large number of glass beads, more than at any other Greek sanctuary. Many of the colorful beads have dots or bumps, which represent apotropaic eyes.[6] They may have been gifts for the goddess, or perhaps strings of beads played a role in the rituals. The architecture of the Kabirion was not extensively developed during the Archaic and Classical periods, in spite of its great popularity: it consisted of the theatral area, some sacrificial pits, and a number of modest *tholoi*, as well as a rectangular building that housed symposiasts.

The Theban Kabirion is best known for a special type of figured vase that was custom made for the sanctuary. The so-called Kabirion ware is decorated with scenes of activity at the sanctuary and was produced from the fifth to the third centuries. The abundant drinking vessels left at the Kabirion show that symposia attended by elite men were an important activity in the sixth century, even before the figured wares appeared. That these symposia had a pederastic focus is suggested by the hundreds of terracottas of boys and youths, which are contemporary with the drinking cups. Participation in the worship, however, was by no means restricted to males. Some dedications were made by women, and vases show family groups participating in sacrifices and other activities which took place both before and after initiation. Initiates wear distinctive ribbons and leafy twigs in their hair. One of the most puzzling features of these scenes is that many individuals are shown with body types and facial features that the Greeks associated with the mythical race of Pygmies. This may reflect the influence of Greek comedy, or some aspect of the cult, such as costumed performances. Another suggestion, supported by Herodotus (3.37), is that the cult images of the Kabiroi themselves had a pygmoid appearance; still, the iconography of the Theban Kabiroi was never fixed. On one vase the senior of the two, labeled Kabiros (Lord), closely resembles Dionysos as he reclines at a symposium, while the junior, Pais (Boy), takes the role of a cupbearer. Another vase shows the elder as Hermes and the younger as Pan.[7]

Several other Kabeiric shrines are mentioned by late authors or revealed in inscriptions. The cult at Lemnos is perhaps the oldest, though its custodians through the Archaic period were so-called Pelasgians, a non-Greek people. Only in the late sixth or early fifth century was the island formally colonized

Figure 13.1 Skuphos from the Theban Kabirion showing initiates, fifth century. Athens, National Archaeological Museum. Bildarchiv Foto Marburg.

173

by the Athenians, who already had in their mother city a thriving cult of the island's most important deity, Hephaistos. The fifth-century historian Acusilaus (*FGrH* 2 F 20) says that Hephaistos produced a son Kamillos with a goddess named Kabeiro. Kamillos in turn fathered the three Kabeiroi and they the three Kabeirid nymphs. The attributes of the Kabeiroi were the smith's hammer and tongs, and the goddess whom they attended was called Lemnos or Megale Theos (Great Goddess). The sanctuary is situated northeast of the capital city Hephaistia. The plentiful inscriptions found there, some as early as the fifth century, give a picture of a Hellenized mystery cult with its staff of priests and financial officers, though the native language persisted and was surely used in the rites. Early versions of the cult probably also existed at Imbros and in the Troad, which were part of the same cultural sphere.[8]

Initiation into the mysteries of Samothrace was said to bestow protection from drowning at sea, and the island with its sanctuary quickly gained a Panhellenic reputation during the Archaic and Classical periods. Filled with votive monuments and tablets presented by grateful survivors, it drew the scorn of the atheist Diagoras of Melos, who remarked that the number of votives would be much greater if all those who did not survive had made dedications.[9] Meticulous excavation of the sanctuary revealed that its first archaeologically visible operations were roughly contemporary with the settlement of the island by Greeks in the seventh century.

Herodotus (2.51) and other sources refer to the Samothracian gods as Kabeiroi, but inscriptions found on the island speak only of Megaloi Theoi (Great Gods) or Theoi (Gods). A Hellenistic historian revealed the secret names of these gods, which are manifestly non-Greek: Axieros, Axiokersa, Axiokersos, and Kasmilos (who is comparable to Lemnian Kamillos).[10] The four have been identified respectively as Demeter, Persephone, Hades, and Hermes, though it is not certain whether Axieros is male or female. As for the content of the mysteries, sources speak of statues with erect *phalloi* at the sanctuary and Herodotus connects these with the sacred story told to initiates.[11] Initiates wore rings of magnetized iron, which were most likely associated with a lodestone in the sanctuary, and the uncanny power of magnetism may have had a role in the mysteries as well. As at Thebes, the focal points of the early sanctuary were a theatral area and natural rock formations, used by the Samothracians as altars. Although the Samothracian mysteries were familiar to Classical Athenians, it is not clear how far their fame had spread by the fifth century. Few structures or artifacts in the sanctuary can be firmly assigned to the Archaic or Classical periods (a sixth-century dining room, previously identified as "the Hall of Votive Gifts," appears to be one). Only in early Hellenistic times did the Samothracian mysteries become a major source of revenue for the islanders.[12]

Ammon

Just as Greek colonists installed the gods of their mother cities in their new homes, they also adopted the cults of indigenous peoples and systematically exported them, in Hellenized form, back to Greece. A good example is the cult of Ammon, which the colonists in Kyrene enthusiastically promoted in Greece. The god Ammon was the result of the blending of Amun-Ra, the main god of Egyptian Thebes, with an indigenous Libyan deity. Because this god was supreme in the pantheon, the Greeks identified him with Zeus. Like Amun-Ra, Ammon was an oracular deity whose responses were determined by the movements of his image, carried in a palanquin on the backs of priests.

During the sixth century, Ammon's oracle in the isolated desert oasis of Siwa began to gain an international reputation, and by about 500, the citizens of Kyrene had struck coins bearing the head of a horned Zeus Ammon, and raised a magnificent temple, comparable in size to the temple of Zeus at Olympia.[13] Most instances of Greek interest in Ammon can be traced back to the colonists of Kyrene. They dedicated monuments of Ammon at Delphi and Olympia, and the elite athletes of the city commissioned Pindar to compose victory odes that acknowledged Ammon's guardianship of the city and its territory. Pindar (*Pyth.* 9.53) calls Kyrene "the finest garden of Zeus," and in his masterpiece, the fourth Pythian ode (14–16), Medeia prophesies that Libya "will be planted with the root of illustrious cities at the foundations of Zeus Ammon." Pindar also expressed his personal devotion to Ammon in a hymn, now lost, and dedicated a statue of the god in his hometown of Thebes.[14]

The Spartans maintained close ties with the Dorian colonists of Kyrene and thus felt a strong affinity for the oracle in the Archaic and Classical periods.[15] According to tradition, Zeus Ammon held the Spartans in high regard, and prophesied that they would colonize Libya. The Spartan general Lysander had a dream vision of Zeus Ammon that caused him to abandon the siege of Aphytis, and he most likely visited Siwa more than once. Temples of Ammon were established at an unknown date in Sparta and its port town of Gythion. To judge from contemporary references in the work of Aristophanes, Euripides, and Herodotus, fifth-century Athenians were also familiar with Ammon, though not as quick to adopt his cult.[16] Plutarch (*Vit. Cim.* 18) tells how the general Kimon, who not coincidentally was a man of pro-Spartan sentiments, attempted to consult the god in 451 during his last campaign in Cyprus. The story goes that he sent a delegation with a secret inquiry, but fell ill and died while the men were traveling. When they arrived at Siwa, the oracle told them their long journey was needless, "for Kimon is already with me." By the early fourth century there is epigraphic evidence of the Athenian state's interest in Ammon, including records of gold sent to

Siwa on behalf of the Athenian people. Its military situation forced Athens to seek alternatives to Delphi during this period, among which Dodona and the oracle of Ammon were favored. Of course the most famous petitioner was Alexander the Great, whose consultation in 331 gave rise to a popular tradition that he was the son of Zeus Ammon.[17]

Bendis

A major Thracian goddess, Bendis came to the notice of Greeks who colonized the northern Aegean in the Archaic period. Thasian settlers on the coast of Thrace frequented at least two sanctuaries (at Neapolis and Oisyme) sacred to a goddess with the title Parthenos (Maiden), who is thought to be Bendis. Too little is known of Bendis as a Thracian deity, but she seems to have been a Great Goddess of the wilderness who like Artemis was associated with springs and cave spirits. On the other hand, an interest in agriculture is suggested by Herodotus' statement (4.33) that the Thracian and Paionian women always sacrificed to "Artemis the Queen" (presumably Bendis) by burning straw. Unlike Artemis, however, Bendis acquired a male cult companion, the hero or deity Deloptes, whose iconography, borrowed from that of Asklepios, suggests that he was viewed as a healer. Bendis' own Hellenized appearance, known to us from fourth-century votive reliefs, was that of a young, athletic woman in a short dress, skin cloak, hunting boots, and

Figure 13.2 Bendis and Deloptes, terracotta votive relief, *c.* 400. Archaeological museum of Chalkis, Greece. Erich Lessing/Art Resource.

Phrygian cap.[18] She typically leans on a spear, and the comic poet Cratinus (fr. 85 Kassel-Austin) called her "twin-speared."

The Athenians too had numerous direct and indirect contacts with Thrace. By 450, most Greek cities of the northern Aegean and Hellespont were allied to or dependencies of Athens, while Athens itself possessed a significant population of Thracian metics (resident foreigners) and slaves. Within another twenty years, the Athenians took the unprecedented step of instituting public worship of Bendis in the Peiraieus, their cosmopolitan port. This event is recorded in the opening lines of Plato's *Republic* (327a–328a), where Sokrates describes how he and a companion walked several miles to say their prayers and see the dual procession: one composed of Athenian citizens, and one of Thracians. Later in the evening, there was a torch race (on horseback, a typically Thracian touch), and an all-night celebration. From later records, it appears that considerable resources were expended on this festival, including the sacrifice of a hundred cattle and the distribution of their meat.[19] The public festival was complemented by private cult organizations of citizens and metics, which conducted their own observances and presumably helped to organize the annual festivities.

Historians have long debated the motivation for the state's highly unusual interest in Bendis, since the Athenians were generally suspicious of foreign gods. The most likely explanation is that they wanted to cement their existing diplomatic, military, and trade relations with the Odrysian Thracians at a time when a major war with the Peloponnesians was imminent.[20]

Britomartis, Diktynna, and Aphaia

In Krete, the worship of a Minoan goddess (or goddesses) of the natural world lingered for centuries. Hellenistic poets and mythographers understood the indigenous Kretan goddesses Britomartis and Diktynna either as companions of Artemis, or as bynames of Artemis herself, but in the realm of cult they continued to be treated as separate deities. Ancient lexicographers tell us that among the Kretans, the name Britomartis meant "sweet maiden." She was worshiped primarily in the eastern half of the island, and her name with the local spelling Britomarpis appears in Hellenistic treaties of Olous, which possessed an Archaic cult statue said to be the work of Daidalos.[21] According to Callimachus (*Hymn* 3.189–203), Britomartis was a nymph, a beloved companion of Artemis who drew the amorous attention of Minos. He pursued her until, in desperation, she threw herself into the sea and was saved in the nets (*diktua*) of some fishermen. Henceforth she was called Diktynna. An alternate version says that she hid from Minos in a grove at Aigina and was afterwards worshiped as Aphaia, the unseen (*aphanēs*) goddess.[22] These tales are constructed around false etymologies, but give us a few hints about the nature of Britomarpis: as her name suggests, she was a virgin, and she was a mistress of the natural world like Artemis.

Diktynna has nothing to do with nets, but rather with the Kretan Mt. Dikte. On the other hand, Dikte lies in the east, while the major centers of Diktynna's cult (Kydonia and Lisos) were in the west of Krete, a fact that has puzzled both ancient and modern commentators. A temple of Diktynna built by Samian colonists in Kydonia (Hdt. 3.59) has been located by archaeologists, and a month name Diktynnaios is attested. During the Classical period, Diktynna was more widely recognized than Britomartis, and her syncretization with Artemis was well underway. Aristophanes (*Ran.* 1359) already thinks of them as identical, and Euripides (*Hipp.* 145) describes Diktynna as a mistress of many beasts. Later we hear of Diktynna or Artemis Diktynna in Lakonia, Phokis, and Athens. The Hellenistic poets' interest in Diktynna coincided with a resurgence of her cult, attested on coins from western Krete starting in the fourth century.[23]

Before the twentieth century, information about Aphaia was strictly limited to a few late literary sources, which recounted how Britomartis/Diktynna fled to the island of Aigina to escape Minos.[24] There, a splendid Doric temple (*c.* 500) had long been assigned to Athena because she appeared as the key figure in both pediments (the east portrays the sack of Troy by Herakles, while the west shows the capture of the city by Aiakid heroes). This temple also contained a cult statue of an Athena-like, spear-wielding goddess, the right arm of which has been recovered. But a sixth-century inscription (*IG* IV 1580) revealed that the predecessor of the Classical temple was dedicated to Aphaia: "In the priesthood of [Th?]eoitas, the house of Aphaia was built and the altar; the ivory was added and a wall was built all around." The ivory in question may refer to ivory components of a cult statue, or plaques of ivory used to adorn the temple interior. A still earlier dedicatory inscription was made to Apha, which is probably the original form of the goddess' name.[25] Aphaia remains an enigmatic deity, and while it is unclear why the fifth-century Aiginetans began to assimilate her to Athena, they may have intended to win for themselves the favor of the better-known goddess who protected their longtime enemy, Athens. They were unsuccessful, for the Athenians eventually expelled the Aiginetans and colonized the island themselves. According to their careful inventory (*IG* IV 39, *c.* 431), the *pronaos* of the temple was full of wooden furniture, chests, and sacrificial implements.

The votive gifts from the sanctuary suggest that Aphaia had a special interest in protecting pregnant and nursing women as well as their babies. This character is apparent even in the Mycenaean objects, which include figurines of women holding infants (though there is, as usual, a gap in the finds between the Mycenaean period and the eighth century). Aphaia's involvement in rituals of maturation is suggested by the presence of sheet bronze rings used to secure offerings of hair, cut when youths reached the threshold of adulthood. Ulrich Sinn suggests that Aphaia's sanctuary was a religious center for a confederation of tribes, and was therefore used for festivals that addressed family and tribal continuity.[26]

Themis and Nemesis

Already in Hesiod's *Theogony*, abstract concepts considered fundamental to human society are treated as divine beings. Worship of these allegorical deities developed in response to the same impulse that made the poets sing of them, but in a much more idiosyncratic fashion, reflecting local needs and preferences. While the great heyday of these cults came during the fourth century and the Hellenistic period, when many personifications like Eirene (Peace) and Tyche (Fortune) were popularized, a religious impulse to acknowledge powerful and culturally weighty concepts through prayer and sacrifice was already active in the Archaic period.

The name Themis refers to "that which has been ordained," the norms of society with respect to politics, social relations, and ritual. In Homer (*Il.* 20.4–6) Themis is the deity who summons and dismisses assemblies, and in cult she sometimes has the epithet Agoraia (of the Meeting Place). Themis also governs the natural world, which likewise functions according to divine laws. Hesiod (*Theog.* 901–4) says her children are Eunomia (Lawfulness), Dike (Justice), Eirene (Peace), and the Moirai (Fates), but also the Horai (Seasons), who ensure the orderly cycle of plant growth and decay.[27] Our sources hint that Themis (like Thetis and perhaps Gaia) once played a more important role in early Greek pantheons and cosmologies. Pindar (fr. 30 Snell-Maehler) made Themis the first wife of Zeus, and she seems to have occupied the place of Hera in the Archaic pantheon of Thessaly. We lack detailed information about her Thessalian worship, but a Thessalian month name Themistios, along with the prevalence of personal names like Themistion and Themistokles in the region, show that her cult was popular in the Archaic period. A fourth-century altar from Pherai, inscribed with the names of six major goddesses, lists Hestia, Demeter, Athena, Aphrodite, Enodia (another important local goddess), and Themis.[28]

As the personification of divine law, Themis was the confidante and frequent companion of Zeus, able to dispense knowledge of future events (hence the verb *themisteuein*, "to pronounce divine law" for the giving of oracles, and Themis' strong mythic, though not cultic, presence at Delphi). In a lost seventh-century epic, the *Cypria*, she and Zeus planned the Trojan war as a way to reduce the population of the overburdened earth. Themis warned Zeus of the prophecy that the Nereid Thetis would bear a son more powerful than his father; hence Thetis was married off to the mortal Peleus, resulting in the birth of Achilles, while Helen, the *casus belli*, was born from the union of Zeus with his own daughter Nemesis. Awareness of Themis' role in these events may account for the construction of a shrine to Themis within the sanctuary of Nemesis at Rhamnous in Attica.[29]

The Attic cult of Nemesis is a rare early example of full-blown worship paid to a personification. Like the cult of Themis in Thessaly, it demonstrates the persistence of idiosyncratic local pantheons in opposition to the trend in poetry toward a canonical, Panhellenized system. Derived from the verb *nemein*, "to deal out, distribute," Nemesis' name evokes that which is allotted by fate, but also whatever is dealt out as just deserts and, finally, the appropriate reaction to wrongdoing: righteous indignation. Hesiod (*Op.* 197–201) pairs Nemesis with Aidos (Right Feeling), and predicts that the two will abandon the earth at the end of the age, leaving a world of shameless criminals. The cult at Rhamnous, however, confounds our expectations about the worship of "abstract concepts" because it emphasizes Nemesis' concrete role in bringing about the Trojan war by giving birth to Helen, in contradiction to the Panhellenic version, which asserted that Helen's mother was the Spartan queen Leda. The two versions were reconciled in the story that Nemesis, having shape-shifted to escape Zeus, was finally raped in goose form at Rhamnous and laid an egg containing Helen, whom Leda then nursed.

The Greek victory against the invading Persians, who burned the little Archaic temple, seems to have positively affected the fortunes of Nemesis' cult, for all agreed that Nemesis had taken a hand in the downfall of the overweening foe, just as in the days of Troy. In the most prosperous period of the Athenian empire, Nemesis was one of the Attic deities selected to receive a lavish new peripteral temple (others outside the city included Poseidon at Sounion and Ares at Acharnai), and the story of Helen's egg enjoyed a spike in popularity. A comedy *Nemesis* by Cratinus, presented around the time the temple was completed (*c.* 430), had Leda attempting to hatch the egg by sitting on it, while Attic and Italian vases also portrayed the story. The ruins of the temple have been excavated, and pieces of the marble cult statue by Agorakritos have been recovered and studied in detail. Twice life-size, the goddess held an apple branch in her left hand and a libation bowl in her right. The statue base was decorated with relief figures of Leda presenting young Helen to her true mother, along with a number of Trojan war heroes. Inscribed dedications from the site show that Themis and Nemesis had their own priestesses, and an annual festival called the Great Nemesia is attested, though only from the late fourth century on.[30]

Damia and Auxesia

Another example of resistance to Panhellenization is the cult of Damia/ Mneia and Auxesia/Azesia, which was roughly equivalent to, but probably independent of, the better-known cult of Demeter and Kore (their names remain mysterious, though the form Auxesia appears to be related to the verb *auxein*, increase). These pre-Dorian goddesses were native to the eastern Peloponnese, particularly the coast of the Saronic gulf. At Epidauros they were worshiped under the names Mneia and Azesia, or as the Theoi Azesioi, and a month Azesios was connected with them.[31] Herodotus (5.83–88), our most detailed source, tells how this worship spread to Aigina and ultimately became symbolic of Aigina's longstanding quarrel with Athens. Previously under the control of Epidauros, Aigina declared its independence in the early seventh century, and absconded with Epidauros' two olivewood statues of the goddesses, installing them in a rural sanctuary with the same annual rites they had enjoyed in the mother city. These included two female "mocking" choruses whose targets were other women, an activity that has been compared to the *aischrologia* (sex talk) and mocking attested in Thesmophoric ritual. The statues, it was said, were made under the guidance of the Delphic oracle, when Epidauros had been stricken with a famine. Told to carve the statues from olive wood, the Epidaurians petitioned Athens for a sacred olive tree, and agreed to bring annual offerings to Athena and Erechtheus in return. After the Aiginetans took away the statues, Epidauros ceased sending offerings, and the angry Athenians were told to seek redress from Aigina. They attacked the island with the intention of repatriating the sacred wood, but found themselves unable to remove the images from their bases. As they dragged the statues toward the Athenian ships, the two goddesses fell to their knees. The Athenians were nearly all killed (either by a supernatural storm and earthquake, or with the aid of the Argives), and the statues thereafter remained frozen in a kneeling posture. Upon returning home, the sole Athenian survivor was murdered by the hostile wives of his comrades, who stabbed him with their dress pins, while the Aiginetans decreed that dress pins should be the main offering in the goddess' sanctuary, and banned all dedications of Attic origin, including pottery.

Clearly, much of this story was fashioned not only to explain details of the cult, but also to provide a religious justification for the Aiginetans' hostility toward Athens. The olive wood of the statues, their kneeling poses, the custom of dedicating dress pins, and the exclusion of Attic objects are all tied to the belief that the Athenians committed an unprovoked, impious attack on an Aiginetan sanctuary, and that the victimized goddesses themselves were therefore anti-Athenian. While the main elements of the legend may be fabricated, the cult is independently attested in a fifth-century temple inventory from Aigina (*IG* IV 1588), which the Athenians produced after expelling the Aiginetans in 431.[32] This inscription indicates that the goddesses shared a temple, and that dress pins (made of iron, in a style not in daily use since the Protogeometric period) were indeed a favorite gift. Other objects of value included bronze lamps, incense burners, chests, wine cups and basins, pedestals, armor (shields and breastplates), and statues of the goddesses. The kneeling pose of the cult statues most likely alludes to childbirth and suggests that the goddesses provided help to women in labor. The dedication of armor, on the other hand, suggests a more bellicose aspect of the goddesses and reminds us of their symbolic role in Aiginetan-Athenian relations.

Further reading

Roller 1999 is especially valuable for its investigation of the prehistoric roots and Phrygian background of the Kybele cult; Borgeaud 2004 is complementary. Schachter 2003 is a concise study of the Theban sanctuary of the Kabiroi by an expert on Boiotian religion, with good illustrations. On the Great Gods at Samothrace, Cole 1984 is still the most detailed discussion in English. Chapter 9 of Parke 1967 provides a thorough introduction to Ammon's cult. On the cult of Bendis at Athens, Simms 1988 is a good discussion of the epigraphic evidence for advanced students with some knowledge of ancient Greek.

14

ANOMALOUS IMMORTALS
Hero-gods and heroine-goddesses

Herakles

Herakles is unique among Greek heroes. He achieved Panhellenic status at such an early date that his origins can no longer be traced, but most likely they lie in the Argolid (his name, which means "glory of Hera," also evokes Argos). The fact that a wide variety of non-Greek populations, from the Lydians to the Phoenicians and Etruscans, adopted this hero is the best evidence of his overwhelming popularity. Much of his story is familiar to Homer, and some scholars believe that he was a Mycenaean hero. In any event, the question of "origins" is perhaps moot for Herakles because the corpus of his myths, and his general character, are the result of a long process of accretion, with contributions from nearly all parts of the Greek world. While some of the myths appear to have Bronze Age and even Stone Age roots, evidence for cults is much more recent, dating from the seventh and sixth centuries or later.[1]

Like Hermes and Apollo, Herakles was a patron of the young men engaged in preparing their bodies for the challenges of campaign and battle. The foremost requirements for a Herakleion, which often did double duty as a gymnasium, were abundant open space, water, and accessibility; many sanctuaries lay just outside the city walls. These same features meant that Herakleia were often used as military encampments. For Pindar, who sang of athletic prowess, he represents the acme of masculine achievement (*Isthm.* 4.11–12): "by their manly deeds, unrivaled, they have set out from home and grasped the Pillars of Herakles." His cults, as well as those of dependent "Herakleian" heroes (Iolaos, Iphikles, and the sons of Herakles) are often found in initiatory and pederastic contexts.[2]

Pindar (*Nem.* 3.22) called Herakles *herōs theos* (hero-god), in recognition of his apotheosis and his unique status among the heroes. Unlike most heroic figures, Herakles was the exclusive possession of no single city or village. None dared to lay claim to his tomb in the normal manner of heroic cult, not even the residents around Mt. Oita where his fiery death was commemorated from the Archaic period with an annual sacrifice and bonfire. Scholars have long debated how his dual nature was handled at the cultic level, citing ancient sources (e.g. Hdt. 2.44 on Thasos or Paus. 2.10.1 on Sikyon) that indicate a "mixed" or dual cult. It is not surprising that some communities enacted Herakles' dual status as god and hero in ritual, but this approach, based in theological speculation, was probably not the norm. A sacrifice more closely approximating the "Olympian" type, with its focus on shared meals and meat consumption, is the mark of Herakles' cults, while the renunciatory mode associated with offerings to the dead, heroes, and chthonian deities seems to be relatively rare.[3]

In antiquity it was generally agreed that Herakles' birthplace was Thebes, though his parents had come from Tiryns. Boiotia's numerous cults focus almost exclusively on a young Herakles, and he often assumes the cultic role of military champion and guardian of city gates. At Thebes, fifth-century coins show the youthful Herakles strangling the snakes sent by Hera, presaging his role as a protector against evils. Our earliest written source for his cult is Pindar (*Isthm.* 4.61–72), who describes a "feast" (*dais*) for Herakles and annual burnt sacrifices for the Alkaidai, warrior sons of Herakles with his Theban wife Megara. This was just one part of the festival, which featured athletic competitions held in the attached gymnasium and stadium. Pausanias (9.11.1–6) gives a more detailed account of the cult complex outside the gate, including the tomb of the warriors, the "house of Amphitryon," and the temple of Herakles. The tomb of Iolaos, an old Theban hero who came to be known as Herakles' nephew, was probably also located here.[4]

In spite of the paucity of Athenian myths about Herakles, his Attic cults were deeply rooted and numerous, arguably benefiting further from the patronage of the Peisistratid tyrants. The Athenian victory over the Persian invaders in 490 only increased his popularity, for one of his oldest Attic shrines was located at Marathon. The Athenians organized their military camp in his sanctuary, which possessed athletic facilities and probably hosted games at the local level. After the battle, the hero-god was credited with aiding the Athenians, and the games quickly developed a following outside of Attica, as we learn from Pindar (e.g. *Ol.* 9.89–90, *Pyth.* 8.79). Vanderpool located the Herakleion in the southern part of the plain of Marathon on the strength of a *stēlē* or marker dating just after 490 (*IG* I³ 2–3), which carried instructions on the organization of the games.[5]

According to Herodotus (6.116), the Athenians rushed back from Marathon to engage the Persian fleet and encamped at Kynosarges, another important sanctuary of Herakles. Located on the Ilissos river in the suburb of Diomeia, Kynosarges had a gymnasium frequented by *nothoi*, youths who were illegitimate or had only one citizen parent. It was also a hothouse of intellectual activity, attracting men like Themistokles and Sokrates. A most unusual feature of this ancient cult was that the *nothoi* were its officiants, and participated as "parasites" in the feasts for the god Herakles; elsewhere such activities were the privilege of full citizens. Pausanias (1.19.3) says that the sanctuary included altars for Herakles and his divine bride Hebe (Youth), as well as one for Alkmene and Iolaos, a combination that suggests Theban influence.[6]

Within the city walls, Herakles' most important shrine was south of the agora, in the deme of Melite. Here, as in several other cities, he had the title of Alexikakos (Warder-Off of Evils), and the Athenians relied on him to repel plagues.[7] As a protector of youths, he received libations from Athenian boys preparing to embark on military training. This ceremony, known as the *oinistēria*, may have taken place at Melite or in the type of neighborhood shrine illustrated on Attic vase paintings and in votive reliefs: four columns stand on a base supporting an unroofed rectangle of beams. Such shrines were probably used often for private sacrifices to Herakles; inscriptions demonstrate that his cult was most frequently observed at the sub-state level. There is abundant fifth- and fourth-century evidence of small cult associations (*thiasoi*), which met regularly to share a banquet in his honor, appointing their own priests and making their own rules.[8]

One of Herakles' oldest known cults belongs to Thasos, an island colonized by Greeks from Paros in the seventh century. A Thasian hymn to Herakles styling him Kallinikos (of Beautiful Victory) was attributed to Archilochus (fr. 324 West *IE²*). Herakles and Dionysos were designated "guardians of the city" in an Archaic inscription on the southern city wall (*IG* XII 8.356), where a relief sculpture depicted Herakles kneeling and taking aim with his bow. According to Herodotus (2.44), it was the Phoenicians who introduced the cult of Herakles – not the Greek hero, but a god of Egyptian origin who was far older. While no evidence from the sanctuary itself supports this idea, the Phoenicians certainly occupied Thasos before the Greeks. Their god Melqart was widely identified with Herakles in the historical period, and the Phoenician background may account for the unusual civic prominence of Herakles on Thasos.[9]

Entering the city from the south, visitors soon encountered the Herakleion, which initially consisted of a space cleared around a rock outcropping, enclosed with stone slabs, which served as an altar. Along its eastern side was a row of pits hewn into the rock, of unknown function (often interpreted as receptacles for offerings, but possibly post-holes for a wooden structure). A small building containing a hearth (the "polygonal *oikos*") was soon added for the purpose of ritual dining; during the fifth century, it was incorporated into a bank of dining rooms. Meanwhile the first identifiable temple was constructed to the north of the altar on a fresh site. A gallery, well, and propylon (entrance) were also added during the fifth century.

As a civic deity, Herakles was worshiped in the Thasian agora. A Classical inscription (*IG* XII Suppl. 414) from the marble-walled "Passage of the Theoroi," a special area in the northeast part of the agora where ritual laws were displayed, announces that it is not permitted to sacrifice goat or pig to Herakles Thasios, nor for a woman to partake of the meat, nor for "a ninth" (a tithe) to be given, nor for *gera* (perquisites) to be cut from the meat, nor for contests to be held (i.e., for prizes of honor to be cut from the meat). These restrictions seem to focus on saving the animal's meat all for one purpose, whether for a holocaust sacrifice in chthonian style, or (more likely) some strictly equal division of meat among a group of privileged men. Other inscriptions mention Thasian festivals of Herakles, including one occasion when athletic competitions were held and the sons of dead soldiers were presented with arms as state compensation for their loss. On the whole, the evidence from Thasos gives us a picture of a warlike Herakles concerned above all with male bonding and commensality.[10]

In spite of (or perhaps because of) his ancient roots in the Peloponnese, the Dorian peoples who settled there appropriated Herakles as an ancestor in order to legitimize their claims to the land. Herakles himself was denied the kingship of Argos, but according to myth, his descendants returned and conquered the land by right. Stories of his exploits overseas similarly served to justify Dorian colonization (first in Rhodes and Kos, later in the West). Thus many an elite family and tribe, including the kings of Sparta, traced their ancestry to him. There is evidence of an Archaic cult at Tiryns, including the report of a statue of Herakles by the sixth-century sculptors Dipoinos and Skyllis.[11] Old Dorian cults of Herakles are not as numerous as we would expect, were he in origin a Dorian hero, and are all but absent in Krete. In fact, Herakles figures far more often as a cult founder than a cult recipient. A surprising number of Spartan monuments and cults are tied to a minor myth, Herakles' feud with the renegade king Hippokoön, who usurped the throne from Tyndareos. Herakles slaughtered Hippokoön and his huge brood of sons, placing Tyndareos in his debt and filling the landscape with tombs, trophies, and sanctuaries thanking the gods for his victory. In the service of the Herakleid ideology, these myths and cults placed Herakles on an equal footing with the native heroes and putative sons of Tyndareos, the Dioskouroi.[12]

The Spartan Herakles was less the club wielding, skin-clad figure familiar from Attic vases, and more an idealized warrior. Spartan youths on the cusp of manhood offered sacrifices to Herakles at the Dromos (course for foot-races) and fought ritual battles at "the Planes," a sacred grove of plane trees where Herakles and Lykourgos were the resident powers. As a tutelary deity of the kings, Herakles often played a role in battle. The Spartan generals' preference for sanctuaries of Herakles as encampments surely owed something to piety as well as expedience. Attacking Mantineia in 418, Agis settled his men at the Herakleion, just as Archidamos III arrayed his men for battle near the Herakleion at Eutresis, interpreting the lightning that flashed over the sanctuary as a good omen.[13]

For the Greeks of the western colonies, Herakles was a trailblazer who traveled to the ends of the earth, a founder of cities and cults, and an apostle of Hellenism. His journey through the western Mediterranean with the cattle of Geryon, celebrated by the Sicilian poet Stesichorus, helped to justify Greek possession of colonized lands. His prominence in the sphere of Phoenician influence was in part a function of his identification with the god Melqart, but this cannot explain the popularity of Italian Hercules, whose cult was ubiquitous. Diodorus Siculus (4.23–25), our main informant for the beliefs of the Sicilian Greeks, says that Herakles made a circuit of the island, battling the indigenes and leaving "imperishable memorials of his presence" in the landscape itself. As elsewhere, he was particularly associated with hot springs, which were known as "Herakleian baths." In Diodorus' native city, Argyrion, Herakles seems to have been a major deity, honored with festivals and splendid sacrifices "on equal terms with the Olympian gods." Youths grew their hair in honor of Iolaos and dedicated it in his precinct when they reached manhood. These offerings were made in connection with annual gymnastic and horse racing contests, and the celebration was extended to slaves, who were allowed to hold their own banquets in Herakles' honor. A private dedication from Selinous shows that Herakles was worshiped in Sicily by the sixth century, while the great temple inscription (*IG* XIV 268, *c.* 450) from the same city names Herakles with major gods such as (Demeter) Malophoros and Zeus.[14]

Pindar repeatedly (*Ol.* 2.1–4, 3.11–38, etc.) credits Herakles with the founding of the sanctuary at Olympia and the establishment of rules for the Olympic games. In later accounts, however, and most conspicuously in Pausanias' (5.7.6–9, 5.14.7) description of the sanctuary, we hear that there was more than one Herakles, and the founding of Olympia is attributed to Idaian Herakles, one of the Daktyls of Kretan Ida who aided Rhea in the upbringing of Zeus. The Daktyls (Fingers) were dwarfish magicians, guardians of mysteries, and experts in metallurgy who would seem to have little in common with the hero-god Herakles. The theory of multiple "Herakleis" goes back to Herodotus' distinction between the god Herakles, of exotic origin, and the Greek hero, son of Alkmene. At Olympia, the custodians of sacred legends exploited the theory in order to bolster the sanctuary's existing connections with Krete, usually acknowledged as the birthplace of Zeus, and to portray the sanctuary as an alternative Ida, where the young Zeus was nurtured. All this is not to say that Idaian Herakles was a complete fabrication. Although there is no sign of him in Krete, it is possible that Herakles the Daktyl has his origin in Bes, the Egypto-Phoenician dwarf god who protected the young. Syncretization of Herakles, Bes, and Melqart, whose kourotrophic and apotropaic functions are similar, has been documented in Cyprus and elsewhere.[15]

Ino-Leukothea

Like Herakles, Ino-Leukothea was widely worshiped and she transcended distinctions between mortal and immortal. The sixth-century philosopher Xenophanes (fr. 21 A 13 *DK*) advised his fellow Eleans that they ought to make up their minds: if Leukothea was a mortal woman, they should not sacrifice (*thuein*) to her. But if she was a goddess, they should not sing laments. This evidence of Archaic dirges for Leukothea was cited by Farnell to support his interpretation of Ino-Leukothea as a vegetation goddess closely associated with Dionysos, for lamentation is often a part of the worship of deities connected with the ebb and flow of the seasons and the cycle of plant growth and death.[16] The myth of Athamas' angry pursuit and Ino's leap into the sea indeed parallels the anger of Lykourgos and the leap of Dionysos recounted in the *Iliad* (6.130–37).

Beneath the myth lies a substrate of ritual, rich in the symbolism of rebirth and transfiguration, which helps us to see how the Theban daughter of Kadmos and the sea-goddess who rescues Odysseus from drowning can be one and the same, an identification already made in Homeric epic (*Od.* 5.333–35). Ino-Leukothea and her son Melikertes-Palaimon derive their power as sea gods from their own experience of drowning, and their dual names may signal not the blending of two originally separate figures, but a passage from one state of existence to another. Like other Dionysiac women, Ino-Leukothea has an ambivalent relationship to children: sometimes she is the maddened killer who dispatches Melikertes, sometimes she attempts to revive his lifeless body through immersion, and sometimes she is the nurturing foster-mother of the infant Dionysos himself.[17]

According to Cicero (*Nat. D.* 3.15), all of Greece worshiped Ino-Leukothea. The evidence for her cults is mostly late, yet they were probably well developed by the Archaic period, given the wide distribution of her worship and her popularity in Archaic poetry. Homer, Alcman (fr. 50b *PMG*), and Pindar (*Pyth.* 11.2) speak of her as a sea goddess, and we must presume that she received prayers and sacrifices from anxious mariners. Antiquarian sources note her presence in Thessaly (where inscribed dedications have been found), Boiotia, the Isthmos, and southern Lakonia, but in contrast to the witness of the Archaic poets, there is little or no indication of a marine character in the cults they describe. A festival at Miletos involving a boys' competition evokes Leukothea's kourotrophic role.[18] Plutarch (*Quaest. Rom.* 267d) mentions her precinct (*sēkos*) in Chaironeia (Boiotia), which was perhaps modeled on the *sēkos* of her sister Semele in Thebes. Near Megara was the Molourian rock from which she leapt, and the Megarians of the Roman period said that her body washed up on their shore, where the two granddaughters of the king found it and laid it to rest, instituting annual sacrifices at the tomb. Whereas the Megarian customs sound like standard heroic cult, we also hear that Ino (like Dionysos at Argos) resided deep in a lake in southern Lakonia. During her annual festival, people threw barley loaves into the water and read omens from the manner in which they sank. Such deep lakes, through which access to the underworld was possible, were the homes of chthonian deities.[19]

The Dioskouroi and Helen

The cult of the Dioskouroi, "youths of Zeus," is already attested in the eleventh book of the *Odyssey* (11.298–304), where we learn that "the life-giving land holds them, living, who beneath the earth have honors from Zeus. On alternate days they live and again are dead, and they have honor equal to the gods." This passage appears to "correct" lines in the *Iliad* (3.243–44) that baldly note the burial of the brothers in Lakedaimon, with no mention of their special status. Together, the passages illustrate a central issue in the cult and myth of the divine twins: the tension between their dual identities as dead heroes and as gods, mortals and immortals. Other poets, including Alcman (fr. 7 *PMG*) and Pindar (*Nem.* 10.55–90), celebrated the paradox of the twins alive under the Lakonian earth, and told how the immortal brother, Polydeukes, would not be separated from his mortal sibling Kastor even by death.

The Tyndaridai (sons of Tyndareos), as the Spartans usually called them, appear at first glance to be typical heroes who exert influence from their tombs. While their Lakonian cult is unquestionably chthonian, however, the Spartans always spoke of them as gods and swore "by the two gods." Other Greeks saw them primarily as divine saviors who rode down from the skies in a blaze of light to give aid in battle or rescue swamped sailors, and their Panhellenic cult developed early in the Archaic period. Already in the seventh century, a hymn of Alcaeus tells how they fly from the Peloponnese to manifest themselves in a ship's rigging as St. Elmo's fire, and "easily rescue men from chilling death," and in the sixth, Poseidon accompanies them on Attic vase paintings. Their Delian cult, established in the seventh or early sixth century, presumably focused on the aid they offered to mariners.[20]

Scholars agree, though not unanimously, that the Dioskouroi have an Indo-European pedigree. The Vedic Asvins, twin riders who give aid in battle and marry the daughter of the Sun, provide a striking parallel to the Greek twins and their divine sister Helen. Anak(t)es (Lords), a third cult title for the Greek twins used in Attica, Boiotia, and Argos, may signal yet another component in their evolution. It was an Argive who dedicated the famous twin statues of the local heroes Kleobis and Biton, now in the Delphi museum, to the Anakes. Thus several strands of tradition, some plausibly Indo-European in origin, coalesced to form the divine persona of the Dioskouroi.[21]

The twins played an important role in the civic lives of the Spartans. Although the Spartan kings claimed to be descendants of Herakles, the dual kingship was intimately connected with the cult of the Tyndaridai. When either king left Sparta on campaign, one of the twins accompanied him, most likely in the form of a statue. The Tyndaridai also served as models for the Spartan youths who aspired to full citizenship. The influence of horse-taming Kastor and the boxer Polydeukes was felt in all the spheres of action appropriate to young Spartan males: there was a Kastorian hunting dog, a

Kastorian battle song, and a choral sword dance invented by the pair. They also provided a model for Spartan matrimony through their capture of the daughters of the Messenian king Leukippos (White Horse). These maidens, Hilaeira (Softly Shining) and Phoibe (Radiant), are ideal female counterparts of the brilliant twins. Spartan marriage customs included a ritual kidnapping that must have evoked this myth, an Archaic favorite often illustrated in Lakonian contexts.[22]

Pindar (*Pyth.* 11.61–64) and other early poets identify Therapne as the site of the brothers' joint burial. There, a complex of related sanctuaries included those of Helen and Menelaos, the shrine of Polydeukes, and "the so-called Phoibaion with a temple of the Dioskouroi in it" (Paus. 3.20.2) where Spartan youths sacrificed to the war god Enyalios. The Phoibaion was probably a shrine of the Leukippides. Unfortunately, none of the cult places of the Tyndaridai have been identified, but we have material evidence of their worship in ten votive reliefs of Archaic and Classical date. They depict the nude twins standing in profile, facing each other and holding spears. Their other attributes are two tall amphoras with peaked lids, a pair of snakes, and a curious monument called the *dokana* (the beams), which consisted of two parallel planks joined by two horizontal crossbars. All of these objects possessed chthonian or sepulchral connotations: the mysterious *dokana* may have served as a tomb marker, or as a schematic representation of the twins in their shrine. The Spartans exported the Tyndaridai to their colony Taras, most likely when it was founded in the eighth century, though our evidence is limited to an important series of terracotta relief plaques dedicated in the fourth and third centuries. These plaques, pierced for suspension on the walls of a shrine or in a grove, include some motifs that are obviously of Spartan origin (the *dokana*, twin amphoras, the rape of the Leukippides) and others that are more generalized (chariots, horse heads).[23]

An aspect of the Panhellenic cult of the Dioskouroi, reflected both in popular legend and in individual devotions, was the belief that the twins gave aid in battle and sometimes appeared on the actual battlefield. Two inscribed spear butts, appropriate gifts for the spear-wielding Dioskouroi, were separately dedicated as battle spoils in Classical Attica and Arkadia.[24] Partisans of Sparta, the Tyndaridai were said to have thwarted Aristomenes, Sparta's great antagonist in the Second Messenian War, on at least two occasions. After they miraculously appeared on their white horses during a clash between Lokroi Epizephyrioi and Kroton beside the Sagra river (*c.* 600), the victorious Lokrians set up altars to them. Over a century later, Simonides elegized the Battle of Plataiai with a description of the Dioskouroi and Menelaos accompanying the Spartans as they rode out to battle against the Persians.[25]

The core ritual in the worship of the Dioskouroi was their reception as guests at a meal. Scholars often refer to the practice as *theoxenia*, but this technical term is only rarely attested. Usually the ritual is described in the same terms used for the entertainment of mortal guests: the hosts receive

190

(*dechesthai*) them or provide hospitality (*xenia*); couches are strewn and tables are set out with food and drink. Herakles, Asklepios, and many other heroes and gods were recipients of such meals, which were often shared with "parasites" in special dining rooms, or as was more often the practice for the Dioskouroi during the Archaic period, set out in private households. According to Pindar (*Ol.* 3.36–40, *Nem.* 10.49–51), the family of Theron of Akragas was favored by the Tyndaridai because "of all mortals they attend them with the most tables of welcome" and Herodotus (6.127) tells of an Arkadian who became famed for his hospitality after he received the Dioskouroi.[26]

Like her siblings the Dioskouroi, Helen was prone to miraculous interventions. Legend had it that she blinded the poet Stesichorus for singing of her adultery at Troy, and then restored his sight when he wrote a recantation denying that she ever traveled there.[27] Herodotus (6.61) says that the nurse of a rich but ugly young Spartan girl took her regularly to the sanctuary of Helen at Therapne and placed her before the cult statue. One day a woman appeared from the shrine and predicted that the child would grow to be the most beautiful woman in Sparta. From that day, her looks improved so dramatically that she ended up marrying one of the Spartan kings. This anecdote illustrates Helen's important role in the lives of Spartan girls and women as a paradigm of female beauty and grace. Like the Dioskouroi, Helen was worshiped both in Sparta proper and in Therapne. The urban cult seems to have involved a girls' footrace or dance on the banks of the Eurotas, and the placing of wreaths on a plane tree sacred to Helen, acts in celebration of Helen's wedding. These rituals were performed at the Dromos and the Planes, the same areas where Spartan youths experienced a separate rite of passage under the protection of Herakles.[28]

Therapne was an important Bronze Age site, revived in the late Geometric period under the impetus of Spartan military victories. Excavations there revealed an enclosure and a small white limestone shrine, begun as early as 700, where statues of Helen and Menelaos probably stood, plus a rich store of votive offerings including jewelry, plentiful bronzes, terracottas, lead figurines, and pottery. A seventh century bronze vase inscribed to "Helen, wife of Menelaos" attests that the royal pair were worshiped together, and other objects are dedicated separately to Menelaos or Helen. The site was centered on a rocky outcropping, hinting at the worship of a prehistoric goddess, a predecessor of the epic Helen. The disappearance and return of a goddess is a familiar motif in Greek religion and presumably gave rise to the myths of Helen's abductions.[29]

Outside of Lakonia, Helen was usually worshiped only in connection with the Dioskouroi. As early as Euripides (*Or.* 1635–43, 1688; *Hel.* 1667–70), we hear of the belief that Helen was a celestial savior of mariners along with her brothers, and that the three received libations and *xenia* (ritual hospitality) as a group. Attica, where Kastor and Polydeukes were worshiped as the Anakes, had its own local traditions of Helen's birth at Rhamnous, her kidnapping by Theseus and her rescue by the Dioskouroi. This rich lore was reflected in various minor cults, such as the sacrifices to the Anakes and Helen recorded in the Thorikos deme calendar.[30]

Asklepios

All the Greeks agreed that Asklepios was a mortal healer who had perished, struck by Zeus' lightning bolt, for presuming to raise the dead. Yet by the Classical period, he was just as unequivocally considered a god, though subordinate to his father Apollo, from whom his healing power was derived. Very little is known of Asklepios before c. 500, when his cult at Epidauros began to develop. During the fifth century, "Asklepiad" was already a familiar synonym for a physician, and Asklepios was considered the father, in a metaphorical sense, of all members of the profession, some of whom probably honored him in private with prayers and offerings; with Apollo and Hygieia, he is one of the witnessing gods in the famous Hippokratic oath. Certainly he was renowned as a culture hero long before the rise of his Panhellenic cult. Homer (Il. 2.729–33, 4.194, etc.) speaks of Asklepios as the "blameless physician" who is father to the heroes Machaon and Podaleirios, and connects the family with Trikka (Thessaly), Ithome, and Oichalia (both in Messenia), where there were early traditions about Asklepios' birth.[31]

Although Asklepios' earliest sanctuary may well have been in Trikka, it was the small Peloponnesian city of Epidauros that developed a cult of Pan-hellenic importance, and from which the worship spread rapidly throughout the Greek world in the fifth and fourth centuries. The peak of Asklepios' popularity, and the heyday of his important Hellenistic sanctuaries at Kos and Pergamon, lie outside the chronological parameters of this discussion. At Epidauros, the early cult of Apollo Maleatas on Mt. Kynortion expanded to the plain as the city grew. One of the earliest installations in this lower sanctuary was an altar to Apollo, beneath which was found a bronze offering bowl dedicated to Asklepios in the early fifth century. A nearby stoa or court-yard ("Building E") contained an ash altar and terminated in a small room supplied with a water channel and a stone couch or table, where the god shared food with his worshipers. A sacred well, which was probably used for ritual baths, became the nucleus of the later *abaton*, the area where incuba-tion (dream cures) took place.[32] These elements formed the core of the early Classical sanctuary, shared by Apollo and Asklepios.

During the fifth century, Asklepios' popularity burgeoned, and his worship began to be exported, often by grateful pilgrims who wished to establish branch cults in their home towns. Important cults at Korinth and Athens were among the early offshoots. Still it was not until the fourth century that the great prosperity of the sanctuary resulted in major architectural elabor-ation, fortunately documented in an unusually full collection of inscriptions detailing the financial and legal arrangements. The new structures, begun as early as 380, included a Doric temple of Asklepios, a large *abaton* that incorporated the sacred well, and a mysterious circular building, the Thymele, which concealed below its floor level a mazelike arrangement of concentric rings around a central chamber. The stadium and famous theater came slightly later, though already in Plato's day (*Ion* 530a), Asklepieia with musical and athletic competitions were held.

Through hymns, dedications, and iconography, we learn that Asklepios was worshiped in conjunction with a family group who personify aspects of healing. The name of his consort Epione refers to the physician's gentle touch, and ancient speculation found the same root in Asklepios' name, though its true etymology is unknown. In addition to his two physician sons, he had a daughter or wife Hygieia (Health) and a trio of nymphlike attendants Akeso (Relief), Iaso (Healing), and Panakeia (Universal Cure).[33] Asklepios possessed certain chthonian characteristics, the most important of which were his epiphany as a snake and the ritual of *enkoimēsis* or incubation, which is generally associated with netherworld powers. The function of the famous Thymele is unknown, but its lower chambers suggest a chthonian component in the Epidaurian cult. In spite of these features, Asklepios lacked the kindly/wrathful dual personality that is typical of chthonian figures. Although he sometimes refused to heal evildoers, he was generally a beneficent, gentle god, extending his gifts even to unbelievers.

The popular and affective element in Asklepios' worship is accessible to us through the famous *iamata* of Apollo and Asklepios, testimonies of cures left

Figure 14.1　Marble votive relief to Asklepios and Hygieia. A family brings a bovine to the altar for sacrifice. Late fourth century. Louvre Museum. Erich Lessing/Art Resource.

by visitors from all over the Aegean. These were set up in the sanctuary in the second half of the fourth century, but they represent a compilation of many older dedications, including a number of painted *pinakes* which are now lost. Perhaps one of the oldest was dedicated by Kleo, whose inscription read: "The size of the tablet is not to be wondered at, but the greatness of the divinity, in that Kleo carried a burden in her womb for five years, until she lay down within and he made her healthy." Another account tells of a local boy who suffered from kidney stones. In his dream, the god asked "what will you give me if I heal you?" The boy offered his collection of knucklebones, the ancient equivalent of dice, and Asklepios laughingly agreed to the bargain. Other tales tell of cures for parasites, blindness, and lameness; they are strikingly similar to the accounts from modern healing shrines such as Lourdes.[34]

Around 420, Athens became home to two sanctuaries of Asklepios, one in the Peiraieus at Zea and one in the city, on the south slope of the Akropolis. Relations between Athens and Epidauros had just been restored through the Peace of Nikias in 421, and Athens was still recovering from the great plague that ravaged the city from 430 to 426. Although a number of older healing cults existed, including those of Apollo Paion, Athena Hygieia, and various physician heroes, the time was ripe for a newer, more potent healing figure. A monument found in the city Asklepieion (*IG* II² 4960–63) proclaims that one Telemachos introduced the god and financed the cult in its earliest years. This large inscribed *stēlē*, topped by a double-sided relief illustrating Asklepios' arrival, says that he came from Zea in 420 at the time of the Eleusinian Mysteries, and was temporarily lodged in the Eleusinion. Damaged lines suggest that Telemachos installed a sacred snake, summoned from Epidauros, in the new sanctuary (other accounts of Asklepios' travels similarly describe how he was conveyed in serpent form to Sikyon, Epidauros Limera, and Rome).[35] There is continuing controversy over which areas of the excavated city Asklepieion, west of the Theater of Dionysos, were included in Tele-machos' original installation. One of the oldest structures, *c.* 420, is a four-room dining area; another is the so-called *bothros*, a stone-lined circular pit covered by a four-columned canopy, which most likely served as a place to deposit offerings. A grotto-spring in the cliff must have been a part of the earliest shrine, since abundant water for ritual and therapeutic bathing was a necessity in all Asklepieia.[36]

Aristophanes' comic account (*Plut.* 633–747) of the healing of Ploutos, set in the Peiraieus Asklepieion, is the earliest description of the incubation ritual. The blind Ploutos (Wealth) is led into the sea to bathe, and inexpensive cakes are burned on the altar. Then he is placed on the temple floor along with the other ailing visitors, and the lamps are extinguished for the night. The god enters, attending to each patient in turn. Assisted by his daughter Panakeia, he covers Ploutos' head with a cloth and calls two huge serpents from the temple to lick his eyes, speedily effecting the cure. This testimony shows that

Asklepios did not demand expensive sacrifices from those he treated. The standard preliminary offering consisted of cakes, while thank offerings after receiving a cure might be more generous: sacrificial sheep, pigs, and cattle are shown in the abundant votive reliefs from the Athens and Peiraieus Asklepieia. Although unusual in other cults, the cock was a common gift to Asklepios, as we learn from Sokrates' last words (Plat. *Phd.* 118a) and the terracotta roosters found in the sanctuaries at Athens and Korinth. Another widespread custom, still practiced at modern healing shrines, was the dedication of metal or clay body parts as thank offerings.

The rise of Asklepios is often called the harbinger of an important shift in Greek religion, a movement away from state and communal worship toward a greater focus on the needs of the individual and the gods who addressed those needs. There is much truth to this, but the available evidence suggests that Asklepios concerned himself with families as much as individuals. More votive reliefs to Asklepios are extant than for any other single deity, and these usually show a family making offerings to the god and Hygieia or other associates. They vary greatly in the number, age, and sex of the family members depicted, showing that the reliefs were custom made, rather than "stock" items.[37]

Further reading

Much of the material in Farnell 1921 is now out of date, yet this book still provides the only comprehensive discussions in English for the cults of several figures treated in this chapter. Woodford 1971 has detailed discussion of the literary and archaeological evidence for Herakles in Attica, and Silk 1985 is complementary. LiDonnici 1995 contributes new insights into the experience of pilgrims and the workings of the sanctuary of Asklepios at Epidauros; Edelstein and Edelstein 1975 contains an important collection of primary sources on Asklepios. Lambrinoudakis 2002 provides a current account of the sanctuary of Apollo Maleatas.

15

THE POWERFUL DEAD

Heroes and heroines

The Greeks sacrificed and prayed to a class of supernatural beings they called the heroes, of which the heroes in Homeric epic formed only a subset. No taxonomy of the heroes and heroines can be completely satisfying because they are a large and varied group, sometimes resembling the medieval saints with respect to the way their relics are manipulated, other times the restless and vengeful dead in their malicious and ghostlike activities, and yet other times functioning as tutelary deities who help shape the identity of the polis and protect its lands. The Greeks looked back with intense interest on their own heroic past, and believed that the first generations of men had possessed godlike powers and stature. Hesiod (*Op.* 123, 141) speaks of early races that died out, yet became "pure ones dwelling on the earth, kindly ones, guardians of mortals" and "blessed ones under the earth." Most of the epic heroes died (*Op.* 166–73), yet a privileged few were brought to the Islands of the Blessed to live an existence like that of the gods. Homer and Hesiod are concerned with Panhellenic, shared traditions about the heroes, so they have little to say about heroic cult, which is a varied phenomenon, distinctive to each place.

Since we must generalize about the worship of heroes and heroines, we can say that their cult places were usually their purported tombs, or ancient structures they supposedly once inhabited. Because they were imagined as dwellers below the earth and were therefore related to the common dead and the underworld gods, they occasionally received sacrifices with what are considered "chthonian" features: a nocturnal setting, a black victim, special blood rituals, and/or the burning of the carcass whole with no attendant feasting. While this grim, renunciatory form of sacrifice "as to a hero" was opposed in the minds of many Greeks to the standard sacrifice "as to a god," the archaeological and epigraphic evidence shows that people were rarely willing to expend resources so lavishly. The prevailing mode of sacrifice for heroes and heroines seems to have been the slaughter of the animal followed by a ritual meal. In these cases the status of the recipient as a hero, hence one of the dead, might be indicated through the blood rituals mentioned above (allowing it to flow on the ground, or pouring into the tomb), the burning of

196

a portion of meat (as opposed to the whole animal), or the requirement that all the meat be eaten on the spot, and not removed from the sanctuary. There was much local variation in sacrifices for the heroes, but the same was true for the gods. In many cases, heroes and heroines were simply "little gods," concerned for the most part with the daily comings and goings in their own neighborhoods. As such, they might be called simply "the hero at the salt-marsh" or "the heroines at the gate." The epigraphic record gives us numerous examples of such minor heroes, whose existence we would not otherwise have suspected.[1]

Heroic cult and tomb cult

Much debate has focused on the origins of heroic cult and to what degree it was influenced by the rise of Homeric epic. Most authorities agree that a major flowering of heroic cult took place in the eighth century, contemporary with the genesis of the Greek city-state and the dissemination of epic poetry in written form. An older scholarly model made epic the impetus for the development of hero cults, while more recent approaches focus on the role of heroes' tombs as "nodes of power" to be contested by different groups claiming land or social status in rapidly changing social and political contexts. During the eleventh through eighth centuries, there was a wave of interest in Bronze Age tombs, particularly in the Argolid and Messenia. In the late Classical and Hellenistic periods, a similar phenomenon is attested over a broader area including Messenia, Lakonia, Boiotia, and Krete. Sometimes the locals reused the ancient tombs for burials, but other times they simply left gifts to honor the tomb occupants. Unlike proper heroic cults, these "tomb cults" usually involved one-time offerings or were sustained only a short while.[2] Special rituals in honor of ancestors also seem to be attested from time to time in the material record, and it is likely that heroic cult evolved from tribal and familial ancestor cults to serve the differing needs of the polis.[3] Unlike the ancestor, who was the actual progenitor of those bringing offerings, the hero was not always a real person, and his cult was not defined by family descent but by other common interests of the group he (or she) represented. In spite of their differences, tomb cult, ancestor cult, and heroic cult are related phenomena, as all share the assumption that, through ritual, the living can carry on a dialogue with the powerful dead, appeasing their anger or benefiting from their goodwill.

There were hundreds, if not thousands of hero and heroine cults in the ancient Greek world. In this chapter, I select a few for more detailed discussion, and information about others appears in the chapters on the gods. The tombs of many heroes and heroines could be found in the very sanctuaries of the gods, overturning the normal prohibition on contact between the Olympian gods and the dead. In such cases, the hero's death was often attributed to the god (Apollo and Hyakinthos, or Artemis and Iphigeneia), yet the identities of deity and mortal might overlap and converge.[4] With a hero or heroine functioning as a sort of alter ego, the festivals of these gods were rich in contrasting rites of mourning and celebration, evoking a full range of emotional experience in the worshipers. The festival of Hyakinthos at Sparta, which opened with a day of mourning for the hero and continued with a festive celebration, is a case in point.

Epic heroes and the archaeological record

Surprisingly few cults of the great mythic and epic heroes can be firmly linked to the material record. The cult of Helen and Menelaos at Therapne is the lone case in which inscribed votives confirm the identity of the recipients as early as the seventh century and the first quarter of the sixth (the cult of Achilles at Olbia, discussed below, may prove to be of similar antiquity). The sanctuary of Alexandra and Agamemnon in Amyklai also produced a rich hoard of votive gifts stretching back to the seventh century, though without identifying inscriptions. The Archaic and Classical offerings include terracotta plaques with the typically Lakonian iconography of heroization: a man and woman are seated on thrones together; the bearded man extends a *kantharos* toward a rearing serpent. Other plaques show Alexandra enthroned, holding a scepter, and accompanied by a snake. The local heroine or goddess Alexandra was identified with the epic Kassandra, possibly as the focus of an expiatory rite that attempted to atone for Kassandra's murder. The introduction of Agamemnon's cult is in keeping with the strong Spartan interest in establishing cultic and mythic claims to the line of Pelops. The Spartans, in fact, seem to be the earliest and most vigorous proponents of heroic cult, promoting the cults of epic heroes as well as Spartan lawgivers and kings.[5]

Often, a cult place can be securely dated to the early Archaic period, but there is no proof of a specific hero's residency until the late Classical or Hellenistic periods. Located about 1 km from the akropolis at Mycenae, the so-called sanctuary of Agamemnon was perhaps the most important cult place in the immediate area, in spite of its modest architecture. While signs of cult begin in the eighth century, only a rubble wall, a sacrificial pit, some roof tiles, and a large votive deposit remain from the Archaic and Classical phases. Inscribed sherds demonstrate that offerings were made to Agamemnon in the fourth century, but this only happened after a significant gap in activity resulting from the Argive sack of Mycenae in 468. Given the female figurines in the deposit, it has been suggested that the site was originally a shrine to Hera, and that the citizens of Archaic Mycenae were more interested in proclaiming their ties to Perseus, ancestor of Herakles, than to Agamemnon. A late Archaic inscription (*IG* IV 493) from the Perseian spring near the entrance to the citadel refers to the judges of youths' contests (probably rites of passage) held for Perseus.[6]

Polis cave in Ithaka has been touted as the site of an old hero cult for Odysseus. This cave, which saw use throughout the Bronze Age, contained the remnants of at least thirteen Geometric tripod cauldrons and a series of other, later votive gifts suggesting female deities. Could it be coincidental that Homer makes Odysseus store away his Phaiakian guest-gifts, including numerous tripods, in an Ithakan cave of the nymphs (*Od.* 13.13–14, 345–50)? Given that some of the tripods go back to the ninth century, Homer's story may be a reference to this wondrous cave and its contents. Some scholars are skeptical about the claim of a cult for Odysseus, as his name does not appear on an object from the cave until the Hellenistic period.[7]

An example of an epic hero who can be more firmly tied to an early shrine is Phrontis son of Onetor, the drowned steersman of Menelaos. Homer must have been aware of this cult, for he goes out of his way to mention that Phrontis was buried on the promontory of Sounion in Attica (*Od.* 3.278–85). When excavators found votive pits containing offerings suitable for a hero (e.g. iron weapons, miniature shields), including a seventh-century terracotta plaque with a painted ship and helmsman, they naturally attributed the cult to the hero. Pots inscribed to Onetor and his son from the sixth century onward confirmed the connection. Phrontis (One Who Watches Over) and son of Onetor (Giver of Advantage) are the perfect names for a hero who looked down on sailors from the cliff of Sounion and took thought for their safety. Still, the minor figure Phrontis is not so much an "epic" hero like Agamemnon as a cult hero who has been absorbed into the epic. There has been much uncertainty about exactly which structures at Sounion can be assigned to Phrontis, for in the same area there are sanctuaries of Poseidon and Athena.[8]

Heroes and politics

Because most heroes were closely identified with specific cities, lineages and/ or ethnic groups, Archaic poleis made extensive use of heroic cult as a symbolic system to convey messages about political relationships. The Athenian tribal *epōnumoi* illustrate how heroes functioned as symbols of group identity, and the extent to which Athens both valued and manipulated heroic cult. Around 500, Kleisthenes reformed the tribal system by restructuring the four old Ionian tribes as ten new units, each containing a balance of citizens from different parts of Attica. The new tribes were political constructs with no kinship bonds to unify them, yet each was assigned a hero as its "founder" and each tribe was named for its hero. In the new democracy, it was by tribe that the Athenians voted, filled public offices, mustered for military service, and commemorated their war dead. With the assistance of Delphi, Kleisthenes selected a group of Attic heroes that heavily favored legendary kings (Kekrops, Pandion, Aigeus, Erechtheus). Others in the list had special connections with places important to Athens, such as Salamis (Ajax), Eleusis

(Hippothoön), and Thrace (Akamas). All had preexisting cults and shrines, which were supplemented by a monument in the agora, a narrow base topped by ten bronze statues of the heroes. On the wall around the base were posted notices of lawsuits, pending legislation, muster rolls, and other information of public interest. In the 460s, statues of the eponymous heroes fashioned by Pheidias were financed by Persian spoils from the battle of Marathon and dedicated at Delphi.[9]

From the sixth century on, there was a widespread belief in the talismanic powers of heroic remains, diligently fostered by the Delphic oracle. The presence of certain heroes and heroines brought prosperity and protected a city from its enemies, just as the Palladion, a famous statue of Athena, once protected Troy until Odysseus penetrated the city's defenses to steal it. Bones served as physical confirmation of a hero's presence, so heroes could be dis-covered, lost, transferred, and stolen via this medium. (Therefore the exact location of some heroic tombs, like those of Dirke in Thebes or Oedipus in Kolonos, was kept secret.) Around 550, the Spartans became embroiled in a war with Tegea. Consulting Delphi about what ritual actions they should take in order to bring about a victory, they were told to "bring in the bones of Orestes" and given a set of riddling directions for finding his grave inside enemy territory (Hdt. 1.67). Spartan propaganda had it that their subsequent hegemony in the Peloponnese was due to the discovery of bones belonging to a ten-foot giant, clearly those of a hero, and the installation of these remains in the Spartan agora. In spite of the Spartans' Dorian ethnicity, they took pains to establish ties with their Achaian, heroic predecessors through culti-vation of the Pelopid heroes: Agamemnon, Menelaos, and Orestes. The Spartan hunger to control the legacy of the Pelopids, and win their favor, even extended to Orestes' son Teisamenos, whose relics were brought from Achaia to Sparta in response to yet another oracle from Delphi.[10]

Heroines too were of interest to the collectors of relics. A Theban tradition held that the body of Herakles' mother Alkmene was miraculously replaced by a stone, which the citizens piously installed in her shrine. At Haliartos in Boiotia, a second purported tomb of Alkmene was opened by Agesilaos (c. 379), who planned to move her remains to Sparta. The Spartans were dis-appointed in the modest contents of the tomb: a stone, a bronze bracelet, two amphoras filled with what appeared to be hardened earth, and a bronze tablet inscribed with strange characters. They went so far as to send the tablet to Egypt for "translation." Disasters and portents followed the violation of the tomb, and attempts were made to propitiate its angry occupant and her husband Aleus, whom the Haliartans identified with the underworld judge Rhadamanthys.[11] The story shows that the fourth-century Spartans main-tained the interest in relics shown by their forefathers, and that they were eager to possess remains associated with Herakleid ancestry.

The heroic founder

Greek mythology and religion held in common a lively interest in the first authors of rituals, founders of cities and sanctuaries, and inventors. Such founder figures, whether real or invented, were often made the objects of cults.[12] One such hero who deserves to be better known is Anios, the priest-king of Delos. His father Apollo taught him divination and established him on Delos, while his grandfather Dionysos gave Anios' daughters Spermo (Grain-Girl), Oino (Wine-Girl), and Elaïs (Oil-Girl) the magical power to create food and drink. The epic *Cypria* told how Anios offered the services of his daughters to provision the Greek armies setting out for Troy.[13] On Delos, however, Anios' importance was far greater than the literary sources suggest. The Delians called him the Archegete (Founder), a title that shows he was considered their first ruler and corporate ancestor. His is one of the few fully excavated and securely identified hero shrines of the Archaic period, and its architectural pattern was often used for heroic cults, though by no means unique to them. Established in the late seventh or early sixth century, Anios' shrine first consisted of a small open-air court, about 10 m by 11 m, edged by a wooden colonnade and wall. Within the court was an altar with a drainage conduit. This was soon tripled in size, and a prohibition on entry by strangers was carved at the thresholds. The sanctuary held numerous dedications including a marble *kouros*; vases deposited at the site were inscribed to Anios, the Archegete, or the King. A few meters away stood a long, multi-chambered building, which surely functioned as a dining facility. Seven Archaic tombs marked with *stēlai*, survivors of the purifications of Delos, were also part of the complex; perhaps they belonged to figures connected with Anios.[14]

A similar but better-known founder-figure is Aiakos, the primordial king of Aigina and son of Zeus. Through the odes of Pindar (e.g. *Ol.* 8, *Nem.* 3–8), who often wrote for elite Aiginetan patrons, we gather that the aristocratic families of the island considered themselves Aiakidai, descendants of Aiakos, and thereby partook of the immense prestige of this mythic lineage, which includes Peleus, Telamon, Achilles, Ajax, and Neoptolemos. Like Anios on Delos, Aiakos had a special priestly relationship with his father. When a drought hit all of Greece, the Delphic oracle told the anxious petitioners that only the prayers and sacrifices of Aiakos could bring rain from Zeus. Thus Aiakos founded the mountain sanctuary of Zeus Hellenios (parts of the Aiakid myth, including the lineage of Peleus, are shared with Thessaly, the ancestral home of the "Hellenes"). Like the hero-shrine of Anios, the Aiakeion seen by Pausanias (2.29.6) was a rectangular enclosure with low walls of stone. Carved at the entrance was the story of the drought, while the interior held a few olive trees and a low altar reputed to be Aiakos' tomb. Here, in Pindar's ode for the victor Pytheas (*Nem.* 5.53–54), a procession brings floral crowns to the "door of Aiakos." During the long struggle between Athens and Aigina, the Athenians attempted to appease Aiakos by building him a hero shrine in Athens. This structure has now been convincingly identified as a large enclosure (the "rectangular *peribolos*") in the southwest corner of the agora. Still later, the Athenians sent a ship to retrieve Aiakos and the Aiakidai (either cult statues or relics) from Aigina before the battle of Salamis, believing that the heroes would function as allies.[15]

The cults of founders were especially important in the Greek colonies, and in these cases the cult was normally observed at the centrally located tomb of the historical oikist, the leader of the original colonial expedition. The founder's death marked the end of the first phase of occupation, and gave the residents their first state cult that was not derivative of the mother-city. The best example of a heroized founder is Battos of Kyrene, who led Theran colonists to the coast of Libya (*c*. 630). Local legend had it that Battos (whose name seems to mean "stammerer") consulted the Delphic oracle to ask about his voice. The Pythia ignored his query and told him to found a city in Libya. Kyrene's subsequent prosperity was attributed in part to the personal qualities of Battos; Pindar describes him (*Pyth*. 5.89–95) as a pious king who founded the groves of the gods and laid a processional road for the celebrations of Apollo. His tomb lay in the agora, set apart from those of his descendants: "Blessed while he dwelled among men, afterwards he was a hero worshiped by the people." The tomb, which has been located and dated to around 600, turned out to be a cremation beneath a large heap of sacrificial ashes, covered in turn by a mound of earth and a ring of stone slabs. Nearby, a preexisting sanctuary contained a one-room structure that was enlarged around the time of the burial. Within it were a sacrificial pit and a number of vases from Battos' time. This has been described as a hero-shrine for Battos, though it could also be an early temple or funerary chapel. In the late Classical period, as the level of the agora rose, the mound was no longer visible, so an elaborate cenotaph was constructed beside it.[16]

The hero as revenant

In Sophocles' *Oedipus at Colonus* (390–415), Apollo tells the Thebans that the safety of their city depends upon gaining control over the deposed king they expelled from the city. Though he still lives, Oedipus is already depicted as a numinous figure whose blessings and curses carry supernatural power, and whose approaching death sets in motion a conflict over possession of his relics. Sophocles recounts the establishment of the Attic cult at Kolonos, and makes the embittered Oedipus resolve never to be of aid to Thebes, but instead vow that if the Athenians protect him, they will gain a "great savior for the city" (459–60). Because of his horrific (though involuntary) crimes against his mother and father, Oedipus was traditionally associated with the Erinyes, chthonian spirits who represent the anger of the dead. Therefore, in the context of rivalry between Athens and Thebes, it is not surprising that claims to the Theban hero were put forward in Kolonos, a deme that possessed a venerable cult of the Erinyes under the euphemistic names of Eumenides (Kindly Ones) or Semnai Theai (Revered Goddesses). Oedipus came as a wanderer and suppliant of the goddesses, and it was in their grove that he mysteriously disappeared, joining his powers to theirs as givers of blessings and curses.

This concept of Oedipus as a suppliant was not the invention of Sophocles, but existed in an independent Boiotian tradition (Lysimachus *FGrH* 382 F 2), according to which the corpse of the hero was denied burial in Thebes. After burial and expulsion by a second Boiotian town, it was finally interred during the night at Eteonos, but in the morning, the people realized that the grave was within the sanctuary of Demeter. Consulting an oracle, they were told not to disturb "the suppliant of the goddess." This story makes clear that even in death, Oedipus was a wanderer, and reflects a conception of the hero as a ghostly revenant whose sufferings will not let him rest in peace. Oedipus the polluted outcast and sufferer derived his powers as a hero from these very qualities. In a fragment of the poet Asios (West *IE*[2] fr. 14), a similar ghostly hero rises from the earth to visit a wedding uninvited, "like a wanderer," squalid and hungry. Such revenant heroes, who both suffer and cause suffering, represent a strand of folk belief that is usually suppressed in the epic and tragic genres.[17]

Revenant heroes were typically persons who died violently or in despair. The Delphic oracle regularly recommended the establishment of annual sacrifices to these restless dead, whose unappeased anger caused famines, illness, and other disasters. A particularly touchy group were the athlete heroes, legendary and historical victors at the Panhellenic games who were already good candidates for heroization because of their superlative physical abilities. During the fifth century, stories of anger and appeasement became attached to athletes such as Kleomedes of Astypalaia (fl. 496), whose fellow citizens tried to stone him, and Oibotas of Dyme, (fl. 756), who supposedly cursed the Achaians to three hundred years of athletic failure because they slighted him, their first Olympic victor.[18] Another revenant was Polites, the hero of Temesa in southern Italy, who had once been a crewman of Odysseus. His spirit terrorized and killed the Temesans because they had stoned him to death for committing a rape. At the behest of Delphi, they agreed to placate him by giving him a maiden to deflower every year. This went on until the Lokrian boxer Euthymos arrived in Temesa and bested the spirit, who sank into the sea and never troubled the city again. Euthymos himself, who won multiple Olympic victories in the early fifth century, became an important cult hero in Lokroi.[19]

Seers and healers

Some "heroes" were clearly local deities absorbed into this category as the pantheon of major Greek gods crystallized. Both Amphiaraos and Trophonios possessed mantic powers, unusual for heroes, which hint at former divine status. Amphiaraos, the Argive seer who fought as one of the Seven Against Thebes, was swallowed into a chasm as he fled the battle in his chariot. Thereafter he lived beneath the earth, still practicing the profession of seer through the medium of a priestess. According to Herodotus (1.46, 1.52, 8.134), his oracle at or near Thebes was well known in the late Archaic period. Though a former enemy, Amphiaraos became a benefactor of Thebes, following a common cult pattern according to which hostile heroic figures are reconciled through worship and appeasement.[20] Later the Athenians popularized their own cult of Amphiaraos at the rival site of Oropos, on the much-contested border area between Attica and Boiotia. The buildings at the site, which has been extensively studied, date no earlier than the late fifth century. Here, the focus of the oracle shifted to healing (a much more common occupation of heroes) and Amphiaraos' cult functioned in many ways like that of Asklepios, except that it charged a fee like an oracular shrine.[21] Pausanias (1.34.1–3) describes the fourth-century altar of Amphiaraos, which was divided into five sections for different groups of gods and heroes. To be healed, visitors made purification sacrifices (normally a piglet was used for this purpose) to all the deities named on the altar, then sacrificed a ram and slept on its fleece in the temple. The resulting dreams were interpreted as prescriptions for the proper treatment of the disease.

Boiotia was a land unusually rich in oracles, and the concept of the hero who is swallowed by the earth seems to have been endemic to this area. Trophonios, the Boiotian master builder who with his brother Agamedes constructed Apollo's first temple at Delphi, disappeared into a chasm at Lebadeia and became an oracular deity. Consultation at this oracle, already renowned in the Archaic period, was a unique and terrifying experience. Pausanias (9.39.2–9.40.3) wrote from personal knowledge about the elaborate purifications and sacrifices required as preparation for an encounter with Trophonios, many of which must have been operative in earlier times. The key preliminary was the sacrifice of a ram at the *bothros* (pit) where Trophonios disappeared, with an invocation to Agamedes and the examination of the entrails to determine the mood of Trophonios. Another Archaic feature was the statue of Trophonios attributed to Daidalos, which was revealed only to those about to consult the oracle. Those who received acceptable omens climbed into a man-made subterranean chamber and poised themselves at a small opening in the floor, carrying honey-cakes as a gift. They were sucked down into "the second place" by means unknown, where they came into personal contact with the divine power. Eventually they were expelled by the same route, dazed and disoriented. Whatever they saw or heard, they were required to record on wooden tablets. In the time of Pausanias, it is clear that consultation of Trophonios was similar to initiation into one of the mystery cults, but in the Archaic period, it may have been more narrowly focused on pragmatic oracular responses.[22]

Figure 15.1 Marble votive relief dedicated to the healing hero Amphiaraos. Background: incubation. The foreground shows the sleeper's dream: the hero treats his shoulder ailment, fourth century. National Archaeological Museum, Athens. Erich Lessing/Art Resource.

Achilles, lord of Leuke

While epic poetry may not have been the stimulus for the earliest worship of heroes, the case of Achilles shows how hero cult could indeed arise as a byproduct of epic. Near Troy, a mound on a promontory at the mouth of the Hellespont was identified with the burial site of Achilles described by Homer (*Od.* 24.80–84). The town of Achilleion, mentioned already by Herodotus (5.94), was founded near the tumulus. According to the late account of Philostratus (*Her.* 53.8–18, third century CE), an ancient oracle of Dodona decreed that the Thessalians send annual offerings to this tomb to recognize their compatriot Achilles. After singing a hymn to Thetis, they sacrificed a black bull "as to the dead" and a white bull "as to a god," using wood brought from the forests of Mt. Pelion. Philostratus says that the Thessalians were carrying out these sacrifices well before the Persian wars, but he also speaks of the repeated suspension and revival of the worship, which means that the earlier history may have been fabricated to provide a pedigree for the cult.

205

Whereas the cult in the Troad was predicated on Homer, the Euxine cults of Achilles show the powerful influence of the post-Homeric *Aethiopis*, which told the story of Achilles' death and funeral. Composed in the seventh century by Arctinus of Miletos, it said that Achilles' body was not buried in the Troad, but snatched from the pyre by Thetis and brought to Leuke, the White Island. Reflecting the current Greek interest in the Black Sea area, the poem probably located this island in the ambit of Skythia, for there was a tradition that Achilles' afterlife existence mirrored that of his enemy Memnon, whose mother Eos removed his body to Ethiopia. A fragment of Alcaeus (354 *LP*), the seventh-century lyric poet, already calls Achilles "ruler of Skythia." According to the geographical knowledge of the time, the two regions were seen as the northernmost and southernmost extremes of the world. Many later authors detail the belief that Achilles continued an immortal existence on Leuke with Helen or Iphigeneia as his companion.

The Greek colonists of the northern Euxine, who came primarily from Miletos during the seventh and sixth centuries, must have been familiar with Arctinus' poem. Excavation of Olbia and surrounding sixth-century settlements revealed that the colonists had a special interest in Achilles. Just as Herakles defined Greek identity for colonists in the West, those in this part of the world seem to have claimed Achilles as their patron and protector in a foreign land. At one site, they buried pots incised with Achilles' name under the floors of their homes, and many such inscribed vessels have been found in Olbia and in the early settlement on the nearby isle of Berezan. Even more mysterious are the pottery disks, about the size of game tokens, bearing full or abbreviated forms of the name Achilles and pictures of snakes, human figures, ships, and weapons, which again come from domestic contexts in Beikush and Olbia. The island of Leuke itself has yielded fifth-century pottery inscribed to Achilles, including a black-glazed *lekuthos* with the message "Glaukos, the son of Posideios, dedicated me to Achilles, ruler of Leuke." Little more than a great limestone boulder standing alone in the midst of the Euxine, Leuke measures only about one-quarter of a square kilometer. Nineteenth-century explorers reported the remains of a structure on the island, possibly the temple mentioned in literary sources. Most information about Achilles on Leuke dates from the Roman period, when Achilles Pontarches (Ruler of the Black Sea) had achieved a godlike status among the Olbians as the patron of the city leaders. Philostratus (*Her.* 55.2–3, 56.2–4), Arrian (*Peripl. M. Eux.* 23), and others tell how sailors passing the island would catch a glimpse of the ghostly Achilles or hear him singing.[23]

Theseus and the Athenian polis

To judge from vase paintings, Theseus achieved a new prominence in late sixth-century Athens. Where before he was the hero who slew the Kretan Minotaur and engaged in some rather disreputable dealings with Ariadne and Helen, he now became a chastiser of brigands and founder of festivals, the just and respected unifier of Attica. Scholars are divided as to whether his elevation came through the patronage of the Peisistratids or a few years later under the nascent democracy, but it is clear that Theseus was to be the Athenian answer to Dorian Herakles (whose cults were already widespread in Attica). Gradually, local traditions about Theseus were expanded, and unrelated cults were provided with Thesean credentials. This process was accelerated when the politically adroit general Kimon, responding to an oracular command to "bring home the bones" of Theseus, contrived to find the hero's remains on the newly conquered island of Skyros (476). Perhaps the bones of some prehistoric behemoth, the remains were ceremoniously laid to rest in a new shrine, the Theseion (the location of which is still unknown) and a levy was passed in order to finance a state cult and annual festival called the Theseia. The resulting ritual cycle, which was readily assimilated into the existing festival calendar, commemorated events in the "biography" of the hero, especially his triumphant return from Krete via Delos and his landing at the port of Phaleron, celebrated in the preexisting vintage festival of the Oschophoria. Theseus' return was placed in the seed-sowing month of Pyanopsion, so the mixture of pulses and cereals consumed in the Apolline festival of the Pyanepsia (Bean Boiling) was explained as the potluck soup created when Theseus and his companions pooled the last of their rations for a homecoming meal.[24] Whereas the Spartans had focused on enlarging a collection of Atreid heroes in order to appropriate their credentials and prestige, the Athenians molded and elevated Theseus to fit the new ideals established by the democracy.

Further reading

Antonaccio 1995 argues from an archaeologist's perspective against the conventional wisdom linking hero cult with the spread of epic and the rise of the polis. Boedeker 1998 discusses the value of Orestes as a "Spartan" hero, while Mayor 2000 (Chapter 3) examines the cults and relics of Pelops, Orestes, and Theseus in the context of ancient fossil discoveries. Kearns 1989 explores the functions of heroic figures, especially as they relate to Attic subgroups such as tribe and deme. Larson 1995b and Lyons 1997 deal with heroines and their cults. Clay 2004 is a valuable discussion of the evidence for the cults of poets, especially Archilochus' cult on Paros and Thasos.

NOTES

1 METHODS, SOURCES, AND CONCEPTS FOR THE STUDY OF ANCIENT GREEK CULTS

1 Graf 1991a; Fowler 2000.
2 Vernant 1980.92–109.
3 Vernant 1983a.
4 Malkin 1994, 2001; Hall 1997, 2002a; papers in Dougherty and Kurke eds 2003.
5 Habicht 1985; Musti and Bingen 1996; Alcock, Cherry and Elsner eds 2001; Arafat 1996.1–79; Hutton 2005.
6 Burkert 1985.227–34; Bell 1997.72–76, 1998.
7 Burkert 1987; Langdon 1987.
8 Meuli 1946; Burkert 1983b.1–72; Girard 1977; Hamerton-Kelly ed. 1987; Robbins 1998.
9 Bérard 1989; Detienne *et al.* 1989.
10 Thomson 1943; Samuel 1972.64–65; Hannah 2005.16–70.
11 Nilsson 1951 Vol 1.166–214; Connor 1987; Graf 1996.
12 Van Straten 1974; Jameson 1988; Pulleyn 1997; Furley and Bremer 2001. See also the papers in Versnel ed. 1981; Linders and Nordquist eds 1987.
13 Yavis 1949; Rupp 1974; Gould 1973; Sinn 2000. See also the papers in Marinatos and Hägg eds 1993.
14 Bergquist 1998, 1990; Bookidis 1993. See also the papers in Murray ed. 1990.
15 Corbett 1970; Burkert 1996; Scheer 2000; Nick 2002.9–99. *Contra* the concept of the cult statue: Donohue 1997.
16 Linders 1972, 1975; Aleshire 1989; Harris 1995; Hamilton 2000.
17 Rouse 1975 [1902]; Van Straten 2000 [1992]; Baumbach 2004. See also the papers in Linders and Nordquist eds 1987.
18 Snodgrass 1980.54; Sourvinou-Inwood 1993; Morris 1997.34–42.
19 de Polignac 1984, 1995. See also the papers in Alcock and Osborne eds 1994.
20 van Gennep 1960.65–115; Brelich 1969; Vidal-Naquet 1986; Dowden 1989. See also the papers in Padilla ed. 1999; Dodd and Faraone eds 2003.
21 Moulinier 1975 [1952]; Parker 1983; Douglas 1994 [1966].
22 Kaestner 1976; Schlesier 1991–92; Scullion 1994, 2000. See also the papers in Hägg and Alroth eds 2005.
23 Sourvinou-Inwood 2000 [1990].15.
24 Beard and North 1990.1–18; Sourvinou-Inwood 2000 [1988], 2000 [1990]; Parker 2005.89–115.

2 PROGENITOR AND KING: ZEUS

1 Kn 02 = PY 172 (Pylos), Fp 05 (Knossos), etc. [Chadwick and Ventris 1973]; Gérard-Rousseau 1968.72–74; Dowden 2006.9–11, 28–29.
2 Paus. 1.32.2; Cook 1964 [1914–] Vol. 2.868–987; Langdon 1976; Dowden 2006.54–64.
3 Isoc. 9.14–15 (Aiakos); Paus. 2.29.6–8 (Hellanios); Ap. Rhod. *Argon.* 2.516–27 with schol.; Callim. fr. 75.32–37 Pf. (Ikmaios); Heraclides Creticus 2.8 [Pfister 1951] (Akraios); Langdon 1976.79–87.
4 Hughes 1991.92–96.
5 Paus. 8.38.2–6; Burkert 1983b.84–93, 109–16; Voutiras and Tiverios 1997, no. 461 (coins).
6 Buxton 1986.67–72; Hughes 1991.102–7. Jost 2002 argues for a real human sacrifice.
7 Hes. fr. 163 M-W; Apollod. *Bibl.* 3.8.1 (further sources in Frazer's 1921 edition, ad loc.); Jost 1985.180–5, 249–69.
8 Cf. Theophrastus in Porph. *Abst.* 2.28–30; other primary sources in Patillon and Bouffartigue eds 1977–, Vol. 2.51–58. Meuli 1975 [1946].954, 1005; Smith 1982.57–65; Burkert 1983b.12–22, 136–43, 2001.10–11.
9 Paus. 3.12.9; West 1969; Pritchett 1971–, Vol. 2.272 n. 78; Jacquemin 2000.62–64.
10 Isoc. 9.57; Plut. *Vit. Arist.* 20.4; Paus. 9.2.5–7; Wycherley 1957.25–30; Rosivach 1978, 1987; Raaflaub 2000.
11 Aesch. *Suppl.* 26–27, *Ag.* 244–47, 1384–87, *Cho.* 244–45, and so on; Ar. *Plut.* 1175–84; Ath. 15.692f–693c (citing comic poets); Garland 1987.137–38; Cole 1988.892; Dowden 2006.80–85.
12 [Dem.] 43.14, 82 (Zeus Phratrios); Apollod. 2.8.4 (Patroös); Sjövall 1931.49–52; Hedrick 1991.241–68; Lambert 1993.205–25.
13 Catling 1990 (Messapeai); Parker 2005.16–18 (Herkeios).
14 Aesch. *Supp.* 443–48; Dem. 21.53; Ath. 11. 473b–c (jar); Sjövall 1931.53–74; Nilsson 1951 Vol. 1.25–34 (snake stele from Boiotia); Parker 2005.15–16.
15 Thuc. 1.126.6 with schol., referring to the seventh century; Jameson 1965.159–72; Dowden 2006.65–67.
16 Eust. *Od.* 22.481; Suda s.v. *Dios kōidion* (fleece); Simon 1983.12–15.
17 Jameson, Jordan, and Kotansky 1993 with Clinton 1996a.
18 Garland 1987.136–37.
19 Bianchi 1953.13–204; Gould 1973; Graf 1985.24–31.
20 Solon fr. 44b Ruschenbusch = Pollux 8.142.
21 Willetts 1962.199–223; Verbruggen 1981.17–26.
22 KN Fp 1.2 [Chadwick and Ventris 1973]; Chadwick 1985.197; Perlman 1995; Sporn 2002.378.
23 *IC* II.2 12–17; West 1965; Furley and Bremer 2001 Vol. 1.65–76, Vol. 2.1–20.
24 MacGillivray, Driessen and Sackett 2000.
25 Verbruggen 1981.71–99; Sakellarakis 1988a, b; Sporn 2002.218–23.
26 Eur. fr. 472 *TrGF* = Porph. *Abst.* 4.19; Willetts 1962.239–43.
27 Porph. *Vit. Pyth.* 17 [Des Places 1982]; Kokolakis 1995; Postlethwait 1999.
28 For Zeus Ammon, see Chapter 13.
29 Parke 1967.1–163; Gartziou-Tatti 1990. An edition of the collected responses from Dodona is in preparation.
30 Stella G. Miller 1988; Stephen G. Miller 2002; Miller *et al.* 2004.50–53, 124–31; Pache 2004.95–134.
31 Morgan 1990.26–56.
32 Pind. *Ol.* 6.64–70; Parke 1967.164–93.

33 Herrmann 1972.67–68; Mallwitz 1988.85–89; Kyrieleis 1990, 2003.55; Antonaccio 1995.170–76.

3 LADY OF GRAND TEMPLES: HERA

1 Of 28 (Thebes), Kn 02 = PY 172 (Pylos) [Chadwick and Ventris 1973]; Pötscher 1961; O'Brien 1993.114 n. 2; Hall 2002b.
2 Hdt. 1.31; Pind. *Ol.* 7.83, *Nem.* 10.22–23, etc.; Burkert 1983b.162–68; O'Brien 1993.142–56; de Polignac 1995.41–45; Hall 1995.592–96.
3 Callim. fr. 66 Pf. (robe, Amymone); Paus. 2.13.3 (Hebe), 2.17.1 (Eleutherion), 2.38.2 (Kanathos); Caskey and Amandry 1952.197–99; Billot 1997.46–47.
4 Schattner 1990.40–86; O'Brien 1993.40–41.
5 Gruben 1986.324–40. Bibliography: Mazarakis Ainian 1997.199–202.
6 Asius in Duris *FGrH* 76 F 60; Kyrieleis 1988, 1993.
7 Menodotus *FGrH* 541 F 1; Burkert 1979.123–42; Kron 1988; O'Brien 1993.54–66.
8 Simon 1986.74–91; de Polignac 1997.
9 Fleischer 1973.202–23; Romano 1980.250–71.
10 Salmon 1972.175–78, Tomlinson 1977, 1992.
11 Eumelus in Paus. 2.3.11 (hide away); Paus. 2.3.6–8 (Glauke/Deima); Schol. Eur. *Med.* 264 [Schwartz]; Johnston 1997; Menadier 2002.
12 Will 1955.103–18, Reichert-Südbeck 2000.167–70.
13 Herrmann 1972.92; Mallwitz 1988.102–3; Moustaka 2002a, b.
14 Paus. 5.16.2–8; Scanlon 1984; Serwint 1993.
15 Cipriani 1997.
16 van Keuren 1989.23–44; de La Genière 1994.
17 Strabo 6.1.1; Pedley 1990.61–75; Zancani-Montuoro and Zanotti-Bianco 1951–; Kossatz-Deissmann 1988, nos. 59–60 (terracottas).
18 Arist. [*Mir. ausc.*] 96, 338a; de Sensi Sestito 1984; Greco 1997.194, 196; Spadea 1997.
19 Aesch. *Eum.* 213–14; Ar. *Thesm.* 973–76; Salviat 1964.
20 Clark 1998; Schachter 1981–, Vol. 1.242–50; Burkert 1988.
21 Paus. 8.22.2; Jost 1985.358–60.

4 MISTRESS OF CITADELS: ATHENA

1 V 52 = KN 208 (Knossos) [Chadwick and Ventris 1973]; Gérard-Rousseau 1968.44–45; Chadwick 1985.194; Nilsson 1927.420–32; Simon 1969.179–84, fig. 163.
2 Herington 1955; Hopper 1963; Demargne 1984 no. 124 (striding Athena); Hurwit 1999.99–137; Ferrari 2002a.
3 Romano 1980.42–53; Kroll 1982.
4 Jeppesen 1979, 1983; Elderkin 1941.
5 Herington 1955.48–59, 1963; Ridgway 1992.131–35; Hurwit 1995.
6 Paus. 1.26.6–7; Harris 1995.104–22.
7 Ridgway 1992.135–37; Mark 1993.
8 Soph. *TrGF* 844 (Athena Ergane); Ridgway 1984; Mansfield 1985.
9 Photius s.v. *Kalluntēria kai Pluntēria*; Mikalson 1975.160, 163–64; Robertson 1996b.48–52.
10 Xen. *Hell.* 1.4.12 (veil); Samuel 1972.104–5, 124. Early (*c.* 700) temple of Athena Poliouchos on Paros: Schilardi 1988.
11 Schol. Lucian *Dial. meret.* 2.1; Deubner 1932.9–17, 40–50; Burkert 1983b.143–54, 2001.37–63; Dillon 2003.124–25, 57–60.

12 These belong to the second century: Mansfield 1985.296–301.
13 Barber 1992.112–16.
14 Harrison 1996 (frieze). The *peplos* is a contested issue: Parker 2005.265–66.
15 Whitehead 1986.179.
16 Hdt. 8.94; Ferguson 1938.18–21.
17 Schlaifer 1943; Stanton 1984.292–98 (list of archons and parasites *c.* 350); Jones 1999.239–41; Jacquemin 2000.16–17, *Mesogaia* 2001.83–84 (temple).
18 Paus. 2.23.5; Plut. *Quaest. Graec.* 302d (Sparta); Robertson 1996a; Billot 1997–98.10–17 and *passim*.
19 Paus. 1.28.8–9; Schol. Dem. 23.71; Nagy 1991; Burkert 2001.85–96.
20 Mallwitz and Schiering 1968; Herrmann 1971.294 n. 6; Simon 1997.126–29.
21 Graf 1985.209–17; Villing 1998.154–59. Weaving at Stymphalos (Arkadia) and Halai (Lokris): see Williams and Schaus 2001.88–89.
22 Akurgal 1983 Vol. 1.111–13, 129–30; Nicholls 1991.
23 Boardman 1967.25–28 (statue); Graf 1985.44–49; Simon 1986.105–7, 111–17.
24 Lehmann and Lehmann1959– (cult in Arkadia); Schachter 1981–, Vol. 1.111–14; Deacy 1995.93–99.
25 Schachter 1981–, Vol. 1.117–27; Deacy 1995.91–93.
26 The earliest sources belong to the fourth century: Aeneas Tacticus 31.24; Timaeus *FGrH* 566 F 12, 146a, b.
27 Vidal-Naquet 1975; Hughes 1991.166–84; Graf 2000; Redfield 2003.85–150.
28 Hdt. 1.66, 9.70; Paus. 8.45.4–47.4.
29 Xen. *Hell.* 6.5.27; Paus. 8.23.1; Jost 1985.151–54, 370–85; Voyatzis 1990, 1998.
30 Paus. 3.12.4, 3.15.6; Otto 1954.53–56 (nearness).
31 Paus. 3.17.1–4; Dickins 1906–7; Woodward 1923–24, 1926–27; Piccirilli 1984; Villing 1997.82–87.
32 Thuc. 1.134; Paus. 3.17.7–9; Ogden 2001.100–107.
33 Thuc. 4.135; Simon 1986.293–95; Villing 1997.82–89, 2002.
34 Sfyroeras 1993.2–16.
35 Hdt. 2.182, 3.47 (Amasis); Cleobulus in Diog. Laert 1.89 (Danaos); Francis and Vickers 1984; Higbie 2003.113–15.
36 Blinkenberg 1980 [1915]; Lippolis 1988–89; Higbie 2003.
37 Yalouris 1950; Detienne 1971.175–84.
38 Hdt. 8.41 (Erichthonios); Paus. 3.11.11, 3.13.6 (Sparta); Neils 2001.

5 RULER OF ELEMENTAL POWERS: POSEIDON

1 Nilsson 1953.155–56.
2 Diod. Sic. 15.49.1 (*aphidrumata*); Paus. 7.24.6; Ael. *NA* 11.19.
3 Nilsson 1906.74–79; Schachter 1981–, Vol. 2.206–7, 214; Hall 2002a.67–69.
4 Robertson 1984.
5 Morgan 1994.109–28; Gebhard 2002a.
6 Broneer 1971 Vol. 1.55, 1976.46. Cf. Paus. 1.41.8.
7 Broneer 1966, 1971 Vol. 1.33–34, Vol. 4.14–61; Gebhard 1993.159–63, 1998; Mylonopoulos 2003.160–210.
8 Gebhard and Dickie 1999; Gebhard 2002b; Pache 2004.135–80.
9 Geagan 1970; Wachter 2001.119–55, 275–330 *passim*.
10 Schol. Pind. *Ol.* 13.159b; Schumacher 1993.
11 Schachermeyr 1950.144, 164; Makkay 1983.
12 Chadwick and Ventris 1973.279–89, 458–62.
13 Themelis 1970; Cartledge 2002.165–66; Mylonopoulos 2003.250–52.

14 Ar. *Ach*. 509–11 with schol. (Tainaria); Thuc. 1.128 (fugitives); Plut. *Mor*. 560e-f (Archilochus); Cummer 1978; Ogden 2001.34–42; Mylonopoulos 2003.229–40.

15 Strabo 8.6.14 (Demosthenes); Penrose Harland 1925; Kelly 1966; Mylonopoulos 2003.70–81.

16 Plut. *Vit. Thes*. 6 (trident); Paus. 2.30.6.

17 Paus. 2.32.7 (Althepos); Robertson 1984. Poseidon was also called Phytalmios in Athens, Erythrai, and Rhodes.

18 Apollod. *Bibl*. 2.1.4 (Amymone), 3.14.1 (flood); Paus. 2.22.4. Cf. Bremmer 1987.38–39.

19 Konsolaki 2002.

20 Sokolowski 1960; Schachter 1981–, Vol. 2.207–21, Teffeteller 2001.

21 Cf. Paus. 8.7.2 (horse sacrifice by drowning in the Argolid).

22 Paus. 8.25.7, Schol. Hom. *Il*. 23.346–47 = *Thebais* fr. 6 Davies *EGF*.

23 *Etym. Magn*. 473.42 s.v. *Hippios*, Hdt. 7.129 (Peneios).

24 Paus. 1.30.4, Detienne 1971, Siewert 1979.

25 Jost 1985.279–317, Mylonopoulos 2003.98–132.

26 Paus. 8.10.3 (Aipytos), 8.8.2 (Rhea).

27 Paus. 8.25.4–10 (Thelpousa), 8.37.10 (Lykosoura), 8.42.1–2 (Phigaleia).

28 Hdt. 8.55, Paus. 2.30.6.

29 Eur. *Erechtheus* fr. 65.59–60 [Austin 1968]; *Ion* 281–82, Elderkin 1941.118; Mikalson 1976; Jeppesen 1979, 1983.

30 Mikalson 1976, Christopoulos 1994. *Contra*: Lacore 1983.

31 Robertson 1984.3–4.

32 Lysias 21.5 (races), Sinn 1992.

<h2 style="text-align:center">6 MISTRESSES OF GRAIN AND SOULS: DEMETER AND KORE/PERSEPHONE</h2>

1 Cole 1994.209; Hinz 1998.232–33.

2 Ath. 3.109e (Delos); Brumfield 1997.

3 Paus. 9.8.1 (Potniai); Lowe 1998; Clinton 1988.72–77.

4 Clinton 1992.29–37, 96–99, 1993.113–14. *Contra*: Parker 1991.

5 *Hom. Hymn. Dem*. 2.202–5 (jests of Iambe); Diod. Sic. 5.4.7; Brumfield 1996.

6 Versnel 1992.37.

7 Thompson 1936; Simon 1983.17–22; Clinton 1996b; Parker 2005.270–83.

8 Brumfield 1981.11–53; Cole 1994.202–3.

9 Schol. Luc. *Dial. meret*. 6.1 is the most detailed and problematic source. It says that the festival was shared with Dionysos, probably a conclusion deduced from the women's consumption of wine and use of *phalloi* in the ritual. Methodological issues: Lowe 1998. Cf. Robertson 1984.5; Parker 2005.199–201.

10 Paus. 1.22.3 (Demeter Chloë); Philochorus *FGrH* 328 F 14 (abstain); Brumfield 1981.156–79; Parker 2005.173–77.

11 Mylonas 1961.23–76; Mazarakis Ainian 1997.147–49; Cosmopoulos 2003b.

12 Parker 1996.25; Sourvinou-Inwood 1997, 2003.

13 Kearns 1989.113–15; Clinton 1974.10–23, 68–71.

14 Schol. Ar. *Ach*. 747 (piglet sacrifice); Clinton 1994.

15 Segal 1961.217–20.

16 The placement of festival events on specific days is in part conjectural; specialists disagree on the exact sequence of events in the Mysteries and on which days they took place. Parke 1977.55–72; Simon 1983.24–35; Burkert 1983b.256–97; Clinton 1993; Foley 1994.65–71.

17 Andoc. 1.110–12 (Solon); Clinton 1980; Miles 1998a.11–23, 33–57.

18 Cavanaugh 1996.36–37, lines 36–40.
19 Paus. 2.4.7; Bookidis and Stroud 1987, 1997.21–51, 85–151, 253–72; Bookidis 1990, 1993; Pemberton 2000.
20 Plut. *Vit. Tim.* 8; Diod. Sic. 16.66.1–5.
21 Hdt. 8.43 (Dryopes); Eur. *Heracl.* 610–15 (Kerberos); Ath. 10.455c–d, 14.624e–f (Lasos); IG IV 683–90; Detienne 1989a.140–42; Jameson *et al.* 1994.592–93.
22 Paus. 8.25.4–7 (Thelpousa); Callim. fr. 652 Pf. (Tilphossa). The two place names have a common origin. Dietrich 1962; Schachter 1981–, Vol.1, 164; Jost 1985.301–14.
23 Paus. 8.42.1–13; Jost 1985.312–17.
24 Jost 1985.326–37, 2003.157–64 (statue).
25 Hdt. 7.153; White 1964.52–80.
26 Hinz 1998.28–30.
27 Orlandini 1968–69; Kron 1992.
28 Holloway 1991.55–60; Hinz 1998.55–79.
29 Le Dinahet 1984; Hinz 1998.70–92.
30 White 1967.335–36; Holloway 1991.61–63, 75–78; Jameson, Jordan and Kotansky 1993.125–36; Curbera 1997.399; Hinz 1998.144–54; Miles 1998b.
31 Prückner 1968; Sourvinou-Inwood 1973, 1978; Lissi Caronna, Sabbione, and Borelli 1996– [*non vidi*].
32 Polyb. 12.5.6–11 (matriliny); Redfield 2003.346–85.
33 Spigo 2000.

7 GUARDING AND GUIDING THE CITY: APOLLO

1 V 52 = KN 208 (Knossos) [Chadwick and Ventris 1973].
2 Faraone 1992.61, 125–27.
3 Burkert 1975a.
4 Farnell 1896–, Vol. 4.371–72; Di Filippo Balestrazz 1984; Faraone 1992.8–9.
5 Ar. *Vesp.* 875 (Agyieus); Fulco 1976.49–54.
6 *SEG* 9 (1944) 72 (third century); Grégoire 1949.52–54, 75–77, 142–47; Faraone 1992.128–32.
7 Jameson 1980; Graf 1985.220–25.
8 *Hymn Hom. Ap.* 3.399–501; Graf 1979a, 1985.56–57; Gorman 2001.168–76.
9 Beyer 1976.18–20; Stewart 1990.105, pl. 16–17; Mazarakis Ainian 1997.216–17; Sporn 2002.81–83.
10 Antonetti 1990.149–99; Mazarakis Ainian 1997.125–35.
11 Hdt. 6.106 (Marathon); 7.206 (Thermopylai); *Anecd. Bekk.* 1.305 s.v. *staphulodromoi*; Paus. 3.13.3–4; Pettersson 1992.57–72; Malkin 1994.143–58.
12 Paus 3.18.6–19.5; Romano 1980.99–114; Pettersson 1992.9–41; Georgoulaki 1994; Faustoferri 1996 (see figs. 1–15, 30 for reconstructions of the "throne").
13 Polycrates in Ath. 4.139d–e; Burkert 1975b; Bruit 1990; S. Morris 1992.113.
14 Thuc. 3.104; Gallet de Santerre 1958.179–92; Calame 1996.116–21.
15 Paus. 2.32.5; Plut *Mor.* 1136a; Prost 1999.
16 Hyperboreans: see Chapter 8 and Hdt. 4.33–35; Sale 1961; Antonaccio 1995.183–86; Larson 1995b.118–21.
17 Arist. [*Ath. Pol.*] 55; Hedrick 1988.
18 Bremmer 2000; Parker 1983.257–80. For more on Ionian *pharmakoi* see Hipponax fr. 5–10 West; Hughes 1991.139–65; Calame 1996.308–10.
19 Parke 1985b.1. General accounts of Delphi: Amandry 1950; Parke and Wormell 1956; Fontenrose 1978, 1988a.
20 Morgan 1990.106–90.

21 Paus. 5.14.10 (Olympia); Morgan 1990.42; Sourvinou-Inwood 1986. Other oracles of Ge: see Chapter 12 (Ge and Helios) and Pliny *HN* 28.41; Paus. 7.25.13.
22 Dyer 1969.
23 Roux 1976.147–64; Maurizio 1995.
24 de Boer, Hale, and Chanton 2001.
25 Furley and Bremer 2001, Vol. 1.334–36.
26 Plut. *Mor.* 293a–b; Nilsson 1906.150–57; Fontenrose 1959.453–61; Roux 1976.166–68.
27 Hdt. 6.57; Paus. 3.11.9 (Sparta); Billot 1989–90 (Argos); Malkin 1987.17–91.
28 Ducat 1971.451–66; Schachter 1981–, Vol. 1.52–73, 1994; Bonnechère 1990.
29 Paus. 2.24.1–2; Kadletz 1978.
30 Callim fr. 194.28–31 Pf.; Clem. Al. *Strom.* 5.8.48 (Branchos); Parke 1985b.118–20.
31 Romano 1980.221–35; Fontenrose 1988b.5–15, 28–44, 115–22; Hägg 1998.54.
32 Translation from Burkert 1994.54. *Contra* the oracle explanation, see Onyshkevych 2002.
33 Parke 1985a; Hammond 1998.
34 Dietrich 1996.
35 Procl. *Chrestomathia* 74–78 [Ferrante 1957]; Burkert 1979.132–38.
36 Auberson 1974; Mazarakis Ainian 1987.10–14, 1997.58–63; Huber 1998a, b.
37 Schachter 1981–, Vol. 1.77–85.
38 Lambrinoudakis 1981, 2002; Gadolou 2002.40–41.
39 *IG* IV² 128; Furley and Bremer 2001.227–40.
40 Sinn 2002.
41 Paus. 8.30.4; Cooper 1996 Vol.1.42–80, 293–95; Jost 1985.90–91, 485–89.

8 THE TENDER AND THE SAVAGE: ARTEMIS

1 Un 11 (Pylos) [Chadwick and Ventris 1973].
2 Polyb. 4.18.10–19.5; Sinn 1992.
3 Marinatos 2000.67–109.
4 Xen. *An.* 3.2.12; Arist. [*Ath. Pol.*] 58 (*polemarchos*); Paus. 1.19.6 (Agrai).
5 Hsch. s.v. *kaprophagos*; Dyggve and Poulson 1948.266, 335–54; Petropoulou 1993. *Contra*: Antonetti 1990.245–62.
6 Paus. 10.1.6–9; Plut. *De mul. vir.* 244b–e; Felsch 1981, 1996; Ellinger 1987, 1993.22–37.
7 Vernant 1991.211–12. *Contra*: Detienne 1989b.9–10.
8 Graf 1979b; Hollinshead 1980.84–112, Bremmer 2002.
9 Paus. 3.16.7 (Tauroi); Plut. *Vit. Lyc.* 18, *Inst. Lac.* 239c–d (Roman spectacle); Lebessi 1991.99–103; Calame 1997.156–69.
10 Cf. the cult of Hera at Samos, where the cult statue was bound with the willow-like *lugos*, most likely the same plant. King 1983.
11 Hsch. s.v. *brudaliga* and *brullichistai* (masked dancers); Carter 1987.
12 Dawkins 1906–7, 1929.192, 199.
13 Paus. 4.4.2–3; de Polignac 1995.33–41; Calame 1997.141–56; Cole 2004.178–230.
14 Paus. 3.10.7 (Karyai), 4.16.9–10 (Aristomenes); Larson 1997; Brulotte 2002.
15 Pind. *Pyth.* 2.7, *Nem.* 1.1–6; Paus. 6.22.8–11 (Letrinoi), 5.14.6 (Olympia); Burkert 1985.150.
16 Hollinshead 1980.30–91, 1985; Lyons 1997.139–57; Themelis 2002.108–12.
17 *IG* II² 1514.15–19; Linders 1972.7–20; Rhodes and Dobbins 1979. Translation adapted from Cole 2004.215.

18 Romano 1980.83–97.
19 Versions of the story were attached to Brauron and Mounichia: Sale 1975.
20 Bevan 1987; Parker 2005.228–48.
21 Brelich 1969.229–311; Kahil 1977, 1983; Perlman 1989; Calame 1997.98–101 with bib. *Contra* the standard initiatory explanation: Sourvinou-Inwood 1988; Faraone 2003, to be read with Hatzopoulos 1994.25–33.
22 Laumonier 1958.62–101; LiDonnici 1992b.
23 Oppenheim 1949; Seltman 1952.42; Fleischer 1973.74–88, 310–24, 1983; Morris 2001.
24 Jacobsthal 1951; Bammer 1974, 1984.165–211, 1990; Simon 1986.27–39.
25 Bammer, Brein, and Wolff 1978.132–38; Bammer 1998.
26 *IK* Bd. 11, 1a.14; *Etym. Magn.* 252.11 s.v. *daitis*; Romano 1980.242–43.
27 LiDonnici 1999. *Contra*: Smith 1996.
28 Hdt. 1.26 (ropes); Xen. *An.* 5.3.6 (bank); Ael. *VH* 3.26; Polyaenus *Strat.* 6.50.
29 Gallet de Santerre 1958.127–34, 252–57, 1975; Desborough 1964.44–46; Snodgrass 2000b.395–96.
30 Romano 1980.197–201; Stewart 1990.108, Figs 34–35.
31 Gallet de Santerre 1958.165–73; Sale 1961; Antonaccio 1995.183–86; Larson 1995b.118–21.

9 THE PERSUASIVE GODDESS: APHRODITE

1 Karageorghis 1977.199–227; Boedeker 1974.1–17; Bonnet and Pirenne-Delforge 1999; Budin 2003.243–82.
2 Paus. 8.5.2 (Agapenor); Tac. *Hist.* 2.3 (Kinyras); Chadwick 1956.
3 Maier 1976.221; Maier and Karageorghis 1984.99.
4 Hurst 1975; Karageorghis 1982.103–4; Budin 2003.163, 173.
5 Phot. *Bibl.* s.v. *Aphroditos*; Philochorus *FGrH* 328 F 184; Sophocleous 1985; Pirenne Delforge 1994.348–56; Ferrari 2002b.108–11; MacLachlan 2002.
6 Paus. 3.23.1; Coldstream and Huxley 1973.34–36, 311–13; Flemberg 1991.19–20, 1995; Bonnet and Pirenne Delforge 1999.264–68.
7 Kato Symi: see Chapter 11. Bousquet 1938; Mazarakis Ainian 1997.215–16; Sporn 2002.386.
8 Servais-Soyez 1983; Edwards 1984.
9 Paus 1.14.7; Knigge 1982; Reese 1989. The altar attributed instead to Hermes: Osanna 1992.
10 Burn 1987.28–44 (Meidias); Pirenne Delforge 1994.48–74; Rosenzweig 2004.29–44.
11 Paus. 6.25.1; Redfield 2003.322–24.
12 Paus. 1.22.3; cf. Philemon in Ath. 13.569d. Pirenne Delforge 1988, 1994.15–62; Rosenzweig 2004.13–28, 59–81.
13 Menander in Ath. 14.659d (*tetradistai*).
14 *IG* II² 4596 (Athens, 284 BCE); Merkelbach 1986 (Erythrai).
15 *IG* XII 5.552; Paus. 9.16.3–4; Sokolowski 1964; Croissant and Salviat 1966.
16 Paus. 3.17.5; Osanna 1990.
17 Paus. 3.15.10–11; Faraone 1992.74–93, 136–40; Pirenne Delforge 1994.193–216; Steiner 2001.160–68.
18 Williams 1986; Reichert-Südbeck 2000.33–53.
19 The text is the late Babylonian *Counsels of Wisdom*: Lambert 1960.102–3. Traditional view: e.g. Yamauchi 1973; MacLachlan 1992.
20 Assante 2003; Westenholz 1989; Henshaw 1994.191–270.
21 *Contra*: Budin 2006.
22 Ath. 13.573c–d; Plut. *Mor.* 871a–b; Simonides 14 Page *FGE*; Brown 1991.

23 Clearchus in Ath. 12.516. Hdt. 1.199, the earliest text to mention the phenomenon, is usually dismissed as a fabrication; cf. the Apocryphal *Epistle of Jeremiah*
(= *Baruch*) 6.42–43.

24 Just. *Epit.* 21.2–3 (vow). Also relevant is Pind. *Pyth.* 2.18–20, possibly a contemporary reference to the vow.

25 Sourvinou-Inwood 1974, 1978.120–21; MacLachlan 1992.161–62; Redfield
2003.332–34, 411–16.

26 Barra Bagnasco 1990; Schindler 1998.15–70; Redfield 2003.210–14.

27 Prückner 1968; Sourvinou-Inwood 1978; Redfield 2003.346–85.

28 Roebuck 1951; Boardman 1999.118–33; Love 1972a.70–76, 1972b.402–5.

29 Asclepiades *FGrH* 12 F 28; *IG* I² 190, 1, 5. (*c.* 420). Cf. Kearns 1989.173;
Rosenzweig 2004.83–89.

30 Eur. *Hipp.* 1424–26; Welter 1941.34; Burkert 1979.111–18; Musti, Beschi, and
Torelli 1982 Vol. 2.320.

31 Ar. *Lys.* 387–96; Atallah 1966; Winkler 1990.188–209; Detienne 1994
[1977].99–122, 133–44; Reed 1995.

32 Paus. 2.34.12 (Hermione), 10.38.12 (Naupaktos), 2.10.4–6 (Sikyon).

10 EPIPHANY AND TRANSFORMATION: DIONYSOS

1 Xa 06, 102, 1419 (Pylos) [Chadwick and Ventris 1973]; Chadwick 1985.194.

2 Zeitlin 1982.129–38; Henrichs 1993; Cole 1993b.

3 Hedreen 1992.67–103.

4 Thomson 1943.58–59.

5 Otto 1965.154–55.

6 Caskey 1981; Caskey and Caskey 1986.39–43.

7 Hedreen 1992.13–66.

8 Jeanmaire 1951.220–28; Casadio 1994.183–91; Simantoni-Bournia 2002.

9 Gallet de Santerre 1958.266; Romano 1980.190–96; Cole 1993a.30–31.

10 Clay 2002; Jameson 1993.

11 Plut. *Quaest. conv.* 655e (Pithoigia); Hamilton 1992.123–46; Ham 1999.

12 Eur. *IT* 947–60 (Orestes); Phanodemus *FGrH* 325 F 11 (Limnaion).

13 Arist. [*Ath. Pol.*] 3.5; Parker 2005.303–4.

14 Segal 1961.221; Noël 1999.150–51.

15 Theopompus *FGrH* 115 F 347 a, b (Hermes Chthonios); Pickard-Cambridge
1968.1–25; Burkert 1983b.213–47; Hamilton 1992; Robertson 1993; Humphreys
2004.223–75; Parker 2005.290–305.

16 Paus. 1.38.8; Schol. Arist. *Ach.* 243a.

17 Burkert 2001.1–36. *Contra*: Winkler 1990.58–62.

18 Xen. *Hipparch.* 3.2 (choruses in agora); Goldhill 1987; Connor 1990; Sourvinou-
Inwood 2002.67–140.

19 Eratosthenes in Schol. Hom. *Il.* 22.29; Apollod. *Bibl.* 3.14.7; Dietrich 1961;
Pickard-Cambridge 1968.42–56; Henrichs 1990.

20 Romano 1982.

21 Arist. [*Ath. Pol.*] 57.1 (King Archon); Schol. Ar. *Ran.* 479; Phot. s.v. *ta ek tōn
hamaxōn*; Wycherley 1965.

22 Frontisi-Ducroux 1991.167–74; Carpenter 1997.70–84; Peirce 1998.

23 Dodds 1951.270–82; Henrichs 1978; Bremmer 1984; Versnel 1990.137–46.

24 Obbink 1993.68–78. *LSAM* no. 48 (Miletos, third century) may attest omophagy.

25 Alcaeus fr. 129.9 *LP*; Ael. *NA* 12.34; Graf 1985.74–80.

26 Clay 1996; Furley and Bremer 2001 Vol. 2. 52–84.

27 E.g. Soph. *Ant.* 1127–30; Eur. *Ion* 1122–31 (blood).
28 Apollod. *Bibl.* 2.2.2; *SEG* 15 (1958) 195; Hsch. s.v. *Agrania* (Iphinoë). In an early variant of the myth, Hera inflicted madness and "the white disease," leprosy, on Proitos' daughters when they jeered at her modest cult statue (Hes. frs. 37.10–15, 130–33 M-W).
29 Paus. 2.22.1, 23.7–8; Burkert 1983b.171–79; Hughes 1991.131–33; Casadio 1994.83–116.
30 Soph. fr. 255 Radt; Eur. *Phoen.* 229–31.
31 Plut. *Vit. Lys.* 28.4 (Kissousa); *Suda* s.v. *astudromia.*
32 Vurtheim 1920; Brown 1982; Mitsopoulos-Leon 1984; Detienne 1989b.40–56, Casadio 1999.20–22; Furley and Bremer 2001, Vol. 1.369–72, Vol. 2.373–77; Scullion 2001.
33 Paus 2.2.6–7 (Korinthians), 2.7.5–6 (Sikyon); Schachter 1981–, Vol. 1.185–92.
34 Longo 1986; Larson 1995b.93–96.
35 *LSS* no. 120 (Cumae); West 1982.
36 Detienne 1979.68–94, to be read with Edmonds 1999.38–49.
37 Bernabé *PEG* II frs. 474, 485–86; Cole, 1993b; Graf 1991b, 1993; Riedweg 2002.
38 Plato *Resp.* 364e–65a; Burkert 1983a, 2004.71–98; Janko 1984.
39 Seaford 1981.

11 DEAR TO THE PEOPLE: HERMES, PAN, AND NATURE DEITIES

1 Kn 02, Un 11 = PY 172, Xn 137 (Pylos), Of 31 (Thebes) [Chadwick and Ventris 1973].
2 Paus. 8.30.6 (Akakesios), 8.47.4 (Aipytos); Athanassakis 1989.40; Jost 1985.439–56.
3 Ar. *Plut.* 1110–30; Teleclides fr. 35 Kassel-Austin = Schol. Ar. *Peace* 1040.
4 Plat. [*Hipparch.*] 228d-229b; Goldman 1942; Rückert 1998.223–26.
5 Thuc. 6.27–28; Andoc. 1.37–38; van Straten 1995.27–30; Osborne 1985.
6 Burkert 1983b.58–72.
7 Philostr. *VA* 6.20; Paus. 6.26.5; Goldman 1942.
8 Herter 1976.221–25.
9 Pind. *Ol.* 6.77–81, 9.97–98; Costa 1982.
10 Willetts 1962.250–51; Lebessi 1976; Lebessi and Schürmann 1985; Lebessi and Muhly 1987; Marinatos 2003.131–44. Cf. the cult of Hermes Kranaios at Patsos: Baldwin Bowsky 2001.270–71; Sporn 2002.247–49.
11 Paus. 9.22.1–2; Schachter 1981–, Vol. 2.44–50.
12 E.g. *BMC* Thrace 77.3.
13 Nilsson 1967.509.
14 *SEG* 51 (2001) 978–79 (curses from Olbia, *c.* 480–40, 400–350); Plut. *Vit. Arist.* 21.5 (prayers); Schol. Ar. *Ach.* 1076a–b. Anthesteria: see Chapter 10.
15 Brommer 1949–50.10–15.
16 Hdt. 2.145 (Penelope); Paus. 8.38.5 (Lykaion); Ael. *NA* 11.6; Jost 1985.456–76; Hübinger 1992.
17 Borgeaud 1988.48–52, 133–62.
18 Photiades 1958.
19 Pind. fr. 96 Snell-Maehler. See also fr. 95, 97–100, *Pyth.* 3.78–79; Borgeaud 1988.88–116, 147–48.
20 Larson 2001.131–34; Leitao 2003; Purvis 2003.15–32.
21 Hes. *Op.* 737–41, 757–59; Hdt. 6.76; Xen. *An.* 4.3.17–19 (sacrifice by an army).
22 Paus. 4.3.10 (kings); Valmin 1938: 417–65.

23 Ephorus *FGrH* 70 F 20 (Dodona); Isler 1970 no. 264 (bronze), no. 51 (mask), 279–310 (jewelry).
24 Larson 1995a, 2001.91–120, 232–33.
25 Connor 1988; Larson 2001.14–20; Purvis 2003.33–63.

12 DIVINE SPECIALISTS: OTHER PANHELLENIC DEITIES

1 Paus. 2.25.1 (Polyneikes); Pötscher 1959; Vian 1963.106–9, 209–10.
2 Paus. 8.44.7–8 (Aphneios), 48.4–6; Plut. *De mul. vir.* 245e (armed women); Graf 1984; Jouan 1990.
3 V 52 = KN 208 (Enyalios at Knossos), Fp 14 = KN 201 (Ares at Knossos) [Chadwick and Ventris 1973]; Aesch. *Sept.* 42–48 (Enyo); Paus. 3.14.9, 3.15.7 (Sparta); *SEG* 11 (1950) 327; Jost 1985.129 (Mantineia).
4 Plut. *Vit. Sol.* 9.4; Poll. 8.91; Tod 1933–, no. 204; Daux 1965; Siewert 1977; Jacquemin 2000.15–20.
5 For Gaia at Delphi see also Chapter 7.
6 *LSCG* 18, 20; Paus. 1.18.7 (with Zeus Olympios); Mikalson 1975.63, 126–27.
7 Carpenter 1991.73–75.
8 Ar. *Peace* 406–11; Nilsson 1967.139–42, 839–40; Gantz 1993.87–88, Reichert-Südbeck 2000.156–59 (Korinth).
9 Paus. 2.4.6 (Korinth); Farnell 1896–, Vol. 5.419–20; Fraser and Bean 1954.130–32; Sfyroeras 1993.
10 Hellanicus *FGrH* 4 F 71 (Sinties); Brelich 1958.325–57; Mustilli 1960; Bernabò-Brea 1961; Faraone 1987.
11 Philostr. *Her.* 53.4–7; Delcourt 1957.171–90; Burkert 1970; Robertson 1985.258–81; Faraone 1992. 55–57.
12 Schol. Ar. *Av.* 436 (kilns); Istros *FGrH* 334 F 2 (torches); Paus. 1.26.5 (altar); Delcourt 1957.191–203.
13 Davies 1967.35–36; Parke 1977.92–93, 171–72.
14 Harrison 1977a, b.
15 Ar. *Vesp.* 846 with schol.; Paus. 5.14.4 (Olympia).
16 Miller 1978 *passim*; Merkelbach 1980; Detienne 1985; Malkin 1987.114–34.
17 Paus. 1.34.3 (Oropos), 5.11.8 (Zeus); Vernant 1983a.
18 MacLachlan 1993.1–12, 41–55.
19 Hes. fr. 71 M-W (Eteokles); Paus. 9.35.1, 9.38.1; Rocchi 1979.10–15; Schachter 1981–, Vol. 1.140–44.
20 Ephoros *FGrH* 70 F 152.
21 Te Riele 1976.
22 Callim. fr. 3–7 Pf.; Apollod. *Bibl.* 3.15.7; Schwarzenberg 1966.4–7 and Pl. 1 (relief); Berranger 1992.195–98; Larson 2001.170 (Thasos).
23 Paus. 1.22.8 (Sokrates); Palagia 1990; Pirenne-Delforge 1996.201–7; Mikalson 1998.174–78.
24 KN 206 = Cg 705 [Chadwick and Ventris 1973]; Willetts 1958; Fauré 1964.82–94; Pingiatoglou 1981.36, 52–53; Marinatos 1996; Sporn 2002.94–96.
25 Paus. 1.18.5, 8.21.3, 9.27.2 (Olen); Bruneau 1970.212–17; Furley and Bremer 2001, Vol. 1.146–51.
26 Paus. 6.20.2–6 (Sosipolis); Hadzisteliou Price 1978.138–47 and *passim*; Kilian 1978.
27 Paus. 2.35.11 (Hermione), 6.20.3 (Olympia).
28 Laumonier 1958.344; Kraus 1960.24–56; Simon 1986.4, 54.
29 Boedeker 1983; Clay 1984.

30 Aesch. *TrGF* 388 (*hekataia*); Soph. *TrGF* 535 (*Rhizotomoi*); Theopompus *FGrH* 115 F 344 (garlands); Johnston 1990.21–28, 1991, 1999.203–49.
31 Dem. 54.14, 39; Parker 1983.30, n. 65.
32 Stesichorus fr. 215 *PMG*; Johnston 1999.238–49.
33 *IG* IX.2 575, 577; Johnston 1999.208–15, n. 42. Cf. Miller 1974.251.
34 Gager 1992 no. 40.
35 Fp 1, Fh 390, V 52 = KN 208 (Knossos) [Chadwick and Ventris 1973]; Chadwick 1985.193; Jost 1985.305.
36 Jameson, Jordan, and Kotansky 1993.79; Johnston 1999.250–87. *Contra*: Clinton 1996a.166.
37 Dem. 21.114–15, 23.67–68; Lloyd-Jones 1990; Henrichs 1983b, 1994.39–54.
38 Paus. 2.11.4 (Sikyon), 7.25.7 (Keryneia), 8.34.1–4 (Megalopolis); Burkert 1996.37.
39 Vollgraff 1944–45; Sarian 1986 no. 118 (votive relief with snakes).

13 STRANGERS AND INDIGENES: LATECOMER AND REGIONAL DEITIES

1 Henrichs 1976.266–76; Roller 1999.119–41; Hermary 2000.
2 Graf 1985.107–15; Roller 1999.163–69.
3 Wycherley 1957.150–51; Parker 1996.188–94; Borgeaud 2004.11–15.
4 Schol. Pind. *Pyth*. 3.137–39; Plut. *Vit. Them*. 30.
5 Roller 1999.143–85; Borgeaud 2004.34–38. "Attis" in the Archaic period: Vermaseren 1977–, Vol. 2, nos. 695–718 (Cyprus).
6 Braun and Haevernick 1981.99–110, Pl. 33–34.
7 Hemberg 1950.184–205; Schachter 1981–, Vol. 2.66–110, 2003; Daumas 1998.19–46, 61–89.
8 Accame 1941–43; Hemberg 1950.160–70; Levi 1966.
9 Diog. Laert. 6.59 (Diagoras).
10 Mnaseas in Schol. Ap. Rhod. 1.916–18b Wendel; Hemberg 1950.303–11.
11 Cic. *Nat. D.* 3.22 (56); Varro *Ling*. 5.58
12 Lehmann and Lehmann 1959–, Vol. 5.267–302; McCredie 1968; Cole 1984.1–20, 30; Bergquist 1990.34, n. 42.
13 Parke 1967.194–241.
14 Paus. 9.16.1 (statue).
15 Malkin 1994.158–68.
16 Hdt. e.g. 1.46, 3.25; Eur. *Alc*. 115; Ar. *Av*. 619–20, 716; Plato *Alc*. 2.149b; Plut. *Vit. Lys*. 25.3; Paus. 3.18.3 (Lysander).
17 Classen 1959; Woodward 1962; Bosworth 1977.
18 Garland 1992.111–14, fig. 25–26; Larson 2001.173.
19 Ferguson 1944.101 (on *IG* II² 1496).
20 Simms 1988; Pache 2004.
21 Paus. 9.40.3; Marinatos 1924–25; Gallet de Santerre 1958,154–55; Willetts 1962.179–93; Sporn 2002.76.
22 Ant. Lib. *Met*. 40.
23 Guarducci 1935.189–92; Sporn 2002.277–78.
24 Ant. Lib. *Met*. 40; Paus. 2.30.3.
25 *IG* IV 1582; Schwandner 1976;Williams 1981, 1982.
26 Sinn 1988; Hoffelner 1999; Figueira 1991.31–39.
27 Rudhardt 1999.43–57.
28 Paus. 9.25.4 (Thebes); Miller 1974; Schachter 1981–, Vol. 3.50–52.
29 Davies *EGF* 31, 37–38 (summary of Proclus and *Cypria* fr. 7); Stafford 2000.45–73.

30 Cratinus frs. 114–27 Kassel-Austin *PCG*; Friendly and Karapanayiotis 1973; Petrakos 1991.14–31; Lapatin 1992; Stafford 2000.75–110.
31 Figueira 1993.57–58.
32 Figueira 1991.31–39.

14 ANOMALOUS IMMORTALS: HERO-GODS AND HEROINE-GODDESSES

1 Burkert 1979.78–98; Salowey 2002 (Mycenaean).
2 Jourdain-Annequin 1986, 1992b.
3 Farnell 1921.95–145, 155–74; Nilsson 1923, 1951 Vol. 1.348–54 (Mt. Oita); Verbanck-Piérard 1989; Lévêque and Verbanck-Piérard 1992; Georgoudi 1998.
4 Pache 2004.49–57; Leitao 2002.
5 Boardman 1972, 1975, 1989; Vanderpool 1942, 1966.
6 Ath. 6.234d–e (parasites); Woodford 1971.215–19.
7 Wycherley 1959; Woodford 1976.218–19; Georgoudi 1998.
8 *IG* I³ 1016; Isaeus 9.30 (*thiasos* of Herakles); Hch. and Phot. s.v. *oinistēria* (libation); Walter 1937; Woodford 1971.214–15 (shrines); Tagalidou 1993.7–49.
9 Bonnet 1985, 1988.346–71. Cf. Paus. 7.5.5–8; Graf 1985.296–316 (Erythrai).
10 Launey 1944; Bergquist 1973, 1998; Courtils and Pariente 1988; Scullion 2000.166–67.
11 Clem. Alex. *Protr.* 42 (statue); Salowey 1995.21.
12 Paus. 3.15.3–9; Malkin 1994.15–45.
13 Thuc. 5.64.5, 5.66.1 (Mantineia); Xen. *Hell.* 7.1.31 (Eutresis); Paus. 3.14.6–8 (Dromos, Planes).
14 Meiggs and Lewis 1969, no. 38; Martin 1979; Jourdain-Annequin 1992b. For Italy, see the sixth-century dedication of Nikomachos: *IG* XIV 652 (Metapontion).
15 Bonnet 1985; Burkert 1992.87, n. 27; Tagalidou 1993.104–22.
16 Farnell 1916, 1921.35–47.
17 Lyons 1997.64–67, 122–24; Pache 2004.149–52.
18 Conon *FGrH* 26 F 1.33 (Miletos); Graf 1985.405–6.
19 Paus. 1.42.7 (Megara), 3.23.8 (Lakonia); Bonnet 1986; Kardulias 2001.
20 Gallet de Santerre 1958.265–66; Hermary 1978.56–62; Furley and Bremer 2001 Vol. 1.166–71, 2.117–19.
21 Ward 1970; West 1975; Sansone 1991.
22 Hdt. 5.75 (kings); Plat. *Leg.* 796b (dance); Plut. *Vit. Lyc.* 15.3 (bride-capture); Farnell 1921.229–33; Pendergraft and Hartigan 1994; Calame 1997.187–91.
23 Tod and Wace 1906 nos. 7–15, 113–18, etc.; Pirzio Birolli Stefanelli 1977; Guarducci 1984; Augé and Linant de Bellefonds 1986 nos. 58–64 (Lakonian reliefs), 66–70 (Tarentine plaques). Another series of plaques in Messene: Themelis 1998.
24 Jeffery 1961.210; Camp 1978.
25 Simon. fr. 11 West *IE*²; Paus. 4.16.5, 9 (Aristomenes); Strabo 6.1.10 (Sagra); van Compernolle 1969; Sordi 1972b; Lorenz 1992; Moscati Castelnuovo 1995; Hornblower 2001.140–47.
26 Cf. Ath. 4.147e; Jameson 1994.
27 Plat. *Phdr.* 243a–b; Isoc. *Helen* 64; Davies 1982.
28 Theoc. *Id.* 18.1–8, 39–44 (Dromos and Planes). Cf. Paus. 3.19.9 (Rhodes); Calame 1997.191–202; Larson 2001.64–70, 80–83.
29 West 1975.5–6; Catling 1976; Antonaccio 1995.155–66.

30 Chapouthier 1935.132–51; Kearns 1989.148, 158.
31 Edelstein and Edelstein 1975.53–64, T 337.
32 Lambrinoudakis 2002.
33 Edelstein and Edelstein 1975.76–91; Stafford 2000.147–71.
34 LiDonnici 1992a, 1995.85, 93.
35 *SEG* 32 (1982) 266; Ov. *Met.* 15.626–744 (Rome); Paus. 2.10.3 (Sikyon), 3.23.7 (Epidauros Limera).
36 Beschi 1967–68, 1985; Aleshire 1989.7–51; Garland 1992.116–35.
37 van Straten 1995.63–72.

15 THE POWERFUL DEAD: HEROES AND HEROINES

1 Ekroth 2000, 2002.140–50, 242–69; Kearns 1989.144, 149, 159, etc.
2 Morris 1988; Alcock 1991; Malkin 1993; Antonaccio 1994, 1995.1–9; Whitley 1994; Snodgrass 2000a [1988].
3 Broneer 1942; Lambrinoudakis 1988; Carter 1997; Antonaccio 1995.199–243.
4 Nagy 1979.142–50; Lyons 1997.71–77.
5 Antonaccio 1994; Larson 1995b.83–84; Salapata 1997, 2002.
6 Jameson 1990; Antonaccio 1995.147–52; Hall 1999.55–57.
7 Antonaccio 1995.152–55.
8 Hägg 1987; Antonaccio 1995.166–69.
9 Mattusch 1988.38–58; Kearns 1989.83–92.
10 Paus. 3.11.10, 7.1.3; Boedeker 1998; McCauley 1999.
11 Pherecydes *FGrH* 3 F 84; Plut. *De gen.* 577e–579a; *Vit. Lys.* 28.4–5; Schachter 1981–, Vol. 1.13–16; Larson 1995.92–93. A third claim by Megara: Paus. 1.41.1.
12 Brelich 1958.129–51.
13 *Cypria* fr. 19 Davies *EGF*; Gantz 1993.577–78.
14 Robert 1953; Gallet de Santerre 1958.173–77, 268–70; Abramson 1978.132–35.
15 Hdt. 5.89.2, 8.64.1; Abramson 1978.115; Figueira 1993.83–84, 277; Stroud 1993, 1998.85–108.
16 Malkin 1987.204–60, 1994.169–80; Antonaccio 1999; Calame 2003.107–8.
17 Edmunds 1981; Henrichs 1983b; Kearns 1989.208–9.
18 Fontenrose 1968.
19 Paus. 6.6.7–10; Visintin 1992.9–30 (other primary sources); Cordiano 1998; Tejeiro and Tejada 2000; Redfield 2003.245–51.
20 Brelich 1958.106–13; Visser 1982.
21 *SEG* 22 (1967) 370; Petropoulou 1981; Schachter 1981–, Vol. 1.19–26.
22 Clark 1968; Schachter 1981–, Vol. 3.66–89, 1984; Bonnechère 1999, 2002.
23 Pind. *Nem.* 4.49–50; Farnell 1921.285–89; Diehl 1953; Nagy 1979.167, 206; Hommel 1980; Pinney 1983; Hedreen 1991.
24 Kearns 1989.117–24; Simon 1996.19–21; Calame 1996.121–30; Connor 1996.

BIBLIOGRAPHY

Abramson, Herbert. 1978. *Greek hero shrines*. Diss. University of California at Berkeley, Berkeley CA.

Accame, Silvio. 1941–43. Iscrizioni del Cabirio di Lemno. *ASAA* 19–21:75–105.

Adamesteanu, D. 1970. ARGOI LITHOI a Metaponto. In *Adriatica praehistorica et antiqua*, ed. G. Novaku *et al.*, 307–24.

Akurgal, Ekrem. 1983. *Alt-Smyrna*. Ankara: Türk Tarih Kurumu Basimevi.

Alcock, Susan E. 1991. Tomb cult and the post-Classical polis. *AJA* 95 (3):447–67.

Alcock, Susan E., and Robin Osborne, eds. 1994. *Placing the gods: sanctuaries and sacred space in ancient Greece*. Oxford: Clarendon Press.

Alcock, Susan E., John F. Cherry, and Jas Elsner, eds. 2001. *Pausanias: travel and memory in Roman Greece*. New York: Oxford University Press.

Aleshire, Sara B. 1989. *The Athenian Asklepieion: The people, their dedications, and the inventories*. Amsterdam: J. C. Gieben.

Amandry, Pierre. 1950. *La mantique apollinienne à Delphes: essai sur le fonctionnement de l'oracle*. Paris: E. de Boccard.

Antonaccio, Carla M. 1994. Contesting the past: Hero cult, tomb cult and epic in early Greece. *AJA* 98 (3):389–410.

——1995. *An archaeology of ancestors: Tomb cult and hero cult in early Greece*, *Greek studies*. Lanham MD: Rowman & Littlefield.

——1999. Colonization and the origins of hero cult. In *Ancient Greek hero cult*, ed. R. Hägg, 109–21.

Antonetti, Claudia. 1990. *Les Étoliens: Image et religion*. Paris: Les Belles Lettres.

Arafat, K. W. 1996. *Pausanias' Greece: Ancient artists and Roman rulers*. Cambridge: Cambridge University Press.

Assante, Julia. 2003. From whores to hierodules: The historiographic invention of Mesopotamian female sex professionals. In *Ancient art and its historiography*, ed. A. A. Donohue and M. D. Fullerton, 13–47.

Assman, J. and A. I. Baumgarten, eds. 2001. *Representation in religion: Studies in honor of Moshe Barasch*. Leiden: E. J. Brill.

Atallah, W. 1966. *Adonis dans la littérature et l'art grecs*. Paris: C. Klincksieck.

Athanassakis, Apostolos. 1989. From the phallic cairn to shepherd god and divine herald. *Eranos* 87:33–49.

Auberson, Paul. 1968. *Temple d'Apollon Daphnéphoros: Architecture*. Eretria; fouilles et recherches, l. Berne: Éditions Francke.

——1974. La reconstitution du Daphnéphoréion d'Érétrie. *AK* 17:60–68.

Augé, C., and P. Linant de Bellefonds. 1986. Dioskouroi. *LIMC* III.1.567–97.

Austin, Colin, ed. 1968. *Nova fragmenta Euripidea*. Berlin: W. de Gruyter.

Avagianou, Aphrodite. 1991. *Sacred marriage in the rituals of Greek religion*. Bern: P. Lang.

Badian, E., ed. 1967. *Ancient society and institutions: Studies presented to Victor Ehrenberg on his 75th birthday*. New York: Barnes & Noble.

Baldwin Bowsky, Martha W. 2001. A temple of Hermes at Sybritos on the road from Gortyn to the Diktynnaion (Crete). *ASAA* 79:263–76.

Bammer, Anton. 1974. Recent excavations at the altar of Artemis in Ephesus. *Archaeology* 27:202–4.

—— 1984. *Das Heiligtum der Artemis von Ephesos*. Graz: Akademische Druck und Verlagsanstalt.

—— 1990. A Peripteros of the Geometric period in the Artemision of Ephesos. *Anatolian Studies* 40:137–60.

—— 1998. Sanctuaries in the Artemision at Ephesus. In *Ancient Greek cult practice from the archaeological evidence*, ed. R. Hägg, 27–47.

Bammer, Anton, and Ulrike Muss. 1996. *Das Artemision von Ephesos: das Weltwunder Ioniens in archaischer und klassischer Zeit*. Mainz am Rhein: P. von Zabern.

Bammer, Anton, Friedrich Brein, and Petra Wolff. 1978. Das Tieropfer am Artemisaltar von Ephesos. In *Studien zur Religion und Kultur Kleinasiens*, ed. S. Sahin, E. Schwertheim, and J. Wagner, 107–57.

Barber, E. J. W. 1992. The peplos of Athena. In *Goddess and polis*, ed. J. Neils, 103–17.

Barra Bagnasco, M. 1990. Nuovi documenti sul culto di Afrodite a Locri Epizefiri. *PP* 45:42–64.

Bats, Michel, and Bruno D'Agostino, eds. 1998. *Euboica: l'Eubea e la presenza euboica in Calcidica e in Occidente*. Napoli: Centre Jean Bérard; Istituto universitario orientale Dipartimento del mondo classico.

Baumbach, Jens David. 2004. *The significance of votive offerings in selected Hera sanctuaries in the Peloponnese, Ionia and western Greece*. Oxford: Archaeopress.

Beard, Mary, and John A. North. 1990. *Pagan priests: Religion and power in the ancient world*. Ithaca NY: Cornell University Press.

Bell, Catherine. 1997. *Ritual: Perspectives and dimensions*. Oxford: Oxford University Press.

—— 1998. Performance. In *Critical terms for religious studies*, ed. M. C. Taylor, 205–24.

Bennett, Michael J., and Aaron J. Paul, eds. 2002. *Magna Graecia: Greek art from South Italy and Sicily*. New York: Hudson Hills Press.

Bérard, Claude. 1989. *A city of images: Iconography and society in Ancient Greece*. Tr. Deborah Lyons. Princeton NJ: Princeton University Press.

Berggreen, B., and Nanno Marinatos, eds. 1995. *Greece and gender*. Bergen: Norwegian Institute at Athens and John Grieg AS.

Bergquist, Birgitta. 1973. *Herakles on Thasos: The archaeological, literary and epigraphic evidence for his sanctuary, status and cult reconsidered*. Uppsala: University of Uppsala; Almquist and Wiksell.

—— 1990. Primary or secondary temple function: The case of Halieis. In *Celebrations of death and divinity in the Bronze Age Argolid*, ed. R. Hägg and G. Nordquist, 225–28.

—— 1992. A particular, Western Greek cult practice? The significance of stele crowned, sacrificial deposits. *OpAth* 19:41–47.

—— 1998. Feasting of worshippers or temple and sacrifice? The case of the Herakleion on Thasos. In *Ancient Greek cult practice from the archaeological evidence*, ed. R. Hägg, 57–72.

Berlingo, I., ed. 2000. *Damarato: Studi di antichità classica offerti a Paola Pelagatti*. Milan: University of Milan.

Bernabò-Brea, L. 1961. Lemnos. In *Enciclopedia dell'arte antica* Vol. 4.542–43.

Berranger, Danièle. 1992. *Recherches sur l'histoire et la prosopographie de Paros à l'époque archaïque*. Clermont-Ferrand: Association des publications de la Faculté des lettres et sciences humaines.

Beschi, L. 1967–68. Il monumento di Telemachos, fondatore dell' Asklepieion Ateniese. *ASAA* 29–30:381–436.

—— 1985. Il rilievo di Telemachos ricompletato. *Archaiologika Analekta ex Athēnōn* 15:31–43.

Bevan, Elinor. 1987. The goddess Artemis and the dedication of bears in sanctuaries. *ABSA* 82:17–21.

Beyer, I. 1976. *Die Tempel von Dreros und Prinias A und die Chronologie der kretischen Kunst des 8. und 7. Jhs. v. Chr.* 2 Vols. Freiberg: Wasmuth.

Bianchi, Ugo. 1953. *[Dios aisa] Destino, uomini e divinità nell'epos, nelle teogonie e nel culto dei Greci*. Rome: A. Signorelli.

Bibauw, Jacqueline, ed. 1969. *Hommages à Marcel Renard*. 3 Vols. Brussels: Latomus.

Billot, Marie-Françoise. 1989–90. Apollon Pythéen et l'Argolide archaïque. Histoire et mythes. *Archaiognosia* 6:35–100.

—— 1997. Recherches archéologiques récentes à l'Héraion d'Argos. In *Héra*, ed. J. de La Genière, 11–56.

—— 1997–98. Sanctuaires et cultes d'Athéna à Argos. *OAth* 22–23:7–52.

Bingen, Jean, Guy Cambier, and Georges Nachtergael, eds. 1975. *Le Monde grec: pensée, littérature, histoire, documents: hommages à Claire Préaux*. Brussels: Éditions de l'Université de Bruxelles.

Blinkenberg, Christian, ed. 1980 [1915]. *Timachidas of Lindus: The Chronicle of the temple of Athena at Lindus in Rhodes = Chronicum Lindium = Die lindische Tempelchronik*. Reprint. Chicago IL: Ares Publishers.

—— 1987 [1911]. *The thunderweapon in religion and folklore: A study in comparative archaeology*. Reprint. New Rochelle NY: Caratzas.

Blomberg, Peter E. 1996. *On Corinthian iconography: The bridled winged horse and the helmeted female head in the sixth century BC*. Uppsala and Stockholm: Swedish Academy of Uppsala; Almquist & Wiksell.

Blundell, Sue, and Margaret Williamson, eds. 1998. *The sacred and the feminine in ancient Greece*. London: Routledge.

Boardman, John. 1963. Artemis Orthia and chronology. *ABSA* 58:1–7.

—— 1967. *Excavations in Chios, 1952–1955: Greek Emporio*. London: British School of Archaeology at Athens; Thames and Hudson.

—— 1972. Herakles, Peisistratos and sons. *RA* 57–72.

—— 1975. Herakles, Peisistratos and Eleusis. *JHS* 95:1–12.

—— 1989. Herakles, Peisistratos and the unconvinced. *JHS* 109:158–59.

—— 1999. *The Greeks overseas*. Fourth ed. London: Thames and Hudson.

Boedeker, Deborah Dickmann. 1974. *Aphrodite's entry into Greek epic*. Leiden: E. J. Brill.

——1983. Hecate. A transfunctional goddess in the Theogony? *TAPhA* 113:79–93.

——1984. *Descent from heaven: Images of dew in Greek poetry and religion*. Chico CA: Scholars Press.

——1998. Hero cult and politics in Herodotus: The bones of Orestes. In *Cultural poetics in Archaic Greece*, ed. C. Dougherty and L. Kurke, 164–77.

Boedeker, Deborah Dickmann, and David Sider, eds. 2001. *The new Simonides: Contexts of praise and desire*. Oxford: Oxford University Press.

Boegehold, Alan L., and Adele C. Scafuro, eds. 1994. *Athenian identity and civic ideology*. Baltimore MD: The Johns Hopkins University Press.

Bolger, Diane R., and Nancy J. Serwint, eds. 2002. *Engendering Aphrodite: Women and society in ancient Cyprus*. Boston MA: American Schools of Oriental Research.

Bonnechère, P. 1990. Les oracles de Béotie. *Kernos* 3:53–65.

——1999. La personnalité mythologique de Trophonios. *RHR* 216 (3):259–97.

——2003. Trophonius of Lebadeia: Mystery aspects of an oracular cult in Boeotia. In *Greek mysteries*, ed. M. B. Cosmopoulos, 169–92.

Bonnet, Corinne. 1985. Melqart, Bès et l'Héraclès Dactyle de Crète. In *Phoenicia and its neighbours*, ed. E. Gubel and E. Lipinski, 231–40.

——1986. Le culte de Leucothéa et de Mélicerte, en Grèce, au Proche-Orient et en Italie. *SMSR* 52:53–71.

——1988. *Melqart: cultes et mythes de l'Héraclès tyrien en Méditerranée*. Leuven: U. Peeters; University Press of Namur.

——1996. Héraclès travesti. In *Héraclès, les femmes et le feminine*, ed. C. Jourdain-Annequin and C. Bonnet, 121–31.

Bonnet, Corinne, and Colette Jourdain-Annequin, eds. 1992. *Héraclès: d'une rive à l'autre de la Méditerranée: bilan et perspectives*. Brussels: Institut Historique Belge de Rome.

Bonnet, Corinne, and André Motte, eds. 1999. *Les syncrétismes religieux dans le monde méditerranéen antique*. Brussels and Rome: Institut historique belge de Rome.

Bonnet, Corinne, and Vinciane Pirenne-Delforge. 1999. Deux déesses en interaction: Astarté et Aphrodite dans le monde égéen. In *Les syncrétismes religieux*, ed. C. Bonnet and A. Motte, 249–73.

Bonnet, Corinne, Colette Jourdain-Annequin, and Vinciane Pirenne-Delforge, eds. 1998. *Le bestiaire d'Héraclès: IIIe Rencontre héracléenne*. Liège: Centre internationale d'étude de la religion grecque antique.

Bookidis, Nancy. 1990. Ritual dining in the sanctuary of Demeter and Kore at Corinth: Some questions. In *Sympotica*, ed. O. Murray, 480–81.

——1993. Ritual Dining at Corinth. In *Greek sanctuaries*, ed. N. Marinatos and R. Hägg, 45–61.

Bookidis, Nancy, and Ronald S. Stroud. 1987. *Demeter and Persephone in ancient Corinth*. Princeton NJ: American School of Classical Studies at Athens.

——1997. *The sanctuary of Demeter and Kore: Topography and architecture*. Corinth Vol. 18, pt. 3. Princeton NJ: American School of Classical Studies at Athens.

Borgeaud, Philippe. 1988. *The cult of Pan in ancient Greece*. Tr. Kathleen Atlass and James Redfield. Chicago IL: University of Chicago Press.

225

——2004. *Mother of the gods: from Cybele to the Virgin Mary*. Tr. Lysa Hochroth. Baltimore MD: The Johns Hopkins University Press.

Borgeaud, Philippe, ed. 1991. *Orphisme et Orphée*. Geneva: Librairie Droz.

Bosworth, A. B. 1977. Alexander and Ammon. In *Greece and the eastern Mediterranean in ancient history and prehistory*, ed. K. Kinzl, 51–75.

Bourriot, Félix. 1976. *Recherches sur la nature du genos: étude d'histoire sociale athénienne, périodes archaïque et classique*. Lille: H. Champion.

Bousquet, Jean. 1938. Le temple d'Aphrodite et d'Arès à Sta Lenikà. *BCH* 62:386–408.

Bowersock, G. W., Walter Burkert, and Michael J. Putnam, eds. 1979. *Arktouros: Hellenic studies presented to Bernard M. W. Knox on the occasion of his 65th birthday*. Berlin: W. de Gruyter.

Boyancé, Pierre. 1972. *Le culte des muses chez les philosophes grecs: études d'histoire et de psychologie religieuses*. Paris: E. de Boccard.

Braun, Karin, and Thea Elisabeth Haevernick. 1981. *Bemalte Keramik und Glas aus dem Kabirenheiligtum bei Theben*. Berlin: de Gruyter.

Breglia Pulci Doria, Luisa. 1984. *Recherches sur les cultes grecs et l'Occident, II*. Naples: Centre Jean Bérard.

Brelich, Angelo. 1958. *Gli eroi greci: un problema storico-religioso*. Rome: Ediziono dell'Ateneo.

——1969. *Paides e Parthenoi*. Rome: Edizioni dell'Ateneo.

Bremer, Jan M., S. L. Radt, and C. J. Ruijgh, eds. 1976. *Miscellanea tragica in honorem J. C. Kamerbeek*. Amsterdam: A. Hakkert.

Bremmer, Jan N. 1984. Greek maenadism reconsidered. *ZPE* 55:267–86.

——1987. "Effigies Dei" in ancient Greece: Poseidon. In *Effigies dei*, ed. D. van der Plas, 35–41.

——1994. *Greek religion*. Oxford: Oxford University Press.

——1999. Transvestite Dionysos. In *Rites of passage in ancient Greece*, ed. M. W. Padilla, 183–200.

——2000. Scapegoat rituals in ancient Greece. In *Oxford readings in Greek religion*, ed. R. G. A. Buxton, 271–93.

——2002. Sacrificing a child in ancient Greece: The case of Iphigeneia. In *The sacrifice of Isaac*, ed. E. Noort and E. Tigchelaar, 21–43.

Bremmer, Jan N., ed. 1986. *Interpretations of Greek mythology*. Totowa NJ: Barnes & Noble.

Brommer, Frank. 1949–50. Pan im 5. und 4. Jahrhundert v. Chr. *Marburger Jahrbuch für Kunstwissenschaft* 15:5–42.

——1957. *Athena Parthenos*. Bremen: W. Dorn.

——1978. *Hephaistos: der Schmiedegott in der antiken Kunst*. Mainz: Ph. von Zabern.

Broneer, Oscar. 1933. Excavations on the north slope of the Acropolis in Athens. *Hesperia* 2:329–417.

——1942. Hero cults in the Corinthian agora. *Hesperia* 11.128–61.

——1966. The temple of Poseidon at Isthmia. In *Charistērion eis Anastasion K. Orlandon*, 3.61–85, pl. 11–24.

——1971. *Isthmia: Excavations by the University of Chicago. Volume 1: The Temple of Poseidon*. Princeton NJ: The American School of Classical Studies at Athens.

—— 1976. The Isthmian sanctuary of Poseidon. In *Neue Forschungen in griechischen Heiligtümern*, ed. U. Jantzen, 39–62.

Brown, C. G. 1982. Dionysus and the women of Elis. *GRBS* 23:305–14.

—— 1991. The prayers of the Corinthian women. *GRBS* 32:5–14.

Bruit, Louise. 1990. The meal at the Hyakinthia: Ritual consumption and offering. In *Sympotica*, ed. O. Murray, 39–62.

Brulé, Pierre. 1988. *La fille d'Athènes: la religion des filles à Athènes à l'époque classique: mythes, cultes et société*. Paris: Belles Lettres.

Brulotte, Eric Lucien. 2002. Artemis: Her Peloponnesian abodes and cults. In *Peloponnesian sanctuaries and cults*, ed R. Hägg, 179–82.

Brumfield, Allaire Chandor. 1981. *The Attic festivals of Demeter and their relation to the agricultural year*. New York: Arno Press.

—— 1996. Aporreta: Verbal and ritual obscenity in the cults of ancient women. In *The role of religion in the early Greek polis*, ed. R. Hägg 67–74.

—— 1997. Cakes in the liknon: Votives from the sanctuary of Demeter and Kore on Acrocorinth. *Hesperia* 66 (1):147–72.

Bruneau, Philippe. 1970. *Recherches sur les cultes de Délos à l'époque hellénistique et à l'époque impériale*. Paris: E. de Boccard.

Bruneau, Philippe, and Jean Ducat. 1983. *Guide de Délos*. Third Edition. Paris: École française d'Athènes; E. de Boccard.

Budin, Stephanie. 2003. *The origin of Aphrodite*. Bethesda MD: CDL Press.

—— 2006. Sacred prostitution in the first person. In *Prostitutes and courtesans in the ancient world*, ed. C. A. Faraone and L. K. McClure, 77–92.

Buitron-Oliver, Diana, ed. 1991. *New perspectives in early Greek art*. Washington and Hanover NH: National Gallery of Art; University Press of New England.

Buitron-Oliver, Diana, and Bernard C. Dietrich. 1996. *The Sanctuary of Apollo Hylates at Kourion: Excavations in the archaic precinct*. Jonsered, Sweden: P. Åström.

Burkert, Walter. 1970. Jason, Hypsipyle and new fire at Lemnos. A study in myth and ritual. *CQ* 20:1–16.

—— 1975a. Apellai und Apollon. *RhM* 118:1–21.

—— 1975b. Resep-Figuren, Apollon von Amyklai und die 'Erfindung' des Opfers auf Cypern. *GB* 4:51–79.

—— 1979. *Structure and history in Greek mythology and ritual*. Berkeley: University of California Press.

—— 1983a. Craft vs. sect: The problem of Orphics and Pythagoreans. In *Jewish and Christian self-definition, Volume 3*, ed. B. Meyer, 1–22.

—— 1983b. *Homo necans: the anthropology of ancient Greek sacrificial ritual and myth*. Berkeley: University of California Press.

—— 1985. *Greek religion*. Cambridge MA: Harvard University Press.

—— 1987. Offerings in perspective: Surrender, distribution, exchange. In *Gifts to the Gods*, ed. T. Linders and G. Nordquist, 43–50.

—— 1988. Katagogia-Anagogia and the goddess of Knossos. In *Early Greek cult practice*, ed. R. Hägg, *et al.*, 81–87.

—— 1992. *The orientalizing revolution: Near Eastern influence on Greek culture in the early archaic age*. Cambridge MA: Harvard University Press.

—— 1994. Olbia and Apollo of Didyma: A new oracle text. In *Apollo*, ed. J. Solomon, 49–60.

——1996. Greek temple builders: Who, where and why? In *The role of religion in the early Greek polis*, ed. R. Hägg, 21–29.

——2000. Private needs and polis acceptance: Purification at Selinous. In *Polis & politics*, ed. P. Flensted-Jensen, T. H. Nielsen, and L. Rubinstein, 207–16.

——2001. *Savage energies: lessons of myth and ritual in ancient Greece*. Chicago IL: University of Chicago Press.

——2004. *Babylon, Memphis, Persepolis: Eastern contexts of Greek culture*. Cambridge MA: Harvard University Press.

Burn, Lucilla. 1987. *The Meidias painter*. Oxford: Clarendon Press.

Buxton, R. G. A. 1986. Wolves and werewolves in Greek thought. In *Interpretations of Greek mythology*, ed. J. N. Bremmer, 60–79.

Buxton, R. G. A., ed. 2000. *Oxford readings in Greek religion*. Oxford: Oxford University Press.

Calame, Claude. 1996. *Thésée et l'imaginaire athénien: légende et culte en Grèce antique*. Second edition. Lausanne: Éditions Payot.

——1997. *Choruses of young women in ancient Greece: Their morphology, religious role, and social functions*. Tr. Derek Collins and Janice Orion. Lanham MD: Rowman & Littlefield.

——2003. *Myth and history in ancient Greece: The symbolic creation of a colony*. Tr. Daniel W. Berman. Princeton NJ: Princeton University Press.

Cameron, Averil, and Amelie Kuhrt, eds. 1983. *Images of women in antiquity*. Revised edition. London: Routledge.

Camp, John M. 1978. A spear butt from the Lesbians. *Hesperia* 47 (2):192–95.

——2001. *The archaeology of Athens*. New Haven CT: Yale University Press.

Cancik, Hubert, and Helmuth Schneider, eds. 1996–. *Der neue Pauly. Altertum: Enzyklopädie der Antike*. Stuttgart: J. B. Metzler.

Caquot, André, and Pierre Canivet, eds. 1989. *Ritualisme et vie intérieure: religion et culture*. Paris : Beauchesne.

Carpenter, Thomas H. 1991. *Art and myth in ancient Greece: A handbook*. London: Thames and Hudson.

——1997. *Dionysian imagery in fifth-century Athens*. Oxford and New York: Clarendon Press; Oxford University Press.

Carpenter, Thomas H., and Christopher A. Faraone, eds. 1993. *Masks of Dionysus: Myth and poetics*. Ithaca NY: Cornell University Press.

Carter, Jane B. 1987. The masks of Ortheia. *AJA* 91:355–83.

——1988. Masks and poetry in early Sparta. In *Early Greek cult practice*, ed. R. Hägg, *et al.*, 89–98.

——1997. Thiasos and marzeah: Ancestor cult in the age of Homer. In *New light on a dark age*, ed. S. H. Langdon, 72–112.

Cartledge, Paul. 2002. *Sparta and Lakonia: A regional history, 1300–362 BC*. Second edition. New York: Routledge.

Cary, Max. 1949. *The geographic background of Greek & Roman history*. Oxford: Clarendon Press.

Casadio, Giovanni. 1994. *Storia del culto di Dioniso in Argolide*. Roma: GEI.

——1999. *Il vino dell'anima: storia del culto di Dioniso a Corinto, Sicione, Trezene*. Rome: Il calamo.

Caskey, John L., and Pierre Amandry. 1952. Investigations at the Heraion of Argos. *Hesperia* 21 (3):165–221.

Caskey, Miriam Ervin. 1981. Ayia Irini: The terracotta statues and the cult in the temple. In *Sanctuaries and cults in the Aegean Bronze Age*, ed. R. Hägg and N. Marinatos, 127–35.

Caskey, Miriam Ervin, and John L. Caskey. 1986. *The temple at Ayia Irini*. Keos Vol. 2. Princeton NJ: American School of Classical Studies.

Catling, H. W. 1976. New excavations at the Menelaion, Sparta. In *Neue Forschungen in griechischen Heiligtümern*, ed. U. Jantzen, 77–90.

——1990. A sanctuary of Zeus Messapeus: Excavations at Aphyssou, Tsakona, 1989. *ABSA* 85:15–35.

Cavanaugh, Maureen B. 1996. *Eleusis and Athens: Documents in finance, religion, and politics in the fifth century* BC. Atlanta GA: Scholars Press.

Chadwick, John. 1956. The Greek dialects and Greek pre-history. *G&R* 3 (1):38–50.

——1985. What do we know about Mycenaean religion? In *Linear B, a 1984 survey*, ed. A. M. Davies and Y. Duhoux, 191–202.

Chadwick, John, and Michael Ventris. 1973. *Documents in Mycenaean Greek*. Second edition. Cambridge: Cambridge University Press.

Chapouthier, Fernand. 1935. *Les Dioscures au service d'une déesse, étude d'iconographie religieuse*. Paris: E. de Boccard.

Charistērion eis Anastasion K. Orlandon. 1965–68. 4 Vols. Athens: Hē en Athēnais Archaiologikē Hetaireia.

Chirassi Colombo, Ileana. 1964. *Miti e culti arcaici di Artemis nel Peloponneso e Grecia centrale*. [Trieste]: Universitá degli studi di Trieste, Facoltá di lettere e filosofia.

Chittenden, J. 1947. The master of animals. *Hesperia* 16:89–114, pl. 15–21.

Christopoulos, Menelaos. 1994. Poseidon Erechtheus and ERECHTHĒIS THALASSA, in *Ancient Greek cult practice from the epigraphical evidence*, ed. R. Hägg, 123–30.

Cipriani, M. 1997. Il ruolo di Hera nel santuario meridionale di Poseidonia. In *Héra*, ed. J. de La Genière, 211–25.

Clark, Isabelle. 1998. The gamos of Hera: Myth and ritual. In *The sacred and the feminine in ancient Greece*, ed. S. Blundell and M. Williamson, 13–26.

Clark, R. J. 1968. Trophonios: the manner of his revelation. *TAPhA* 99:63–75.

Classen, C. J. 1959. The Libyan god Ammon in Greece before 331 BC. *Historia* 8: 349–61.

Classical studies in honor of William Abbott Oldfather. 1943. Urbana: The University of Illinois Press.

Clauss, James Joseph, and Sarah Iles Johnston, eds. 1997. *Medea: Essays on Medea in myth, literature, philosophy, and art*. Princeton NJ: Princeton University Press.

Clay, Diskin. 2002. The scandal of Dionysos on Paros: The Mnesiepes inscription E3. *Prometheus* 27:97–111.

——2004. *Archilochos Heros: The cult of poets in the Greek polis*. Cambridge: Center for Hellenic Studies; distributed by Harvard University Press.

Clay, Jenny Strauss. 1984. The Hecate of the Theogony. *GRBS* 25:27–38.

——1996. Fusing the boundaries: Apollo and Dionysos at Delphi. *Metis* 11:83–100.

Clinton, Kevin. 1974. *The sacred officials of the Eleusinian Mysteries*. Philadelphia PA: American Philosophical Society.

——1979. IG I² 5, the Eleusinia, and the Eleusinians. *AJP* 100 (1):1–12.

——1980. A law in the city Eleusinion concerning the Mysteries. *Hesperia* 49 (3):258–88.

——1988. Sacrifice at the Eleusinian Mysteries. In *Early Greek cult practice*, ed. R. Hägg, *et al.*, 69–80.

——1992. *Myth and cult: the iconography of the Eleusinian mysteries*. Stockholm: Swedish Institute at Athens; distributed by P. Åström.

——1993. The Sanctuary of Demeter and Kore at Eleusis. In *Greek Sanctuaries*, ed. N. Marinatos and R. Hägg, 110–24.

——1994. The Epidauria and the arrival of Asclepius in Athens. In *Ancient Greek cult practice from the epigraphical evidence*, ed. R. Hägg, 17–34.

——1996a. A new lex sacra from Selinus: Kindly Zeuses, Eumenides, Impure and Pure Tritopatores, and Elasteroi. *CP* 91.2:159–79.

——1996b. The Thesmophorion in central Athens and the celebration of the Thesmophoria in Attica. In *The role of religion in the early Greek polis*, ed. R. Hägg, 111–25.

Coldstream, J. N. 2003. *Geometric Greece: 900–700 BC*. Second edition. London: Routledge.

Coldstream, J. N., and Malcolm A. R. Colledge, eds. 1979. *Greece and Italy in the classical world*. London: National Organizing Committee, XI International Congress of Classical Archaeology.

Coldstream, J. N., and George Leonard Huxley. 1973. *Kythera: Excavations and studies conducted by the University of Pennsylvania Museum and the British School at Athens*. Park Ridge NJ: Noyes Press.

Cole, Susan Guettel. 1980. New evidence for the mysteries of Dionysos. *GRBS* 21:223–38.

——1984. *Theoi Megaloi: The cult of the great gods at Samothrace*. Leiden: E. J. Brill.

——1988. Greek cults. In *Civilization of the ancient Mediterranean*, ed. M. Grant and R. Kitzinger, 887–908.

——1993a. Procession and celebration at the Dionysia. In *Theater and society in the classical world*, ed. R. Scodel, 25–38.

——1993b. Voices from beyond the grave: Dionysus and the dead. In *Masks of Dionysus*, ed. T. H. Carpenter and C. A. Faraone, 276–95.

——1994. Demeter in the ancient Greek city and its countryside. In *Placing the Gods*, ed. S. E. Alcock and R. Osborne, 199–216.

——1998. Domesticating Artemis. In *The sacred and the feminine in ancient Greece*, ed. S. Blundell and M. Williamson, 27–43.

——2000. Landscapes of Artemis. *CW* 93 (5):471–81.

——2003. Landscapes of Dionysos and Elysian fields. In *Greek mysteries*, M. B. Cosmopoulos ed., 193–217.

——2004. *Landscapes, gender, and ritual space: The ancient Greek experience*. Berkeley: University of California Press.

Connolly, Andrew. 1998. Was Sophocles heroised as Dexion? *JHS* 118:1–21.

Connor, W. Robert. 1987. Tribes, festivals and processions: Civic ceremonial and political manipulation in archaic Greece. *JHS* 107:140–50.

——1988. Seized by the nymphs: Nympholepsy and symbolic expression in Classical Greece. *ClAnt* 7:155–89.

——1990. City Dionysia and Athenian democracy. In *Aspects of Athenian democracy*, ed. W. R. Connor *et al.*, 7–32.

——1996. Theseus and his city. In *Religion and power in the ancient Greek world*, ed. P. Hellström and B. Alroth, 115–20.

Connor, W. Robert, H. Hansen Mogens, Kurt A. Raaflaub, and Barry S. Strauss. 1990. *Aspects of Athenian democracy*. Copenhagen: Museum Tusculanum Press University of Copenhagen.

Cook, Arthur Bernard. 1964 [1914–]. *Zeus: A study in ancient religion*. Cambridge: Cambridge University Press. 2 Vols in 3. Reprint. New York: Biblo and Tannen.

Cooper, Frederick A. 1983. *The Temple of Zeus at Nemea, perspectives and prospects: A guide to the exhibition, Benaki Museum, April 1983*. [Athens]: Benaki Museum and American School of Classical Studies.

Cooper, Frederick A., ed. 1996. *The Temple of Apollo Bassitas*. 4 Vols. Princeton NJ: American School of Classical Studies at Athens.

Corbett, P. E. 1970. Greek temples and Greek worshipers: The literary and archaeological evidence. *BICS* 17:149–58.

Cordiano, Giuseppe. 1998. La saga dell'eroe di Temesa. *QUCC*:177–83.

Cosmopoulos, Michael B., ed. 2003a. *Greek mysteries: The archaeology of ancient Greek secret cults*. London: Routledge.

——2003b. Mycenaean religion at Eleusis: The architecture and stratigraphy of Megaron B. In *Greek mysteries*, ed. M. B. Cosmopoulos, 1–24.

Costa, Giacomo. 1982. Hermes dio delle iniziazioni. *CCC* 3:277–95.

Craik, Elizabeth M., ed. 1990. *Owls to Athens: Essays on classical subjects presented to Sir Kenneth Dover*. Oxford and New York: Clarendon Press; Oxford University Press.

Croissant, F., and F. Salviat. 1966. Aphrodite gardienne des magistrats. *BCH* 90:460–71.

Cummer, W. 1978. The sanctuary of Poseidon at Tainaron, Lakonia. *MDAI(A)* 93:35–43.

Curbera, Jaime B. 1997. Chthonians in Sicily. *GRBS* 38:397–408.

Dalfen, J., G. Petersmann, and F. F. Schwarz, eds. 1993. *Religio Graeco-Romana: Festschrift für Walter Pötscher*. Horn: Berger.

Daremberg, Charles, and E. Saglio, eds. 1877–1919. *Dictionnaire des antiquities grecques et romains d'apres les textes et les monuments*. Paris: Hachette.

Daumas, Michèle. 1998. *Cabiriaca: Recherches sur l'iconographie du culte des Cabires, de l'archéologie à l'histoire*. Paris: De Boccard.

Daux, Georges. 1965. Deux stèles d'Acharnes. In *Charistērion eis Anastasion K. Orlandon*, 1.78–90.

Davies, Anna Morpurgo, and Yves Duhoux. 1985. *Linear B, a 1984 survey*. Louvain-la-Neuve: Cabay.

Davies, J. K. 1967. Demosthenes on liturgies: A note. *JHS* 87:33–40.

Davies, M. 1982. Derivative and proverbial testimonia concerning Stesichorus' palinode. *QUCC* 41:7–16.

Dawkins, Richard McGillivray. 1906–7. The sanctuary of Artemis Orthia. *ABSA* 13:77–108.

——1929. *The sanctuary of Artemis Orthia at Sparta*. *JHS* Supplement 5. London: The Council; Macmillan and Co.

Deacy, Susan. 1995. Athena in Boiotia: Local tradition and cultural identity. In *Boeotia antiqua V: Studies in Boiotian topography, cults and terracottas*, ed. J. Fossey and P. J. Smith, 91–103.

Deacy, Susan, and Alexandra Villing, eds. 2001. *Athena in the classical world*. Leiden: E. J. Brill.

de Boer, J. Z., J. R. Hale, and J. Chanton. 2001. New evidence for the geological origins of the ancient Delphic oracle (Greece). *Geology* 29:707–10.

de La Genière, Juliette. 1994. Note sur le sanctuaire de Hera au Sele. *CRAI*:305–14.

——ed. 1997. *Héra: images, espaces, cultes*. Naples: Centre Jean Bérard.

Del Chiaro, Mario A., and William R. Biers, eds. 1986. *Corinthiaca: Studies in honor of Darrell A. Amyx*. Columbia: University of Missouri Press.

Delcourt, Marie. 1957. *Héphaistos, ou, la légende du magicien*. Paris: Belles Lettres.

——1992. *Légendes et cultes de héros en Grèce*. Second edition. Paris: Presses universitaires de France.

Demargne, P. 1984. Athena. *LIMC* II.1.955–1044.

de Polignac, François. 1984. *La naissance de la cité grecque: cultes, espace et société VIIIe–VIIe siècles avant J.-C.* Paris: Éditions la Découverte.

——1995. *Cults, territory, and the origins of the Greek city-state*. Tr. Janet Lloyd. Revised edition. Chicago IL: University of Chicago Press.

——1997. Héra, le navire et la demeure: offrandes, divinité et société en Grèce archaïque. In *Héra*, ed. J. de La Genière, 113–22.

des Courtils, J., and A. Pariente. 1988. Excavations in the Heracles sanctuary at Thasos. In *Early Greek cult practice*, ed. R. Hägg, *et al.*, 121–23.

Desborough, V. R. 1964. *The last Mycenaeans and their successors: An archaeological survey, c. 1200–c. 1000 BC*. Oxford: Clarendon Press.

de Sensi Sestito, G. 1984. La funzione politica dell'Heraion del Lacinio al temp delle lotte contro i Lucani e Dionisio I. In *I santuari e la guerra nel mondo classico*, ed. M. Sordi, 41–50.

Des Places, Edouard, ed. 1982. *Porphyre. Vie de Pythagore. Lettre à Marcella*. Paris: Belles Lettres.

Detienne, Marcel. 1971. Athena and the mastery of the horse. *History of Religions* 11:161–84.

——1979. *Dionysos slain*. Tr. Mireille Muellner and Leonard Muellner. Baltimore MD: Johns Hopkins University Press.

——1985. La cité en son autonomie. Autour d'Hestia. *QS* 11 (22):59–78.

——1989a. The violence of wellborn ladies: Women in the Thesmophoria. In M. Detienne *et al.*, *The cuisine of sacrifice among the Greeks*, 129–47.

——1989b. *Dionysos at large*. Tr. Arthur Goldhammer. Cambridge MA: Harvard University Press.

——1994 [1977]. *The gardens of Adonis: Spices in Greek mythology*. Tr. Janet Lloyd. Princeton NJ: Princeton University Press.

——1998. *Apollon le couteau à la main: Une approche expérimentale du polythéisme grec*. Bibliothèque des sciences humaines. [Paris]: Gallimard.

Detienne, Marcel, and Jean Pierre Vernant. 1989. *The cuisine of sacrifice among the Greeks*. Tr. Paula Wissig. Chicago IL: University of Chicago Press.

——1991 [1978]. *Cunning intelligence in Greek culture and society*. Tr. Janet Lloyd. Reprint. Chicago IL: University of Chicago Press.

Deubner, L. 1932. *Attische Feste*. Berlin: H. Keller.

Dickins, G. 1906–7. The hieron of Athena Chalkioikos. History and nature of the sanctuary. *ABSA* 13:137–54.

Diehl, E. 1953. Pontarches. *RE* 22, cols. 1–18.

Dietrich, Bernard C. 1961. A rite of swinging during the Anthesteria. *Hermes* 89:36–50.

——1962. Demeter, Erinys, Artemis. *Hermes* 90:129–48.

——1965. *Death, fate, and the gods; the development of a religious idea in Greek popular belief and in Homer*. [London]: University of London, Athlone Press.

——1986. *Tradition in Greek religion*. Berlin: W. de Gruyter.

——1996. The sanctuary of Apollo at Kourion. In *The Sanctuary of Apollo Hylates at Kourion*, ed. D. Buitron-Oliver and B. C. Dietrich. 17–38.

Di Filippo Balestrazz, Elena. 1984. l'Agyeus e la città. In *Religione e città nel mondo antico*, 90–108.

Dillon, Matthew. 1996. *Religion in the ancient world: New themes and approaches*. Amsterdam: A.M. Hakkert.

——2003. *Girls and women in classical Greek religion*. London: Routledge.

Dodd, David Brooks, and Christopher A. Faraone, eds. 2003. *Initiation in ancient Greek rituals and narratives: New critical perspectives*. London: Routledge.

Dodds, Eric R. 1951. *The Greeks and the irrational*. Berkeley: University of California Press.

Donohue, A. A., and Mark D. Fullerton. 2003. *Ancient art and its historiography*. Cambridge: Cambridge University Press.

Donohue, Alice. 1988. *Xoana and the origins of Greek sculpture*. APA American Classical Studies. Atlanta: Scholars Press.

——1997. Greek images of the gods: Considerations on terminology and methodology. *Hephaistos* 15:31–45.

Dougherty, Carol, and Leslie Kurke. 1998. *Cultural poetics in Archaic Greece: Cult, performance, politics*. Cambridge: Cambridge University Press.

——2003. *The cultures within ancient Greek culture: Contact, conflict, collaboration*. Cambridge: Cambridge University Press.

Douglas, Mary. 1994 [1966]. *Purity and danger: An analysis of the concepts of pollution and taboo*. London: Routledge.

Dow, Sterling, and Robert F. Healey. 1965. *A sacred calendar of Eleusis*. Cambridge MA: Harvard University Press.

Dowden, Ken. 1989. *Death and the maiden: Girls' initiation rites in Greek mythology*. London: Routledge.

——1992. *The uses of Greek mythology*. London: Routledge.

——2006. *Zeus*. London: Routledge.

Drees, Ludwig. 1968. *Olympia: Gods, artists and athletes*. New York: Frederick A. Praeger.

Ducat, Jean. 1971. *Les Kouroi du Ptoion, le sanctuaire d'Apollon Ptoieus à l'époque archaïque*. Paris: E. de Boccard.

Dyer, R. R. 1969. The evidence for Apolline purification ritual at Delphi and Athens. *JHS* 89:38–56.

Dyggve, E., and Frederik Poulsen. 1948. *Das Laphrion, der Tempelbezirk von Kalydon*. Copenhagen: E. Munksgaard.

Easterling, P. E., and J. V. Muir, eds. 1985. *Greek religion and society*. Cambridge: Cambridge University Press.

Edelstein, Emma Jeannette Levy, and Ludwig Edelstein. 1975. *Asclepius: A collection and interpretation of the testimonies*. 2 Vols. New York: Arno Press.

Edmonds, Radcliffe. 1999. Tearing apart the Zagreus myth: A few disparaging remarks on Orphism and original sin. *ClAnt* 18.1.35–73.

Edmunds, Lowell. 1981. The cults and the legend of Oedipus. *HSCP* 85:221–38.

Edwards, Charles M. 1984. Aphrodite on a ladder. *Hesperia* 53 (1):59–72.

Ekroth, Gunnel. 2000. Offerings of blood in Greek hero-cults. In *Héros et héroïnes dans les mythes et les cultes grecs*, ed. V. Pirenne-Delforge and E. Suárez de la Torre, 263–80.

——2002. *The sacrificial rituals of Greek hero-cults in the Archaic to the early Hellenistic periods*. Liège: Centre international d'étude de la religion grecque antique.

Elderkin, G. W. 1941. The cults of the Erechtheion. *Hesperia* 10 (2):113–24.

Ellinger, Pierre. 1987. Hyampolis et le sanctuaire d'Artemis Elaphébolos dans l'histoire, la légende et l'espace de la Phocide. *AA*:88–99.

——1993. *La légende nationale phocidienne: Artémis, les situations extrêmes et les récits de guerre d'anéantissement*. Athens and Paris: École française d'Athènes; distributed by E. de Boccard.

Enciclopedia dell'arte antica, classica e orientale [EAA] 1958–. 7 Vols. Rome: Istituto della Enciclopedia italiana.

Evjen, Harold D., ed. 1984. *Mnemai: Classical studies in memory of Karl K. Hulley*. Chico CA: Scholars Press.

Fabre, Georges, ed. 1990. *La montagne dans l'antiquité*. Pau: Université de Pau et des Pays de l'Adour.

Faraone, Christopher A. 1987. Hephaestus the magician and the Near Eastern parallels for the gold and silver dogs of Alcinous (Od. 7.91–94). *GRBS* 28:257–80.

——1992. *Talismans and Trojan horses: Guardian statues in ancient Greek myth and ritual*. Oxford: Oxford University Press.

——2003. Playing the bear and the fawn for Artemis: female initiation or substitute sacrifice? In *Initiation in ancient Greek rituals and narratives*, ed. D. B. Dodd and C. A. Faraone, 43–68.

Faraone, Christopher A., and Laura K. McClure, eds. 2006. *Prostitutes and courtesans in the ancient world*. Madison: University of Wisconsin Press.

Faraone, Christopher A., and Dirk Obbink, eds. 1991. *Magika hiera: Ancient Greek magic and religion*. New York: Oxford University Press.

Farnell, Lewis Richard. 1896–. *The cults of the Greek states*. 5 Vols. Oxford: Clarendon Press.

——1916. Ino-Leukothea. *JHS* 36:36–44.

——1921. *Greek hero cults and ideas of immortality. The Gifford lectures delivered in the University of St. Andrews in the year 1920*. Oxford: Clarendon Press.

Fauré, Paul. 1964. *Fonctions des cavernes crétoises*. Paris: E. de Boccard.

Faustoferri, Amalia. 1996. *Il trono di Amyklai e Sparta: Bathykles al servizio del potere*. Napoli: Edizioni scientifiche italiane.

Felsch, Rainer C. S. 1981. Mykenischer Kult im Heiligtum bei Kalapodi? In *Sanctuaries and cults in the Aegean Bronze Age*, ed. R. Hägg and N. Marinatos, 81–89.

——1996. *Kalapodi: Ergebnisse der Ausgrabungen im Heiligtum der Artemis und des Apollon von Hyampolis in der antiken Phokis*. Mainz: P. von Zabern.

Felsch, Rainer C. S., H. J. Kienast, and H. Schuler. 1980. Apollon und Artemis oder Artemis und Apollon? Bericht von den Grabungen im neu entdeckten Heiligtum bei Kalapodi, 1973–77. *AA*:38–123.

Ferguson, John. 1989. *Among the gods: An archaeological exploration of ancient Greek religion*. London: Routledge.

Ferguson, William S. 1938. The Salaminioi of Heptaphylai and Sounion. *Hesperia* 7 (1):1–74.

—— 1944. The Attic Orgeones. *HThR* 37:61–140.

Ferrante, D., ed. 1957. *Proclo Crestomazia*. Naples: Armanni.

Ferrari, Gloria. 2002a. The ancient temple on the Acropolis at Athens. *AJA* 106:11–35.

—— 2002b. *Figures of speech: Men and maidens in ancient Greece*. Chicago IL: University of Chicago Press.

Figueira, Thomas J. 1986 [1981]. *Aegina, society and politics*. Reprint. Salem NH: Ayer Company.

—— 1991. *Athens and Aigina in the age of imperial colonization*. Baltimore MD: Johns Hopkins University Press.

—— 1993. *Excursions in epichoric history: Aiginetan essays*. Lanham MD: Rowman & Littlefield.

Finkelberg, Margalit. 2005. *Greeks and pre-Greeks: Aegean history and Greek heroic tradition*. Cambridge: Cambridge University Press.

Fisher, Nick, and Hans van Wees, eds. 1998. *Archaic Greece: New approaches and new evidence*. London, Swansea and Oakville CT: Duckworth and the Classical Press of Wales; distributed by David Brown.

Fleischer, Robert. 1973. *Artemis von Ephesos und verwandte Kultstatuen aus Anatolien und Syrien*. Leiden: E. J. Brill.

—— 1983. Neues zu kleinasiatischen Kultstatuen. *AA* 98:81–93.

Flemberg, Johan. 1991. *Venus armata: Studien zur bewaffneten Aphrodite in der griechisch-römischen Kunst*. Stockholm and Göteborg: Swedish Institute at Athens; distributed by P. Åström.

—— 1995. The transformations of the armed Aphrodite. In *Greece and Gender*, ed. B. Berggreen and N. Marinatos.

Flensted-Jensen, Pernille, Thomas Heine Nielsen, and Lene Rubinstein, eds. 2000. *Polis & politics: Studies in Ancient Greek history presented to Mogens Herman Hansen on his sixtieth birthday, August 20, 2000*. Copenhagen: Museum Tusculanum Press University of Copenhagen.

Foley, Helene P. 1994. *The Homeric Hymn to Demeter: Translation, commentary, and interpretive essays*. Princeton NJ: Princeton University Press.

Fontenrose, Joseph Eddy. 1959. *Python; a study of Delphic myth and its origins*. Berkeley: University of California Press.

—— 1968. The hero as athlete. *California Studies in Classical Antiquity* 1:73–104.

—— 1978. *The Delphic oracle, its responses and operations, with a catalogue of responses*. Berkeley: University of California Press.

—— 1988a. The cult of Apollo and the games at Delphi. In *The Archaeology of the Olympics*, ed. W. J. Raschke, 121–40. Madison: University of Wisconsin Press.

—— 1988b. *Didyma: Apollo's oracle, cult, and companions*. Berkeley: University of California Press.

Fossey, John M. 1987. The cults of Artemis in Argolis. *Euphrosyne* 15:71–88.

Fossey, John M., and Albert Schachter, eds. 1979. *Proceedings of the Second International Conference on Boiotian Antiquities = Actes du deuxième Congres international sur la Béotie antique (McGill University, Montréal, 2–4.11.1973)*. Montreal: Dept. of Classics. McGill University.

Fossey, John M. and Philit J. Smith, eds. 1995. *Boeotia antiqua V: Studies in Boiotian topography, cults and terracottas*. Amsterdam: J. C. Gieben.

Foucart, Paul F. 1975 [1873]. *Des associations religieuses chez les Grecs, thiases, éranes, orgéons*. Reprint. New York: Arno Press.

Fowler, Robert L. 2000. Greek magic, Greek religion? In *Oxford readings in Greek religion*, ed. R. G. A. Buxton, 317–43.

Francis, E. D., and Michael Vickers. 1984. Green goddess: A gift to Lindos from Amasis of Egypt. *AJA* 88 (1):68–69.

Fraser, P. M., and George Ewart Bean. 1954. *The Rhodian Peraea and islands*. London: Oxford University Press.

Frazer, James George, ed. 1921. *Apollodorus: The library*. 2 Vols. Cambridge MA: Harvard University Press.

Fridh-Haneson. 1988. Hera's wedding on Samos: A change of paradigms. In *Early Greek cult practice*, ed. R. Hägg, *et al.*, 205–13.

Friedrich, Paul. 1978. *The meaning of Aphrodite*. Chicago IL: University of Chicago Press.

Friendly, A., and E. Karapanayiotis. 1973. Nemesis. *Expedition* 15 (1):10–14.

Froning, Heide, Tonio Hölscher, and Harald Mielsch. 1992. *Kotinos: Festschrift für Erika Simon*. Mainz/Rhein: P. von Zabern.

Frontisi-Ducroux, Françoise. 1991. *Le dieu-masque: une figure du Dionysos d'Athènes*. Paris and Rome: Éditions La découverte; École française de Rome.

Fulco, William J. 1976. *The Canaanite God Resep*. New Haven CT: American Oriental Society.

Furley, William D., and Jan Maarten Bremer. 2001. *Greek hymns: Selected cult songs from the Archaic to the Hellenistic period*. 2 Vols. Tübingen: Mohr Siebeck.

Gadolou, A. 2002. The formation of the sacred landscapes of the Eastern Argolid, 900–700 BC. A religious, social and political survey. In *Peloponnesian sanctuaries and cults*, ed. R. Hägg, 37–43.

Gager, John G. 1992. *Curse tablets and binding spells from the ancient world*. New York: Oxford University Press.

Gallet de Santerre, Hubert. 1958. *Délos primitive et archaïque*. Paris: E. de Boccard.

——1975. Notes Déliennes. *BCH* 99:247–65.

Gantz, Timothy. 1993. *Early Greek myth: A guide to literary and artistic sources*. Baltimore MD: Johns Hopkins University Press.

Garland, Robert. 1987. *The Piraeus: From the fifth to the first century BC*. London: Duckworth.

——1992. *Introducing new gods: The politics of Athenian religion*. London: Duckworth.

Gartziou-Tatti, A. 1990. L'oracle de Dodone, mythe et rituel. *Kernos* 3:175–84.

Geagan, H. A. 1970. Mythological themes on the plaques from Penteskouphia. *AA*:31–48.

Gebhard, Elizabeth R. 1993. The evolution of a pan-Hellenic sanctuary: from archaeology towards history at Isthmia. In *Greek Sanctuaries*, ed. N. Marinatos and R. Hägg, 154–77.

—— 1998. Small dedications in the Archaic temple of Poseidon at Isthmia. In *Ancient Greek cult practice from the archaeological evidence*, ed. R. Hägg, 91–115.

—— 2002a. The beginnings of Panhellenic games at the Isthmus. In *Olympia 1875–2000*, ed. H. Kyrieleis, 221–37.

—— 2002b. Caves and cults at the Isthmian sanctuary of Poseidon. In *Peloponnesian sanctuaries and cults*, ed. R. Hägg, 63–74.

Gebhard, Elizabeth R., and Matthew W. Dickie. 1999. Melikertes-Palaimon, Hero of the Isthmian Games. In *Ancient Greek Hero Cult*, ed. R. Hägg, 159–65.

Geerard, Maurice, Jan Desmet, and Roel van der Plaetse. 1990. *Opes Atticae: Miscellanea philologica et historica Raymondo Bogaert et Hermanno van Looy oblata*. Steenbrugge and The Hague: Uitgave van de Sint-Pietersabdij; M. Nijhoff.

Gentili, Bruno, and Franca Perusino, eds. 2002. *Le orse di Brauron: un rituale di iniziazione femminile nel santuario di Artemide*. Pisa: ETS.

Georgoudi, S. 1998. Héraclès dans les pratiques sacrificielles des cités. In *Le bestiaire d'Héraclès*, ed. C. Bonnet, C. Jourdain-Annequin, and V. Pirenne-Delforge, 301–17.

Georgoulaki, E. 1994. Le type iconographique de la statue cultuelle d'Apollon Amyklaios: Un emprunt oriental? *Kernos* 7:95–118.

Gérard-Rousseau, Monique. 1968. *Les mentions religieuses dans les tablettes mycéniennes*. Rome: Edizioni dell'Ateneo.

Gernet, Louis. 1981. *The anthropology of ancient Greece*. Tr. John Hamilton and Blaise Nagy. Baltimore MD: Johns Hopkins University Press.

Giangiulio, M. 1993. La dedica ad Eracle di Nicomaco (*IG*. XIV 652). Un'iscrizione arcaica di Lucania ed i rapporti fra greci ed indigeni nell'entroterra di metaponto. In *Ercole in occidente*, ed. A. Mastrocinque, 29–52.

Gigon, A. A., ed. 1946. *Phyllobolia für Peter von der Mühll*. Basel: B. Schwabe.

Gill, David. 1991. *Greek cult tables*. New York: Garland.

Girard, René. 1977. *Violence and the sacred*. Tr. Patrick Gregory. Baltimore MD: Johns Hopkins University Press.

Golden, Mark, and Peter Toohey, eds. 1997. *Inventing ancient culture: Historicism, periodization and the ancient world*. London: Routledge.

Goldhill, Simon. 1987. The Great Dionysia and civic ideology. *JHS* 107:58–76.

Goldman, H. 1942. The origin of the Greek herm. *AJA* 46 (1):58–68.

Goodison, Lucy, and Christine Morris, eds. 1998. *Ancient goddesses: The myths and the evidence*. London: British Museum Press.

Gordon, R. L., ed. 1981. *Myth, religion, and society: Structuralist essays*. Cambridge: Cambridge University Press.

Gorman, Vanessa B. 2001. *Miletos, the ornament of Ionia: A history of the city to 400 BCE*. Ann Arbor: University of Michigan Press.

Gorman, Vanessa B., and Eric W. Robinson, eds. 2002. *Oikistes: Studies in constitutions, colonies, and military power in the ancient world, offered in honor of A.J. Graham. Mnemosyne* Supplement 234. Leiden: E. J. Brill.

Gould, John. 1973. Hiketeia. *JHS* 93:74–103.

—— 2001a. Dionysus and the hippy convoy: Ritual, myth and metaphor in the cult of Dionysus. In J. Gould, *Myth, ritual, memory and exchange*, 269–82.

—— 2001b. *Myth, ritual, memory, and exchange: Essays in Greek literature and culture*. Oxford: Oxford University Press.

Graf, Fritz. 1974. Zum opferkalender des Nikomachos. *ZPE* 14:139–44.

——1979a. Apollon Delphinios. *MH* 36:2–22.

——1979b. Das Götterbild aus dem Taurerland. *AW* 10 (4):33–41.

——1984. Women, war and warlike divinities. *ZPE* 55:245–54.

——1985. *Nordionische Kulte: religionsgeschichtliche und epigraphische Untersuchungen zu den Kulten von Chios, Erythrai, Klazomenai und Phokaia*. Rome: Schweizerisches Institut in Rom.

——1991a. Prayer in magic and religious ritual. In *Magika hiera*, ed. C. A. Faraone and D. Obbink, 188–97.

——1991b. Textes orphiques et ritual bacchique. À propos des lamelles de Pélinna. In *Orphisme et Orphée*, ed. P. Borgeaud, 87–102.

——1993. Dionysian and Orphic eschatology: New texts and old questions. In *Masks of Dionysus*, edited by T. H. Carpenter and C. A. Faraone, 239–58.

——1996. Pompai in Greece. Some considerations about space and ritual in the Greek polis. In *The role of religion in the early Greek polis*, ed. R. Hägg, 55–65.

——2000. The Locrian maidens. In *Oxford readings in Greek religion*, ed. R. G. A. Buxton, 250–70.

Grant, Michael, and Rachel Kitzinger, eds. 1988. *Civilization of the ancient Mediterranean: Greece and Rome*. New York: Scribner's.

Greaves, Alan M. 2002. *Miletos: A history*. New York: Routledge.

Greco, G. 1997. Des étoffes pour Héra. In *Héra*, ed. J. de La Genière, 185–99.

Grégoire, Henri. 1949. *Asklépios, Apollon Smintheus et Rudra; études sur le dieu à la taupe et le dieu au rat dans la Grèce et dans l'Inde*. [Brussels]: Palais des académies.

Griffith, Mark, and Donald J. Mastronarde, eds. 1990. *Cabinet of the muses: Essays on classical and comparative literature in honor of Thomas G. Rosenmeyer*. Atlanta, GA: Scholars Press.

Gruben, Gottfried. 1986. *Die Tempel der Griechen*. Munich: Hirmer.

Guarducci, Margherita. 1935. Diktynna. *SMSR*:187–203.

——1984. Le insegne dei Dioscuri. *ArchClass* 36:133–54.

Gubel, E., and Edward Lipinski, eds. 1985. *Phoenicia and its neighbours*. Leuven: Peeters.

Habicht, Christian. 1985. *Pausanias' Guide to ancient Greece*. Berkeley: University of California Press.

Hadzisteliou Price, Theodora. 1978. *Kourotrophos: Cults and representations of the Greek nursing deities*. Leiden: E. J. Brill.

Hägg, Robin. 1987. Gifts to the heroes in Geometric and archaic Greece. In *Gifts to the gods*, ed. T. Linders and G. Nordquist, 93–99.

——1998. Osteology and Greek sacrificial practice. In *Ancient Greek cult practice from the archaeological evidence*, ed. R. Hägg, 49–56.

Hägg, Robin, ed. 1983. *The Greek renaissance of the eighth century* BC: *Tradition and innovation*. Stockholm: Swedish Institute at Athens; distributed by P. Åström.

——ed. 1992. *The iconography of Greek cult in the Archaic and Classical periods*. Athens: Centre d'étude de la religion grecque antique.

——ed. 1994. *Ancient Greek cult practice from the epigraphical evidence*. Stockholm: Swedish Institute at Athens; distributed by P. Åström.

——ed. 1996. *The role of religion in the early Greek polis*. Stockholm and Göteborg: Swedish Institute at Athens; distributed by P. Åström.

——ed. 1998. *Ancient Greek cult practice from the archaeological evidence*. Stockholm and Göteborg: Swedish Institute at Athens; distributed by P. Åström.

——ed. 1999. *Ancient Greek hero cult*. Stockholm: Swedish Institute at Athens; distributed by P. Åström.

——ed. 2002. *Peloponnesian sanctuaries and cults*. Stockholm and Göteborg: Swedish Institute at Athens; distributed by P. Åström.

Hägg, Robin, and Brita Alroth, eds. 2005. *Greek sacrificial ritual, Olympian and chthonian*. Sävedalen, Sweden: Swedish institute at Athens; distributed by P. Åström.

Hägg, Robin, and Nanno Marinatos, eds. 1981. *Sanctuaries and cults in the Aegean Bronze Age*. Stockholm and Lund: Swedish Institute at Athens; distributed by P. Åström.

Hägg, Robin, and Gullög Nordquist, eds. 1990. *Celebrations of death and divinity in the Bronze Age Argolid*. Stockholm: Swedish Institute at Athens; distributed by P. Åström.

Hägg, Robin, Nanno Marinatos, and Gullög Nordquist, eds. 1988. *Early Greek cult practice*. Stockholm and Göteborg: Swedish Institute at Athens; distributed by P. Åström.

Hall, Jonathan M. 1995. How Argive was the "Argive" Heraion? The political and cultic geography of the Argive plain, 900–400 BC. *AJA* 99:577–613.

——1997. *Ethnic identity in Greek antiquity*. Cambridge: Cambridge University Press.

——1999. Beyond the polis: The multilocality of heroes. In *Ancient Greek hero cult*, ed. R. Hägg, 49–56.

——2002a. *Hellenicity: Between ethnicity and culture*. Chicago IL: University of Chicago Press.

——2002b. Heroes, Hera and Herakleidai in the Argive plain. In *Peloponnesian sanctuaries and cults*, ed. R. Hägg, 93–8.

Halliday, W. R., ed. 1975 [1928]. *The Greek questions of Plutarch with a new translation & commentary*. Reprint. New York: Arno Press.

Ham, Greta L. 1999. The Choes and Anthesteria reconsidered: Male maturation rites and the Peloponnesian wars. In *Rites of passage in ancient Greece*, ed. M. W. Padilla, 201–18.

Hamerton-Kelly, Robert, ed. 1987. *Violent origins: Walter Burkert, René Girard & Jonathan Z. Smith on ritual killing and cultural formation*. Stanford CA: Stanford University Press.

Hamilton, Richard. 1992. *Choes and anthesteria: Athenian iconography and ritual*. Ann Arbor: University of Michigan Press.

——2000. *Treasure map. A guide to the Delian inventories*. Ann Arbor: University of Michigan Press.

Hammond, N. G. L. 1998. The Branchidae at Didyma and in Sogdiana. *CQ* 48 (2):339–44.

Hannah, Robert. 2005. *Greek and Roman calendars: Constructions of time in the Classical world*. London: Duckworth.

Harris, Diane. 1995. *The Treasures of the Parthenon and Erechtheion*. Oxford and New York: Clarendon Press; Oxford University Press.

Harrison, Evelyn B. 1977a. Alkamenes' sculptures for the Hephaisteion: Part I, the cult statues. *AJA* 81 (2):137–78.

——1977b. Alkamenes' sculptures for the Hephaisteion: Part III, iconography and style. *AJA* 81 (4):411–26.

——1996. The web of history: A conservative reading of the Parthenon frieze. In *Worshipping Athena*, ed. J. Neils, 198–214.

Hatzopoulos, Miltiade B. 1994. *Cultes et rites de passage en Macédoine*. Athens: Centre de recherches de l'antiquité grecque et romaine; De Boccard.

Hedreen, Guy Michael. 1991. The cult of Achilles in the Euxine. *Hesperia* 60.313–30.

——1992. *Silens in Attic black-figure vase-painting: Myth and performance*. Ann Arbor: University of Michigan Press.

Hedrick, C. W., Jr. 1988. The temple and cult of Apollo Patroos in Athens. *AJA* 92:185–210.

——1991. Phratry shrines of Attica and Athens. *Hesperia* 60:241–68.

Hellström, Pontus, and Brita Alroth. eds. 1996. *Religion and power in the ancient Greek world*. Uppsala and Stockholm: Ubsaliensis S. Academiae; Almqvist & Wiksell.

Hemberg, Bengt. 1950. *Die Kabiren*. Uppsala: Almquist & Wiksell.

Henrichs, Albert. 1976. Despoina Kybele: Ein Beitrag zur religiösen Namenkunde. *HSCP* 80:253–86.

——1978. Greek maenadism from Olympias to Messalina. *HSCP* 82:121–60.

——1983a. Changing Dionysiac identities. In *Jewish and Christian self-definition, Volume 3*, ed. B. F. Meyer, 137–60.

——1983b. The "sobriety" of Oedipus: Sophocles OC 100 misunderstood. *HSPh* 87:87–100.

——1984. Male intruders among the maenads: The so-called male celebrant. In *Mnemai*, ed. H. D. Evjen, 69–91.

——1990. Between country and city: Cultic dimensions of Dionysus in Athens and Attica. In *Cabinet of the Muses*, ed. M. Griffith and D. J. Mastronarde, 257–77.

——1993. "He has a god in him": Human and divine in the modern perception of Dionysus. In *Masks of Dionysus*, ed. T. H. Carpenter and C. A. Faraone, 13–43.

——1994. Anonymity and polarity: Unknown gods and nameless altars at the Areopagos. *ICS* 19:27–58.

Henshaw, Richard A. 1994. *Female and male: the cultic personnel. The Bible and the rest of the ancient Near East*. Allison Park PA: Pickwick Pub.

Herington, C. J. 1955. *Athena Parthenos and Athena Polias: A study in the religion of Periclean Athens*. [Manchester]: Manchester University Press.

——1963. Athena in Athenian literature and cult. *G&R* 10 Supplement:61–73.

Hermary, A. 1978. Images de l'apothéose des Dioscures. *BCH* 102:51–76.

——2000. De la mère des dieux à Cybèle et Artémis: Les ambiguïtés de l'iconographie grecque archaïque. In *Agathos daimôn*, ed. P. Linant de Bellefonds, 193–203.

Herrmann, Hans-Volkmar. 1972. *Olympia. Heiligtum und Wettampfstatte*. Munich: Hirmer Verlag.

Herrmann, Peter. 1971. Athena Polias in Milet. *Chiron* 1:291–98.

Herter, Hans. 1976. Hermes. Ursprung und Wesen eines griechischen Gottes. *RhM* 119:193–241.

Higbie, Carolyn. 2003. *The Lindian chronicle and the Greek creation of their past*. Oxford: Oxford University Press.

Hill, Bert Hodge, Lewey T. Lands, and Charles K. Williams. 1966. *The Temple of Zeus at Nemea*. Princeton NJ: American School of Classical Studies at Athens.

Hinz, Valentina. 1998. *Der Kult von Demeter und Kore auf Sizilien und in der Magna Graecia*. Wiesbaden: Dr. Ludwig Reichert Verlag.

Hoffelner, Klaus. 1999. *Das Apollon-Heiligtum: Tempel, Altare, Temenosmauer, Thearion*. Alt-Ägina Vol. I.3. Mainz: Philipp von Zabern.

Hoffelner, Klaus, and Michael Kerschner. 1996. *Die Sphinxsäule: Votivträger, Altäre, Steingeräte*. Alt-Ägina Vol. II.4. Mainz/Rhein: Philipp von Zabern.

Hoffner, Harry A. 1973. *Orient and Occident. Essays presented to Cyrus H. Gordon on the occasion of his sixty-fifth birthday*. Kevelaer: Butzon & Bercker.

Hollinshead, Mary B. 1980. Legend, cult and architecture at three sanctuaries of Artemis. Diss. Bryn Mawr College, Bryn Mawr PA.

——1985. Against Iphigeneia's adyton in three mainland temples. *AJA* 89:419–40.

——1999. "Adyton," "opisthodomos," and the inner room of a Greek temple. *Hesperia* 68 (2):189–218.

Holloway, R. Ross. 1991. *The archaeology of ancient Sicily*. London: Routledge.

Hommel, Hildebrecht. 1980. *Der Gott Achilleus*. Heidelberg: Winter.

Hopper, R. J. 1963. Athena and the early Acropolis. *G&R* 10 Supplement:1–16.

Hornblower, Simon. 2001. Epic and epiphanies: Herodotus and the "New Simonides". In *The new Simonides*, ed. D. D. Boedeker and D. Sider, 135–47.

Horstmanshoff, H. F. J., ed. 2002. *Kykeon: Studies in honour of H.S. Versnel*. Leiden: E. J. Brill.

Huber, Sandrine. 1998a. Une aire sacrificielle proche du sanctuaire d'Apollon Daphné-phoros à Érétrie. In *Ancient Greek cult practice from the archaeological evidence*, ed. R. Hägg, 141–55.

——1998b. Érétrie et la Méditerranée à la lumière des trouvailles provenant d'une aire sacrificielle au Nord du sanctuaire d'Apollon Daphnéphoros. In *Euboica*, ed. M. Bats and B. D'Agostino, 109–33.

Hübinger, Ulrich. 1992. On Pan's iconography and the cult in the 'Sanctuary of Pan' on the slopes of Mount Lykaion. In *The iconography of Greek cult in the Archaic and Classical periods*, ed. R. Hägg, 189–212.

Hughes, D. D. 1991. *Human sacrifice in ancient Greece*. London: Routledge.

Humphreys, S. C. 2004. *The strangeness of gods: Historical perspectives on the interpretation of Athenian religion*. Oxford: Oxford University Press.

Hurst, André. 1975. L'huile d'Aphrodite. In *Chypre des origines au moyen – âge*, ed. D. van Berchem, 92–95.

Hurwit, Jeffrey. 1995. Beautiful evil: Pandora and the Athena Parthenos. *AJA* 99:171–86.

——1999. *The Athenian Acropolis: History, mythology, and archaeology from the Neolithic era to the present*. Cambridge: Cambridge University Press.

Hutton, William. 2005. *Describing Greece: Landscape and literature in the Periegesis of Pausanias*. Cambridge: Cambridge University Press.

Huxley, George Leonard. 1967. Troy VIII and the Lokrian maidens. In *Ancient society and institutions*, ed. E. Badian, 147–64.

Isler, Hans Peter. 1970. *Acheloos. Eine Monographie*. Bern: Francke.

Jacobsthal, P. 1951. The date of the Ephesian foundation deposit. *JHS* 71:85–95, pl. 31–36.

Jacquemin, Anne. 2000. *Guerre et religion dans le monde grec (490–322 av. J. C.).* Paris: Sedes.

Jameson, Michael H. 1965. Notes on the sacred calendar from Erchia. *BCH* 89:159–72.

——1980. Apollo Lykeios in Athens. *Archaiognosia* 1:213–35.

——1982. The submerged sanctuary of Apollo at Halieis in the Argolid of Greece. *National Geographic Research Reports* 14:362–67.

——1988. Sacrifice and ritual: Greece. In *Civilization of the ancient Mediterranean,* ed. M. Grant and R. Kitzinger, 959–79.

——1990. Perseus, the hero of Mykenai. In *Celebrations of death and divinity in the Bronze Age Argolid,* ed. R. Hägg and G. Nordquist, 213–23.

——1993. The asexuality of Dionysus. In *Masks of Dionysus,* ed. T. H. Carpenter and C. A. Faraone, 44–64.

——1994. Theoxenia. In *Ancient Greek cult practice from the epigraphical evidence,* ed. R. Hägg, 35–57.

Jameson, Michael H., David R. Jordan, and Roy D. Kotansky. 1993. *A Lex Sacra from Selinous.* Durham NC: Duke University Press.

Jameson, Michael H., Curtis N. Runnels, and Tjeerd H. van Andel. 1994. *A Greek countryside: The southern Argolid from prehistory to the present day.* Stanford CT: Stanford University Press.

Janko, Richard. 1984. Forgetfulness in the golden tablets of Memory. *CQ* 34.89–100.

Jantzen, Ulf, ed. 1976. *Neue Forschungen in griechischen Heiligtümern.* Tübingen: Ernst Wasmuth.

Jeanmaire, Henri. 1975 [1939]. *Couroi et courètes. Essai sur l'éducation spartiate et sur les rites d'adolescence dans l'antiquité hellénique* Lille: Bibliothèque universitaire. Reprint. New York: Arno Press.

——1951. *Dionysos. Histoire du culte de Bacchus.* Paris: Payot.

Jeffery, L. H. 1961. *The local scripts of archaic Greece. A study of the origin of the Greek alphabet and its development from the eighth to the fifth centuries BC.* Oxford: Clarendon Press.

Jeppesen, K. 1979. Where was the so-called Erechtheion? *AJA* 83 (4):381–94.

——1983. Further inquiries on the location of the Erechtheion and its relationship to the Temple of the Polias 1. Prostomiaion and Prostomion. *AJA* 87 (3):325–33.

——1987. *The theory of the alternative Erechtheion: Premises, definition and implications.* Århus: Aarhus University Press.

Johnston, Patricia A. 1996. Cybele and her companions on the northern littoral of the Black Sea. In *Cybele, Attis and related cults,* ed. E. Lane, 101–16.

Johnston, Sarah Iles. 1990. *Hekate soteira: A study of Hekate's roles in the Chaldean oracles and related literature.* Atlanta GA: Scholars Press.

——1991. Crossroads. *ZPE* 88:217–24.

——1997. Corinthian Medea and the cult of Hera Akraia. In *Medea,* ed. J. J. Clauss and S. I. Johnston, 44–70.

——1999. *Restless dead: Encounters between the living and the dead in ancient Greece.* Berkeley: University of California Press.

Johnston, Sarah Iles, ed. 2004. *Religions of the ancient world: A guide.* Cambridge MA: Belknap Press.

Jones, Nicholas F. 1999. *The associations of Classical Athens: The response to democracy.* New York: Oxford University Press.

Jost, Madeleine. 1985. *Sanctuaires et cultes d'Arcadie.* Paris: J. Vrin.

——1990. La vie religieuse dans les montagnes d'Arcadie. In *La montagne dans l'antiquité,* ed. G. Fabre, 55–67.

——1992. Sanctuaires ruraux et sanctuaires urbains en Arcadie. In *Le Sanctuaire grec,* ed. A. Schachter and J. Bingen, 205–45.

——2002. À propos des sacrifices humains dans le sanctuaire de Zeus du mont Lycée. In *Peloponnesian sanctuaries and cults,* ed. R. Hägg, 183–86.

——2003. Mystery cults in Arcadia. In *Greek mysteries,* ed. M. B. Cosmopoulos, 143–68.

Jouan, F. 1989. Le dieu Arès. Figure rituelle et image littéraire. In *Ritualisme et vie intérieure,* ed. A. Caquot and P. Canivet, 125–40.

Jourdain-Annequin, Colette. 1986. Heracles Parastates. In *Les grandes figures religieuses,* 283–331.

——1989. *Héraclès aux portes du soir: mythe et histoire.* [Besançon] Paris: Université de Besançon; Les Belles Lettres.

——1992a. Héraclès en Occident. In *Héraclès,* ed. C. Bonnet and C. Jourdain-Annequin, 263–91.

——1992b. À propos d'un ritual pour Iolaos à Argyrion: Héraclès et l'initiation des jeunes gens. In *L'Initiation,* ed. A. Moreau, 121–41.

Jourdain-Annequin, Colette, and Corinne Bonnet, eds. 1996. *Héraclès, les femmes et le féminin.* Brussels and Turnhout: Institut historique belge de Rome; distributed by Brepols Publishers.

Kadletz, E. 1978. The cult of Apollo Deiradiotes. *TAPhA* 108:93–101.

Kaestner, D. W. 1976. The Coan festival of Zeus Polieus. *CJ* 71:344–8.

Kahil, L. 1965. Autour de l'Artémis attique. *AK* 8:20–33.

——1977. L'Artemis de Brauron: rites et mystère. *AK* 20:86–98.

——1983. Mythological repertoire of Brauron. In *Ancient Greek art and iconography,* ed. W. G. Moon, 231–44.

Karageorghis, Jacqueline. 1977. *La grande déesse de Chypre et son culte à travers l'iconographie de l'époque néolithique au VIème s.a.C.* Lyon and Paris: Maison de l'Orient; distributed by E. de Boccard.

Karageorghis, Vassos. 1969. *The ancient civilization of Cyprus.* New York: Cowles Education Corp.

——1976. *Kition: Mycenaean and Phoenician discoveries in Cyprus.* London: Thames and Hudson.

——1982. *Cyprus: from the stone age to the Romans.* London: Thames and Hudson.

Kardulias, D. R. 2001. Odysseus in Ino's veil: Feminine headdress and the hero in Odyssey 5. *TAPhA* 131:23–51.

Kearns, Emily. 1989. *The heroes of Attica. BICS* Supplement 57. London: University of London Institute of Classical Studies.

Keesling, Catherine. 2003. *The votive statues of the Athenian Acropolis.* Cambridge: Cambridge University Press.

Kelly, Thomas. 1966. The Calaurian amphictiony. *AJA* 70 (2):113–21.

Kerényi, Karl. 1959. *Asklepios; archetypal image of the physician's existence.* Tr. Ralph Manheim. [New York]: Pantheon Books.

Kilian, I. 1978. Weihungen an Eileithyia und Artemis Orthia. *ZPE* 31:219–22.

King, Helen. 1983. Bound to bleed: Artemis and Greek women. In *Images of women in antiquity*, ed. A. Cameron and A. Kuhrt, 109–27.

Kinzl, Konrad, ed. 1977. *Greece and the eastern Mediterranean in ancient history and prehistory: Studies presented to Fritz Schachermeyr on the occasion of his eightieth birthday*. Berlin: W. de Gruyter.

Knigge, U. 1982. Ho astēr tēs Aphroditēs. *MDAI(A)* 97:153–70.

Kokolakis, M. 1995. Zeus' tomb: An object of pride and reproach. *Kernos* 8:123–38.

Konsolaki, E. 2002. A Mycenaean sanctuary at Methana. In *Peloponnesian sanctuaries and cults*, ed. R. Hägg, 25–36.

Kossatz-Deismann, A. 1988. Hera. *LIMC* IV.1.659–719.

Kraus, Theodor. 1960. *Hekate; Studien zu Wesen und Bild der Göttin in Kleinasien und Griechenland*. Heidelberg: C. Winter.

Kroll, John H. 1982. The ancient image of Athena Polias. In *Studies in Athenian architecture, sculpture and topography presented to Homer A. Thompson. Hesperia* Supplement 20. 65–76.

Kron, Uta. 1988. Kultmahle im Heraion von Samos archaischer Zeit. In *Early Greek cult practice*, ed. R. Hägg, *et al.*, 135–47.

——1992. Frauenfeste in Demeterheiligtümern. Das Thesmophorion von Bitalemi: eine archäologische Fallstudie. *AA*:611–50.

Kyrieleis, Helmut. 1980. Archaische Holzfunde aus Samos. *MDAI(A)* 95:87–147.

——1988. Offerings of the common man in the Heraion at Samos. In *Early Greek cult practice*, ed. R. Hägg, *et al.*, 215–21.

——1990. Neue Ausgrabungen in Olympia. *AntW* 21:177–88.

——1993. The Heraion at Samos. In *Greek sanctuaries*, ed. N. Marinatos and R. Hägg, 125–53.

——2003. The German excavations at Olympia: An introduction. In *Sport and festival in the ancient Greek world*, ed. D. J. Phillips and D. Pritchard, 41–60.

Kyrieleis, Helmut, ed. 2002. *Olympia 1875–2000: 125 Jahre deutsche Ausgrabungen*. Mainz am Rhein: Philipp von Zabern.

Lacore, M. 1983. Euripide et la culte de Poseidon-Erechtheé. *REA* 85:215–34.

Laffineur, Robert, and Robin Hägg, eds. 2001. *Potnia: Deities and religion in the Aegean Bronze Age*. Liège and Austin: Université de Liège; University of Texas at Austin.

Lalonde, Gerald V. 2006. *Horos Dios: An Athenian shrine and cult of Zeus*. Leiden: E. J. Brill.

Lambert, S. D. 1993. *The phratries of Attica*. Ann Arbor: University of Michigan Press.

Lambert, W. G. 1960. *Babylonian wisdom literature*. Oxford: Clarendon Press.

Lambrinoudakis, Vassilis. 1981. Remains of the Mycenaean period in the sanctuary of Apollon Maleatas. In *Sanctuaries and cults in the Aegean Bronze Age*, ed. R. Hägg and N. Marinatos, 59–65.

——1988. Veneration of ancestors in Geometric Naxos. In *Early Greek cult practice*, ed. R. Hägg, *et al.*, 235–45.

——2002. Conservation and research: new evidence on a long-living cult. The Sanctuary of Apollo Maleatas and Asklepios at Epidauros. In *Excavating classical culture*, ed. M. Stamatopoulou and M. Yeroulanou, 213–24.

Lane, Eugene, ed. 1996. *Cybele, Attis and related cults: Essays in memory of M. J. Vermaseren*. Leiden: E. J. Brill.

Langdon, Merle K. 1976. *A sanctuary of Zeus on Mount Hymettos*. Princeton NJ: American School of Classical Studies at Athens.

Langdon, Susan Helen. 1987. Gift exchange in the Geometric sanctuaries. In *Gifts to the Gods*, ed. T. Linders and G. Nordquist, 107–13.

——ed. 1997. *New light on a dark age: Exploring the culture of geometric Greece*. Columbia MO: University of Missouri Press.

Lapatin, Kenneth D. S. 1992. A family gathering at Rhamnous? Who's who on the Nemesis base. *Hesperia* 61 (1):107–19.

——2001. *Chryselephantine statuary in the ancient Mediterranean world*. Oxford: Oxford University Press.

Larson, Jennifer. 1995a. The Corycian nymphs and the Homeric Hymn to Hermes. *GRBS* 86:341–57.

——1995b. *Greek heroine cults*. Madison: University of Wisconsin Press.

——1997. Handmaidens of Artemis? *CJ* 92 (3):249–58.

——2001. *Greek nymphs: Myth, cult, lore*. Oxford: Oxford University Press.

Laumonier, Alfred. 1958. *Les cultes indigènes en Carie*. Paris: E. de Boccard.

Launey, Marcel. 1937. Le verge d'Héraklès à Thasos. *BCH* 61:380–409.

——1944. *Le sanctuaire et le culte d'Héraklès à Thasos*. Paris: E. de Boccard.

Laurens, Annie France, ed. 1989. *Entre hommes et dieux: le convive, le héros, le prophète*. Besançon and Paris: Université de Besançon; distributed by Les Belles Lettres.

Lebessi, A. 1976. A sanctuary of Hermes and Aphrodite in Crete. *Expedition* 18 (3):1–13.

——1991. Flagellation ou autoflagellation: données iconographiques pour une tentative d'interprétation. *BCH* 115:99–123.

Lebessi, A., and P. Muhly. 1987. The sanctuary of Hermes and Aphrodite at Syme, Crete. *National Geographic Research Reports* 3:102–12.

Lebessi, A., and Wolfgang Schürmann. 1985. *To hiero tou Hermē kai tēs Aphroditēs stē Symē Viannou*. 2 Vols. Athens: Hē en Athēnais Archaiologikē Hetaireia.

Le Dinahet, M. T. 1984. Sanctuaires chthoniens de Sicile de l'époque archaïque à l'époque classique. In *Temples et sanctuaires*, ed. G. Roux, 137–52.

Lehmann, Karl. 1959. A bronze pail of Athena Alalkomenia. *Hesperia* 28:153–61.

——1975. *Samothrace: A guide to the excavations and the museum*. Fourth edition. Locust Valley NY: J. J. Augustin.

Lehmann, Karl, and Phyllis Williams Lehmann. 1959–. *Samothrace: Excavations conducted by the Institute of Fine Arts of New York University*. 11 Vols. New York: Pantheon Books.

Leitao, David. 1995. The perils of Leukippos: Initiatory transvestism and male gender ideology in the Ekdysia. *ClAnt* 14 (1):130–63.

——2002. The legend of the Sacred Band. In *The sleep of reason*, ed. M. Nussbaum and J. Sihvola, 143–69.

——2003. Adolescent hair-growing and hair-cutting rituals in ancient Greece: A sociological approach. In *Initiation in ancient Greek rituals and narratives*, ed. D. B. Dodd and C. A. Faraone, 109–29.

Les grandes figures religieuses, fonctionnement pratique et symbolique dans l'antiquité: Besançon 25–26 avril 1984. 1986. Paris: Les Belles Lettres.

Lévêque, Pierre, and A. Verbanck-Piérard. 1992. Héraclès héros ou dieu? In *Héraclès: d'une rive à l'autre de la Méditerranée*, ed. C. Bonnet and C. Jourdain-Annequin. 43–65.

Levi, D. 1966. Il Cabirio di Lemno. In *Charistērion eis Anastasion K. Orlandon*, 3.110–32.

Lewis, David M., Robin Osborne, and Simon Hornblower, eds. 1994. *Ritual, finance, politics: Athenian democratic accounts presented to David Lewis*. Oxford and New York: Clarendon Press; Oxford University Press.

Lexicon iconographicum mythologiae classicae (LIMC). 1981–. Zurich: Artemis.

LiDonnici, Lynn R. 1992a. Compositional background of the Epidaurian Iamata. *AJPh* 113 (1):25–41.

——1992b. The images of Artemis Ephesia and Greco-Roman worship: A reconsideration. *HThR* 85 (4):389–415.

——1995. *The Epidaurian miracle inscriptions*. Atlanta GA: Scholars Press.

——1999. The Megabyzos priesthood and religious diplomacy at the end of the Classical period. *Religion* 29(3):201–14.

Limet, Henri, and J. Ries, eds. 1983. *Le mythe, son langage et son message: actes du colloque de Liège et Louvain-la-Neuve, 1981*. Louvain-la-Neuve: Centre d'Histoire des Religions.

Linant de Bellefonds, P., ed. 2000. *Agathos daimôn. Mythes et cultes: Études d'iconographie en l'honneur de Lilly Kahil*. BCH Supplément 38. Paris: E. De Boccard; École française d'Athènes.

Linders, Tullia. 1972. *Studies in the treasure records of Artemis Brauronia found in Athens*. Lund: P. Åström.

——1975. *The treasurers of the other gods in Athens and their functions*. Meisenheim am Glan: Hain.

Linders, Tullia, and Gullög Nordquist, eds. 1987. *Gifts to the Gods: Proceedings of the Uppsala symposium 1985*. Uppsala: Almquist & Wiksell.

Lippolis, E. 1988–89. Il santuario di Athana a Lindo. *ASAA* 66–67.97–157.

Lissi Caronna, E., C. Sabbione, and L. V. Borelli. 1996–. *I Pinakes di Lokri Epizefiri*. Rome: Società Magna Grecia.

Lloyd, Alan B., ed. 1997. *What is a god? Studies in the nature of Greek divinity*. London: Duckworth; Classical Press of Wales.

Lloyd-Jones, Hugh. 1983. *The justice of Zeus*. Second edition. Berkeley: University of California Press.

——1990. Erinyes, Semnai Theai, Eumenides. In *Owls to Athens*. ed. E. M. Craik, 203–11.

——1990. *Greek comedy, Hellenistic literature, Greek religion, and miscellanea: The academic papers of Sir Hugh Lloyd-Jones*. Oxford: Clarendon Press; Oxford University Press.

Longo, Oddone. 1986. Dionysos à Thebes. In *Les grandes figures religieuses*, 93–106.

Loraux, Nicole. 1995. *The experiences of Tiresias: The feminine and the Greek man*. Princeton NJ: Princeton University Press.

Lorenz, Thuri. 1992. Die Epiphanie der Dioskuren. In *Kotinos*, ed. H. Froning, T. Hölscher, and H. Mielsch, 114–22.

Love, Iris. 1972a. A preliminary report of the excavations at Knidos, 1970. *AJA* 76 (1):61–76.

——1972b. A preliminary report of the excavations at Knidos, 1971. *AJA* 76 (4):393–405.

Lowe, N. J. 1998. Thesmophoria and Haloa: Myth, physics and mysteries. In *The Sacred and the Feminine in Ancient Greece*, ed. S. Blundell and M. Williamson, 149–73.

Lyons, Deborah J. 1997. *Gender and immortality: Heroines in ancient Greek myth and cult*. Princeton NJ: Princeton University Press.

McCauley, Barbara. 1999. Heroes and power: the politics of bone transferral. In *Ancient Greek hero cult*, ed. R. Hägg, 85–98.

McCredie, J. 1968. Samothrace: Preliminary report on the campaigns of 1965–67. *Hesperia* 37:200–234.

MacGillivray, J. A., J. M. Driessen, and L. H. Sackett. 2000. *The Palaikastro Kouros: A Minoan chryselephantine statuette and its Aegean Bronze Age context*. London: The British School at Athens.

MacLachlan, Bonnie. 1992. Sacred prostitution and Aphrodite. *Studies in Religion* 21 (2):145–62.

——1993. *The age of grace: Charis in early Greek poetry*. Princeton NJ: Princeton University Press.

——2002. The ungendering of Aphrodite. In *Engendering Aphrodite*, ed. D. R. Bolger and N. J. Serwint, 365–78.

Maier, Franz Georg. 1976. Das Heiligtum der Aphrodite in Paphos. In *Neue Forschungen in griechischen Heiligtümern*, ed. U. Jantzen, 220–38.

Maier, Franz Georg, and Vassos Karageorghis. 1984. *Paphos: History and archaeology*. Nicosia: A.G. Leventis Foundation.

Makkay, J. 1983. Metal forks as symbols of power and religion. *AArchHung* 35:313–44.

Malkin, Irad. 1987. *Religion and colonization in ancient Greece*. Leiden: E. J. Brill.

——1993. Land ownership, territorial possession, hero cults, and scholarly theory. In *Nomodeiktes*, ed. R. M. Rosen and J. Farrell, 225–34.

——1994. *Myth and territory in the Spartan Mediterranean*. Cambridge: Cambridge University Press.

——2001. *Ancient perceptions of Greek ethnicity*. Washington D.C. and Cambridge MA: Center for Hellenic Studies; distributed by Harvard University Press.

Mallwitz, Alfred. 1988. Cult and competition locations at Olympia. In *The Archaeology of the Olympics*, ed. W. J. Raschke, 79–109.

Mallwitz, Alfred, and Wolfgang Schiering. 1968. Der alte Athena-Temple von Milet. *MDAI(I)* 18:87–160.

Mansfield, John Magruder. 1985. *The robe of Athena and the Panathenaic peplos*. Diss. University of California at Berkeley, Berkeley CA.

Marconi, Clemente. 1994. *Selinunte: le metope dell'Heraion*. Modena: Franco Cosimo Panini.

Marinatos, Nanno. 1996. Cult by the seashore: What happened at Amnisos? In *The role of religion in the early Greek polis*, ed. R. Hägg, 135–39.

——2000. *The goddess and the warrior: The naked goddess and mistress of animals in early Greek religion*. London: Routledge.

——2003. Striding across boundaries: Hermes and Aphrodite as gods of initiation. In *Initiation in ancient Greek rituals and narratives*, ed. D. B. Dodd and C. A. Faraone, 130–51.

Marinatos, Nanno, and Robin Hägg, eds. 1993. *Greek sanctuaries: New approaches*. London: Routledge.

Marinatos, Spyridon. 1924–25. Epigraphē eis Britomarpin ek Chersonēsou. *AD* 9:79–84.

——1936. Le temple geométrique de Dréros. *BCH* 60:214–85, pl. 26–31.

Mark, Ira S. 1993. *The sanctuary of Athena Nike in Athens: Architectural stages and chronology*. Princeton NJ: American School of Classical Studies at Athens.

Martin, Roland. 1979. Introduction à l'étude du culte d'Héraclès en Sicile. In *Recherches sur les cultes grecs et l'occident, 1*. Naples: Centre Jean Bérard, 11–17.

Mastrocinque, Attilio, ed. 1993. *Ercole in occidente*. Trento: Dipartimento di scienze filologiche e storiche.

Mattusch, Carol C. 1988. *Greek bronze statuary: From the beginnings through the fifth century* BC. Ithaca NY: Cornell University Press.

Maurizio, Lisa. 1995. Anthropology and spirit possession: A reconsideration of the Pythia's role at Delphi. *JHS* 115.69–86.

Mayor, Adrienne. 2000. *The first fossil hunters: Paleontology in Greek and Roman times*. Princeton NJ: Princeton University Press.

Mazarakis Ainian, Alexander. 1987. Geometric Eretria. *AK* 30:3–24.

——1997. *From rulers' dwellings to temples: Architecture, religion and society in early iron age Greece (1100–700 BC)*. Jonsered: P. Åström.

Meiggs, Russell, and David M. Lewis. 1969. *A Selection of Greek historical inscriptions to the end of the fifth century* BC. Oxford: Clarendon Press.

Menadier, B. 2002. The sanctuary of Hera Akraia and its religious connections with Corinth. In *Peloponnesian sanctuaries and cults*, ed. R. Hägg, 85–91.

Merkelbach, Reinhold. 1980. Der Kult der Hestia im Prytaneion der griechischen Städte. *ZPE* 37:77–92.

——1986. Volksbeschluss aus Erythrai über den Bau eines Tempels der Aphrodite Pandemos. *Epigraphica Anatolica* 8:15–18.

Mesogaia: History and culture of Mesogeia in Attica. 2001. Athens: Eleftherios Venizelos.

Meuli, Karl. 1946. Griechische Opferbräuche. In *Phyllobolia für Peter von der Mühll*, ed. A. A. Gigon, 185–288.

——1975. *Gesammelte Schriften*. Ed. T. Gelser. 2 Vols. Basel: B. Schwabe.

——1975 [1946]. Griechische Opferriten. In *Gesammelte Schriften*, ed. T. Gelser, 2.907–1021.

Meyer, Ben F., ed. 1983. *Jewish and Christian self-definition, Volume 3: Self-definition in the Graeco-Roman world*. London: SCM Press Limited.

Mikalson, Jon D. 1975. *The sacred and civil calendar of the Athenian year*. Princeton NJ: Princeton University Press.

——1976. Erechtheus and the Panathenaia. *AJPh* 97:141–53.

——1998. *Religion in Hellenistic Athens*. Berkeley: University of California Press.

——2004. *Ancient Greek Religion*. Oxford: Blackwell.

Miles, Margaret Melanie. 1998a. *The city Eleusinion*. The Athenian Agora Vol. 31. Princeton NJ: American School of Classical Studies.

——1998b. The propylon to the sanctuary of Demeter Malophoros at Selinous. *AJA* 102 (1):35–57.

Miller, Margaret C. 1999. Reexamining transvestism in Archaic and Classical Athens: The Zewadski stamnos. *AJA* 103:223–53.

Miller, Stella G. 1988. Excavations at the Panhellenic site of Nemea: Cults, politics and games. In *The Archaeology of the Olympics*, ed. W. J. Raschke, 141–51.

Miller, Stephen G. 1974. The altar of the six goddesses from Thessalian Pherai. *California Studies in Classical Antiquity* 7:231–56.

——1978. *The prytaneion: Its function and architectural form.* Berkeley: University of California Press.

——2002. The shrine of Opheltes and the earliest stadium of Nemea. In *Olympia 1875–2000*, ed. H. Kyrieleis, 239–50.

Miller, Stephen G. 2004. *Nemea: A guide to the site and museum.* Athens: Archaeological Receipts Fund Directorate of Publications.

Mitsopoulos-Leon, Veronika. 1984. Zur Verehrung des Dionysos in Elis. *MDAI(A)* 99:275–90.

Mitten, David Gordon, John Griffiths Pedley, and Jane Ayer Scott, eds. 1971. *Studies presented to George M. A. Hanfmann.* Cambridge MA: Fogg Art Museum.

Moon, Warren G., ed. 1983. *Ancient Greek art and iconography.* Madison: University of Wisconsin Press.

Moreau, A., ed. 1992. *L'Initiation: actes du colloque international de Montpellier, 11–14 Avril 1991.* 2 Vols. Montpellier: Université Paul Valéry.

Morgan, Catherine. 1990. *Athletes and oracles: The transformation of Olympia and Delphi in the eighth century* BC. Cambridge: Cambridge University Press.

——1994. The evolution of a sacral landscape: Isthmia, Perachora and the early Corinthian state. In *Placing the gods*, ed. S. E. Alcock and R. Osborne. 105–42.

Morris, Ian. 1988. Tomb cult and the Greek Renaissance: The past in the present in the 8th c. *Antiquity* 62:750–61.

——1997. The art of citizenship. In *New light on a dark age*, ed. S. H. Langdon, 9–43.

——2000. *Archaeology as cultural history: Words and things in Iron Age Greece.* Malden MA: Blackwell.

Morris, Sarah P. 1992. *Daidalos and the origins of Greek art.* Princeton NJ: Princeton University Press.

——2001. The prehistoric background of Artemis Ephesia: A solution to the enigma of her "breasts"? In *Der Kosmos der Artemis von Ephesos*, ed. U. Muss, 135–51.

Moscati Castelnuovo, L. 1995. Sparta e le tradizioni crotoniati e locresi sulla battaglia della Sagra. *QUCC*:141–63.

Moulinier, Louis. 1975 [1952]. *Le pur et l'impur dans la pensée des Grecs d'Homère à Aristote.* Reprint. New York: Arno Press.

Moustaka, A. 2002a. On the cult of Hera at Olympia. In *Peloponnesian sanctuaries and cults*, ed. R. Hägg, 199–205.

——2002b. Zeus und Hera im Heiligtum von Olympia. In *Olympia 1875–2000*, ed. H. Kyrieleis, 301–15.

Mullen, W. 1986. The Herakles theme in Pindar. In *Herakles*, ed. J. P. Uhlenbrock, 29–33.

Murray, Oswyn, ed. 1990. *Sympotica: A symposium on the symposion.* Oxford: Clarendon Press.

Muss, Ulrike, ed. 2001. *Der Kosmos der Artemis von Ephesos.* Vienna: Österreichisches Archäologisches Institut.

Musti, Domenico, and Jean Bingen, eds. 1996. *Pausanias historien.* Geneva: Fondation Hardt.

Musti, Domenico, Luigi Beschi, and M. Torelli. 1982. *Guida della Grecia. Pausania.* 2 Vols. [Rome and Milan]: Fondazione Lorenzo Valla; A. Mondadori.

Mustilli, D. 1960. Efestia. In *Enciclopedia dell'arte antica, classica e orientale*, Vol. 3.230–31.

Mylonas, George E. 1943. The Lykaian altar of Zeus. In *Classical Studies in honor of William Abbott Oldfather*, 122–33.

——1961. *Eleusis and the Eleusinian mysteries.* Princeton NJ: Princeton University Press.

Mylonopoulos, Joannis. 2003. *Peloponnēsos oikētērion Poseidōnos = Heiligtümer und Kulte des Poseidon auf der Peloponnes. Kernos.* Supplement 13. Liège: Centre International d'Étude de la Religion Grecque Antique.

Nagy, Blaise. 1991. The procession to Phaleron. *Historia* 40:288–306.

Nagy, Gregory. 1979. *The best of the Achaeans: Concepts of the hero in archaic Greek poetry.* Baltimore MD: The Johns Hopkins University Press.

Neils, Jenifer. 1992. The Panathenaia: An introduction. In *Goddess and polis*, ed. J. Neils, 13–27.

——2001. Athena, alter ego of Zeus. In *Athena in the classical world*, ed. S. Deacy and A. Villing, 219–32.

Neils, Jenifer, ed. 1992. *Goddess and polis: the Panathenaic Festival in ancient Athens.* Hanover NH and Princeton NJ: Hood Museum of Art Dartmouth College; Princeton University Press.

——ed. 1996. *Worshipping Athena: Panathenaia and Parthenon.* Madison: University of Wisconsin Press.

Nicholls, Richard V. 1991. Early monumental religious architecture at Old Smyrna. In *New perspectives in early Greek art*, ed. D. Buitron-Oliver, 151–71.

Nick, Gabriele. 2002. *Die Athena Parthenos: Studien zum griechischen Kultbild und seiner Rezeption. MDAI(A)* Supplement 19. Mainz: P. von Zabern.

Nilsson, Martin P. 1906. *Griechische Feste von religiöser Bedeutung mit Ausschluss der attischen.* Second edition. Stuttgart: B. G. Teubner.

——1923. Fire-festivals in ancient Greece. *JHS* 43 (2):144–48.

——1927. *The Minoan-Mycenaean religion and its survival in Greek religion.* Lund: C. W. K. Gleerup.

——1951. *Opuscula selecta.* 3 Vols. Lund: C. W. K. Gleerup.

——1953. Poseidon und die Entstehung des griechischen Gotterglaubens [Review]. *AJP* 74 (2):161–68.

——1967. *Geschichte der griechischen Religion.* Third edition. 2 Vols. Munich: Beck.

——1975 [1957]. *The Dionysiac mysteries of the Hellenistic and Roman age.* Reprint. New York: Arno Press.

Noël, Daniel. 1999. Les Anthestéries et le vin. *Kernos* 12.125–52.

Noort, Ed, and Eibert Tigchelaar, eds. 2002. *The sacrifice of Isaac: The Aqedah (Genesis 22) and its interpretations.* Boston: E. J. Brill.

Novaku, Grgi, V. Mirosavljevic, D. Rendic-Miocevic, and M. Suic, eds. 1970. *Adriatica praehistorica et antiqua.* Zagreb: Sveuciliste-Arheoloski institut Filozofskog fakulteta.

Nussbaum, Martha, and Juha Sihvola, eds. 2002. *The sleep of reason: Erotic experience and sexual ethics in ancient Greece and Rome.* Chicago IL: University of Chicago Press.

Obbink, Dirk. 1993. Dionysus poured out: Ancient and modern theories of sacrifice and cultural formation. In *Masks of Dionysus*, ed. T. H. Carpenter and C. A. Faraone, 65–86.

O'Brien, Joan V. 1993. *The transformation of Hera: A study of ritual, hero, and the goddess in the Iliad*. Lanham MD: Rowman & Littlefield.

Ogden, Daniel. 2001. *Greek and Roman necromancy*. Princeton NJ: Princeton University Press.

Onyshkevych, Lada. 2002. Interpreting the Berezan bone graffito. In *Oikistes*, ed. Vanessa B. Gorman and Eric W. Robinson, 161–77.

Oppenheim, A. L. 1949. The golden garments of the gods. *JNES* 8:172–93.

Orgogozo, J. 1949. L'Hermès des Achéens. *RHR* 136.10–30, 139–79.

Orlandini, P. 1968–69. Diffusione del culto di Demetra e Kore in Sicilia. *Kokalos* 14–15:334–38.

Osanna, Massimo. 1990. Sui culti arcaici di Sparta e Taranto: Afrodite Basilis. *PP* 45:81–94.

——1992. Il culto di Hermes Agoraios ad Atene. *Ostraka* 10(2): 215–22.

Osborne, Robin. 1985. The erection and mutilation of the hermai. *PCPhS* 31:65–75.

——1993. Women and sacrifice in ancient Greece. *CQ* 43 (2):392–405.

Otto, Walter Friedrich. 1954. *The Homeric gods. The spiritual significance of Greek religion*. Tr. Moses Hadas. [New York]: Pantheon.

——1965. *Dionysos: Myth and cult*. Tr. R. F. Palmer. Bloomington: Indiana University Press.

Pache, Corinne Ondine 2004. *Baby and child heroes in ancient Greece*. Urbana: University of Illinois Press.

Padilla, Mark William, ed. 1999. *Rites of passage in ancient Greece: Literature, religion, society*. Lewisburg PA: Bucknell University Press.

Palagia, O. 1990. A new relief of the Graces and the Charites of Socrates. In *Opes Atticae*, ed. M. Geerard, J. Desmet, and R. van der Plaetse, 347–56.

Papademetriou, J. 1963. The Sanctuary of Artemis at Brauron. *Scientific American* (June):110–20.

Parke, H. W. 1967. *The oracles of Zeus: Dodona, Olympia, Ammon*. Cambridge MA: Harvard University Press.

——1977. *Festivals of the Athenians*. Ithaca NY: Cornell University Press.

——1985a. The massacre of the Branchidae. *JHS* 105:59–68.

——1985b. *The oracles of Apollo in Asia Minor*. London: Croom Helm.

Parke, H. W., and Donald Ernest Wilson Wormell. 1956. *The Delphic oracle*. Oxford: Blackwell.

Parker, Robert. 1983. *Miasma: Pollution and purification in early Greek religion*. Oxford: Clarendon Press.

——1988. Demeter, Dionysus and the Spartan pantheon. In *Early Greek cult practice*, ed. R. Hägg, *et al.*, 99–103.

——1991. The "Hymn to Demeter" and the "Homeric Hymns". *G&R* 38 (1):1–17.

——1996. *Athenian religion: A history*. Oxford and New York: Clarendon Press; Oxford University Press.

——2000 [1985]. Greek states and Greek oracles. In *Oxford readings in Greek religion*, ed. R. G. A. Buxton, 76–108.

——2005. *Polytheism and society at Athens*. Oxford: Oxford University Press.

Patillon, Michel, and Jean Bouffartigue, eds. 1977–. *Porphyre: De l'Abstinence.* 3 Vols. Paris: Les Belles Lettres.

Paulson, Ivar. 1964. The animal guardian: A critical and synthetic view. *HR* 3:202–19.

Pauly, A. G. Wissowa, and W. Kroll, eds. 1893–1972. *Real-encyclopädie der classischen Altertumswissenschaft (RE).* Stuttgart: J.B. Metzler.

Payne, Humfry, and Thomas James Dunbabin. 1940. *Perachora: The sanctuaries of Hera Akraia, and Limenia.* Oxford: Clarendon Press.

Pedley, John Griffiths. 1990. *Paestum: Greeks and Romans in Southern Italy.* London: Thames and Hudson.

——2005. *Sanctuaries and the sacred in the ancient Greek world.* Cambridge: Cambridge University Press.

Peirce, Sarah. 1998. Visual language and concepts of cult on the "Lenaia Vases". *ClAnt* 17 (1):59–104.

Pemberton, Elizabeth G. 2000. Wine, women and song: Gender roles in Corinthian cult. *Kernos* 13:85–106.

Pendergraft, M., and Karelisa Hartigan. 1994. Naming the figures: A controversial stele in the Spartan museum. *Maia* 46:283–89.

Penrose Harland, J. 1925. The Calaurian amphictyony. *AJA* 29 (2):160–71.

Perdrizet, E. 1903. Hermès Criophore. *BCH* 27:300–313.

Perlman, Paula. 1989. Acting the she-bear for Artemis. *Arethusa* 22:111–33.

——1995. Invocatio and imprecatio: The hymn to the greatest Kouros from Palaikastro and the oath in ancient Crete. *JHS* 115:161–67.

Petrakos, Vasileios. 1991. *Ramnous.* Athens: Tameio Archaiologikōn Porōn.

Petropoulou, Angeliki. 1981. The Eparche documents and the early oracle at Oropus. *GRBS* 22:39–63.

——1993. The Laphrian holocaust at Patrai and its Celtic parallel: a ritual with Indo-European components? In *Religio Graeco-Romana*, ed. J. Dalfen, G. Petersmann, and F. F. Schwarz, 313–34.

Pettersson, Michael. 1992. *Cults of Apollo at Sparta: The Hyakinthia the Gymnopaidiai and the Karneia.* Stockholm and Göteborg: Swedish Institute at Athens; distributed by P. Åström.

Pfister, Friedrich. 1951. *Die Reisebilder des Herakleides.* Vienna: R. M. Rohrer.

David J. Phillips and David Pritchard, eds. 2003. *Sport and festival in the ancient Greek world.* London: Classical Press of Wales; Oakville, Conn.: Dist. in the USA by David Brown.

Photiades, P. 1958. Pan's prologue to the *Dyskolos* of Menander. *G&R* 5:108–22.

Picard, Charles. 1922. *Éphèse et Claros: recherches sur les sanctuaires et les cultes de l'Ionie du Nord.* Paris: E. de Boccard.

Piccirilli, L. 1984. Il santuario, la funzione guerriera della dea, la regalità: il caso di Atena Chalkioikos. In *I santuari e la guerra nel mondo classico*, ed. M. Sordi, 3–19.

Pickard-Cambridge, Arthur Wallace. 1968. *The dramatic festivals of Athens.* Second edition. Rev. John Gould and David M. Lewis. Oxford: Clarendon Press.

Pierart, Marcel. 1996. Le culte de Dionysos à Argos [review essay]. *Kernos* 9:423–29.

Pingiatoglou, Semeli. 1981. *Eileithyia.* Würzburg: Königshausen and Neumann.

Pinney, Gloria Ferrari. 1983. Achilles lord of Skythia. In *Ancient Greek art and iconography*, ed. W. G. Moon, 127–46.

Pirenne-Delforge, Vinciane. 1988. Épithètes cultuelles et interprétation philosophique à propos d'Aphrodite Ourania et Pandémos à Athènes. *AC* 57:142–57.

—— 1994. *L'Aphrodite grecque: contribution à l'étude de ses cultes et de sa personnalité dans le panthéon archaïque et classique*. Athens: Centre International d'Étude de la Religion Grecque Antique.

—— 1996. Les Charites à Athènes et dans l'île de Cos. *Kernos* 9:195–214.

Pirenne-Delforge, Vinciane, and Emilio Suárez de la Torre, eds. 2000. *Héros et héroïnes dans les mythes et les cultes grecs. Kernos* Supplement 10. Liège: Centre International d' Étude de la Religion Grecque Antique.

Pirzio Birolli Stefanelli, L. 1977. Tabelle fittili tarentine relative al culto dei Dioscuri. *ArchClass* 29:310–98, pl. 64–111.

Poikilia: études offertes à Jean-Pierre Vernant. 1987. Paris: Editions de l'École des hautes études en sciences sociales.

Postlethwait, N. 1999. The death of Zeus Kretagenes. *Kernos* 12:85–98.

Pötscher, Walter. 1959. Ares. *Gymnasium* 66:5–14.

—— 1961. Hera und Heros. *RhM* 104:302–55.

Price, Simon. 1999. *Religions of the ancient Greeks*. Cambridge: Cambridge University Press.

Pritchett, W. Kendrick. 1971–. *The Greek state at war.* 5 Vols. Berkeley: University of California Press.

—— 1979. Plataiai. *AJP* 100 (1):145–47, 150–52.

Prost, Francis. 1999. La statue cultuelle d'Apollon à Délos. *REG* 112 (1):37–60.

Prückner, Helmut. 1968. *Die lokrischen Tonreliefs. Beitrag zur Kultgeschichte.* Mainz am Rhein: P. von Zabern.

Pugliese Carratelli, Giovanni. 1985. *Sikanie: Storia e civiltà della Sicilia greca.* Milan: Istituto Veneto di Arti Grafiche.

Puhvel, Jaan, ed. 1970. *Myth and law among the Indo-Europeans: Studies in Indo-European comparative mythology.* Berkeley: University of California Press.

Pulleyn, Simon. 1997. *Prayer in Greek religion.* Oxford and New York: Clarendon Press; Oxford University Press.

Purvis, Andrea. 2003. *Singular dedications: Founders and innovators of private cults in classical Greece.* New York: Routledge.

Quantin, F. 1999. Aspects épirotes de la vie religieuse antique. *REG* 112.1:61–98.

Raaflaub, Kurt A. 2000. Zeus Eleutherios, Dionysos the Liberator, and the Athenian tyrannicides. Anachronistic uses of fifth-century political concepts. In *Polis & Politics*, ed. T. H. N. P. Flensted-Jensen, T. H. Nielsen, and L. Rubinstein, 249–75.

Raingeard, Pierre. 1935. *Hermès psychagogue; essai sur les origines du culte d'Hermès.* Paris: Les Belles Lettres.

Raschke, Wendy J, ed. 1988. *The Archaeology of the Olympics: The Olympics and other festivals in antiquity.* Madison: University of Wisconsin Press.

Redfield, James M. 2003. *The Locrian maidens: Love and death in Greek Italy.* Princeton NJ: Princeton University Press.

Reed, Joseph D. 1995. The sexuality of Adonis. *ClAnt* 14 (2):317–45.

Reese, David S. 1989. Faunal remains from the altar of Aphrodite Ourania, Athens. *Hesperia* 58 (1):63–70.

Reichert-Südbeck, Petra. 2000. *Kulte von Korinth und Syrakus: Vergleich zwischen einer Metropolis und ihrer Apoikia*. Dettelbach: J. H. Röll.

Religione e città nel mondo antico. 1984. Rome: "l'Erma" di Bretschneider.

Rhodes, R. F., and J. J. Dobbins. 1979. The sanctuary of Artemis Brauronia on the Athenian Akropolis. *Hesperia* 48:325–41.

Ridgway, B. 1984. The fashion of the Elgin Kore. *The J. Paul Getty Museum Journal* 12:29–58.

—— 1992. Images of Athena on the Acropolis. In *Goddess and polis*, ed. J. Neils, 119–42.

Riedweg, Christoph. 2002. Poésie orphique et rituel initiatique. *RHR* 219 (4):459–81.

Robbins, Jill. 1998. Sacrifice. In *Critical terms for religious studies*, ed. M. C. Taylor, 285–97.

Robert, Fernand. 1939. *Thymélè; recherches sur la signification et la destination des monuments circulaires dans l'architecture religieuse de la Grèce*. Paris: E. de Boccard.

—— 1953. Le sanctuaire de l'Archégète Anios à Délos. *RA* 41:8–40.

Robertson, Noel. 1984. Poseidon's festival at the winter solstice. *CQ* 34 (1):1–16.

—— 1985. The origins of the Panathenaia. *RhM* 128:231–95.

—— 1992. *Festivals and legends: The formation of Greek cities in the light of public ritual*. Toronto: University of Toronto Press.

—— 1993. Athens' festival of the new wine. *HSCP* 95:197–250.

—— 1996a. Athena and early Greek society: Palladium shrines and promontory shrines. In *Religion in the ancient world*, ed. M. Dillon, 383–475.

—— 1996b. Athena's shrines and festivals. In *Worshipping Athena*, ed. J. Neils, 27–77.

—— 2002. The religious criterion in Greek ethnicity: The Dorians and the festival Carneia. *AJAH* 1 (2):5–74.

Robinson, H. S. 1976. Temple hill, Corinth. In *Neue Forschungen in griechischen Heiligtümern*, ed. U. Jantzen, 239–60.

Rocchetti, Luigi. 1994. *Sybrita, la valle di Amari fra Bronzo e Ferro*. Rome: Gruppo editoriale internazionale.

Rocchi, M. 1979. Contributi allo culto delle Charites (I). *StudClas* 18:5–16.

—— 1980. Contributi allo culto delle Charites (II). *StudClas* 19:19–28.

Roebuck, Carl. 1951. The organization of Naukratis. *CP* 46 (4):212–20.

Roebuck, Carl, and F. J. de Waele. 1951. *The Asklepieion and Lerna*. Princeton NJ: American School of Classical Studies at Athens.

Rohde, Erwin. 1987 [1925]. *Psyche: The cult of souls and belief in immortality among the ancient Greeks*. Tr. W. B. Hillis. Reprint. Chicago IL: Ares Publishers.

Roller, Lynn E. 1999. *In search of god the mother: The cult of Anatolian Cybele*. Berkeley: University of California Press.

Romano, Irene Bald. 1980. *Early Greek cult images*. Diss. University of Pennsylvania, Philadelphia PA.

—— 1982. The archaic statue of Dionysos from Ikarion. *Hesperia* 51 (4):398–409.

—— 1988. Early Greek cult images and cult practices. In *Early Greek Cult Practice*, ed. R. Hägg, *et al.*, 127–34.

Rosen, Ralph Mark, and Joseph Farrell, eds. 1993. *Nomodeiktes: Greek studies in honor of Martin Ostwald*. Ann Arbor: University of Michigan Press.

Rosenzweig, Rachel. 2004. *Worshipping Aphrodite: Art and cult in classical Athens*. Ann Arbor: University of Michigan Press.

Rosivach, V. J. 1978. The altar of Zeus Agoraios in the *Heracleidae*. *PP* 33:32–47.

——1987. The cult of Zeus Eleutherios at Athens. *PP* 42:262–85.

Rouse, W. H. D. 1975 [1902]. *Greek votive offerings; an essay in the history of Greek religion*. Reprint. New York: Arno Press.

Roux, Georges. 1976. *Delphes, son oracle et ses dieux*. Paris: Les Belles Lettres.

Roux, Georges, ed. 1984. *Temples et sanctuaires: séminaire de recherche 1981–1983*. Lyon and Paris: GIS-Maison de l'Orient; distributed by E. de Boccard.

Roy, J. 1967. The mercenaries of Cyrus. *Historia* 16:287–323.

——1972. Arcadian nationality as seen in Xenophon's *Anabasis*. *Mnemosyne* 25:129–36.

Rückert, Birgit. 1998. *Die Herme im öffentlichen und privaten Leben der Griechen. Untersuchungen zur Funktion der griechischen Herme als Grenzmal, Inschriften-träger und Kulturbild des Hermes*. Regensburg: Roderer Verlag.

Rudhardt, Jean. 1958. *Notions fondamentales de la pensée religieuse et actes constitutifs du culte dans la Grèce classique; étude préliminaire pour aider à la compréhension de la piété athénienne au IVme siècle*. Geneva: E. Droz.

——1975. Quelques notes sur les cultes chypriotes, en particulier sur celui d'Aphrodite. In *Chypre des origines au moyen-âge*, ed. D. van Berchem, 109–36.

——1999. *Thémis et les Hôrai: recherche sur les divinités grecques de la justice et de la paix*. Geneva: Droz.

Rupp, David William. 1974. *Greek altars of the Northeastern Peloponnese, c. 750/725 BC to c. 300/275 BC*. Diss. Bryn Mawr College, Bryn Mawr PA.

——1976. The altars of Zeus and Hera on Mt. Arachnaion in the Argeia, Greece. *JFA* 3:261–68.

Ruschenbusch, Eberhard. 1983. *Solonos Nomoi: die Fragmente des solonischen Gesetzeswerkes mit einer Text-und Uberlieferungsgeschichte*. Wiesbaden: F. Steiner.

Sahin, Sencer, Elmar Schwertheim, and Jörg Wagner eds. 1978. *Studien zur Religion und Kultur Kleinasiens: Festschrift für Friedrich Karl Dörner zum 65. Geburtstag am 28. Februar 1976*. 2 Vols. Leiden: E. J. Brill.

Sakellarakis, J. A. 1988a. The Idaean cave: Minoan and Greek worship. *Kernos* 1:207–14.

——1988b. Some Geometric and Archaic finds from the Idaean cave. In *Early Greek cult practice*, ed. R. Hägg, *et al.*, 173–93.

Salapata, Gina. 1997. Hero warriors from Corinth and Lakonia. *Hesperia* 66.245–60.

——2002. Myth into cult: Alexandra/Kassandra in Lakonia. In *Oikistes*, ed. V. B. Gorman and E. W. Robinson, 131–59.

Sale, W. 1961. The Hyperborean maidens on Delos. *HThR* 54 (2):75–89.

——1975. The Temple Legends of the Arkteia. *RhM* 118:265–84.

Salmon, J. 1972. The Heraeum at Perachora and the early history of Corinth and Megara. *ABSA* 67:159–204.

Salowey, C. 1995. *The Peloponnesian Herakles: Cult and labors*. Diss. Bryn Mawr College, Bryn Mawr PA.

——2002. Herakles and healing cult in the Peloponnesos. In *Peloponnesian sanctuaries and cults*, ed. R. Hägg, 171–77.

Salviat, F. 1964. Les théogamies attiques, Zeus Téleios et l'*Agamemnon* d'Eschyle. *BCH* 88:647–54.

Samuel, Alan Edouard. 1972. *Greek and Roman chronology: Calendars and years in classical antiquity*. Munich: Beck.

Sansone, D. 1991. Cleobis and Biton at Delphi. *Nikephoros* 4:121–32.

Sarian, S. 1986. Erinys. *LIMC* III.1.825–43.

Scanlon, Thomas F. 1984. The footrace of the Heraia at Olympia. *AncW* 9:77–90.

——1988. Virgineum Gymnasium. In *The archaeology of the Olympics*, ed. W. J. Raschke, 185–216.

Schachermeyr, Fritz. 1950. *Poseidon und die Entstehung des grieschen Götterglaubens*. Bern: A. Francke.

Schachter, Albert. 1979. The Boiotian Heracles. In *Proceedings of the Second International Conference on Boiotian Antiquities*, ed. J. M. Fossey and A. Schachter, 37–43.

——1981–. *Cults of Boiotia*. 4 Vols. London: University of London, Institute of Classical Studies.

——1984. A consultation of Trophonios (IG 7.4136). *AJPh* 105 (3):258–70.

——1994. The politics of dedication: Two Athenian dedications at the sanctuary of A. Ptoieus in Boeotia. In *Ritual, finance, politics*, ed. D. M. Lewis, R. Osborne and S. Hornblower, 291–306.

——2003. Evolutions of a mystery cult: The Theban Kabeiroi. In *Greek mysteries*, ed. M. B. Cosmopoulos, 112–42.

Schachter, Albert, and Jean Bingen, eds. 1992. *Le Sanctuaire grec*. Vandoeuvres: Fondation Hardt.

Schattner, Thomas G. 1990. *Griechische Hausmodelle: Untersuchungen zur frühgriechischen Architektur*. Berlin: Gebr. Mann.

Scheer, Tanja Susanne. 2000. *Die Gottheit und ihr Bild: Untersuchungen zur Funktion griechischer Kultbilder in Religion und Politik*. Munich: C. H. Beck.

Schilardi, Demetrios U. 1988. The temple of Athena at Koukounaries. In *Early Greek cult practice*, ed. R. Hägg, et al., 41–48.

Schindler, Rebecca Karina. 1998. *The archaeology of Aphrodite in the Greek West, c. 650–480 BC*. Diss. University of Michigan, Ann Arbor MI.

Schlaifer, Robert. 1943. The cult of Athena Pallenis: (Athenaeus VI 234–35). *HSCP* 54:35–67.

Schlesier, R. 1991–92. Olympian versus chthonian religion. *SCI* 11:38–51.

Schmitt, Pauline. 1977. Athéna Apatouria et la ceinture: Les aspects feminins des Apatouries. *Annales: économies, sociétés, civilisations* 32:1059–73.

Schmitt Pantel, Pauline. 1992. *La cité au banquet: histoire des repas publics dans les cités grecques*. Rome: Ecole française de Rome.

Schumacher, Rob W. M. 1993. Three related sanctuaries of Poseidon: Geraistos, Kalaureia and Tainaron. In *Greek sanctuaries*, ed. N. Marinatos and R. Hägg, 62–87.

Schwandner, E.-L. 1976. Der Ältere Aphaiatempel auf Aegina. In *Neue Forschungen in griechischen Heiligtümern*, ed. U. Jantzen, 103–20.

Schwarzenberg, Erkinger. 1966. *Die Grazien*. Bonn: Habelt.

Scodel, Ruth. 1993. *Theater and society in the classical world*. Ann Arbor: University of Michigan Press.

Scullion, S. 1994. Olympian and chthonian. *ClAnt* 13:75–119.

——2000. Heroic and chthonian sacrifice: New evidence from Selinous. *ZPE* 132:163–71.

——2001. Dionysos at Elis. *Philologus* 145(2): 203–18.

Seaford, Richard. 1981. Dionysiac drama and the Dionysiac mysteries. *CQ* 31 (2):252–75.

Segal, Charles. 1961. The character and cults of Dionysus and the unity of *The Frogs*. *HSCP* 65:207–42.

Seltman, C. 1952. The wardrobe of Artemis. *Numismatic Chronicle* 12:33–51 with pl. 5–6.

Servais-Soyez, Brigitte. 1983. Aphrodite Ouranie et le symbolisme de l'echelle, Un message venue d'Orient. In *Le mythe, son langage et son message*, ed. H. Limet and J. Ries, 191–207.

Serwint, Nancy J. 1993. The female athletic costume at the Heraia and prenuptial initiation rites. *AJA* 97 (3):403–22.

Sfyroeras, Pavlos. 1993. Fireless sacrifices: Pindar's Olympian 7 and the Panathenaic festival. *AJP* 114 (1):1–26.

Shapiro, H. A. 1999. Cult warfare: the Dioskouroi between Sparta and Athens. In *Ancient Greek hero cult*, ed. R. Hägg, 99–107.

——2002. Demeter and Persephone in western Greece: Migrations of myth and cult. In *Magna Graecia*, ed. M. Bennett and A. J. Paul, 82–95.

Sherwin-White, Susan M. 1978. *Ancient Cos: An historical study from the Dorian settlement to the imperial period*. Göttingen: Vandenhoeck und Ruprecht.

Siewert, Peter. 1977. The ephebic oath in fifth-century Athens. *JHS* 97:102–11.

——1979. Poseidon Hippios am Kolonos und die athenischen Hippeis. In *Arktouros*, ed. G. W. Bowersock, W. Burkert, and M. J. Putnam, 280–89.

Silk, M. S. 1985. Heracles and Greek tragedy. *G&R* 32 (1):1–22.

Simantoni-Bournia, Eva. 2002. The early phases of the Hyria Sanctuary on Naxos. An overview of the pottery. In *Excavating classical culture*, ed. M. Stamatopoulou and M. Yeroulanou, 269–80.

Simms, Ronda R. 1988. The cult of the Thracian goddess Bendis in Athens and Attica. *AncW* 18:59–76.

Simon, Christopher George. 1986. *The archaic votive offerings and cults of Ionia*. Diss. University of California at Berkeley, Berkeley CA.

——1997. The archaeology of cult in Geometric Greece: Ionian temples, altars and dedications. In *New light on a dark age*, ed. S. H. Langdon, 125–43.

Simon, Erika. 1969. *Die Götter der Griechen*. Munich: Hirmer.

——1972. Hera und die Nymphen. Ein Böotischer Polos in Stockholm. *RA*:205–20.

——1983. *Festivals of Attica: An archaeological commentary*. Madison: University of Wisconsin Press.

——1996. Theseus and Athenian festivals. In *Worshipping Athena*, ed. J. Neils, 9–26.

Sinn, Ulrich. 1981. Das Heiligtum der Artemis Limnatis bei Kombothekra. *MDAI(A)* 96:25–71.

——1988. Der Kult der Aphaia auf Aegina. In *Early Greek cult practice*, ed. R. Hägg, et al., 149–59.

——1992. Sunion: Das befestige Heiligtum der Athena und des Poseidon an der "Heiligen Landspitze Attikas". *AW* 23:175–90.

——1993. Greek sanctuaries as places of refuge. In *Greek sanctuaries*, ed. N. Marinatos and R. Hägg, 88–109.

——2000. *Olympia: Cult, sport and ancient festival*. Princeton NJ: Markus Wiener.

——2002. Artemis in the sanctuary on Mount Kotilion. In *Peloponnesian sanctuaries and cults*, ed. R. Hägg, 193–98.

Sjövall, Harald. 1931. *Zeus im altgriechischen Hauskult*. Lund: H. Ohlsson.

Smith, James O. 1996. The high priests of the temple of Artemis at Ephesus. In *Cybele, Attis and related cults*, ed. E. Lane, 323–35.

Smith, Jonathan Z. 1982. *Imagining religion: From Babylon to Jonestown*. Chicago IL: University of Chicago Press.

Smith, W. Robertson. 1907. *Lectures on the religion of the Semites. First Series*. Revised Edition. London: A&C Black.

Snodgrass, Anthony M. 1980. *Archaic Greece: The age of experiment*. London: J. M. Dent.

——2000a [1988]. The archaeology of the hero. In *Oxford readings in Greek religion*, ed. R. G. A. Buxton, 180–90.

——2000b. *The dark age of Greece: An archaeological survey of the eleventh to the eighth centuries BC*. New York: Routledge.

Sokolowski, Franciszek. 1955. *Lois sacrées de l'Asie Mineure*. Paris: E. de Boccard.

——1960. On the episode of Onchestus in the Homeric Hymn to Apollo. *TAPhA* 91:376–80.

——1962. *Lois sacrées des cités grecques. Supplément*. Paris: E. de Boccard.

——1964. Aphrodite as guardian of Greek magistrates. *HThR* 57 (1):1–8.

——1969. *Lois sacrées des cités grecques*. Paris: E. de Boccard.

Solomon, Jon. 1994. *Apollo: Origins and influences*. Tucson: University of Arizona Press.

Sophocleous, S. 1985. L'Aphrodite en tant qu'androgyne. *Archaeologia Cypria* 1:79–96, pl. 15–16.

Sordi, M. 1972a. La leggenda dei Dioscuri nella battaglia della Sagra e di Lago Regillo. In *Contributi dell'Istituto di storia antica*, ed. M. Sordi, 47–70.

Sordi, M., ed. 1972b. *Contributi dell'Istituto di storia antica*. Vol. 1. Milan: Università Cattolica del Sacro Cruore.

——ed. 1984. *I santuari e la guerra nel mondo classico. Contributi dell'Istituto di storia antica*. Milano: Università Cattolica del Sacro Cruore.

Soren, David, ed. 1987. *The Sanctuary of Apollo Hylates at Kourion, Cyprus*. Tucson: University of Arizona Press.

Sourvinou-Inwood, Christiane. 1973. The young abductor of the Locrian pinakes. *BICS* 20:12–21.

——1974. The votum of 477/6 BC and the foundation legend of Locri Epizephyrii. *CQ* 24 (2):186–98.

——1978. Persephone and Aphrodite at Locri: A model for personality definition in Greek religion. *JHS* 98:101–21.

——1986. Myth as history: The previous owners of the Delphic oracle. In *Interpretations of Greek mythology*, ed. J. N. Bremmer, 215–41.

——1988. *Studies in girls' transitions: Aspects of the arkteia and age representation in Attic iconography*. Athens: Kardamitsa.

——1993. Early sanctuaries, the eighth century and ritual space: fragments of a discourse. In *Greek sanctuaries*, ed. N. Marinatos and R. Hägg, 1–17.

——1997. Reconstructing change: Ritual and ideology at Eleusis. In *Inventing ancient culture*, ed. M. Golden and P. Toohey, 132–64.

——2000 [1988]. Further aspects of polis religion. In *Oxford readings in Greek religion*, ed. R. G. A. Buxton, 38–55.

——2000 [1990]. What is polis religion? In *Oxford readings in Greek religion*, ed. R. G. A. Buxton, 13–37.

——2002. *Tragedy and Athenian religion, Greek studies.* Lanham MD: Lexington Books.

——2003. Festival and mysteries: Aspects of the Eleusinian cult. In *Greek mysteries*, ed. M. B. Cosmopoulos, 25–49.

Spadea, Roberto. 1996. *Il tesoro di Hera: scoperte nel Santuario di Hera Lacinia a Capo Colonna di Crotone.* Milano: Edizioni ET.

——1997. Santuari di Hera a Crotone. In *Héra*, ed. J. de La Genière, 235–59.

Spigo, Umberto. 2000. I pinakes di Francavilla di Sicilia. Nuova classificazione e brevi note sugli aspetti cultuali. In *Damarato,* ed. I. Berlingo, 208–19.

Sporn, Katja. 2002. *Heiligtümer und Kulte Kretas in klassischer und hellenistischer Zeit.* Heidelberg: Verlag Archäologie und Geschichte.

Stafford, Emma. 2000. *Worshipping virtues: Personification and the divine in ancient Greece.* London: Duckworth; The Classical Press of Wales.

Stamatopoulou, Maria, and Marina Yeroulanou, eds. 2002. *Excavating classical culture: Recent archaeological discoveries in Greece.* Oxford: Beazley Archive and Archaeopress.

Stanton, G. R. 1984. Some Attic inscriptions. *ABSA* 79.289–306.

Steiner, Deborah. 2001. *Images in mind: Statues in archaic and classical Greek literature and thought.* Princeton NJ: Princeton University Press.

Stewart, Andrew F. 1990. *Greek sculpture: An exploration.* 2 Vols. New Haven CT: Yale University Press.

Strom, I. 1988. The early sanctuary of the Argive Heraion and its external relations. *Acta Archeologica* 59:173–203.

Stroud, Ronald S. 1993. The sanctuary of Aiakos in the Athenian Agora. *AJA* 97:308–9.

——1998. *The Athenian grain-tax law of 374/3 BC.* Princeton NJ: American School of Classical Studies at Athens.

Tagalidou, Efpraxia. 1993. *Weihreliefs an Herakles aus klassischer Zeit.* Jonsered: P. Åström.

Taylor, Mark C., ed. 1998. *Critical terms for religious studies.* Chicago IL: University of Chicago Press.

Te Riele, G.-J. M.-J. 1976. Charitésia. In *Miscellanea tragica in honorem J. C. Kamerbeek*, ed. J. M. Bremer, S. L. Radt, and C. J. Ruijgh, 285–91.

Teffeteller, A. 2001. The chariot rite at Onchestos: Homeric Hymn to Apollo 229–38. *JHS* 121:159–66.

Tejeiro, M. G., and M. T. M. Tejada. 2000. Les héros méchants. In *Héros et héroïnes dans les mythes et les cultes grecs*, ed. V. Pirenne-Delforge and E. Suárez de la Torre, 111–23.

Themelis, Petros G. 1970. Archaikē epigraphē ek tou hierou tou Poseidōnos eis Akovitika. *AD* 25:109–25.

——1971. *Brauron: Guide to the site and museum.* Athens: Apollo.

——1994. Artemis Ortheia at Messene: The epigraphical and archaeological evidence. In *Ancient Greek cult practice from the epigraphical evidence*, ed. R. Hägg, 101–22.

——1998. The sanctuary of Demeter and the Dioscuri in Messene. In *Ancient Greek cult practice from the archaeological evidence*, ed. R. Hägg, 157–86.

——2002. Contribution to the topography of the sanctuary at Brauron. In *Le orse di Brauron*, ed. B. Gentili and F. Perusino, 103–16.

Thompson, Homer A. 1936. Pnyx and Thesmophorion. *Hesperia* 5 (2):151–200.

Thompson, Homer A., and R. E. Wycherley. 1972. *The Agora of Athens; the history, shape and uses of an ancient city center*. Princeton NJ: The American School of Classical Studies at Athens.

Thomson, George. 1943. The Greek calendar. *JHS* 63:52–65.

Tod, Marcus Niebuhr, ed. 1933–. *A selection of Greek historical inscriptions*. Oxford: Clarendon Press.

Tod, Marcus Niebuhr, and A. J. B. Wace. 1906. *A catalogue of the Sparta Museum*. Oxford: Clarendon Press.

Tomlinson, R. A. 1977. The upper terraces at Perachora. *ABSA* 72:197–202.

——1983. *Epidauros*. Austin: University of Texas Press.

——1992. Perachora. In *Le Sanctuaire grec*, ed. A. Schachter and J. Bingen, 321–51.

Tournavitou, I. 1995. The Mycenaean ivories from the Artemision of Delos. *BCH* 119 (2):479–527.

Travlos, J. 1976. Treis naoi tēs Artemidos: Aulidias, Tauropolou, kai Braurōnias. In *Neue Forschungen in griechischen Heiligtümern*, ed. U. Jantzen, 197–205.

Trell, Bluma L. 1945. *The Temple of Artemis at Ephesos*. New York: The American Numismatic Society.

Tuchelt, Klaus. 1976. Tempel, Heiligtum, Siedlung. Probleme zur Topographie von Didyma. In *Neue Forschungen in griechischen Heiligtümern*, ed. U. Jantzen, 207–17.

Turner, Judy Ann. 1988. Greek priesthoods. In *Civilization of the ancient Mediterranean*, ed. M. Grant and R. Kitzinger, 925–31.

Tylor, Edward Burnett. 1903. *Primitive culture: Researches into the development of mythology, philosophy, religion, language, art and custom*. Fourth edition. London: Murray.

Uhlenbrock, Jaimee Pugliese. 1986. *Herakles: Passage of the hero through 1000 years of classical art*. New Rochelle NY and Annandale-on-Hudson NY: Aristide D. Caratzas; Edith C. Blum Art Institute.

Valmin, Mattias Natan. 1938. *The Swedish Messenia expedition*. Lund: C. W. K. Gleerup.

van Berchem, D., ed. 1975. *Chypre des origines au moyen-âge: séminaire interdisciplinaire, semestre d'été, 1975*. Geneva: University of Geneva, Département des sciences de l'antiquité.

van Compernolle, R. 1969. Ajax et les Dioscures au secours des Locriens sur les rives de la Sagra (*c.* 575–565 av. notre ère). In *Hommages à Marcel Renard, II*, ed. J. Bibauw, 733–66.

van der Plas, Dirk. 1987. *Effigies dei: Essays on the history of religions*. Leiden: E. J. Brill.

Vanderpool, E. 1942. An archaic inscribed stele from Marathon. *Hesperia* 11 (4):329–37.

——1966. The deme of Marathon and the Herakleion. *AJA* 70 (4):319–23.

van Gennep, Arnold. 1960. *The rites of passage*. Tr. Monika B. Vizedom and Gabrielle L. Caffee. Chicago, IL: University of Chicago Press.

van Keuren, Frances Dodds. 1989. *The frieze from the Hera I temple at Foce del Sele*. Rome: G. Bretschneider.

van Straten, F. T. 1974. Did the Greeks kneel before their gods? *BABesch* 49:159–89.

——1995. *Hiera kala: Images of animal sacrifice in archaic and classical Greece*. Leiden: E. J. Brill.

——2000 [1992]. Votives and votaries in Greek sanctuaries. In *Oxford readings in Greek religion*, ed. R. G. A. Buxton, 191–223.

van Windekens, A. J. 1961. Réflexions sur la nature e l'origine du dieu Hermès. *RhM* 104:289–301.

Verbanck-Piérard, A. 1989. Le double culte d'Héraklès: Légende ou réalité? In *Entre hommes et dieux*, ed. A. F. Laurens, 43–64.

——1992. Herakles at feast in Attic art: A mythical or cultic iconography? In *The iconography of Greek cult in the Archaic and Classical periods*, ed. R. Hägg, 85–106.

Verbruggen, H. 1981. *Le Zeus crétois. Collection d'études mythologiques*. Paris: Les Belles Lettres.

——1985. *Sources pertaining to the cult of Zeus in Crete: A geographical survey*. Leuven: [n.p.].

Vermaseren, M. J. 1977–. *Corpus cultus Cybelae Attidisque (CCCA)*. Leiden: E. J. Brill.

——1977. *Cybele and Attis: The myth and cult*. London: Thames and Hudson.

Vernant, Jean Pierre. 1980. *Myth and society in ancient Greece*. Tr. Janet Lloyd. Sussex, England and Atlantic Highlands NJ: Harvester Press; Humanities Press.

——1982. *The origins of Greek thought*. Ithaca NY: Cornell University Press.

——1983a. Hestia-Hermes: The religious expression of space and movement in ancient Greece. In *Myth and thought among the Greeks* 127–75.

——1983b. *Myth and thought among the Greeks*. London: Routledge & Kegan Paul.

——1990. *Figures, idoles, masques*. Paris: Julliard.

——1991. *Mortals and immortals: Collected essays*. Ed. Froma Zeitlin. Princeton NJ: Princeton University Press.

Vernant, Jean Pierre, Jean Rudhardt, and Olivier Reverdin, eds. 1981. *Le Sacrifice dans l'Antiquité*. Geneva: Fondation Hardt.

Versnel, H. S. 1981. *Faith, hope and worship: Aspects of religious mentality in the ancient world*. Leiden: E. J. Brill.

——1990. *Inconsistencies in Greek and Roman religion*. 2 Vols. New York: E. J. Brill.

——1992. The festival for Bona Dea and the Thesmophoria. *G&R* 39.31–55.

Vian, Francis. 1963. *Les origines de Thébes; Cadmos et les Spartes*. Paris: C. Klincksieck.

Vidal-Naquet, Pierre. 1975. Les esclaves immortelles d'Athéna Ilias. In *Le Monde grec*, ed. J. Bingen, G. Cambier, and G. Nachtergael, 496–507.

——1986. *The black hunter: Forms of thought and forms of society in the Greek world*. Tr. Andrew Szegedy-Maszak. Baltimore MD: Johns Hopkins University Press.

Villing, Alexandra. 1997. Aspects of Athena in the Greek polis: Sparta and Corinth. In *What is a god?* ed. A. B. Lloyd, 81–100.

—— 1998. Athena as Ergane and Promachos: The iconography of Athena in archaic East Greece. In *Archaic Greece*, ed. N. R. E. Fisher and H. van Wees, 147–68.

—— 2002. For whom did the bell toll in ancient Greece? Archaic and classical Greek bells at Sparta and beyond. *ABSA* 97:223–95.

Visintin, Monica. 1992. *La vergine e l'eroe: Temesa e la leggenda di Euthymos di Locri*. Bari: Edipuglia.

Visser, M. 1982. Worship your enemy: aspects of the cult of heroes in ancient Greece. *HThR* 75 (4):403–38.

Vollgraff, Carl Wilhelm. 1944–45. Inscriptions d'Argos. *BCH* 68–69:395–96, pl. 36.

—— 1956. *Le sanctuaire d'Apollon Pythéen à Argos*. Paris: J. Vrin.

Voutiras, E., and M. Tiverios. 1997. Zeus. *LIMC* VIII.1.310–74.

Voyatzis, M. E. 1990. *The early sanctuary of Athena Alea at Tegea and other archaic sanctuaries in Arcadia*. Göteborg: P. Åström.

—— 1998. From Athena to Zeus: An A-Z guide to the origins of Greek goddesses. In *Ancient goddesses*, ed. L. Goodison and C. Morris, 133–47.

—— 1999. The role of temple-building in consolidating Arcadian communities. *CPCActs* 6:130–68.

Vurtheim, J. 1920. The miracle of the wine at Dionysos advent: On the Lenaia festival. *CQ* 14 (2):92–96.

Wachter, Rudolf. 2001. *Non-Attic Greek vase inscriptions*. Oxford: Oxford University Press.

Waldstein, Charles. 1902. *The Argive Heraeum*. Boston MA: Houghton Mifflin.

Walter, O. 1937. Der Säulenbau des Herakles. *MDAI(A)* 62:41–51, pl. 25–28.

Ward, D. J. 1970. The separate functions of the Indo-European Divine Twins. In *Myth and law among the Indo-Europeans*, ed. J. Puhvel, 193–202.

Welter, Gabriel. 1941. *Troizen und Kalaureia*. Berlin: Gebr. Mann.

West, M. L. 1965. The Dictaean hymn to the Kouros. *JHS* 5:149–59.

—— 1975. *Immortal Helen*. London: Bedford College, University of London.

—— 1982. The Orphics of Olbia. *ZPE* 45:17–29.

West, William C. III. 1969. The trophies of the Persian wars. *CP* 64 (1):7–19.

Westenholz, Joan Goodnick. 1989. Tamar, Qedesa, Qadistu, and sacred prostitution in Mesopotamia. *HThR* 82 (3):245–65.

Wheeler, James Rignall. 1903. Two lexicographical notes. *CR* 17 (1):28–29.

White, Donald. 1963. *Hagne thea: A study of Sicilian Demeter*. Diss. Princeton University, Princeton NJ.

—— 1964. Demeter's Sicilian cult as a political instrument. *GRBS* 5:261–79.

—— 1967. The post-classical cult of Malophorus at Selinus. *AJA* 71 (4):335–52.

White, Donald, and Gerald P. Schaus. 1984. *The extramural sanctuary of Demeter and Persephone at Cyrene, Libya: Final reports*. Philadelphia: University Museum University of Pennsylvania in association with the Libyan Department of Antiquities.

Whitehead, David. 1986. *The demes of Attica, 508/7–c. 250 BC: A political and social study*. Princeton NJ: Princeton University Press.

Whitley, J. 1994. The monuments that stood before Marathon: Tomb cult and hero cult in Archaic Attica. *AJA* 98 (2):213–30.

Wide, Samuel Karl Anders. 1893. *Lakonische kulte*. Leipzig: B. G. Teubner.

Wide, Samuel Karl Anders, and L. Kjellberg. 1895. Ausgrabungen auf Kalaureia. *MDAI(A)* 20:267–326.

Wilamowitz-Moellendorff, Ulrich von. 1931. *Der glaube der Hellenen*. 2 Vols. Berlin: Weidmannsche buchhandlung.

Will, Edouard. 1955. *Korinthiaka: recherches sur l'histoire et la civilization de Corinthe des origines aux guerres médiques*. Paris: E. de Boccard.

Willetts, R. F. 1958. Cretan Eileithyia. *CQ* 8 (34):221–3.

—— 1962. *Cretan cults and festivals*. London: Routledge and Kegan Paul.

Williams, Charles Kaufman. 1986. Corinth and the cult of Aphrodite. In *Corinthiaca*, ed. M. A. Del Chiaro and W. R. Biers.

Williams, Charles K., and Nancy Bookidis. 2003. *Corinth, the centenary, 1896–1996*. Corinth Vol. 20. [Princeton NJ]: American School of Classical Studies at Athens.

Williams, Dyfri. 1981. Aphaia. *LIMC* II.876–77.

—— 1982. Aegina. Aphaia-Tempel, IV. The inscription commemorating the construction of the first limestone temple and other features of the sixth century temenos. *AA*:55–68.

Williams, Hector, and Gerald P. Schaus. 2001. The sanctuary of Athena at ancient Stymphalos. In *Athena in the classical world*, ed. S. Deacy and A. Villing, 75–94.

Winkler, John J. 1990. *The constraints of desire: The anthropology of sex and gender in ancient Greece*. New York: Routledge.

Winkler, John J., and Froma I. Zeitlin. 1990. *Nothing to do with Dionysos? Athenian drama in its social context*. Princeton NJ: Princeton University Press.

Woodford, S. 1971. Cults of Heracles in Attica. In *Studies presented to George M. A. Hanfmann*, ed, D. G. Mitten, J. G. Pedley, and J. A. Scott, 211–25.

—— 1976. Heracles Alexikakos reviewed. *AJA* 80 (3):291–94.

Woodward, A.M. 1923–24. Excavations at Sparta 1924–25. 4. The Acropolis. *ABSA* 26:240–76, pl. 17–22.

—— 1926–27. Excavations at Sparta, 1927. *ABSA* 28:37–95.

—— 1962. Athens and the oracle of Ammon. *ABSA* 57:5–13.

Wright, J. 1982. The old temple terrace at the Argive Heraion and the early cult of Hera in the Argolid. *JHS* 102:186–201.

Wycherley, R. E. 1957. *Literary and epigraphical testimonia*. Athenian Agora Vol. 3. Princeton NJ: American School of Classical Studies at Athens.

—— 1959. Two Athenian shrines. *AJA* 63 (1):67–72.

—— 1965. Lenaion. *Hesperia* 34 (1):72–76.

Yalouris, N. 1950. Athena als Herrin der Pferde. *MH* 7:19–101.

—— 1979. Problems relating to the Temple of Apollo Epikourios at Bassai. In *Greece and Italy in the classical world*, ed. J. N. Coldstream and M. A. R. Colledge, 89–104.

Yamauchi, E. M. 1973. Cultic prostitution: A case study in cultural diffusion. In *Orient and occident*, ed. H. A. Hoffner, 213–22.

Yavis, Constantine George. 1949. *Greek altars, origins and typology, including the Minoan-Mycenaean offertory apparatus; an archaeological study in the history of religion*. St. Louis MO: St. Louis University Press.

Zaidman, Louise Bruit, and Pauline Schmitt Pantel. 1992. *Religion in the ancient Greek city*. Cambridge: Cambridge University Press.

Zancani Montuoro, Paola, and Umberto Zanotti-Bianco. 1951–. *Heraion alla foce del Sele*. Rome: Libreria dello Stato.

Zeitlin, Froma I. 1982. Cultic models of the female: Rites of Dionysus and Demeter. *Arethusa* 15 (1982):129–57.

Zuntz, Günther. 1971. *Persephone: Three essays on religion and thought in Magna Graecia*. Oxford: Clarendon Press.

INDEX OF
PRIMARY SOURCES

In most cases, entries for longer citations of ancient authors are inclusive of shorter citations. For example, the entry for Aesch. *Eum.* 1–8 includes pages for citations of Aesch. *Eum.* 1–2.

INDEX OF DIVINE, HEROIC,
AND MYTHIC FIGURES

276

GENERAL INDEX

59, 93, 98, 199; vases 191, 192 (bronze), 9, 26–7, 31, 73, 77, 81–2, 89, 119, 121–2, 123, 128, 151, 172–3, 181, 191, 199, 201, 202, 206 (ceramic), 107 (glass), 164; weapon 99, 112, 190; wool 80, 163

Wach, Joachim 7
war 86, 94; and Ares 119, 156–7; and Artemis 101–2, 103; and Athena 41, 50, 55; between Athens and Aigina 181; between Athens and Eleusis 67, 73; dead 133, 149, 157, 186, 199; and Dorians 57, 91; and Enyalios 102, 156–7, 190; game of 105; between Lokroi and Rhegion 121; Messenian 62, 190; Peloponnesian 130, 146, 177; Persian 96, 97, 149, 171, 205; between Phokis and Thessaly 103–4; between Sparta and Tegea 200; spoils of 9, 28, 49, 50, 52, 156, 190, 200; Trojan 30, 51, 61, 115, 179, 180; and Zeus 19–20; see also battle, truce
warrior 54, 184, 186; and Artemis 101, 102, 113; and Athena 41; and Hera 30; Kouretes as 24–5; ritual roles of 46, 54, 91, 102; training of 10, 18, 20, 41, 88, 105; women 109, 156; see also hoplite
water 21, 131, 142, 183, 188; and Artemis 102, 106, 107; channel for 83, 192; and Charites 162; and Hera 31; jars for 70, and Poseidon 57, 63–8

passim; in purification 11, 31, 48, 59, 94, 194; see also bath, flood, libation, river, spring
weaving 41, 45, 47, 49, 52; see also clothing
wedding see bride, marriage
werewolf see lycanthropy
white, color 34; of clothing 25, 32, 45, 78, 107; goddesses 168, 187–8, 190; horse 190; Island 206; sacrificial victim 158, 205
widow 40, 125
wine 62, 126, 201; in Aegean islands 127–8; and Dionysos 126–40 passim; consumed by men 130–1, 133; consumed by women 72, 78, 212n9; introduction of 133; miracles of 139–40; mixing of 131; new 128, 130; prohibited 12, 168; serving and storage of 34, 78, 128, 130, 131, 135, 136 fig. 10.2, 181; vintage of 128; see also libation, symposium
witchcraft 1, 166–7; see also magic, curse
wolf 18, 88, 97, 151
wreath see garland

Xenokrateia 152
Xenophon (of Korinth) 120
Xerxes 53
xoanon 8

Zea 194